February 12–13, 2015
Santa Fe, New Mexico, USA

I0031384

**Association for
Computing Machinery**

Advancing Computing as a Science & Profession

HotMobile'15

The 16th International Workshop on
Mobile Computing Systems and Applications

Sponsored by:
ACM SIGMOBILE

Supported by:
Google, HP, IBM Research and AT&T Labs

Association for
Computing Machinery

Advancing Computing as a Science & Profession

The Association for Computing Machinery
2 Penn Plaza, Suite 701
New York, New York 10121-0701

Notice to Past Authors of ACM-Published Articles

ISBN: 978-1-4503-3391-7 (Digital)

ISBN: 978-1-4503-3764-9 (Print)

Additional copies may be ordered prepaid from:

ACM Order Department
PO Box 30777
New York, NY 10087-0777, USA

Phone: 1-800-342-6626 (USA and Canada)
+1-212-626-0500 (Global)
Fax: +1-212-944-1318
E-mail: acmhelp@acm.org
Hours of Operation: 8:30 am – 4:30 pm ET

Printed in the USA

Message from the Chairs

It is our great pleasure to welcome you to the *Sixteenth International Workshop on Mobile Computing Systems – HotMobile '15*. This year's workshop continues the tradition of previous years, being a highly selective venue for mobile computing research. *HotMobile '15* again serves its mission as an interactive workshop focused on mobile applications, systems, and environments, as well as their underlying state-of-the-art technologies.

The call for papers attracted 85 submissions from Asia, Australia, Europe, North America, and South America. The program committee accepted 23 across a variety of topics, including: understanding human gestures, the Internet-of-things, mobile energy requirements, cellular networks, network monitoring and imaging, location, mobile platforms, learning, and privacy. The program also includes a keynote speech by Mark Corner of Fiksu Inc. and The University of Massachusetts at Amherst examining the tradeoffs between academia and the startup world, the challenges in starting companies, and the calculus for joining them -- along with his startup experience in mobile advertising technology. 16 posters and 7 demos were accepted for display.

We must thank our colleagues who helped organize the workshop, including the steering committee (chaired by Nigel Davies), the poster and demo chair (Eric Rozer), the sponsorship chair (Nic Lane), the publicity chair (Xia Zhou), the student grants and volunteers chair (Eduardo Cuervo), the publication chair (Wenjun Hu), and the web chair (Christos Efstratiou). Thanks also to our support at ACM.

We must also thank our authors for providing an outstanding technical program. We are grateful for the time and experience of our program committee, who worked tirelessly in reviewing submissions and providing earnest feedback. Finally, we thank our sponsors, without whom *HotMobile '15* could not continue as inclusively to both professional researchers and students from institutions around the world.

We hope that you will enjoy both the technical program as well as opportunities afforded by *HotMobile '15* to exchange ideas with the global research community.

Justin Manweiler
HotMobile '15 General Chair
IBM Research, USA

Romit Roy Choudhury
HotMobile '15 Program Chair
Univ. of Illinois Urbana Champaign, USA

Table of Contents

HotMobile'15 Organization List vii

HotMobile'15 Sponsor & Supporters ix

Session: Keynote Address

- **Academia, Startups and Mobile Advertising** 1
  Mark Corner *(Fiksu Inc. and University of Massachusetts at Amherst)*

Session: Gesture

- **Memory Stones: An Intuitive Information Transfer Technique
  between Multi-Touch Computers** 3
  Kaori Ikematsu, Itiro Siio *(Ochanomizu University)*
- **Finger-Writing with Smartwatch: A Case for Finger
  and Hand Gesture Recognition Using Smartwatch** 9
  Chao Xu, Parth H. Pathak, Prasant Mohapatra *(University of California, Davis)*
- **Mobile Touch-Free Interaction for Global Health** 15
  Nicola Dell, Krittika D'Silva, Gaetano Borriello *(University of Washington)*

Session: IoT

- *Retro-VLC:* **Enabling Battery-Free Duplex Visible Light Communication
  for Mobile and IoT Applications** 21
  Jiangtao Li *(Microsoft Research)*, Angli Liu *(University of Washington)*,
  Guobin Shen, Liqun Li, Chao Sun, Feng Zhao *(Microsoft Research)*
- **The Internet of Things Has a Gateway Problem** 27
  Thomas Zachariah, Noah Klugman, Bradford Campbell, Joshua Adkins, Neal Jackson,
  Prabal Dutta *(University of Michigan)*

Session: Energy

- **Reducing Energy Consumption of Alarm-Induced Wake-Ups
  on Android Smartphones** 33
  Sewook Park, Dongwon Kim, Hojung Cha *(Yonsei University)*
- **Energy-Efficiency Comparison of Mobile Platforms and Applications:
  A Quantitative Approach** 39
  Grace Metri, Weisong Shi, Monica Brockmeyer *(Wayne State University)*

Session: Cellular

- **CQIC: Revisiting Cross-Layer Congestion Control for Cellular Networks** 45
  Feng Lu, Hao Du, Ankur Jain *(Google)*, Geoffrey M. Voelker, Alex C. Snoeren *(University of California, San Diego)*,
  Andreas Terzis *(Google)*
- **The Case for Offload Shaping** 51
  Wenlu Hu, Brandon Amos, Zhuo Chen, Kiryong Ha, Wolfgang Richter *(Carnegie Mellon University)*,
  Padmanabhan Pillai *(Intel Labs)*,
  Benjamin Gilbert, Jan Harkes, Mahadev Satyanarayanan *(Carnegie Mellon University)*
- **Can Accurate Predictions Improve Video Streaming in Cellular Networks?** 57
  Xuan Kelvin Zou *(Princeton University)*,
  Jeffrey Erman, Vijay Gopalakrishnan, Emir Halepovic, Rittwik Jana *(AT&T Labs -- Research)*,
  Xin Jin, Jennifer Rexford *(Princeton University)*, Rakesh K. Sinha *(AT&T Labs -- Research)*

Session: Network Monitoring and Imaging

- *CrowdREM:* **Harnessing the Power of the Mobile Crowd for Flexible Wireless Network Monitoring**..................................63
  Andreas Achtzehn, Janne Riihihjärvi, Irving Antonio Barría Castillo, Marina Petrova, Petri Mähönen *(RWTH Aachen University)*

- **A Wireless Spectrum Analyzer in Your Pocket**..................................69
  Tan Zhang, Ashish Patro, Ning Leng, Suman Banerjee *(University of Wisconsin-Madison)*

- **60GHz Mobile Imaging Radar**..................................75
  Yibo Zhu, Yanzi Zhu, Zengbin Zhang, Ben Y. Zhao, Haitao Zheng *(University of California, Santa Barbara)*

Session: Location

- **Indoor Person Identification Through Footstep Induced Structural Vibration**..................................81
  Shijia Pan, Ningning Wang *(Carnegie Mellon University)*,
  Yuqiu Qian *(University of Science and Technology of China)*,
  Irem Velibeyoglu, Hae Young Noh, Pei Zhang *(Carnegie Mellon University)*

- **Human Assisted Positioning Using Textual Signs**..................................87
  Bo Han, Feng Qian, Moo-Ryong Ra *(AT&T Labs - Research)*

- **Step-By-Step Detection of Personally Collocated Mobile Devices**..................................93
  Animesh Srivastava *(Duke University)*, Jeremy Gummeson, Mary Baker, Kyu-Han Kim *(HP Labs Palo Alto)*

Session: Mobile Platforms

- **The Missing Numerator: Toward a Value Measure for Smartphone Apps**..................................99
  Anudipa Maiti, Geoffrey Challen *(University at Buffalo)*

- **maybe We Should Enable More Uncertain Mobile App Programming**..................................105
  Geoffrey Challen, Jerry Antony Ajay, Nick DiRienzo, Oliver Kennedy, Anudipa Maiti, Anandatirtha Nandugudi, Sriram Shantharam, Jinghao Shi, Guru Prasad Srinivasa, Lukasz Ziarek *(University at Buffalo)*

- **The Case for Operating System Management of User Attention**..................................111
  Kyungmin Lee, Jason Flinn, Brian Noble *(University of Michigan)*

Session: Learning

- **Can Deep Learning Revolutionize Mobile Sensing?**..................................117
  Nicholas D. Lane *(Microsoft Research)*, Petko Georgiev *(University of Cambridge)*

- **Mobile Ad(D): Estimating Mobile App Session Times for Better Ads**..................................123
  John P. Rula, Byungjin Jun, Fabián Bustamante *(Northwestern University)*

Session: Privacy

- **Policy-Carrying Data: A Privacy Abstraction for Attaching Terms of Service to Mobile Data**..................................129
  Stefan Saroiu, Alec Wolman, Sharad Agarwal *(Microsoft Research)*

- **Sound Shredding: Privacy Preserved Audio Sensing**..................................135
  Sumeet Kumar, Le T. Nguyen, Ming Zeng, Kate Liu, Joy Zhang *(Carnegie Mellon University)*

Author Index

Author Index..................................141

2015 International Workshop on Mobile Computing Systems and Application

General Chair:	Justin Manweiler *(IBM Research – TJ Watson, USA)*
Program Chair:	Romit Roy Choudhury *(University of Illinois at Urbana Champaign, USA)*
Posters & Demos Chair:	Eric Rozner *(IBM Research – Austin, USA)*
Sponsorship Chair:	Nicholas Lane *(Microsoft Research, China)*
Publicity Chair:	Xia Zhou *(Dartmouth College, USA)*
Student Grants and Volunteers Chair:	Eduardo Cuervo *(Microsoft Research, USA)*
Publication Chair:	Wenjun Hu *(Yale University, USA)*
Web Chair:	Christos Efstratiou *(University of Kent, UK)*
Steering Committee Chair:	Nigel Davies *(Lancaster University, UK)*
Steering Committee:	Sharad Agarwal *(Microsoft Research, USA)*
	Ramón Cáceres *(AT&T Labs, USA)*
	Mahadev Satyanarayanan *(Carnegie Mellon University, USA)*
	Stefan Sariou *(Microsoft Research, USA)*
	Alexander Varshavsky *(Google, USA)*
	Roy Want *(Google, USA)*
	Matt Welsh *(Google, USA)*
Program Committee:	Suman Banerjee *(University of Wisconsin-Madison, USA)*
	Andrew Campbell *(Dartmouth College, USA)*
	Landon Cox *(Duke University, USA)*
	Christos Efstratiou *(University of Kent, UK)*
	Marco Gruteser *(Rutgers University, USA)*
	Robin Kravets *(University of Illinois at Urbana Champaign, USA)*
	Mo Li *(Nanyang Technological University, Singapore)*
	Qin Lv *(University of Colorado, USA)*
	Tamer Nadeem *(Old Dominion University, USA)*
	Vinayak S. Naik *(Indraprastha Institute of Information Technology, India)*
	Srihari Nelakuditi *(University of South Carolina, USA)*
	Lili Qiu *(University of Texas, USA)*
	Eric Rozner *(IBM Research – Austin, USA)*
	Mahadev Satyanarayanan *(Carnegie Mellon University, USA)*
	Souvik Sen *(HP Labs, USA)*
	Alex Snoeren *(University of California, San Diego, USA)*
	Kannan Srinivasan *(Ohio State University, USA)*
	Mani Srivastava *(University of California, Los Angeles, USA)*

HotMobile 2015 Sponsor & Supporters

Sponsor:

Supporters:
Gold

Silver

Bronze

IBM Research

Academia, Startups and Mobile Advertising

Mark Corner

Fiksu Inc. and University of Massachusetts at Amherst

mcorner@fiksu.com, mcorner@cs.umass.edu

Abstract

Should more academics be making the leap to startups? I have been lucky enough to have that experience: going from a tenured professor position in mobile systems at UMass Amherst to a CTO job at a $100M+ startup in the mobile advertising space, Fiksu Inc. This talk examines some of the tradeoffs between academia and the startup world, the challenges in starting companies, and the calculus for joining them. Startups abound in the world of mobile advertising technology, which provides the economic foundation of the free-to-play internet and the continuing growth of e-commerce. We will delve into the murky world of advertising technology and discuss the unique opportunities that mobile presents.

ACM Classification

K.7 The Computing Profession

Keywords

Advertising Technology; Mobile Advertising; Startups; Academia.

Short Bio

Mark Corner is an expert in the areas of mobile and pervasive computing, mobile advertising technology, real-time bidding (RTB), large-scale systems, networking, file systems, and security. He is a tenured Associate Professor in the School of Computer Science at the University of Massachusetts Amherst and has been there since 2003. After tenure Mark put his research career on hold to be an early-stage founder and CTO at Fiksu Inc., a Boston-based mobile advertising technology company.

As a professor he has authored dozens of publications on mobile systems, holds two patents, and has been awarded millions of dollars in federal and industrial research grants. He was selected for DARPA's prestigious Computer Science Study Panel in 2009.

He was the recipient of an NSF CAREER award in 2005, Best Paper awards at USENIX FAST 2007, ACM Multimedia 2005, and ACM Mobicom 2002. Prof. Corner also serves on the editorial board of IEEE Pervasive and IEEE Transactions on Mobile Computing. Mark holds a PhD in Electrical Engineering from the University of Michigan and BS and MS degrees from the University of Virginia. At UMass he teaches the Operating Systems course and a course on Usability.

The 50+ person team that Mark built enabled revenue growth from 0 to more than $100 million / year. He oversees the development of a massively scalable infrastructure on Ruby on Rails, Postgresql, and AWS that processes thousands of events per second from Real Time Bidding and in-app telemetry. The SDK that the team built touches more than half of all mobile devices, the RTB platform bids in excess of 500k times per second using proprietary optimization techniques, and Fiksu's large-scale analytics system summarizes data from hundreds of billions of in-app events.

HotMobile'15, February 12–13, 2015, Santa Fe, New Mexico, USA.
ACM 978-1-4503-3391-7/15/02.
http://dx.doi.org/10.1145/2699343.2699368

Memory Stones: An Intuitive Information Transfer Technique between Multi-touch Computers

Kaori Ikematsu
Ochanomizu University
g0920502@gmail.com

Itiro Siio
Ochanomizu University
siio@acm.org

ABSTRACT

Owners of multiple personal computing devices, such as mobile phones, tablet PCs, laptops, or desktop PCs, may frequently want to transfer information from one device to another. Whereas a drag-and-drop function on the same computing device is easy to achieve, it becomes cumbersome in an environment with multiple computing devices. We have to first locate and then select the target device from a list of devices on a network, even when the device is right in front of us. In this paper, a novel direct manipulation technique for executing drag-and-drop operations between multi-touch devices is proposed. Under our interface concept, dubbed "Memory Stones," a user can "pick up" a data object displayed on one device screen, "carry" it to another device screen, and "put it down" on that device using only their fingers. During this drag-and-drop operation, the user is invited to pantomime the act of carrying a tangible object (a "stone") while keeping their fingertip positions unchanged. The system identifies both the source and target devices by matching the shape of the polygon formed by the fingertips when touching each respective screen. We have developed a prototype system for small-to-large sized multi-touch computers including smartphones, tablet PCs, laptops, and desktop PCs, and have carried out a preliminary evaluation of its feasibility.

Keywords

Graphical User Interfaces (GUI); Drag-and-drop; Multi-touch Interaction; Gesture Input; User Interface for Multiple Computing Environment.

Categories and Subject Descriptors

H.5.2. [**Information Interfaces and Presentation (e.g. HCI)**]: Interaction Styles (e.g., commands, menus, forms, direct manipulation)

1. INTRODUCTION

As computing devices become ubiquitous commodities in everyday life, the number of users who own multiple devices is sharply increasing, and it is no longer exceptional for a user to operate more than one computing device at the same time. Given this use scenario, there is an increasing need for an easy and intuitive user interface method for operations among multiple computing environments, such as drag-and-drop capability between two devices [14]. For example, if a user finds a dinner recipe on a Web page using a desktop or notebook PC, and wants to follow out the recipe in the kitchen while using a tablet PC, they have to find some way to drag-and-drop the URL of the Web page from the first device to the other. Similar needs arise frequently in everyday use: for example, presenting pictures or documents to friends or colleagues, using a nearby printer to make a hard copy of a document on a mobile device, or presenting a document on a laptop or tablet PC using a projection device in a meeting room. Such scenarios are already common in daily life and are likely to become more common in the near future. Although there are ways to transfer documents between two different computers, such as using a device-to-device network connection or a portable memory device, most of these methods include cloud file service involve cumbersome or complicated procedures and may be uncomfortable for average users. In this paper, we propose a new method we call "Memory Stones." This method involves the direct manipulation of multi-touch devices using finger gestures, metaphorically allowing the user to "pick up" a data object from one computing device, "carry" it to a nearby device, and "put it down" the data on that device.

2. RELATED WORK

Many methods have been developed for facilitating the transfer of information between multiple computers. In this section, we discuss previous work conducted in this area, which we have grouped into two categories: systems that allow a simple pairing between two computers before a conventional data transfer via a computer network, and systems that allow a seamless pairing and data transfer with a single operation.

2.1 Simple pairing

Several methods have been proposed for achieving an easy pairing between two computers before a conventional data transfer through a computer network takes place. For example, tranSticks [2] uses a pair of memory card devices and connects them in a one-to-one fashion by inserting them into

Figure 1: Proposed drag-and-drop method between two computing devices. A user picks up a data object (left) from one device using their fingers, (center) brings it to another device, and (right) puts it down on that device.

(a)   (b)   (c)

Figure 2: Examples of Copy-and-paste actions (a) from a laptop to a tablet PC, (b) from a smartphone to a tablet PC, and (c) from a tablet PC to a printer.

two different PCs. Using the accelerometer that is normally embedded in modern smartphones, Shake Well Before Use [10] establishes a network connection when the user holds two different mobile devices and shakes them both at the same time. In a similar way, Smart-Its Friends[8] and Synchronous Gestures [6] also use the accelerometer. To establish a connection, Smart-Its Friends uses a shaking gesture of two mobile devices held together, and Synchronous Gestures establish a connection when the user bumps two devices into each other. Point&Connect [13] uses a combination of the microphone and loudspeaker on a mobile phone, to allow the user to point their phone at a target phone with which they want to establish a link. Seeing-Is-Believing [11] uses a camera-equipped mobile device to identify a target device to which an optical ID marker is attached. Gaze-link [1] allows a use can establish a virtual connection over a network (e.g, Bluetooth or Ethernet) by looking at the target device through a device attached to a camera. SyncTap [15] links two computers together when the user taps or presses the input devices of both computers simultaneously. That one there! [17] uses infrared tags to identify paired computers. Finally, some commercial products and proposed methods facilitate computer pairing methods, including using NFC equipment or tags [1], or detecting printers on the same network and listing them in a selection menu [2].

2.2 Seamless pairing and data transfer

A number of user-interface methods have also been proposed for achieving seamless drag-and-drop capability between two devices using implicit pairing functions. In Pick-

and-Drop [14], using a pen device, a user can "pick up" a data object, such as an icon visible on a computer display, and "drop" it onto another computer display. This system uses an identifiable pen device to pair the two computers within a local area network. In Stitching [7], connection between two mobile devices is established by using a stroking gesture across both devices. This interaction technique requires the two devices to be contiguous. Therefore, a data transfer between two large desktop PCs or fixed displays is difficult to achieve. In Toss-It [19], an information transfer is achieved when a user makes a throwing gesture with the source device aiming for the target device. A background process identifies and spatially locates all computers within the shared physical space, and calculates a landing spot for the virtual object thrown by the user. The computer nearest to the landing spot will receive the virtual object. Hassan developed a similar technique that with a tilt-based interaction for sharing a document from a mobile device to a public display [5]. As a further examples of an information transfer technique in a multiple device environment, Wilson [18] uses multiple Kinect and projectors to enable users to establish connections through tracking gestures (e.g, swiping and grabbing). In addition, Andrew explored a meeting environment [3] for sharing and manipulating information across multiple mobile devices and public displays. Finally, using Touch & Interact [4], a user is able to share data between an NFC phone and a large display using a mesh of NFC tags.

Our proposed Memory Stones technique also aims to provide both information transfer capability and implicit pairing in a single, seamless operation. To develop a practical user-interface method, we restricted our technique to commonplace hardware devices or sensors that are available in consumer computing products. Therefore, we avoided meth-

---

[1]http://www.nfc-forum.org/resources/AppDocs/
NFCForum_AD_BTSSP_1_0.pdf
[2]http://www.apple.com/iphone/features/airprint.html

ods that require infrared transceivers [17], cameras [18][3][9], or identifiable pen devices [14][12]. Moreover, because we also intended to support larger computing devices such as desktop PCs, laptops, and large-sized tablet PCs, acceleration-based methods [19][10], tilt-based method [5], and aim-based methods [13][11][17] were also avoided. Considering that multi-touch devices are becoming widespread in a wide variety of computers (smartphones, tablet PCss, laptops, and desktops) and are supported by many different OSs (iOS, Mac OS X, Android, Windows, Windows RT, and Windows Phone), we believe our proposed method has a practical application.

3. MEMORY STONES

In the real world, we can transfer objects such as printed documents by picking them up from one desktop and putting them down onto another. If the object we pick up is a solid material, such as a stone, the form of our fingertips will be unchanged over the course of such again. Our proposed Memory Stones method applies these common actions to a drag-and-drop operation between two devices equipped with multi-touch input. Using our method, a user can drag-and-drop an information object using the same actions they would normally apply to a physical object:"picking up" the information object from one device screen, "carrying" it to another device screen, and "putting it down" onto that screen. This is a more intuitive user interface method [16] than conventional methods that requiring a network connection processes, because it is based on more basic human activity than the use of a tool such as sticky pen [14] for bringing an object above a display surfac.

Figure 1 illustrates this sequence of user actions for copying a Web page. The user first picks up the Web page up by touching the screen with three fingers (Fig. 1(a)). Next, the user moves their hand to the target computer while keeping the fingertip positions unchanged, similar to carrying a solid object. (Fig. 1(b)). Finally, the user touches the target computer display using the same fingers and fingertip positions, at which point the Web page is copied to that computer (Fig. 1(c)) within few(2-3) seconds. Using this method, the user can drag-and-drop intangible information as if moving a tangible object. We have added visual feedback in the form of a virtual stone (a "Memory Stone") to both the source and target displays as an indication that the drag-and-drop action was accepted and completed. This visual feedback also reinforces the metaphor of carrying something tangible from one device to another.

Before and after the steps shown in Fig. 1 , the user can select the object to copy, and specify the location where it should be pasted, respectively. That is, after a user selects and starts to drag an object conventionally using a single finger, they can trigger the Memory Stone method by placing additional fingers onto the computer surface. Once the copied objects shown up on the target computer, the user can also trigger a conventional single-finger drag-and-drop operation by lifting all but one finger from the computer surface. This seamless transition between our method and a conventional drag-and-drop action enables a wide variety of operations, such as copying multiple icons and texts, and pasting them to specific locations on the target surface.

Since our method is essentially an extension of a basic drag-and-drop operation to include nearby devices as paste

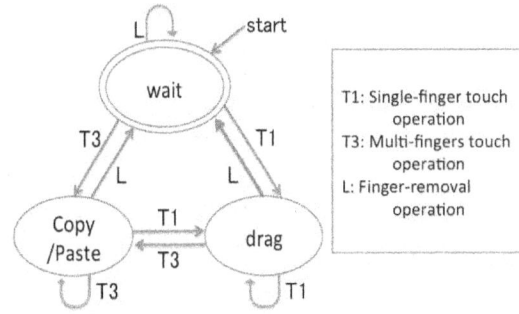

Figure 3: Deterministic finite automaton.

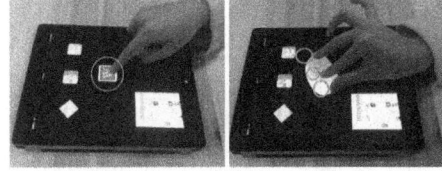

Figure 4: Object (icon) transfer method. After conventional dragging of an object (left), our method is activated by touching with multiple fingers (right).

destinations, it has many possible applications. Fig.2 shows some examples.

4. IMPLEMENTATION

To test the feasibility of our Memory Stones method, we implemented a prototype system in Objective-C for use on the iOS 5 and Mac OS X 10.7 operating systems. These platforms use a single programming framework to support multi-touch input on a wide range of devices, including smartphones (iPhones), tablet PCs (iPads), laptops (MacBooks), and desktop PCs (Macs and iMacs).

4.1 Client applications

One of our prototypes, shown in the Fig.1, functions as a simplified Web browser for computing devices running an iOS or OS X operating system. When a user touches a multi-touch display or trackpad of a device with multiple fingers, the URL of the Web page is copied to the system. The URL

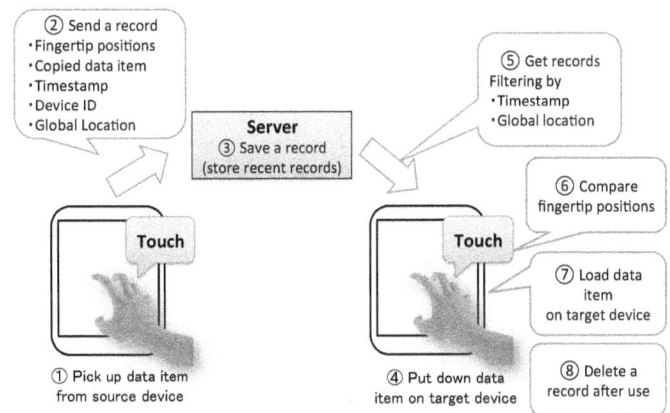

Figure 5: System configuration and operation.

is then pasted to the target device when the user touches the multi-touch display or trackpad of the target device with the same fingertip pattern, after which the pasted URL is loaded into the simplified Web browser running on the target device.

We developed other prototypes that support object selection before transferring data between devices. In these prototypes, a conventional drag-and-drop method is seamlessly combined before and after our data transfer method is applied. Figure 4 shows the method used to transfer selected objects. As shown on the left side of Fig.4, the conventional dragging of an icon is performed after it is selected. When the user places extra fingers on the touch surface (Fig. 4, right), a stone appears and the inter-device drag-and-drop process is activated. When the user touches the destination device using the same finger shape, the stone image reappears (Fig. 4, right), and conventional dragging starts when the user removes all but her one finger (Fig. 4, left, in this case the user uses an index finger). The user can place the icon at the desired position using a conventional drag-and-drop method. As with a conventional text drag-and-drop method, the dragging of the characters starts when the user drags part of the selected text.When the user put extra fingers on the touch surface, a stone is appeared and our inter-device drag-and-drop process is activated. When the user touches the destination device by the same finger shape, the stone image also appears, and conventional dragging starts when the user lifts fingers other than one finger. The user can then place part of the text to the desired insertion point on the target device.

The transition state for these prototypes are shown in Fig. 3. T1 indicates a single-finger operation, T3 represents a multi-finger operation, and L refers to a finger-removal operation. When a user touches the computer surface with multiple fingers (T3), an inter-device drag or drop process starts. To indicate that the drag-and-drop operation was successful, the system displays the image of a stone on both the source and target device screen. The stone, which is scaled to fit within the polygon formed by the user's fingers, appears on the screen, and then disappears when the user lifts their fingers from the display (L). The same stone reappears when the user touches the destination device (T3) with a near-identical fingertip pattern, indicating a successful completion of the drag-and-drop operation.

Touching multiple fingers (T3) during a waiting state will activate the receiving or sending operations depending on the existence of valid data on the server. When no valid data is stored on the server, the application can select content(s) covered by the fingers and activate the transfer process to the destination device. This operation is adopted in a Web browser prototype (Fig. 1) for sending the whole page on the display.

In the current prototype, the user must apply a drag-and-drop operation using more than two fingers to avoid a conflict with other commonly adopted multi-touch two-finger operations, including pinching (zooming), rotating, sliding (scrolling), and tapping.

4.2 Server

Figure 5 shows the series of operations between devices when a user performs a drag-and-drop action. When a user touches the source computer to pick up an information object (e.g., Web page or image file), the client application

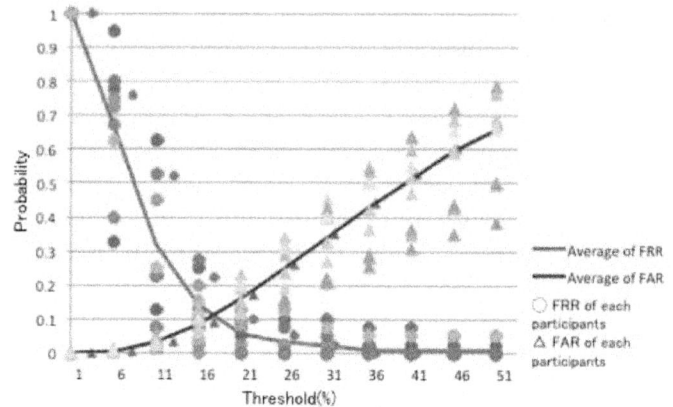

Figure 6: Matching threshold for the mean squared error of the distance between fingers and the average FAR and FRR values among the participants.

pushes the following data to a prepared server: the timestamp, the global position of the computer, the URL of the data object, the unique device ID and the fingertip positions. The server preserves these data [3].

When the user touches the destination device to drop the information object, the client application on that device fetches the recent records [4] from the server. From these recent records received, those that are physically the farthest from the destination device (based on global positioning) are removed. After excluding unqualifying records, the program uses a polygonal congruence condition to try to find a record with a matching fingertip shape. Specifically, if the square summation of the difference between the lengths of the corresponding sides is less than a given threshold, then the two fingertip shapes are considered a match. If a match is found, the client application fetches the URL from the matched record and loads it into the browser, thereby completing the drag-and-drop procedure. In the current prototype, the URL fetch starts within 3.0 second after the user touches the destination device.

Global location information is used to prevent the establishment of an unintentional connection by accident. In addition to timestamp filtering, global location filtering prevents malfunction. We use the CoreLocation framework (supported by iOS and Mac OS, version10.6 or higher) to obtain the global location information. Windows, can also support Memory Stones since Windows PCs include Windows Sensor and Location (Windows 7) or a built-in position acquisition system (Windows 8). Our technique can be used even in non-GPS equipped PCs because the location acquisition served by the OS supports alternative positioning methods such as the use of the signal intensities of Wi-Fi base stations.

4.3 Threshold for Identification

Once the fingertip position data are acquired at the source and destination computers, the system matches the polygon formed by the fingertips as follows First, it calculates the distances between each pair of fingers, and sorts them by

---

[3]Five records are maintained in the current implementation.
[4]Finishes recording within 5 s in the current implementation.

length. Second, it calculates the mean squared error between each distance pair of the same order. If the polygons formed by the fingertips are exactly congruent, the mean squared error should be zero. Finally, in the third step, the system determines that the fingertip positions are identical if the mean squared error is less than the given threshold.

To determine an appropriate threshold, we asked ten female students (one graduate and nine undergraduate, nine right-handed and one left-handed) to perform a drag-and-drop action 40 times each (a total of 400 actions) between two tablet PCs (iPads), and obtained their fingertip position data. Using this data, we calculated the False Acceptance Rate (FAR) and False Rejection Rate (FRR), as shown in the following equations, to obtain several threshold candidates.

$$FAR = \frac{\text{Number of incorrect acceptances}}{\text{Number of trials}} \quad (1)$$

$$FRR = \frac{\text{Number of incorrect rejections}}{\text{Number of trials}} \quad (2)$$

FAR is the probability that the system incorrectly matches the fingertip position pattern to a non-matching pattern in the server, while FRR is the probability that the system fails to detect a match between the fingertip position pattern and a matching pattern in the server.

Figure 6 shows the average FAR and FRR values for all of the participants. The horizontal axis shows the threshold (% of length between fingers) for the mean squared error comparison. If the threshold is extremely low, the required matching accuracy is such that even a correct user's finger pattern may be rejected, and the FRR value is increased. On the other hand, if the threshold is very high, the required matching accuracy may be low enough to allow an incorrect user finger pattern to be accepted, and the FAR value is increased. We determined the threshold to be approximately 18% such that the value of FAR and FRR are equal; as a worst case, the Equal Error Rate (EER), which is the error rate at this point, is less than 11.0%. In addition, as we mentioned before, the actual system is expected to provide lower FAR value than the result of this experiment by using timestamp and location filtering. Furthermore we can expect an improvement in FRR when the user masters operation gestures. In that case, the system can provide a strict threshold option for skilled users to allow a more secure operation.

If a large number of people in a meeting room or classroom try to transfer data using the Memory Stones method, reliable data transfers may be difficult to achieve. One of our ideas to solve the problem is temporally place a stricter judgment on the fingertip-pattern similarity when a large number of requests arrive at the server at short intervals from the same location.

5. USER EVALUATION

In addition to the gesture performance experiment mentioned in the earlier threshold design section, we carried out two user-evaluation experiments. The first was to evaluate the mental effect of displaying a stone image when a user performs a drag-and-drop operation between devices. The other was to estimate the influence of an inclined touch surface, because in certain applications, such as those operat-

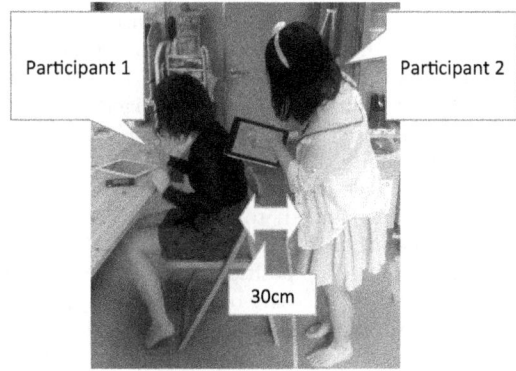

Figure 7: Setup of the shoulder surfing experiment.

ing on a printer control panel (Fig.2) or public display, the input surface may not be placed horizontally. In these experiments, we asked five female graduate students (all right handed) to participate in the following experiments. All participants were familiar with smartphones, tablet PCs, and laptops with trackpads, and all had experience using multi-touch devices.

5.1 Stone Image Effect

For the experiment on evaluating the stone image effect, we assigned each participant sixteen drag-and-drop tasks between two tablet PCs (iPads). Tasks with and without using stone image were conducted in turn. After the tasks were completed, we asked each participant the following question: "Of the two methods of interaction methods, (a) with the stone image and (b) without, which gives you a greater feeling of really transferring an object with your hand" The grading was based on a four-point scale: 4 = strongly agree, 3 = agree, 2 = disagree, and 1 = strongly disagree.

Each of the participants positively evaluated our method as intuitive and easy to use. The mean scores of the questionnaire results are 4.0 and 2.6 for with and without a stone image respectively. This shows that the task with a stone image is relatively more intuitive than without a stone image.

For the experiment on estimating the influence of an inclined touch surface, we assigned the participants data transfer tasks between an iPad placed on a table and another iPad tilted (90 or 45 degrees) relative to the horizontal surface. Each participant performed the task five times for both inclination angles (a total of 50 tasks), and we observed the influence of the operationality on the drag and drop operation based on the inclination angles of the devices. The success rate of the task for the 90-degree tilted iPad was 88.0% and for the 45-degree tilted iPad was 92.0%. Considering that the FRR is 10.0% for horizontally placed devices using the threshold mentioned in the previous section, the angle of the devices are not an obstacle, and it is therefore believed that Memory Stones can be applied to an inclined or wall-mounted display such as on a printer (Fig. 2) or a touch surface attached to a wall).

5.2 Shoulder surfing experiment

Although the proposed method facilitates secure drag-and-drop operations using temporal-personal fingertip positions, timestamps, and locations, there still remains the possibility that a malicious user can steal data by mimicking the fingertip action of an authorized user. One problem with the proposed application that information may be "stolen" by mimicking the formation of a user's fingertip positions. We therefore carried out a "shoulder surfing" experiment to estimate the possibility of data theft by an eavesdropper.

We asked five female undergraduate students (four right-handed and one left-handed) to participate in our experiment. We assigned them shoulder surfing tasks where they had to imitate the fingertip position of a user who was copy-and-pasting a data object using our proposed system. Figure 7 shows the experimental setup. Participant 2 executed shoulder surfing on iPad A 30-cm behind participant 1, who was sitting and copying-and-pasting data from a smartphone to iPad B, placed on a table, using three fingers. Participant 2 was allowed to move from side to side provided that she did not enter participant 1âĂŹs field of view. Each participant took the role of both participants 1 and 2, as shown in Fig. 9, and had 40 attempts at shoulder surfing. As a result, we recorded 200 trial datasets in this experiment, and the mimicked users were encouraged to simply "pick up a stone."

The results of this shoulder surfing experiment showed a success rate of about 4.0%. This value is less than one-half of the EER discussed in the previous section. Furthermore, because we employed both timestamp and location factors, as well as fingertip patterns, in the coupling process of the source and target computers, the person engaging in successful shoulder surfing had to conduct a false paste operation close to the target user within several seconds after the target user touched the transmitting device. Thus, we consider the threat of shoulder surfing to be acceptably low in practical situations.

6. CONCLUSION AND FUTURE WORK

We proposed a novel user-interface method called Memory Stones for executing drag-and-drop operations between nearby devices equipped with multi-touch inputs. We implemented a prototype of Memory Stones that runs on smartphones, tablet PCs, laptops, and desktop PCs, and carried out usability experiments. The participants of the usability experiments rated the proposed technique positively, and we found that users tend to move their fingers inward while performing drag-and-drop actions. The success rate of a shoulder surfing experiment was about 4.0%, and we therefore consider our method to be sufficiently secure for practical use.

We plan to enhance the scalability of our system by developing a more functional server-side application for managing, filtering, and searching the fingertip information, allowing the system to be used by larger numbers of users, and eventually becoming a worldwide service.

7. ACKNOWLEDGEMENT

This work was supported by JSPS KAKENHI Grant Number 26330210.

8. REFERENCES

[1] Ayatsuka, Y., M. N., and Rekimoto, J. Gaze-link: A new metaphor of real-world oriented user interface. *IPSJ Journal 42*, 6 (2011), 1330–1337.(in Japanese).

[2] Ayatsuka, Y., and Rekimoto, J. transticks: physically manipulatable virtual connections. CHI '05, ACM (2005), 251–260.

[3] Bragdon, A., DeLine, R., Hinckley, K., and Morris, M. R. Code space: Touch + air gesture hybrid interactions for supporting developer meetings. ITS '11, ACM (2011), 212–221.

[4] Hardy, R., and Rukzio, E. Touch & interact: Touch-based interaction of mobile phones with displays. MobileHCI '08, ACM (2008), 245–254.

[5] Hassan, N., Rahman, M. M., Irani, P., and Graham, P. Chucking: A one-handed document sharing technique. INTERACT '09, Springer-Verlag (2009), 264–278.

[6] Hinckley, K. Synchronous gestures for multiple persons and computers. UIST '03, ACM (2003), 149–158.

[7] Hinckley, K., Ramos, G., Guimbretiere, F., Baudisch, P., and Smith, M. Stitching: Pen gestures that span multiple displays. AVI '04, ACM (2004), 23–31.

[8] Holmquist, L. E., Mattern, F., Schiele, B., Alahuhta, P., Beigl, M., and Gellersen, H.-W. Smart-its friends: A technique for users to easily establish connections between smart artefacts. UbiComp '01, Springer-Verlag (2001), 116–122.

[9] Lee, H., Jeong, H., Lee, J., Yeom, K.-W., Shin, H.-J., and Park, J.-H. Select-and-point: A novel interface for multi-device connection and control based on simple hand gestures. CHI EA '08, ACM (2008), 3357–3362.

[10] Mayrhofer, R., and Gellersen, H. Shake well before use: authentication based on accelerometer data. PERVASIVE'07, Springer-Verlag (2007), 144–161.

[11] McCune, J. M., Perrig, A., and Reiter, M. K. Seeing-is-believing: using camera phones for human-verifiable authentication. *Int. J. Secur. Netw. 4*, 1/2 (Feb. 2009), 43–56.

[12] Ogata, M., Sugiura, Y., Osawa, H., and Imai, M. Flashtouch: data communication through touchscreens. CHI '13, ACM (New York, NY, USA, 2013), 2321–2324.

[13] Peng, C., Shen, G., Zhang, Y., and Lu, S. Point&connect: intention-based device pairing for mobile phone users. MobiSys '09, ACM (2009), 137–150.

[14] Rekimoto, J. Pick-and-drop: a direct manipulation technique for multiple computer environments. UIST '97, ACM (New York, NY, USA, 1997), 31–39.

[15] Rekimoto, J. Synctap: synchronous user operation for spontaneous network connection. *Personal Ubiquitous Comput. 8*, 2 (May 2004), 126–134.

[16] Shneiderman, B. Designing the user interface 2nd edition.

[17] Swindells, C., Inkpen, K. M., Dill, J. C., and Tory, M. That one there! pointing to establish device identity. UIST '02, ACM (2002), 151–160.

[18] Wilson, A. D., and Benko, H. Combining multiple depth cameras and projectors for interactions on, above and between surfaces. UIST '10, ACM (2010), 273–282.

[19] Yatani, K., Tamura, K., Hiroki, K., Sugimoto, M., and Hashizume, H. Toss-it: intuitive information transfer techniques for mobile devices. CHI EA '05, ACM (2005), 1881–1884.

Finger-writing with Smartwatch: A Case for Finger and Hand Gesture Recognition using Smartwatch

Chao Xu, Parth H. Pathak, Prasant Mohapatra
Computer Science Department, University of California, Davis, CA, 95616, USA
Email: {haxu, phpathak, pmohapatra}@ucdavis.edu

ABSTRACT

Smartwatch is becoming one of the most popular wearable device with many major smartphone manufacturers such as Samsung and Apple releasing their smartwatches recently. Apart from the fitness applications, the smartwatch provides a rich user interface that has enabled many applications like instant messaging and email. Since the smartwatch is worn on the wrist, it introduces a unique opportunity to understand user's arm, hand and possibly finger movements using its accelerometer and gyroscope sensors. Although user's arm and hand gestures are likely to be identified with ease using the smartwatch sensors, it is not clear how much of user's finger gestures can be recognized. In this paper, we show that motion energy measured at the smartwatch is sufficient to uniquely identify user's hand and finger gestures. We identify essential features of accelerometer and gyroscope data that reflect the movements of tendons (passing through the wrist) when performing a finger or a hand gesture. With these features, we build a classifier that can uniquely identify 37 (13 finger, 14 hand and 10 arm) gestures with an accuracy of 98%. We further extend our gesture recognition to identify the characters written by the user with her index finger on a surface, and show that such finger-writing can also be accurately recognized with nearly 95% accuracy. Our presented results will enable many novel applications like remote control and finger-writing-based input to devices using smartwatch.

Categories and Subject Descriptors: C.5.3 [Computer System Implementation]: Microcomputers – portable devices

Keywords: Wearables; Gesture Recognition; Mobile Computing.

1. INTRODUCTION

There has been a sharp increase in the popularity of smartwatches in last one year. With recent release of smartwatches from Apple [1], LG [2], Motorola [3] and Samsung

HotMobile '15, February 12 – 13 2015, Santa Fe, NM, USA
Copyright 2015 ACM 978-1-4503-3391-7/15/02$15.00
http://dx.doi.org/10.1145/2699343.2699350.

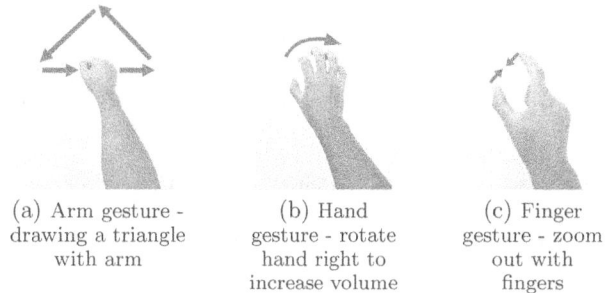

Figure 1: Examples of arm, hand and finger gestures

(a) Arm gesture - drawing a triangle with arm

(b) Hand gesture - rotate hand right to increase volume

(c) Finger gesture - zoom out with fingers

[4], it is expected that they will be at the forefront in adaptation of wearable devices. Apart from the fitness applications (which are also available in wrist-bands such as Fitbit [5]), the smartwatches provide a rich user interface to interact via voice or touch. Current smartwatches support applications like email, instant messaging, calendar, navigation by connecting to user's smartphone over Bluetooth.

This increasing popularity of smartwatch presents a unique opportunity. Because the smartwatch is worn on the wrist, it is possible to understand user's hand and arm movement better than ever before. Most of today's smartwatch have accelerometer and gyroscope sensors built in them. If we can capture and analyze these sensors' data, we can understand user's arm, hand and finger gestures. It is expected that smartwatch sensors would be able to identify user's arm gestures (when the gesture involves the movement of shoulder or elbow joint) with ease, however, it is not clear if it can recognize user's hand and finger gestures. The finger gestures are especially challenging to be detected using smartwatch since the movement in the wrist when doing a finger gesture is very small and it is not clear whether it can be recognized uniquely. If this is feasible, there can be a plethora of applications. A user wearing a smartwatch can remotely control nearby television, computer, smartphone or any smart device using the finger gestures. If the finger movements are captured by the smartwatch, user can write with her finger (in the air or on a surface) to input text on smartwatch or any other connected device.

In this paper, we investigate the following questions: Can accelerometer and gyroscope sensors in smartwatch be used for identifying user's arm, hand and finger gestures? Although it is likely that arm and hand gestures can be recognized using smartwatch sensors, how accurately can we determine user's *finger gestures* e.g. zoom-in, zoom-out etc. (Fig. 1)? Even further, can we identify the characters when user writes with her index finger in air or on the surface by simply monitoring smartwatch sensors? Our study provides affirmative answers to all these questions. The contributions of our work are as follows:

(1) We first show that measured motion energy in accelerometer and gyroscope of smartwatch can be used to distinguish the *type of a gesture* - arm, hand or finger. We then show that even low-intensity finger gestures such as moving index finger up and down is captured with corresponding motion energy in the smartwatch sensors. This motivates us to design a hand and finger gesture recognition technique using smartwatch.

(2) We show that due to the tendons passing through human's wrist, it is possible to *uniquely* identify a finger gesture using the smartwatch. We provide essential features derived from accelerometer and gyroscope data that can be used to identify the gestures. Our machine learning classifier can identify 37 (13 finger, 14 hand and 10 arm) gestures with an accuracy of 98%.

(3) We then extend our gesture recognition technique to identify the characters when user writes with her index finger on a surface while wearing the watch. Our classifier can identify the characters from 26 alphabets with an accuracy of nearly 95%.

The rest of the paper is organized as follows. In Section 2, we provide the details of our experiment settings and describe how motion energy can be used to distinguish the type of gestures. Section 3 provides the details of our gesture recognition technique and Section 4 shows how finger-writing characters can be detected when wearing the smartwatch. Additional challenges and our ongoing work are described in Section 5. Section 6 discusses the related work and Section 7 concludes the paper.

2. MOTION ENERGY AND GESTURE TYPE

In this section, we describe our experiment settings and show how we can determine the gesture type using the measured motion energy from the smartwatch.

2.1 Experiment Settings

Sensor Data Collection: We use a Shimmer [6] device attached to a wristband as the smartwatch as shown in Fig. 2a. The Shimmer contains an accelerometer sensor and a gyroscope sensor. The sensor data is collected at 128 Hz on Shimmer and transferred to a smartphone via Bluetooth. We use the Shimmer instead of any commercially available smartwatch because most smartwatch available in market provide only a limited API support for collecting accelerometer and gyroscope data. The sampling frequency of 128 Hz for Shimmer is not too high since the typical sampling frequency for accelerometer on current smartphones and smartwatches is 200 Hz [10] and 100 Hz [7] respectively. This means that a Shimmer closely resembles a smartwatch in terms of the motion sensors.

Gesture Experiments: Although our primary focus in this work is to identify finger and hand gestures using smartwatch, we also consider arm gestures for comparison. This way, we classify all the gestures in three types: arm, hand and finger. The list of all gestures we tested in our experiments is provided in Table 1. A total of 37 gestures are considered in our work which consists of 13 finger gestures, 14 hand gestures and 10 arm gestures. The data is collected for each gesture by repeating it for 10 times. Apart from the gestures, we also recognize characters when user writes on

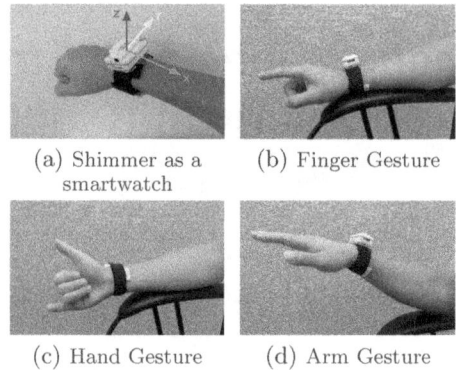

(a) Shimmer as a smartwatch (b) Finger Gesture

(c) Hand Gesture (d) Arm Gesture

Figure 2: Experiment settings showing how we perform different types of gestures

the surface while wearing the Shimmer. These experiments are described in Section 4.

Type	Gestures
Arm	ThumbsDown, Push, Left, Right, Up, ClockwiseCircle, Cross, AntiClockwiseCircle, LeftTwice, RightTwice
Hand	AntiClockwiseCircle, ClockwiseCircle, DownOnce, DownTwice, GunShoot, LeftOnce, LeftTwice, PhoneCall, RightOnce, RightTwice, RotateLeftVolumeDown, RotateRightVolumeUp, UpOnce, UpTwice
Finger	IndexFingerClick, ZoomIn, ZoomOut, One, Two, Three, Four, Five, OneTwice, ThumbsUp, Singleclick, DoubleClick, TwoTwice

Table 1: List of gestures used in our experiments

In order to maintain consistency across the gestures of each type, we adhere to the following guidelines. As shown in Fig. 2b, while doing the finger gestures, the wrist and the arm are affixed to the chair arm. For the hand gestures, the arm is affixed, however, the wrist is free to move and/or rotate (Fig. 2c). The arm gestures have the highest freedom of movement where only user's elbow is assumed to be touching the chair arm (Fig. 2d). Note that other arm gestures with movement of shoulder joint can also be recognized using our approach without requiring any major modifications.

2.2 Classifying Gesture Type - Finger, Hand or Arm

In this section, we answer the following question: can we determine if a given gesture is a finger, hand or arm gesture based on the smartwatch sensor data?

The motion energy behind the movement in different types of gesture is likely to be different. We can expect that motion energy observed during the arm gesture to be the highest, followed by hand gestures and then the finger gestures. The motion energy (or simply energy) can be measured for smartwatch's accelerometer and gyroscope as shown in [11]. The energy is computed as

$$\text{Energy} = \sum_{i=1}^{\text{window\_length}/2} \text{magnitude}_i^2 \qquad (1)$$

where magnitude values are the Fast Fourier Transform (FFT) coefficients calculated over the time window. Because all gestures considered in this work last for very small duration, we set the window size to be the time of the complete gesture. The energy is only calculated for half the window since the remaining magnitude values are redundant which follows from the symmetry of FFT. Also, we only choose to

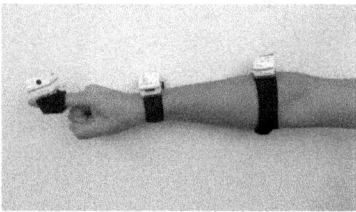

Figure 3: 3 Shimmers used to measure finger, wrist and forearm motion

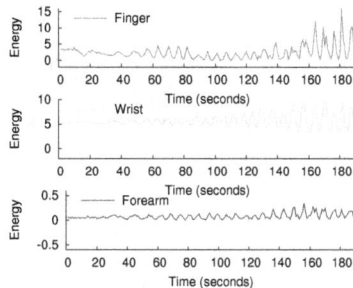

Figure 4: Motion energy in finger, wrist and forearm when doing a finger gesture

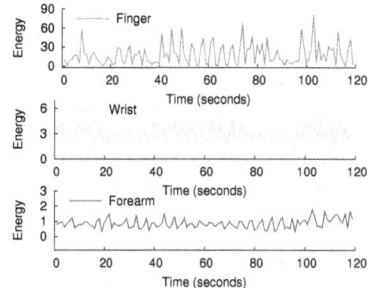

Figure 5: Motion energy in finger, wrist and forearm when doing a hand gesture

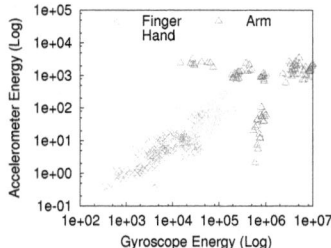

Figure 6: Accelerometer and gyroscope motion energy can be used to differentiate the type of gesture: arm, hand or finger

Classified as ->	Finger	Hand	Arm
Finger	129	1	0
Hand	3	136	1
Arm	0	0	100

Table 3: Confusion matrix for logistic regression classifier

calculate the energy within the lower frequency range of 0 to 1 Hz which is known to indicate low intensity activities and minor changes in posture [11].

Fig. 6 shows the energy of accelerometer and gyroscope for different gestures. We calculate the energy for all three axis and show the highest among the three axis in Fig. 6. It can be seen that the energy values can clearly distinguish the type of gesture. The finger and arm gestures have the lowest and the highest accelerometer and gyroscope energy respectively, while the energy values of hand gestures fall between the two. Arm gestures that involve more wrist rotation (such as ThumbsDown) will result in higher gyroscope energy. On the other hand, the arm gestures with more motion but less rotation (e.g. up or down) have more accelerometer energy and less gyroscope energy.

Using these attributes, we build machine learning classifiers to classify gestures in the three types. We use three different machine learning methods - Naive Bayes, Logistic Regression and Decision Tree - for comparison. We will use these three methods along with 10-fold cross-validation to present our evaluation throughout the paper. The results of the classifications are presented in Table 2. It can be observed that the True Positive Rate (TP Rate) for arm gesture classification is 100% while the classification accuracy is slightly lower in finger and hand gestures. Logistic regression-based classifier achieves the highest overall accuracy (maximum weighed TP rate) among all three methods. Table 3 provides the confusion matrix for the logistic regression-based classifier. It shows that hand and finger gestures are often misclassified among each other especially when some hand gestures such as UpOnce or DownOnce have similar motion energy as the finger gestures.

Classifier	TP Rate		
	Finger	Hand	Arm
Naive Bayes	91.50%	81.40%	100.00%
Logistic Regression	99.20%	97.10%	100.00%
Decision Tree	99.20%	93.60%	100.00%

Table 2: Gesture type classification accuracy

2.3 Motion Energy in Wrist from Finger and Hand Gesture

We now investigate the resultant motion energy in wrist when performing a finger or a hand gesture. Higher resultant energy would mean that wrist motion is a good representation of the finger/hand gesture and it might be possible to *uniquely identify* the gesture itself.

For analyzing this, we use three separate Shimmer sensors - one on the index finger, the second on wrist (like the smartwatch as before) and the third one on the forearm. The setup is shown in Fig. 3. When the user performs a finger or a hand gesture, measured motion energy in index finger Shimmer sensor would be the highest. However, it is not clear how much of this motion is reflected by the motion energy measured at the wrist and the forearm Shimmer sensors. We study the forearm case because it was shown by [8] that forearm muscles are good representatives of the hand movements.

With this setup of three sensors, the user performs a finger gesture and data is collected from all the three sensors. The user moves her index finger up and down with increasing the frequency of up-down with time. This is shown in Fig. 4. We can observe that motion energy measured in index finger sensor is very high, and it increases with time as user increases the frequency of motion. The motion energy at the wrist and the forearm sensors are also shown in Fig. 4. It is observed that forearm has lesser motion energy compared to the wrist sensor. We also see that the motion energy measured in the wrist sensor is a good indication of finger movements. Since the finger motion energy is the highest while doing a finger gesture, we can use a wearable ring (such as [9]) to identify the gestures, however, its limitation is that it can only be used to understand gestures of one specific finger on which the ring is worn. While with smartwatch, it is possible to recognize gestures of all fingers as we will show in Section 3.

We repeat the experiment with a hand gesture where user continuously makes a fist and releases the fist. The results of measured motion energy are presented in Fig. 5. Compared to the finger gesture, more motion energy is observed in the index finger sensor. We conclude the same phenomenon as Fig. 4 that motion energy in wrist is more compared to the forearm and it is also a good representative of the hand movement.

3. GESTURE RECOGNITION

We know from the previous section that there is a noticeable motion energy observed in the wrist when performing a finger or a hand gesture. In this section, we leverage this to build a gesture recognition technique. We first provide a brief description of anatomy of human hand and wrist to describe how tendons are responsible for creating a unique signature of different gestures.

3.1 Anatomy of Hand and Wrist

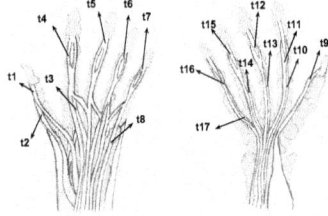

Figure 7: Tendons in posterior (left) and anterior (right) view of human hand and wrist

There are a total of seven different muscles in the forearm which are responsible for extension (releasing a fist) and flexion (making a fist) motions. These muscles include five extensor muscles and two flexor muscles. Each of these muscles are responsible for movements of different sets of fingers. The movement itself, however, is carried out using the tendons which are tissues that connect the muscles with the finger bones (refer Fig. 7). There are seventeen tendons on the front and back of the wrist. When user moves a finger or the hand, these tendons get pushed or pulled, resulting in some movement around the wrist area. As we show next, this movement is sufficiently rich to recognize different finger and hand gestures.

3.2 Primitive Gestures

To demonstrate that movement of tendons can be used to distinguish different gestures, we first take examples of primitive gestures and show how smartwatch accelerometer and gyroscope data is different for each of them. Fig. 8 shows the accelerometer data for Y-axis when the four fingers and the thumb individually perform a simple up-down gesture once. Simple visual inspection reveals that each finger (or the thumb) has clearly distinct pattern when performing the same gesture. This is because different tendons are involved in the movement of different fingers and the thumb. For example, for the index finger, extensor tendons t3 and t4 (Fig. 7) enable the up movement, while for the little finger, extensor tendons t7 and t8 create the up movement.

We also test how the accelerometer pattern is different when performing different gestures using the same finger. For this, user performs three different gestures - up-down, circular motion and left-right - using her index finger. Fig. 9 shows that the accelerometer data from smartwatch is sufficiently different for each gesture even when performed using the same finger.

3.3 Gesture Recognition

After our preliminary study with primitive gestures, we now attempt to identify each gesture (finger, hand or arm) uniquely given the accelerometer and gyroscope data from smartwatch. In order to perform this gesture recognition, we collect the data of all gestures listed in Table 1 (each gesture

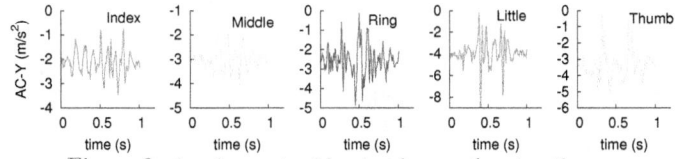

Figure 8: Accelerometer Y-axis when performing the same up-down gesture with four fingers and the thumb

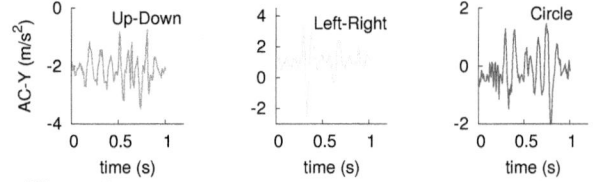

Figure 9: Accelerometer Y-axis when doing three different primitive gestures with index finger

repeated 10 times). Since each gesture has a different time duration, we use a time interval between two gestures where user's hand is stationary to delimit the gesture boundaries for both training and testing.

Feature Extraction and Evaluation: After collecting the data for all gesture instances, we calculate various features using the data. The complete list of features is provided in Table 4. This forms a subset of features extracted from [11]. In [11], it was shown that these features closely correlate to human activity (e.g. walking, running etc) and various postures (e.g. sleeping, sitting etc.). Because these features were initially proposed for smartphone to evaluate human body movement, it is not clear that their direct application to smartwatch gesture recognition would be useful or not. To calculate the worth of these features, we use Information Gain-based feature evaluation.

Type	Features
Motion Energy	ACEnergy, ACLowEnergy
Posture	DCMean, DCTotalMean, DCArea, DCPostureDist
Motion Shape	ACAbsMean, ACAbsArea, ACTotalAbsArea
Motion Variation	ACVar, ACAbsCV, ACIQR, ACRange

Table 4: Features selected from [11]; refer [11] for complete definitions and full names; all features are calculated for both accelerometer and gyroscope; some features calculated across all three axis while the others for all three axis individually

Information gain [13] measures the number of bits of information obtained in predicting a gesture in presence of a feature compared to the feature being absent. It is measured by calculating the entropy. Let F be a feature and G be the set of gestures then Equ. 2 and Equ. 3 calculate the entropy of G in absence and presence of feature F respectively.

$$E(G) = -\sum_{g \in G} p(g) \log_2 p(g) \qquad (2)$$

$$E(G|F) = -\sum_{f \in F} p(f) \sum_{g \in G} p(g|f) \log_2 p(g|f) \qquad (3)$$

Here, $p(g)$ is the fraction of instances for gesture $g \in G$, $p(f)$ is the probability that feature F has the value f and $p(g|f)$ is the fraction of instances of g given $F = f$. The information gain of F is then calculated as $E(G) - E(G|F)$.

We calculate the information gain for all features in Table 4 and order them in decreasing order of their information gain. Fig. 10a shows the information gain of top 10 features. It is observed that features of motion energy, posture and shape have high information gain in distinguishing the gestures, while motion variation features are of little use in classification. This is expected given that motion shape and posture related features are likely to be useful in distinguishing among the gestures of one type - arm, hand or finger, and as we saw in Section 2, motion energy is useful in classifying the gesture type itself. Hence, we only use motion energy, posture and shape related features in our identification.

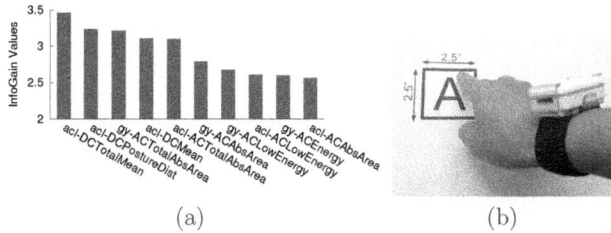

Figure 10: (a) Top 10 features with highest information gain; *acl-* and *gy-* indicate features calculated for accelerometer and gyroscope respectively (b) Experiment settings of how user writes alphabets on a surface while wearing the smartwatch

Identification Performance: Using the features selected from previous section, we build three classifiers as before - Naive Bayes (NB), Logistic Regression (LR) and Decision Tree (DT). The results of the gesture identification are presented in Tables 5 and 6. Table 5 shows the maximum, minimum and average TP rate for all gestures, and top three most misidentified gestures for each classifier. We observe that Naive Bayes outperforms the other two classifiers with an overall accuracy of 98%. The top 3 misidentified gestures of NB and DT suggest that finger gestures recognition is comparatively more difficult than hand and arm gestures. For the LR classifier, the model performs well to classify finger and hand gestures but the accuracy of arm gestures recognition is relatively lower (top 3 misidentified are arm gestures). Since in this paper, we are interested in understanding the feasibility of gesture recognition, we only use the data collected from a single person. However, the method can be extended for more than one user where a separate classifier is trained for each user based on how she performs the given gesture. We leave the accuracy evaluation of such user-specific classifier to future work.

Table 6 shows the confusion matrix for each gesture type for the NB classifier. The arm gestures have high TP rate of identification and they are only misidentified as other arm gestures. This is in line with our results in Table 3 where arm gestures were not misclassified as other types of gestures. The hand gestures have the highest TP rate in Table 6 although they had the lowest classification accuracy in Table 3. This means that they were often misclassified but with additional set of features, they are rarely misidentified. The finger gestures, on the other hand, have the lowest classification and identification accuracy.

4. FINGER WRITING WITH SMARTWATCH

We saw in the previous section that even finger gestures can be identified with a very high accuracy. Motivated by this, we now take a look at detecting finger writing using the smartwatch. Writing with the index finger (on a surface or in the air) is one of the most intuitive way of human-computer interaction. If we can detect what a user is writing with her

| Classifier | TP Rate | | | Top 3 Misidentified |
	Max.	Min.	Avg.	
NB	100%	80.00%	98.11%	Finger-One, Arm-Left, Finger-Two
LR	100%	60.00%	94.60%	Arm-Up, Arm-ClockwiseCircle, Arm-Cross
DT	100%	80.00%	95.41%	Finger-One, Arm-Left, Finger-TwoTwice

Table 5: Gesture recognition accuracy and top three misclassified gestures

| Gesture Type | TP Rate | Misidentified as | | |
		Finger	Hand	Arm
Finger	93.85%	2	1	0
Hand	98.57%	0	1	0
Arm	96.00%	0	0	2

Table 6: TP rate of each type of gestures in NB classifier; finger gestures have the lowest TP rate among the three types

index finger using her smartwatch, it can be used to input text to smartwatch itself or other connected nearby devices such as a smartphone. For example, a user can finger-write an instant message to her smartwatch or an email to her smartphone. In this section, we investigate the question: can we detect the characters written by the user with her index finger using the smartwatch accelerometer and gyroscope sensors?

Finger-writing on Surface: A user can write with her index finger on a surface or in the air. Writing on the surface (on a desk, on a wall or on one's thigh) is often preferred as it provides a touch-based feedback to the user, allowing her to be more accurate in writing. In this work, we have focused on detecting writing on the surface and we are currently extending this to air-writing as discussed in Section 5. The touch-based feedback received by the user when writing on the surface generates a counter-acting force, pushing and pulling the index finger tendons in different ways. This movement of tendons is reflected in the smartwatch accelerometer and gyroscope, and it allows us to detect the characters.

To collect the sensor data, we use the settings shown in Fig. 10b where user writes a character on any surface. The size of the alphabet written by the user is approximately 2.5" in width and height, however, user writes on a surface without any printed characters or box. The accelerometer and gyroscope data is collected when user writes all 26 alphabets 10 times. We calculate the same set of features as in the gesture recognition and put them to test for classification.

Classification Performance: Table 7 shows the results for character classification using the three machine learning methods. It is observed that logistic regression outperforms the other two classifiers in overall accuracy. It shows that characters in finger-writing can be uniquely identified with an accuracy of 94.6%. Table 7 also shows that "D" and "U" are the most often misclassified alphabets in all three classifiers. In our classification, "D" and "U" are most often misclassified as "B" and "V" respectively. This is because these alphabets have similar primitive strokes. Some of the other misclassified instances include "W" as "N" and "R" as "A". In general, the classification accuracy of approximately 95% means that finger-writing on a surface while wearing a smartwatch can be an accurate way of inputting text to

Classifier	TP Rate			Top 3 Misclassified
	Max.	Min.	Avg.	
NB	100%	70.00%	90.00%	"D", "U", "W"
SL	100%	80.00%	94.62%	"D", "U", "R"
DT	100%	70.00%	88.08%	"D", "U", "A"

Table 7: Classification accuracy of recognizing finger-written alphabets and top three misclassified alphabets

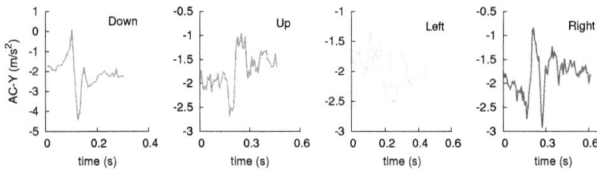

Figure 11: Accelerometer Y-axis data for four primitive strokes when writing in the air using the index finger

smartwatch itself (e.g. instant messaging) or other devices connected to the smartwatch (e.g. smartphone).

5. POTENTIAL AND CHALLENGES

During this research, we discovered that smartwatch has a great potential in enabling gesture recognition and finger-writing. Our findings suggest that the smartwatch can also be used to detect fine-grained movements of user's fingers. This opens a new avenue for research where the smartwatch can be used for many novel applications such as virtual touch screen and interaction with smart-environment.

There are numerous challenges in realizing the true potential of smartwatch. First, in this paper, we have only explored finger gesture recognition when user's wrist and arm are affixed to the chair arm. Recognizing finger gestures while the arm and wrist are allowed to move freely is challenging as it requires a method that can cancel the noise due to arm/wrist movement to distill the signals of finger movement. Another challenge is that different people write and perform different gestures in different ways. Such user-specific characteristics (e.g. right vs. left handed user etc.) require a separate user-specific classifier to be trained. Reducing the computational complexity, memory requirements and energy consumption of training and testing such a classifier is an important direction of future work. Additional challenges are introduced when extending our finger-writing on surface to finger-writing in the air due to unconstrained movement of user's finger. In our ongoing work, we are pursuing to design such air-writing system. Fig. 11 shows some preliminary results where we can see how different primitive strokes in the air are different in terms of smartwatch's accelerometer data. We are also addressing additional challenges such as detecting continuous writing to form words and sentences. The same framework will be further extended to create a virtual touch-screen where user can interact with remote devices by simply moving her fingers in the air.

6. RELATED WORK

Gesture recognition related research has gained a lot of interest in recent years. The research can be classified in two types: motion sensor-based approaches and RF-based approaches. Similar to our work, in the motion sensor-based gesture recognition, accelerometer and gyroscope sensors embedded in various devices are used for gesture recognition. In [9], authors presented a wearable ring platform which can be used to understand user's finger gestures and writing. However, this limits the gestures to a specific finger, and gestures using other fingers like little finger or thumb can not be identified. In this work, we showed that smartwatch-based gesture recognition is more general as it allows us to recognize gestures from all fingers and hand. Similarly, [8] introduced an arm-band which is worn on the forearm to be able to recognize many arm and hand gestures. As we showed in Section 2.2, more motion energy is observed in the wrist compared to the forearm, making smartwatch a more accurate way of gesture recognition. Also, due to limited motion energy in forearm, it can not be used for detecting finger gestures or writing. In RF-based gesture recognition, [12] showed how Doppler shift can be used to detect user's arm gestures even when user is not equipped with any device. In our previous work [14], we showed how an access point can detect user's arm gestures performed while holding the smartphone. Such device-free gesture recognition is difficult to be applied to identify low-intensity finger gestures and writing.

7. CONCLUSIONS

In this work, we explored how smartwatch can be used for gesture recognition and finger-writing. We showed that smartwatch sensors can accurately detect arm, hand and even finger gestures. It was also demonstrated that smartwatch can detect the characters when user writes on a surface using her index finger. Gesture recognition and finger-writing using smartwatch can be used to create novel applications for interacting with nearby devices and remotely controlling them. As part of our ongoing work, we are designing a virtual touch-screen and techniques to detect user's finger-writing in the air based on smartwatch sensors.

Acknowledgements

We thank Muchen Wu for his help in feature calculation. We also thank our shepherd, Kannan Srinivasan and anonymous reviewers for their insightful comments.

8. REFERENCES

[1] http://www.apple.com/watch.
[2] http://www.lg.com/global/gwatch.
[3] https://moto360.motorola.com/.
[4] http://www.samsung.com/us/mobile/wearable-tech.
[5] https://www.fitbit.com/.
[6] http://www.shimmersensing.com.
[7] http://developer.getpebble.com.
[8] https://www.thalmic.com/en/myo/.
[9] J. Gummeson, B. Priyantha, and J. Liu. An energy harvesting wearable ring platform for gestureinput on surfaces. In *Mobisys*. ACM, 2014.
[10] Y. Michalevsky, D. Boneh, and G. Nakibly. Gyrophone: Recognizing speech from gyroscope signals. In *USENIX Security 2014*.
[11] E. Munguia Tapia. *Using machine learning for real-time activity recognition and estimation of energy expenditure*. PhD thesis, MIT, 2008.
[12] Q. Pu, S. Gupta, S. Gollakota, and S. Patel. Whole-home gesture recognition using wireless signals. In *Mobicom*. ACM, 2013.
[13] I. H. Witten, E. Frank, and M. A. Hall. *Data Mining: Practical Machine Learning Tools and Techniques*. Morgan Kaufmann Publishers Inc., 2011.
[14] Y. Zeng, P. H. Pathak, C. Xu, and P. Mohapatra. Your ap knows how you move: fine-grained device motion recognition through wifi. In *HotWireless*. ACM, 2014.

Mobile Touch-Free Interaction for Global Health

Nicola Dell, Krittika D'Silva, Gaetano Borriello
Department of Computer Science & Engineering
University of Washington
{nixdell, kdsilva, gaetano}@cs.washington.edu

ABSTRACT

Health workers in remote settings are increasingly using mobile devices to assist with a range of medical tasks that may require them to handle potentially infectious biological material, and touching their mobile device in these scenarios is undesirable or potentially harmful. To overcome this challenge, we present Maestro, a software-only gesture detection system that enables touch-free interaction on commodity mobile devices. Maestro uses the built-in, forward-facing camera on the device and computer vision to recognize users' in-air gestures. Our key design criteria are high gesture recognition rates and low power consumption. We describe Maestro's design and implementation and show that the system is able to detect and respond to users' gestures in real-time with acceptable energy consumption and memory overheads. We also evaluate Maestro through a controlled user study that provides insight into the performance of touch-free interaction, finding that participants were able to make gestures quickly and accurately enough to be useful for a variety of motivating global health applications. Finally, we describe the programming effort required to integrate touch-free interaction into several open-source mobile applications so that it can be used on commodity devices without requiring changes to the operating system. Taken together, our findings suggest that Maestro is a simple and practical tool that could allow health workers in remote settings to interact with their devices touch-free in demanding settings.

Keywords

Touch-free interaction; mobile device; smartphone; situational impairment; global health; mHealth.

1. INTRODUCTION

The field of mobile health is an emerging area of research that encompasses the use of mobile devices, such as smartphones or tablet computers, to deliver health services and information. The rapid increase in mobile device penetration throughout the world, and particularly in developing

HotMobile '15, February 12 - 13 2015, Santa Fe, NM, USA
ACM 978-1-4503-3391-7/15/02 ... $15.00
http://dx.doi.org/10.1145/2699343.2699355

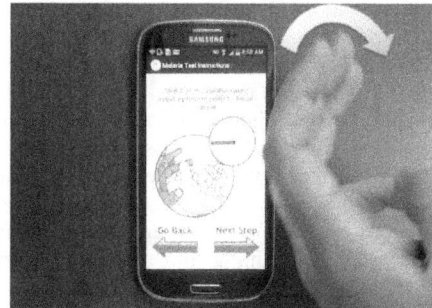

Figure 1: Maestro uses the forward-facing camera on mobile devices to detect users' in-air gestures.

countries, has resulted in the creation of a large number of mobile health applications designed to increase access to healthcare and health-related information, improve disease diagnosis and tracking, and provide health workers with ongoing medical education and training. However, many of the medical tasks that these mobile applications are designed to assist with also require health workers to handle potentially infectious biological material. For example, health workers using a mobile device to process rapid diagnostic tests for infectious diseases must handle blood samples [4]. Although health workers typically wear latex gloves when handling this potentially harmful material, touching a mobile device in these scenarios risks contamination of both the device from the gloves, or the gloves from the device. In these situations, it would be beneficial if health workers were able to interact with the device without touching it at all.

Fortunately, modern mobile devices come equipped with a range of sensors, including cameras, that can be used to create alternate methods of interaction with devices. A device's programming interface gives developers access to raw data from these sensors, but significant programming effort from the developer, unrelated to the application's core functionality, is needed to facilitate a touch-free experience. To overcome this barrier, we created Maestro, a software library for Android that uses computer vision to detect in-air gestures (see Figure 1). The Maestro API provides application developers with easy, high-level access to a variety of touch-free gestures that can be detected using any commodity smartphone equipped with a basic forward-facing camera.

Many of the global health scenarios that we target lack reliable Internet connectivity. As a result, we focus on recognizing a minimal set of touch-free gestures using image processing algorithms that run entirely on the device. This simple and intuitive gesture set is appropriate for a variety of global health applications, including mobile job aids for clinical procedures and applications that assist with disease diagnosis [4], and a range of diverse users can achieve high enough gesture recognition rates to be practical in demanding public health settings.

Key results from our work demonstrate that Maestro can successfully enable touch-free interaction for a range of mobile applications. In addition, the energy consumption and memory usage overheads imposed by the system are acceptable for practical use. The system is also capable of processing image data obtained from the device's camera fast enough to detect and respond to users' gestures in real-time, with the overall speed of interaction limited by how fast users move their hands, rather than by the speed of computation. Furthermore, findings from a user evaluation with 18 participants show that, within minutes of first being introduced to Maestro's gestures, many participants were able to sustain speeds of over 40 correct touch-free gestures per minute. Finally, participants were also able to use Maestro's touch-free gestures to successfully perform a range of common interactions (e.g., scrolling, swiping and selecting targets) and navigate our target global health applications touch free.

This paper makes the following contributions: (1) the identification of key design principles required to make a touch-free system appropriate for global health scenarios in low-resource settings; (2) the design of Maestro, a software-only gesture detection system that uses the forward-facing camera on commodity mobile devices to detect and respond to users' in-air gestures; (3) an inspection-based evaluation that details the programming effort required to add touch-free interaction to several open-source mobile applications; (4) a performance evaluation that quantifies the responsiveness of the system and the energy and memory usage overheads incurred by Maestro's algorithms; and (5) a user evaluation that shows Maestro's gestures are easy-to-learn and that people are capable of using them to successfully navigate a variety of user interfaces and realistic applications. Our findings suggest that Maestro is a simple and practical tool that allows users in a range of global health scenarios to interact with commodity mobile devices touch free.

2. RELATED WORK

Gestural input for natural human-computer interaction has for decades inspired research that explores potential future scenarios [1]. We wanted to create a practical working solution that runs on commodity mobile devices and that is viable for immediate use in the field.

A large number of existing desktop-based vision systems focus on detecting and segmenting the hand from the background using shape or skin color [11]. Systems have been designed to detect both static hand poses and dynamic gestures [18] and many of these systems have been useful for sign-language recognition [16]. The reliability of hand-tracking systems depends heavily on the specific features used for tracking and segmentation and on powerful machine-learning algorithms for recognition [11]. The sophistication of these algorithms enables many of these systems to recognize between 5 and 50 gestures. However, developing a vision-based

touch-free system for use by health workers in low-resource settings requires a different approach for several reasons. First, most prior solutions run on computationally powerful desktop computers. Our work focuses on mobile devices with limited computational capabilities, which makes it more difficult to meet real-time requirements using such intensive approaches. In addition, these systems generally expect users to dedicate both hands (and their full attention) to interacting with the system. However, in global health scenarios, users' hands may be occupied with other tasks, such as holding a biological sample, and their attention should be primarily on patients and not on the system. These constraints suggest that, rather than focusing on a large and complex gesture set, a system targeting global health scenarios should instead focus on recognizing simple, intuitive and easy-to-remember gestures that can be performed while the health worker's hands are occupied with other tasks and the device is on a surface.

A variety of other existing systems use additional hardware to perform gesture detection. Glove-based systems, like ImageGlove [10], require users to wear a special glove and map motion changes in the glove to gestures. Another class of systems use specialized sensing devices designed to be worn on the body, like Abracadabra [5]. There are also systems that augment commodity devices with additional sensors, such as Hoverflow [7] and SideSight [3]. PalmSpace [8] uses a depth camera to track 3D hand positions, while Pouke et al. [14] use a Bluetooth-connected sensor attached to the hand. Although the use of additional hardware can lead to powerful solutions, users must purchase and set up the additional components. This may be particularly challenging for non-technical users in developing countries and the additional components only increase the likelihood that something may get lost, broken, or exhaust its own batteries. By using a self-contained commodity device, Maestro greatly simplifies deployments and training.

Finally, a number of specialized consumer devices, like Leap Motion's Leap [9] enable touch-free interaction with large displays or televisions. In addition, several specific mobile device models, like the Samsung Galaxy S4 [15], also offer some built-in touch-free capabilities. However, the algorithms and APIs that provide this functionality have not been documented or released, and no rigorous system or user evaluations have been presented that describe the usability of these systems. We wanted to create a solution that works on a wide range of commodity devices that are affordable and available in developing countries, rather than force users to purchase a specific device model.

3. SCENARIO AND DESIGN PRINCIPLES

We focus on the following usage scenario for Maestro: a health worker in a rural clinic in Africa has been issued a mobile device to assist with medical duties. The health worker enters a patient exam room to perform a medical procedure, such as administering a rapid diagnostic test for HIV [4]. She removes the mobile device from a pocket and places it flat on the table. She also collects and prepares any necessary medical equipment, like syringes, gauzes and protective gloves. When ready, she starts the appropriate mobile application on the device and activates touch-free interaction. Then, she puts on a pair of protective latex gloves and moves through the steps of the procedure, interacting with the patient and with the device touch-free by passing a hand over it as if "swiping in mid-air." When instructed to by the application, she collects the necessary blood sample from the patient and places it on the test. After completing the procedure, she disposes of any infectious material, removes her gloves, and can then touch the device again.

Our key design principles are informed by current literature and the constraints presented by global health scenarios.

Camera-Based Input: We considered a variety of input modalities, including sound and voice, before settling on camera-based gesture detection. Clinics in developing countries are usually noisy, busy and crowded, which could decrease the accuracy of voice recognition. In addition, collecting blood or biological samples from patients (especially children) may result in crying or other noises that could interfere with a voice or sound-based system. Moreover, we wanted to build a system that works for diverse populations who speak different languages. This made it undesirable to require users to speak voice commands in a potentially unfamiliar language. We also wanted to ensure that health workers are free to speak clearly to patients, and issuing voice commands to the system could interfere with health worker-patient conversations. Finally, camera-based input is already used in clinical settings for a range of tasks, including data collection [6], microscopy [2], and disease diagnosis [4].

Flexible and Easy-to-Learn: Users need to be able to interact with a device while their hands are occupied, such as holding a biological sample. Thus, Maestro does not rely on users being able to make specific shapes with their fingers or hands and instead targets a simple and flexible, although limited, gesture set. Furthermore, to prevent contamination users need not touch other objects, such as a stylus or tapping a tabletop. Touch-free interaction should be intuitive and easy to learn. We specifically target a simple gesture set that people would quickly understand and easily remember but provide basic navigation and selection primitives.

No Additional Hardware and Device-Independent: Requiring that people purchase and setup additional hardware is a significant barrier for many potential users in developing countries and increases the likelihood that hardware will get lost or broken or not be properly connected or powered. Maestro only uses hardware that is integral to a range of commodity mobile devices readily available around the world. Health programs in developing countries have diverse needs and budgets, thus, we do not want to constrain users to specific models (*e.g.*, the Samsung Galaxy S4). Instead, Maestro is a software-only solution that enables touch-free interaction on a wide variety of different device models.

Local Computation and Calibration-Free: Many remote clinics in developing countries do not have reliable Internet access. Thus, all of the computation required to detect and respond to touch-free gestures must be performed locally on the device. Maestro targets global health applications that will be used by a diverse range of people in a variety of scenarios. In addition, in many developing countries, multiple users often share a single device. Thus, the system must work "out of the box" for a wide range of people (including different skin tones) and not require per user calibration.

Application-Level and Developer-Friendly: Enabling touch-free interaction should not require users to make changes to a device's underlying operating system because many commercially available mobile devices are locked by manufacturers and system-level changes may void manufacturer warranties. Maestro exposes a robust and usable API that developers can use to enable touch-free interaction on existing applications with only minimal modifications.

4. MAESTRO

Touch-free interaction will be useful for a range of specific applications in which it is undesirable or potentially harmful for users to touch a device. We are not suggesting that touch-free interaction will replace touch, nor have we tried to fully replicate multi-touch gestures provided by many touch-screen devices. Instead, Maestro provides much of the same functionality as a desktop mouse, allowing users to move a cursor around the screen, scroll, and select user interface targets. We expect that this limited gesture set will achieve simplicity and ease-of-use while also providing sufficient expressivity and flexibility for our target applications and many others. At a high-level, Maestro monitors image data from a device's front-facing camera in real-time and detects five basic gestures: up, down, left, right and dwell. The directional gestures are triggered by moving any object, including a finger or hand, across the camera's field of view in the desired direction. The speed of the gesture is recorded and can be used to add further expressivity to the motion commands. The dwell gesture is triggered when the user covers the camera's field of view for a short period of time. This gesture is used to indicate a click or tap.

4.1 Algorithm

In keeping with our design principles, Maestro's gesture recognition algorithm is relatively simple, both conceptually and computationally. The first stage of the algorithm works by comparing pairs of consecutive grayscale video frames captured by the forward-facing camera. For each pair of frames, we calculate the absolute value of the per-pixel difference between the images. This gives us the number of pixels at which movement occurred between the two frames. We then find the moment that the number of moving pixels exceeds a dynamically adjusted threshold, and consider that point in time to be the start of a gesture. Once the number of moving pixels drops below the threshold, the gesture is considered complete. To calculate an appropriate threshold, we keep a running average of the amount of motion between consecutive pairs of frames for the last few hundred frames and pick a value that is substantially larger (*e.g.*, 15% higher) than the average current motion. We also calculate the duration of the gesture by recording the time at which the motion started and ended. Gestures that are classified as being either too short or too long are filtered as noise. In addition, we enforce a minimum between-gesture time to minimize the chances that backswing, secondary, or recovery motions are falsely detected as gestures. After detecting a gesture, the next step is to determine whether the gesture is directional, or whether the user paused over the camera for a dwell gesture. To differentiate between gesture types, we analyze the average grayscale intensity of each frame that makes up the gesture. In a directional gesture, the intensities of the frames get darker as the user moves towards the camera, and then lighter again as the user moves away. By contrast, with a dwell gesture, the intensities of the frames get darker as the user covers the camera and stay dark until the motion has stopped. To detect this difference, the system again keeps a running average of the grayscale intensity for the last few hundred frames. This average constitutes a background intensity value. If the intensity of the final gesture frame is sufficiently lower (*e.g.*, 15% lower) than the current background intensity, it is classified as a dwell gesture. If a dwell gesture is not detected, the gesture is deemed to be directional and to determine its direction, we compute the average geometric coordinates of all the pixels at which motion was detected at the start of the gesture. This computation results in a single point at which movement was centered when the gesture began. We then compute the corresponding center of motion at the end of the gesture. If the distance covered along one of the axes is sufficiently large (*e.g.*, 20% of the screen's width), the gesture is classified as being in that direction.

4.2 Mapping Gestures to Interactions

UI targets include buttons, checkboxes, and lists. Typically, these have listeners that trigger an action when the element is selected. Although users can touch anywhere on the screen, it often only makes sense to touch a target. Target-awareness has been exploited in prior work, including using the tab key to navigate the focus of an application from one target to the next. Maestro also exploits the focus property of UI targets. Directional gestures can move the application's focus to the next target in the specified direction and the dwell gesture used to select the target currently in focus. In addition to navigating UI elements, touch-free gestures can be directly mapped to horizontal and vertical scrolling. The speed of the gesture can control the speed of scrolling. A dwell gesture can be used to activate scrolling, and another dwell or timeout used for deactivation. Finger-based touch gestures, such as swipes and flicks, have become popular in touchscreen applications and provide a natural style of user interaction. Maestro's directional gestures provide a similar interaction style and developers can choose to map Maestro's gestures (*e.g.*, using their speed) to these finger-based touch gestures to achieve similar effects.

4.3 Implementation

We implemented Maestro as an application-level software library on the Android platform. The image processing components of the library were implemented in native code using OpenCV [13], an open-source computer vision library. Gesture detection and classification were implemented using Android's Java framework and use the JNI to communicate with OpenCV's native image processing algorithms. All of the computation is performed locally on the device.

5. ADDING TOUCH-FREE INTERACTION TO EXISTING MOBILE APPLICATIONS

Maestro exposes an API that developers can use to map touch-free gestures to UI interactions. Any application module or activity that will respond to touch-free gestures should contain a small amount of code to initialize the camera and the UI, and five methods that specify the actions to be taken when each of the five touch-free gesture types is detected. This section describes the programming effort required to integrate Maestro into several popular open-source applica-

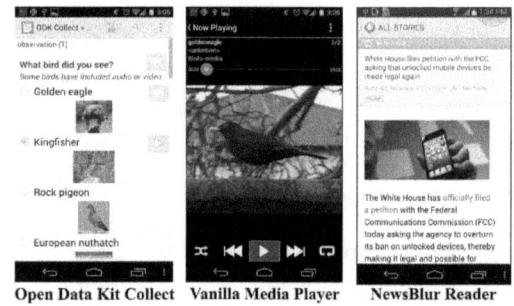

Open Data Kit Collect   **Vanilla Media Player**   **NewsBlur Reader**

Figure 2: Screenshots from existing applications that we modified to enable touch-free interaction.

tions: Open Data Kit (ODK) Collect [6], the Vanilla media player [17] and NewsBlur [12] (see Figure 2).

ODK Collect has thousands of users and is the preferred mobile data collection tool for many global health applications [6]. Users navigate through screens of the application using swipe gestures, enter data, and read text. Vanilla [17] is a popular media player that provides lists of albums, artists and songs and an interface for playing tracks. NewsBlur [12] is a personal newsreader that allows users to subscribe to news feeds and to read, tag and share stories. We did not attempt to make every module or activity in each application touch free. Instead, we focused on activities in which touch-free interaction would be most useful. For ODK Collect, we added touch-free interaction to the activities for navigating menus and lists, swiping through screens, and entering, editing and saving data. For Vanilla, we added touch-free interaction to the activities for browsing and selecting artists, albums and songs, and for playing and navigating tracks. For NewsBlur, we added touch-free interaction to the activities for browsing, reading and navigating articles.

The code to integrate Maestro into these applications was written by a second-year undergraduate who was familiar with Maestro but not with the target applications. Enabling touch-free interaction required a small amount of code to be added to each module or activity that will respond to touch-free gestures. This code can be divided into four tasks that were common to all activities across all applications: (1) system initialization of the camera (30 lines of code identical across all apps); (2) initialization to make UI elements "focusable" (2-20 lines per activity); (3) focus navigation required four routines for each of the directional gestures (14-20 lines of code); and, (4) target selection to handle dwell gestures (4 lines - identical across all activities). Although we realize that the amount of code added to each application does not necessarily translate to ease of integration, we wanted to include these measurements to provide readers with a rough indication of the effort required (*i.e.*, enabling touch-free interaction required tens of lines of code rather than hundreds or thousands of lines of code).

In summary, we added touch-free interaction to five activities in ODK Collect. These activities averaged 793 lines of code each without Maestro. We added an average of 66 lines of code to each activity, 34 of which were identical to all five activities. In addition, two sets of two activities shared the exact same code. We added touch-free interaction to two activities in Vanilla that averaged 1008 lines of code each without Maestro. We added an average of 59 lines to each activity, 34 of which were common to both activities. Furthermore, the code added to one of the Vanilla activities was exactly the same as that added to two of the ODK Collect activities. Finally, we added touch-free interaction to three activities in NewsBlur that averaged 325 lines of code each without Maestro. We added an average of 50 lines of code to each activity, 34 of which were common to all activities. In addition, two NewsBlur activities shared identical code.

6. EVALUATION

We performed experiments to evaluate the responsiveness of the system as well as the energy and memory overhead added by Maestro. Our experiments were conducted using a Samsung Galaxy S3 device running Android v.4.1. All of the computation was performed locally on the device using a 1.4 GHz processor, 1 GB RAM and a 4.8 inch capacitive touchscreen. Touch-free gestures were detected using the built-in 1.9 mega-pixel forward-facing camera.

Responsiveness: We performed several experiments to quantify the responsiveness of the system to the user. The data for these experiments was collected by running Maestro on the device and recording all of the system timing data for five sets of 100 random touch-free gestures. Our data set thus consisted of the timing data for a total of 15,199 captured image frames and 500 touch-free gestures. The system is able to operate at 29 frames/second. Maestro's per-frame computation is 6.5ms including all image/motion processing to determine a gesture's start. An average of 184.5ms is spent detecting the end of a gesture but this is mostly due to human motion rather than computation. Only 0.2ms are needed to classify the gesture and trigger the application callback. Taken together, these findings indicate that the system is able to perform all of the computation required for gesture detection and classification in a fraction of the time that it takes a user to move a hand over the camera.

Energy: Since mobile devices are battery powered, energy consumption is a critical factor in assessing the viability of a system for practical, daily use. To compute Maestro's energy overhead, we measured the battery consumption of a system running Maestro and continuously processing image data for a period of four hours. We then measured the battery consumption of the same system without Maestro. In both cases, the device was fully charged prior to the start of the experiment. In addition, the screen was kept on for the duration of the experiment and no other applications were running. At the end of four hours of continuous processing, the system running Maestro had a remaining battery level of 28%, while the system without Maestro had a remaining battery level of 53%. It is important to note that these percentages represent the worst case energy consumption of Maestro. In most cases, the device would also be running other applications that would be consuming energy, and this would lower the percentage of battery usage due to Maestro. In addition, this experiment shows energy consumption resulting from continuously running Maestro for a long period of time. In reality, we expect that Maestro would be activated only when touch-free interaction is necessary, used for a short period of time, and then deactivated when it is safe for the user to touch the device again.

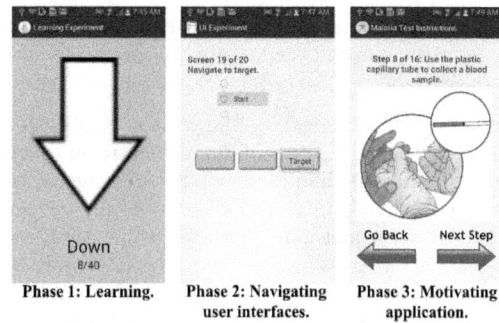

Phase 1: Learning.   Phase 2: Navigating user interfaces.   Phase 3: Motivating application.

Figure 3: Screenshots from our usability experiments: learning drills, UI navigation, and app use.

Memory Overhead: We ran each version of the application for four hours and computed the maximum resident set size in each case. Our findings show that Maestro imposes an 8% memory overhead when compared to the same application not using Maestro. On a mobile device with 1GB of RAM, we do not consider this to be of significance.

User Evaluation: Although we anticipate that touch-free interaction will primarily be useful in scenarios where it is undesirable or potentially harmful to touch the device, we wanted to provide readers with a way to understand the performance of touch-free interaction in comparison to a known point of reference: touch interaction. We expected that touch-free interaction would be slower than touch, but we wanted to quantify the difference to provide readers with context and insight into the usability of touch-free interaction. In addition, we were unable to identify a viable alternative touch-free system with which to compare Maestro. We conducted a controlled laboratory study with 18 participants to: (1) evaluate the speed and accuracy with which users learn to interact touch free; (2) evaluate how well people can use touch-free gestures to interact with user interfaces (UIs); and (3) understand whether people are able to navigate a realistic clinical application - processing a rapid diagnostic test for HIV - without touching the device. Participants completed the experiments while seated with the device flat on a table in front of them. They first watched a two-minute video introducing the gesture techniques and were given one minute to practice making gestures. They then completed three study phases: learning, UI navigation, and completing a clinical application touch-free (see Fig. 3).

Learning: As expected, participants made touch gestures significantly faster than touch-free gestures, 0.66 seconds for touch vs. 1.63 seconds for touch-free. Their accuracy as they learned the touch-free gestures increased leveling out at only 7.5% errors vs. 1% for touch. The learning task encouraged participants to make gestures as fast as possible and it was encouraging that, within minutes of learning the touch-free gestures, many participants were able to sustain speeds of over 40 touch-free gestures per minute. This finding suggests that touch-free gestures were intuitive and easy to learn.

Navigating: Participants took longer to navigate the UI screens using touch-free gestures than touch gestures, spending an average of 1.70 seconds per screen with touch and 6.67 seconds with touch-free. The magnitude of the difference (approximately 4x) between touch and touch-free gestures was expected and can be explained by two factors. First, successfully completing the tasks required participants to make twice as many touch-free gestures as touch gestures. Second, as we saw during the learning phase each touch-free gesture takes roughly 2.5x as long as each touch gesture.

Using the App: For navigating the clinical application, we expected to see a smaller time difference between touch and touch-free interaction than in previous experiments for two reasons. First, participants needed to make only one gesture per screen for both methods. Second, rather than making gestures as fast as possible, the experiment required participants to read a sentence of text on each screen, which increased the task time for both methods. There turned out to be no detectable difference in the times taken to navigate the app using touch and touch-free gestures as the time was dominated by reading (doing the work) rather than by the speed of interaction.

Participant Feedback: A common theme voiced by many participants was *"I was surprised how well [touch-free gestures] worked. For how much this type of technology has been in sci-fi for years, I've never seen it actually used. I always suspected that's because it's not reliable, but it was."* Although this positive feedback is highly encouraging, further research is needed to assess the performance of the system in real global health settings. Integrating Maestro into health workers' clinical routines will likely present a range of additional challenges that will need to be addressed. Moreover, care will need to be taken to ensure that patients are comfortable with health workers using the system during clinical procedures and that patient privacy is properly protected.

7. CONCLUSION

It is important to note that there is no requirement for an application to choose between touch and touch-free interaction. Instead, applications can incorporate both gesture types and switch between them as circumstances warrant. Maestro's simplicity offers a number of advantages. Since the algorithm looks for movement alone (not color or shape), it can recognize any object, including a hand regardless of skintone or covering. Maestro's gesture set also allows novice users to quickly interact touch-free with minimal training. Finally, the computational simplicity of the algorithm makes the system highly responsive. However, the current implementation also has several limitations. For example, the gesture set is limited and does not provide an easy way to simulate more advanced multi-touch gestures like pinch. In addition, our current design is not well suited to text entry. Instead, touch-free interaction is better suited to tasks like scrolling and swiping, while text entry is better suited to touch interaction. Another limitation is that adding touch-free interaction to an application requires that the Maestro library be incorporated into the application's code. We are unable to interact touch-free with closed-source applications already installed on the device. Redirecting gesture input to these applications would require system-level changes that we have specifically avoided because of usage constraints for public health scenarios in the developing world.

Health workers in global health scenarios are increasingly using mobile devices to assist with a range of medical tasks. However, touching the device when performing these tasks may be undesirable or potentially harmful. We identified key design principles for a mobile touch-free system that targets these scenarios. We then presented Maestro, a vision-based system that recognizes in-air gestures using the built-in forward-facing camera on commodity mobile devices. We described the programming effort required to integrate touch-free functionality into three widely-used mobile applications. We also show that the system is capable of responding to users' gestures in real-time while imposing acceptable energy and memory overheads. Finally, we presented a user evaluation that shows people were able to quickly learn touch-free gestures and use them to complete a variety of tasks without touching the device. We conclude that Maestro is a practical tool that could allow users in global health scenarios to interact with commodity mobile devices touch free.

8. ACKNOWLEDGEMENTS

This work was funded by NSF grant 1111433. We also thank Leeran Raphaely and Jacob Wobbrock.

9. REFERENCES

[1] R. A. Bolt. "Put-that-there": Voice and Gesture at the Graphics Interface. In *Computer Graphics and Interactive Techniques*, pages 262–270, 1980.

[2] D. Breslauer, R. Maamari, N. Switz, W. Lam, and D. Fletcher. Mobile phone based clinical microscopy for global health applications. *Plos One*, 4(7), 2009.

[3] A. Butler, S. Izadi, and S. Hodges. Sidesight: Multi-"touch" interaction around small devices. In *User Interface Software and Technology*, UIST '08, pages 201–204, 2008.

[4] N. Dell, I. Francis, H. Sheppard, R. Simbi, and G. Borriello. Field Evaluation of a Camera-Based Mobile Health System in Low-Resource Settings. In *Human-Computer Interaction with Mobile Devices and Services*, 2014.

[5] C. Harrison and S. E. Hudson. Abracadabra: Wireless, high-precision, and unpowered finger input for very small devices. In *User Interface Software and Technology*, 2009.

[6] C. Hartung, Y. Anokwa, W. Brunette, A. Lerer, C. Tseng, and G. Borriello. Open Data Kit: Building Information Services for Developing Regions. In *Information and Communication Technologies and Development*, 2010.

[7] S. Kratz and M. Rohs. Hoverflow: Exploring around-device interaction with ir distance sensors. In *Human-Computer Interaction with Mobile Devices and Services*, 2009.

[8] S. Kratz, M. Rohs, D. Guse, J. Müller, G. Bailly, and M. Nischt. Palmspace: Continuous around-device gestures vs. multitouch for 3d rotation tasks on mobile devices. In *Working Conference on Advanced Visual Interfaces*, 2012.

[9] Leap Motion. https://www.leapmotion.com.

[10] C. Maggioni. A novel gestural input device for virtual reality. In *Virtual Reality Annual Symposium*, 1993.

[11] G. Murthy and R. Jadon. A Review of Vision-Based Hand Gestures Recognition. *Information Technology and Knowledge Management*, 2(2):405–410, 2009.

[12] NewsBlur. http://www.newsblur.com/.

[13] OpenCV. http://opencv.willowgarage.com/wiki/.

[14] M. Pouke, A. Karhu, S. Hickey, and L. Arhippainen. Gaze tracking and non-touch gesture based interaction method for mobile 3d virtual spaces. In *Australian Computer-Human Interaction Conference*, 2012.

[15] Samsung Galaxy S4. http://www.samsung.com/GalaxyS4.

[16] T. Starner, A. Pentland, and J. Weaver. Real-time american sign language recognition using desk and wearable computer based video. *IEEE Trans. Pattern Anal. Mach. Intell.*, 20(12):1371–1375, 1998.

[17] Vanilla Media Player. https://play.google.com/store/apps/details?id=ch.blink enlights.android.vanilla.

[18] Z. Yang, Y. Li, Y. Zheng, W. Chen, and X. Zheng. An interaction system using mixed hand gestures. In *Asia Pacific Conference on Computer Human Interaction*, 2012.

Retro-VLC: Enabling Battery-free Duplex Visible Light Communication for Mobile and IoT Applications

Jiangtao Li
Microsoft Research, Beijing
jangtao.li@gmail.com

Angli Liu
University of Washington
anglil@cs.washington.edu

Guobin Shen
Microsoft Research, Beijing
jacky.shen@microsoft.com

Liqun Li
Microsoft Research, Beijing
liqul@microsoft.com

Chao Sun
Microsoft Research, Beijing
v-csun@microsoft.com

Feng Zhao
Microsoft Research, Beijing
zhao@microsoft.com

ABSTRACT

The ubiquity of the lighting infrastructure makes the visible light communication (VLC) well suited for mobile and Internet of Things (IoT) applications in the indoor environment. However, existing VLC systems have primarily been focused on one-way communications from the illumination infrastructure to the mobile device. They are power demanding and not applicable for communication in the opposite direction. In this paper, we present Retro-VLC, a duplex VLC system that enables a battery-free device to perform bi-directional communications over a shared light carrier across the uplink and downlink. The design features a retro-reflector fabric that backscatters light, an LCD modulator, and several low-power optimization techniques. We have prototyped a working system consisting of a credit card-sized battery-free tag and an illuminating LED reader. Experimental results show that the tag can achieve $10kbps$ downlink speed and $0.5kbps$ uplink speed over a distance of $2.4m$. We outline several potential applications and limitations of the system.

Categories and Subject Descriptors

C.2.1 [**Network Architecture and Design**]: Wireless communication

General Terms

Design, Experimentation, Security

Keywords

Visible Light Communication, Internet of Things, Retro-reflector, Smart Tag, Bi-directional VLC

1. INTRODUCTION

White LEDs are deployed ubiquitously for the illumination purpose for its high energy efficiency, long lifetime, and environmental friendliness. As semiconducting devices, LEDs also possess another feature; *i.e.*, they can be turned on and off *instantaneously*.

This effectively turns LED lights into a communication carrier and gives rise to a new "dual-paradigm" – simultaneous illumination and communication, and has inspired significant research interests in visible light communication (VLC) systems. However, existing VLC systems are usually one-directional, i.e. from the LED to the device (downlink), due to the asymmetric capabilities on its two ends: on one end is the externally powered LED; on the other is the power-constrained mobile or IoT devices that are usually battery empowered. With existing VLC techniques, the mobile/IoT devices cannot afford a power-intensive LED for the uplink transmission. In fact, some early VLC-based mobile systems such as ByteLight [2], which exploits LED lighting infrastructure for both communication and localization [16, 24], have adopted Bluetooth Low Energy (BLE), for the uplink device-to-LED communication. This unfortunately incurs additional cost and system complexity.

In this paper, we present the design and implementation of *Retro-VLC– a battery-free duplex VLC system* that consists of a reader (termed *ViReader*) residing in the lighting infrastructure and a tag (termed *ViTag*) integrated in mobile devices or IoT devices such as sensor nodes. Inspired by recent work on backscattering communication systems [10, 22], we avoid using power-intensive LEDs on the ViTag for the uplink communication. Rather, we choose to backscatter the incoming light from the externally-powered illuminating LED of the ViReader. Central to the Retro-VLC is the adoption of a retro-reflective fabric that bounces light back to its source from arbitrary incidence angles *along its incoming direction*. The retro-reflected light forms the carrier of the visible light uplink.

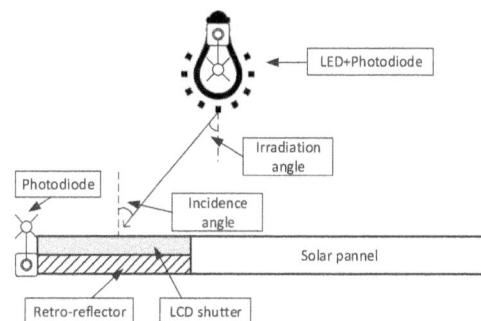

Figure 1: System architecture.

We have implemented a prototype that demonstrates the effectiveness of our Retro-VLC design, as shown in Fig. 1. We have built a ViReader by adding a photodiode and some control circuits to an off-the-shelf LED bulb, and a battery-free ViTag device that operates by harvesting energy from the light. The ViTag consists of a photodiode, a retro-reflector fabric, an LCD shutter, solar cells, and control circuits. It is the same size as a credit card, one-third of the area being the retro-reflector and two-thirds the polycrystalline silicon solar cell.

We evaluate our system in a normal office environment with typical lighting, and also in a dark chamber for comparison. We measure the maximum communication range between the ViReader and the ViTag with various LED illumination levels, device orientations, solar panel areas and retro-reflector areas. Experiments show that the prototype system can achieve a $10kbps$ downlink speed and a $0.5kbps$ uplink speed over distances of up to $1.7m$ in dark chambers and $2.4m$ in office environments. The current at which the tag works is around $90\mu A$. To manifest its advantage in secure communication, we also measure the range within which the uplink transmission from a ViTag may be sniffed.

2. PRINCIPLE AND CHALLENGES

2.1 Explanation on Uplink of Retro-VLC

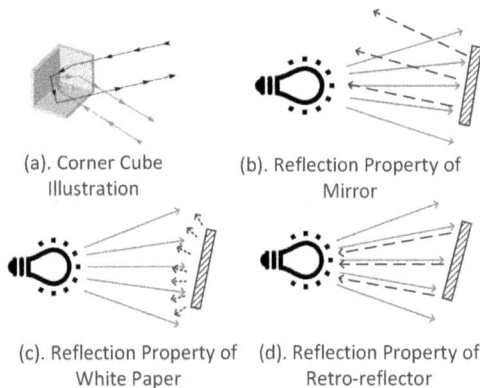

(a). Corner Cube Illustration

(b). Reflection Property of Mirror

(c). Reflection Property of White Paper

(d). Reflection Property of Retro-reflector

Figure 2: Illustration of the principle of retro-reflector reflection. The line in dash is the reflected light.

The major difference between Retro-VLC and traditional VLC systems is the uplink. An easy-to-think solution is duplicate the downlink, *i.e.* to use an LED. However, as Retro-VLC is powered by solar cells, the power consumption of LED would demand an unacceptable solar cell size. Alternatively, if a tag can send information bits by reflecting the light generated the externally-powered LED lamp of the reader, we could preserve significant amount of energy. A mirror could be used for this purpose. However, due to the reflection characteristics, as Fig. 2(b) depicts, a mirror must be perpendicular to the incident light in order for the reader to receive signals effectively. This would be hard to tune and impose significant constraints in the usage. White paper with diffuse reflection may mitigate this problem, as depicted in Fig. 2(c), the signal received by the reader would however be extremely weak due to the low reflection rate of white paper.

In response, we choose to use retro-reflectors. Retro-reflectors are devices or surfaces that, unlike mirrors, reflect light back to its source reversely along its incoming direction with little scattering. A retro-reflector can be produced using spherical lens or using a corner reflector, which consists of a set of cubes each with three mutually perpendicular reflective surfaces, as shown in Fig. 2(a). A large yet relatively thin retro-reflector is possible by combining many small corner reflectors, using the standard triangular tiling. Such thin retro-reflectors are widely used on road signs, bicycles, and clothing for safety. In addition, an LCD, which has an ultra low quiescent current, closely fitting together with the retro-reflector, is used to modulate the reflected light carrier.

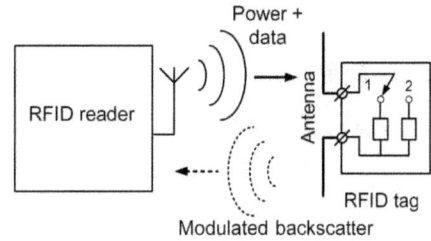

Figure 3: A typical backscatter system illustration

2.2 Comparison with Backscatter RF System

By harvesting energy from the reader to power the tag, and modulating the reflected carrier wave from the reader to avoid power-consuming carrier generation, Retro-VLC is similar to the existing backscatter coupling or inductive coupling technologies at HF and UHF radio frequency, which is widely used in passive RFID systems. But the medium of visible light brings Retro-VLC many differences in the way it is implemented. In this section, we compare Retro-VLC with existing RF backscatter system, mainly in 3 aspects: energy harvesting, magnitude of signal received by reader and bandwidth.

It is not easy to achieve long range communication with batter-free devices such as passive RFID tags. Basically there are 2 limitations, energy harvesting and signal-to-noise ratio (SNR), both of which attenuate rapidly as the distance between the reader and the tag increases. The tag of a backscatter-based systems can only harvest energy from the reader through the antenna. The energy is inverse proportionally to the square of the communication range [21]. Retro-VLC, on the other hand, can harvest energy form ambient light in addition to harvesting energy from the reader. Our prototype shows that with typical office lights, the power harvested only from the ambient light is enough to power the ViTag.

The magnitude of the backscattered signal received by the reader is much weaker than the downlink, which makes up the bottleneck of the system. As shown in Fig. 3, for a backscatter system, the carrier transmitted by the reader distributes to part of the spherical surface, so its energy attenuates proportionally to the square of the communication range. The backscattered (uplink) signal received by the reader from the tag also attenuates proportionally to the square of the reader-tag distance. As a result, the final received signal energy attenuates proportionally to the fourth power of the communication range in total. The formula is also explained in paper [21]. However, in Retro-VLC, the energy of the final signal received by the reader attenuates roughly proportionally to the square of the distance, as revealed in our measurement. This is due to the retro-reflection property, *i.e.* reflecting light back to the source (the reader) from any incoming direction. For a scattering light source, the retro-reflector actually converges the light energy back, as illustrated in Fig. 2(d). Therefore, Retro-VLC has potential to achieve longer communication distance than other systems.

As for bandwidth, the uplink of Retro-VLC is limited by the LCD switching speed. The response time of the LCD we used is $1.5ms$, and we choose 500Hz as the maximum shuttering rate. However, as the technology evolves, much faster light modulating methods may be used.

2.3 Challenges of Retro-VLC System

The actual design of Retro-VLC faces several major challenges, because of the slow switching speed of LCD, low power requirement and the size constraint.

On the ViReader side, due to the small size of the retro-reflector and possibly long communication range, the reflected signal is extremely weak. Also, it is severely interfered by leakage and reflection of the strong downlink carrier, and FM radio signals around 1MHz due to relatively long transmission lines from the photodiode to the demodulation and decoding circuits. In addition, clock drifts exist because there is no clock synchronization between the ViReader and the ViTag. In Retro-VLC, the internal RC oscillator of the MCU is employed as clock to avoid high energy cost and overly large size of crystal oscillators. On the ViTag side, the low power consumption requirement entails careful design as well. In particular, as an LCD is equivalent to a capacitor, toggling (*i.e.* charging and discharging) the LCD at high rate would consume considerable amount of energy.

To address the challenges, we apply following design principles:

- Use analog components for signal detection. This is to avoid use of expensive ADC and relieve the MCU from heavy digital signal processing.
- Make the transistors in the circuit work at a low DC operation point (*e.g.* close to cut-off state). This is an exploitation of the nonlinear relationship between the amplification gain and DC work current (hence energy consumption) of a triode.
- Reuse energy as much as possible. In particular, we recycle the discharging current of the LCD to reduce energy consumption.

3. SYSTEM DESIGN

Fig. 4 shows the block diagram of Retro-VLC. It consists of a ViReader and a ViTag. The ViReader resides in the lighting infrastructure, consisting of an illuminating LED and transmission logic (termed ViReader-Tx hereafter), a photodiode and subsequent receiving circuits (ViReader-Rx). The ViTag consists of a photodiode, receiving circuits (ViTag-Rx), a retro-reflector, a modulating LCD and other circuitry components for transmission (ViTag-Tx).

3.1 Design Overview

For the downlink communication, the ViReader sends information by modulating the carrier. This signal is captured by a ViTag, amplified, demodulated and decoded by ViTag-Rx in analog domain. On the uplink, the MCU on the ViTag controls the LCD to modulate (block or pass) the light carrier reflected by the retro-reflector fabric. The reflected light travels back to the ViReader. Upon capture, the weak signal is amplified, demodulated, digitized and finally decoded. Special logic has been designed to address the possible clock drift on the reflected carrier caused by the ViTag.

Normally, when there is no traffic, the ViReader-Tx sends out the carrier by switching the LED light at a high frequency f_0 (1MHz in our implementation). Both the receiving logic on the ViReader and the ViTag (when turned on) keep on monitoring the incoming light channel, so a ViTag can initiate the communication to the ViReader. An alternative mode is turning on the ViTag-Tx only when ViTag receives certain information. This is the half-duplexing mode where only the ViReader can initiate a communication session, similar to how existing RFID systems work.

We now elaborate the design of major modules.

3.2 ViReader Design

The ViReader-Tx has a standard design – toggle the LED light using an MCU to perform encoding and control the power amplifier gain. Specifically, we use a 1MHz carrier with Manchester coding and On/Off keying (OOK) modulation. In the rest part of this section we focus on the ViReader-Rx design.

As the photodiode is collocated with the lighting LED, received signal from a tag is severely interfered by the leaked and the re-flected carriers; the photo-current is also interfered by other electromagnetic waves (including FM radio around 1MHz). These interferences could cause the ViReader-Rx amplifiers to saturate without careful design. In practice, the movement of human and other objects around can also lead to interferences with very high dynamic range.

Amplification and Demodulation: As shown in Fig. 4, in our design, we first try to isolate the receiving path, both the circuit and the light sensor, from the transmitting path. An external light sensor with a parallel inductor captures the ViTag signal and performs preliminary band-pass filtering. The photocurrent is then amplified by a subsequent preamplifier and further transmitted to the internal (*i.e.* on the ViReader board hosted within the lamp) amplifier and then the processing circuit.

The pair of transmission lines is relatively long, decoupling the front end and the subsequent processing unit. As the two wires are equally affected by the common-mode noise, we design a tuned differential amplifier to eliminate common-mode noises early. Amplified signals then go through a high precision envelope detector that picks up the baseband signal from the carrier. The baseband signal is them further amplified and fed to the ADC of the MCU.

Decoding: Clock drifts caused by the MCU internal RC-clock of the ViTag poses challenges to extracting the timing information from the signal and performing the decoding at the same time. Due to the high dynamic range of the light interference and the non-liner property of the modulator (*i.e.* LCD), distortions are heavy. We develop an improved match filter to handle these problems. The method extends a normal match filter such that the clock is estimated and adjusted per symbol through a 3-symbol matching filter. By matching all possible patterns of the waveform that may result from Manchester encoding, and iteratively adjusting the local clock in every bit period, this method avoids the biased timing caused by skewed correlation peaks in the conventional symbol-based match filter method.

3.3 ViTag-Rx Design

As shown in Fig. 4, the incoming light is first captured by the light sensor. Then a preliminary LC filter and two triode amplifiers successively amplify the received signal.

Our demodulator contains a constant voltage source and a low-pass amplifier. The constant voltage source sets an ultra-low quiescent current that flows into the base of the triode in the low-pass amplifier, making it work at a critical conduction mode. The positive half of the signal can pass through and amplified. Hence, the 1MHz AC carrier is turned into an unipolar signal with a low frequency DC bias which can represent its primary envelope. Finally, the envelope signal is obtained by a smoothing capacitor and then fed into a comparator for digitization.

Digitization and Decoding: We digitize the analog signal with a comparator instead of using ADC. The Manchester-encoded signal uses edges to denote bits. To align with this pattern, we design a comparator to detect *changes* of the voltage. First, using a resister and a capacitor, the comparator sets a time constant that captures its detection delay that corresponds to the input symbol rate. The comparator consistently compares the current (analog) signal voltage V_{now} with that of the last symbol V_{prev}. If $V_{now} > V_{prev}$, the comparator outputs '1'; otherwise, it outputs '0'. V_{prev} is updated with V_{now} subsequently.

In summary, we achieve low energy reception at ViTag by using only analog elements and a low-power MCU (MSP430). In the analog circuit design, we further set the transistors to work at a lower DC operating point to maximally reduce energy consumption.

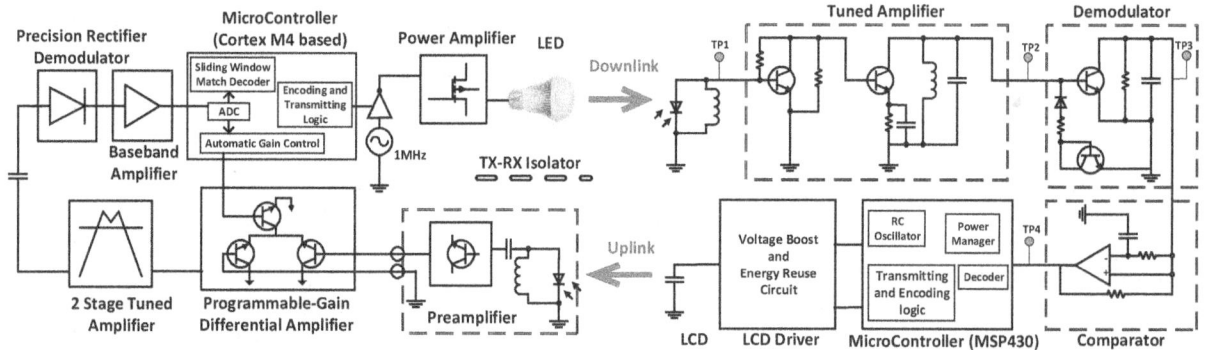

Figure 4: Retro-VLC system diagram. The left part is the ViReader and the right part is the ViTag.

3.4 ViTag-Tx Design

Our ViTag transmitter transmits by passively backscattering the incoming light. The core of the transmitter is the combination of an LCD and a retro-reflector that serves as a modulator. The LCD requires a voltage high enough (*e.g.* at least $5.5V$) to achieve desired polarization level. This voltage is nearly 3 times of solar cell's voltage. So a voltage boosting circuit is adopted.

More than 70% of the power consumption during transmission is caused by LCD. The reason is that the LCD has a considerable capacitance ($9nF$), which must be charged to $5.5V$ so as to turn the LCD off and discharged to turn the LCD on. The discharging process wastes the energy charged to the capacitor. So we design an energy reuse module to recycle the discharging current.

Energy Reuse: The design of the energy reuse module is depicted in Fig. 5. In the charging phase, the DC/DC boosts the voltage supplied by solar cells to be high enough for driving the LCD towards a blocking state. The MCU sets this high voltage and activates the transistor Q_0 This operation puts the LCD into the charging mode and pumps up the voltage of the LCD.

In the discharging phase, the MCU sets the Q_0 to the cut-off state and thus closes the charging path, and activates the NPN transistor Q_1 on the discharging path. With the help of diode D_0, which prevents the LCD from discharging to the solar cell capacitor, the current flows back to the input of DC/DC circuits. Measurements show that the total power consumed by LCD decreases from $84uA$ to $46uA$ when switched at 0.5kHz.

3.5 Prototype Implementation

To demonstrate the effectiveness of our design, we have implemented Retro-VLC according to the diagram shown in Fig. 4, using printed circuit boards (PCBs) and off-the-shelf circuit components. In particular, we pay special attention on isolation. We use a 4-layer PCB with two layers being fully copper coated and connected to the ground. Transmission lines are also similarly isolated. We also shield the light sensor to avoid leakage of the downlink signals. The retro-reflector fabric is Scotchlite from 3M [1] and the LCD shutter is from a 3D glass. Our prototype is shown in Fig. 6. The ViTag is battery-free and operates by harvesting light energy using solar cells. The size of ViTag is $8.2cm \times 5.2cm$, the same as a credit card. About two-thirds of the area is for solar cells and the rest for the LCD and retro-reflector.

4. EVALUATION

Testing Environments: We evaluate the Retro-VLC prototype in a typical office environment with a typical ambient luminance level around $300lx$. The ViTag harvests energy not only from the ViReader, but also from ambient lights. In the baseline experiment,

We also evaluate it in a dark chamber with the LED being the only light source. The LED on the ViReader is 12 watt, externally powered. Indeed, the downlink signal is strong. The the following evaluation experiments, we focus on measuring the uplink performance.

4.1 Packet Loss Rate

We measure the impact of the distance on packet loss rate (PLR) by varying the distance between the ViReader and the ViTag. The ViReader faces squarely to the ViTag, and ViTag continuously sends packets for 20 minutes to the ViReader at a constant rate. Each packet is consisted of *4bytes* ID data. Fig. 7 shows the resulting PLR versus distance.

In Fig. 7, we see that in the dark chamber, the PLR remains below 3% up to $1.5m$. After $1.5m$, the PLR increases dramatically. That is caused by the energy gained from the solar cell turns insufficient at long distances. In contrast, we see PLR increases slower in the office environment as the ViTag harvests energy from ambient light in addition to that from the LED on the ViReader.

We then evaluate the PLR with various incidence/irradiation angles. We fix the distance between the reader and the tag plane (the plane where the ViTag resides in 3D space), and move ViTag along the plane. In this setting, the incidence angle always equals the irradiation angle. In our evaluation, we fix the distance at 100cm. The measured results are shown in Fig. 8. We note that despite the seemingly high PLR (*e.g.* 20%), we were still able to obtain information after a few trials. This is similar to RFID systems.

4.2 Working Range

We define the working range as the area within which the ViTag can harvest enough energy and talk with the ViReader with a chance above 20%. We measure the working range in office environment, and show the result in Fig. 9. The working range in Fig. 9 is the area within the closed blue curve. With an upright orientation of the ViTag, the maximum working distance is $2.6m$. With ViReader perpendicular to the ViTag plane, the field of view (FoV) is around $50°$ (*i.e.* $\pm 25°$). The main constraint is the manual made cover shelter around the light sensor to prevent direct light leakage from the LED lamp. A better shelter would increase the FoV significantly. Also, in our evaluation, we always guarantee the same incidence angle and irradiation angle, thus the measured working range is a conservative estimate.

4.3 Eavesdropping Range

Eavesdropping attacks in our system refer to a device secretly listening to the conversation between a ViTag and a ViReader. It is shown that eavesdropping is usually an early step of other attacks like man-in-the-middle attacks [15].

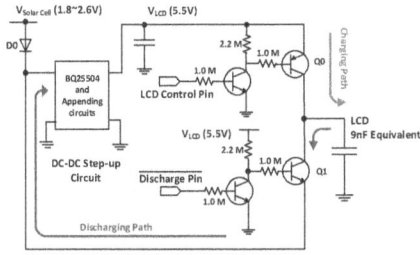

Figure 5: Energy reuse design for LCD driver.

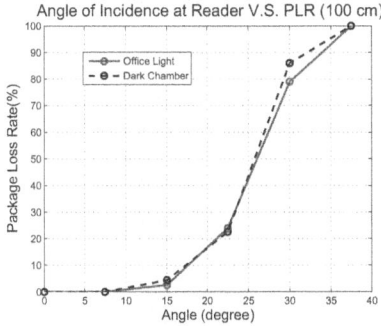

(a) Front   (b) Back

Figure 6: ViTag prototype.

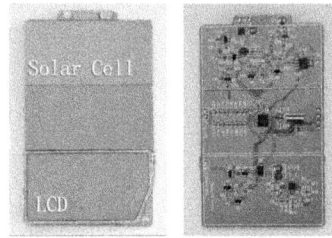

Figure 7: PLR vs. distance.

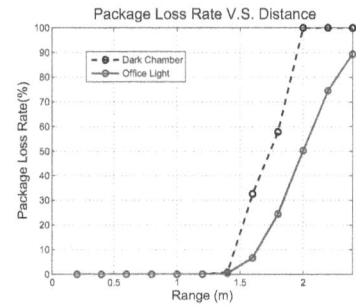

Figure 8: PLR vs. incidence angle.

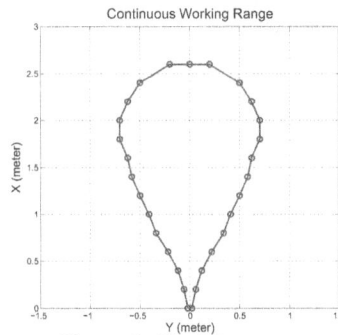

Figure 9: Working range.

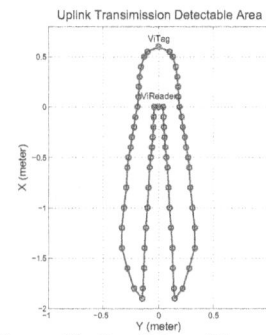

Figure 10: Possible sniffing range.

A key feature of Retro-VLC when compared with RFID/NFC is that the tag-to-reader communication is *directional*. Therefore, the conversation between a ViTag and a ViReader can only be detected within a narrow range along the tag-reader direction. It is shown in [28] that one can overhear NFC communication 1 meter away on the side. In our evaluation, we place a ViReader and a ViTag pair $0.6m$ apart from each other. The ViTag is held upright and faces directly to the ViReader. We use the receiving part of another reader (*i.e.* without lighting LED) as the sniffer and measure the range in which the sniffer can sniff the uplink transmission from the ViTag. The area is plotted in Fig. 10. We see that the shape of possible sniffing area is very narrow; the area behind the legislate reader is also sniffing-free as the light is blocked by the legislate reader). These make it easy for the user to discern the sniffer.

4.4 Power Consumption

Component\Voltage	2.0V	2.6V
Receiving Circuit	$43.8\mu A$	$48.4\mu A$
Transmitting Circuit	$45.1\mu A$	$36.7\mu A$
Total	$91.9\mu A$	$90.0\mu A$

Table 1: Energy consumption of ViTag.

The ViReader transmitter is implemented using a $12W$ white light bulb. The energy consumption of ViTag is related to the voltage output of the solar cell. We measure the overall and component-specific energy consumption for ViTag for two typical operating voltages, as shown in Table 1. The measurement shows that the ViTag prototype indeed achieves ultra-low power consumption.

5. POTENTIAL APPLICATIONS

Retro-VLC has the promise of enabling a rich variety of applications. We give the following examples.

Visible-light identification (VLID): This is similar to RFID, while using visible light as the communicating media. It is more secure due to the visibility of the light sources and the directional property

of Retro-VLC. It can also serve as a more secure alternative means for near-field communication (NFC).

Home IoT applications: The ViTag can serve as a home sensor bearer. Energy-efficient sensors, such as motion, temperature, humidity can be integrated with ViTag and benefit from the battery-free property. Sensor data can be streamed to a ViReader-capable illuminating LED.

Intelligent traffic systems: We can design interactive road side traffic signs using Retro-VLC technology. The battery-free design can enable traffic sign to communicate with headlights on cars. Similarly, we may design smart plates and use them for inter-vehicle communications. It can be used for automatic tollgates.

6. DISCUSSIONS

Tag size trade-off: The surface of ViTag consists of the backscattering area (retro-reflector and LCD) and the energy harvesting area (solar cells). For a fixed tag size, there exists an optimal ratio between the two areas in terms of communication range. The optimal ratio seems to also depend on the power level, the desired maximal working range, and also the ambient luminance of the targeted working environment. We leave this for future work.

Interference between carriers: The light reflected by other objects will interfere with the uplink signals. The slow response of the LCD modulator prevents Retro-VLC from performing a secondary modulation. This is a major difference from other radio backscattering systems. Due to the low-pass filter at the ViReader, the major impact of the interference is on the AGC circuit – If the reflected light is overly strong, it may saturate the receiver circuits. This is a limitation in our design.

Uplink data rate: The uplink data rate is low, due to the slow response of the LCD modulator. To increase the data rate, one way is to use a fast modulator, *e.g.* faster LCDs, MEMS retro-reflector or new material like low power electro-optical crystal [26] or ferroelectric liquid crystal [12]. Another possibility is to use more advanced modulation schemes such as multi-level modulation. As in other radio communication systems, the bit rate can be adapted according to the signal-to-noise ratio (*i.e.* the working range).

7. RELATED WORK

Our work is related to prior work in VLC systems and backscatter communication systems:

(a) VLC Systems: Existing work on VLC has primarily focused on improving the throughput for one-way link using power hungry, expensive, dedicated devices [4, 19, 23]. Few focus on mobile or IoT applications. These efforts, however, either deal with only one-way communication without an uplink [7, 14], or appear in a two-way fashion with both ends supplied by battery [6, 9]. Specifically, LED-to-phone systems [16, 17, 24] only support downlink transmissions, targeted at phone localization. LED-to-LED systems [25, 27] consider visible light networks, where each end is not meant to be mobile. By contrast, our work augments the existing systems with an additional uplink channel from the mobile device to the LED on the same band as the downlink, with elimination of artificial power supply and addition of system robustness.

(b) Backscatter Systems: Backscattering is a way in which to provide transmission capability for extremely low-power devices, eliminating the need for devices actively generating signals. The technique has been primarily taken by RFID tags [11]. Recently Wi-Fi [13] and TV-based [18,22] systems employed and advanced this techniques as well. Our Retro-VLC system employs a similar idea to achieve low-energy design and further shares the same principle with [13, 18, 22], *i.e.* using analog components and circuits for extreme energy-efficiency. The difference is that we are dealing with visible lights. In addition, unlike other backscattering systems that would require intensive tricks and overhead to achieve full-duplex due to their shared antenna and front-end design [3, 5, 8], Retro-VLC can easily achieve duplex communication. Furthermore, the scattering nature of these backscattering systems tends to expose their transmissions to a wide area, leaving a good chance for side readers to overhear the information [13, 18, 22]. By contrast, ViTag relies on visible light, which implies eavesdroppers are discernible. The use of retro-reflectors further focuses the uplink transmission to the tag-reader path. As a result, our system comes with better security properties inherently while other systems have to be more secure with extra efforts [20, 28].

8. CONCLUSION

In this paper, we have presented a bi-directional VLC system, Retro-VLC, that consists of a LED lamp(ViReader) and a tag device (ViTag). The tag can run battery-free by harvesting energy via solar cells from ViReader and ambient light. The ViTag transmits by reflecting and modulating incoming light using a retro-reflector and an LCD modulator. The system overcomes the power consumption challenge on the ViTag and interferences and clock offsets on the LED end, achieving $10kbps$ downlink rate and $0.5kbps$ uplink rate over a distance up to $2.4m$. The system also shows security advantages, preventing readers nearby from overhearing uplink data. Potential applications, such as VLID and Home IoT are also outlined. We believe our work opens the opportunity that VLC can be applied to power constrained scenarios such as IoT and mobile applications.

9. REFERENCES

[1] 3M Retro-reflector.
    http://qxwujoey.tripod.com/lcd.htm.

[2] ByteLight. http://www.bytelight.com/.

[3] D. Bharadia and S. Katti. Full duplex mimo radios. *Self*, 1(A2):A3, 2014.

[4] T. K. Chan and J. E. Ford. Retroreflecting optical modulator using an mems deformable micromirror array. *Journal of lightwave technology*, 2006.

[5] J. I. Choi, M. Jain, K. Srinivasan, P. Levis, and S. Katti. Achieving single channel, full duplex wireless communication. In *MobiCom'10*.

[6] C. Chow, C. Yeh, Y. Liu, and Y. Liu. Improved modulation speed of led visible light communication system integrated to main electricity network. *Electronics letters*, 2011.

[7] K. Cui, G. Chen, Z. Xu, and R. D. Roberts. Line-of-sight visible light communication system design and demonstration. In *CSNDSP'10*, 2010.

[8] M. Duarte and A. Sabharwal. Full-duplex wireless communications using off-the-shelf radios: Feasibility and first results. In *ASILOMAR'10*.

[9] D. Giustiniano, N. O. Tippenhauer, and S. Mangold. Low-complexity visible light networking with led-to-led communication. In *Wireless Days, 2012 IFIP*, 2012.

[10] P. Hu, P. Zhang, and D. Ganesan. Leveraging interleaved signal edges for concurrent backscatter. 2014.

[11] S. Jeon, Y. Yu, and J. Choi. Dual-band slot-coupled dipole antenna for 900 mhz and 2.45 ghz rfid tag application. *Electronics letters*, 2006.

[12] T. Joshi, A. Kumar, J. Prakash, and A. Biradar. Low power operation of ferroelectric liquid crystal system dispersed with zinc oxide nanoparticles. *Applied Physics Letters*, 96(25):253109, 2010.

[13] B. Kellogg, A. Parks, S. Gollakota, J. R. Smith, and D. Wetherall. Wi-fi backscatter: internet connectivity for rf-powered devices. In *SIGCOMM'14*.

[14] T. Komine and M. Nakagawa. Integrated system of white led visible-light communication and power-line communication. *Consumer Electronics, IEEE Transactions on*, 2003.

[15] K. Koscher, A. Juels, V. Brajkovic, and T. Kohno. Epc rfid tag security weaknesses and defenses: passport cards, enhanced drivers licenses, and beyond. In *CCS'09*.

[16] Y.-S. Kuo, P. Pannuto, K.-J. Hsiao, and P. Dutta. Luxapose: Indoor positioning with mobile phones and visible light. *MobiCom'14*.

[17] L. Li, P. Hu, C. Peng, G. Shen, and F. Zhao. Epsilon: a visible light based positioning system. In *NSDI'14*.

[18] V. Liu, A. Parks, V. Talla, S. Gollakota, D. Wetherall, and J. R. Smith. Ambient backscatter: wireless communication out of thin air. In *SIGCOMM'13*.

[19] D. N. Mansell, P. S. Durkin, G. N. Whitfield, and D. W. Morley. Modulated-retroreflector based optical identification system, 2002. US Patent 6,493,123.

[20] R. Nandakumar, K. K. Chintalapudi, V. Padmanabhan, and R. Venkatesan. Dhwani: secure peer-to-peer acoustic nfc. In *SIGCOMM'13*.

[21] P. V. Nikitin and K. S. Rao. Theory and measurement of backscattering from rfid tags. *Antennas and Propagation Magazine, IEEE*, 48(6):212–218, 2006.

[22] A. N. Parks, A. Liu, S. Gollakota, and J. R. Smith. Turbocharging ambient backscatter communication. In *SIGCOMM'14*.

[23] W. S. Rabinovich, R. Mahon, P. Goetz, E. Waluschka, D. Katzer, S. Binari, and G. Gilbreath. A cat's eye multiple quantum well modulating retro-reflector. Technical report, DTIC Document, 2006.

[24] N. Rajagopal, P. Lazik, and A. Rowe. Visual light landmarks for mobile devices. In *IPSN'14*.

[25] S. Schmid, G. Corbellini, S. Mangold, and T. R. Gross. Led-to-led visible light communication networks. In *MobiHoc'13*.

[26] T. Tanabe, K. Nishiguchi, E. Kuramochi, and M. Notomi. Low power and fast electro-optic silicon modulator with lateral p-i-n embedded photonic crystal nanocavity. *Optics express*, 17(25):22505–22513, 2009.

[27] Q. Wang, D. Giustiniano, and D. Puccinelli. Openvlc: software-defined visible light embedded networks. In *VLCS'14*.

[28] R. Zhou and G. Xing. nshield: a noninvasive nfc security system for mobiledevices. In *MobiSys'14*.

The Internet of Things Has a Gateway Problem

Thomas Zachariah, Noah Klugman, Bradford Campbell,
Joshua Adkins, Neal Jackson, and Prabal Dutta
Electrical Engineering and Computer Science Department
University of Michigan
Ann Arbor, MI 48109
{tzachari,nklugman,bradjc,adkinsjd,nealjack,prabal}@umich.edu

ABSTRACT

The vision of an Internet of Things (IoT) has captured the imagination of the world and raised billions of dollars, all before we stopped to deeply consider how all these *Things* should connect to the *Internet*. The current state-of-the-art requires application-layer gateways both in software and hardware that provide application-specific connectivity to IoT devices. In much the same way that it would be difficult to imagine requiring a new web browser for each website, it is hard to imagine our current approach to IoT connectivity scaling to support the IoT vision. The IoT gateway problem exists in part because today's gateways conflate network connectivity, in-network processing, and user interface functions. We believe that disentangling these functions would improve the connectivity potential for IoT devices. To realize the broader vision, we propose an architecture that leverages the increasingly ubiquitous presence of Bluetooth Low Energy radios to connect IoT peripherals to the Internet. In much the same way that WiFi access points revolutionized laptop utility, we envision that a worldwide deployment of IoT gateways could revolutionize application-agnostic connectivity, thus breaking free from the stove-piped architectures now taking hold. In this paper, we present our proposed architecture, show example applications enabled by it, and explore research challenges in its implementation and deployment.

Categories and Subject Descriptors

C.2.1 [**Computer-Communication Networks**]: Network Architecture and Design

General Terms

Design, Documentation, Management, Performance, Standardization

Keywords

Internet of Things, Gateway, Mobile Phones, Bluetooth Low Energy, Sensor Networks, Low-Powered Devices

HotMobile'15, February 12–13, 2015, Santa Fe, New Mexico, USA.
ACM 978-1-4503-3391-7/15/02
http://dx.doi.org/10.1145/2699343.2699344

1. INTRODUCTION

Mobile computers, including laptops, tablets, and smartphones, have experienced unparalleled success due in no small part to an abundance of wireless connectivity. Widespread Wi-Fi and cellular networks provide universal and transparent access to the Internet and cloud-powered applications. This has driven the success of mobile computing. The coming wave of tiny, embedded, low-power, wireless, mobile, and wearable devices, however, does not currently enjoy the same level of ubiquitous and universal access to the Internet. Due to battery constraints and lifetime considerations, these devices tend to rely on low-power wireless communications like Bluetooth Low Energy (BLE) instead of more well-connected, but also more power intensive, Wi-Fi and 3G/4G cellular radios, despite their increasing ubiquity. To connect to the Internet, these devices require an *application layer gateway*—a system capable of translating data from the low-power link to the Internet at large. However, current implementations of these low-power links do not provide an *Internet gateway*, but rather, as Figure 1 depicts, a narrow connection to a device-specific application that must be installed on a smartphone or laptop. Opening a new webpage on a laptop does not require a new application on the Wi-Fi router, but connecting a new IoT device does require a new smartphone app, a new laptop dongle, or a new basestation device, as Figure 2 illustrates.

From smartwatches that interoperate with only a small subset of smartphones to wearable health monitors that cease communicating when their paired phone dies, it is clear that the Internet of Things (IoT) has a gateway problem. While the global network of well-connected smartphones provides a promising foundation for ubiquitous, low-power, last-inch networking, the current siloed, segmented, and application-specific approach to wireless connectivity is hampering the growth potential of this emerging device class.

Addressing this problem requires a new networking architecture for low-power wireless devices that better leverages the opportunities provided by the worldwide network of smartphones. Such an architecture would need to provide convenient and transparent access to the Internet for low-power devices while offering data integrity, security, throughput, and lifetime for the phone and device.

Our approach uses BLE, common on modern smartphones, as the primary link between low-power peripherals and capable smartphones. In contrast to the application-specific design of device-phone interactions, however, we envision an open, two-prong gateway model. First, we envision that any BLE device could leverage any smartphone as a temporary IP router and act as a normal IP end host. Second, any phone could proxy a Bluetooth profile to the cloud on behalf of a device. The former allows for a high degree of flexibility while the latter may be better suited to the power and processing constraints of the device. Both can be implemented as part of an independent app or OS service on the phone.

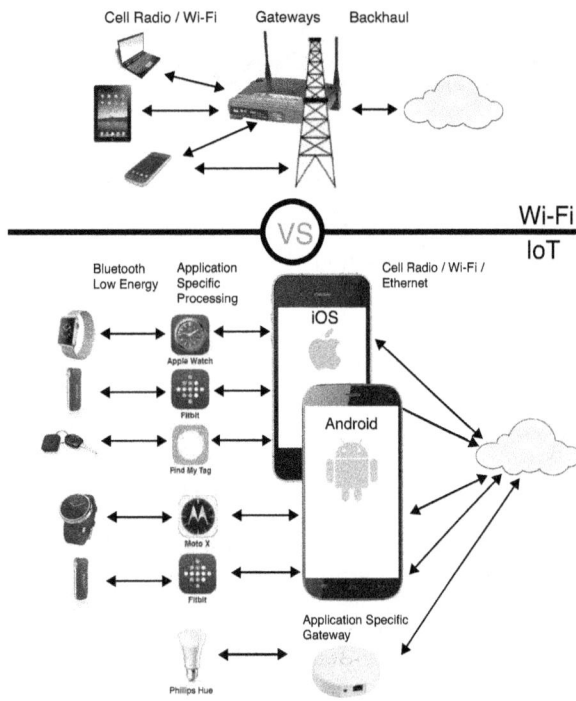

Figure 1: The IoT Gateway Problem. Currently, a separate physical router or smartphone application must be provided in order to enable gateway services for each type of IoT device deployed. This contrasts with any mobile computer's ability to connect to the Internet via a single Wi-Fi router.

Current applications cannot be entirely replaced by transparent gateways, however. The asymmetry in capabilities between smartphones and peripherals leads to some application-specific functionality, like location information or user interfaces, being handled by the phone. To support some such usage scenarios, we propose to extend the architecture to allow devices to request certain services from the paired smartphone, such as the phone's location or the current time. Services like these may be critical to the application but difficult for a cost and energy constrained peripheral device to acquire on its own. This suggests a possible new role for the smart phone—as an opportunistic context server for nearby devices.

A worldwide collection of Internet-connected smartphones provides an unprecedented opportunity to provide last-inch connectivity for the billions of IoT devices expected to emerge in the next few years, crucially, without requiring each phone to load every application-specific gateway app. A simpler (than IPv6) approach might be to provide a generic BLE gateway and a set of common services. Such a network could also provide Internet access to stationary sensors tasked with monitoring homes, offices, cities, or other areas. Instead of requiring nodes to form mesh networks to relay data back to a few Internet-connected gateways, each node could piggyback on passing smartphones to offload or receive data. Indeed we are witnessing siloed versions of such approaches from Fitbit [8] and Tile [23].

This network architecture—of shared access using untrusted, crowd-sourced gateways—raises many questions concerning usability, availability, incentives, security, privacy, and deployability. In this paper, we identify some of the key issues and begin to explore them, with the goal of raising awareness and generating discussion about both the opportunities and challenges.

2. APPLICATIONS

To motivate the need for a well-defined, cross-platform architecture for connecting low-power devices and sensors to the Internet, we describe several applications that are enabled or improved by our proposed gateway architecture.

2.1 Ambient Data Collection

Sensors installed in buildings, homes, cities, remote environments, and other locations can provide invaluable streams of data for monitoring, control, analysis, and prediction applications. Retrieving data from each device, however, is often challenging due to sensor power constraints, poor wireless connectivity, or expensive data links. One solution that has been extensively studied is to mesh-network sensors to allow data packets to hop through the network, but this often fails in areas with poor RF characteristics, and the demands of packet forwarding take a substantial toll on sensor lifetime.

In contrast, our BLE gateway architecture would leverage the smartphones that people already carry to collect data from installed sensors. As an example, consider scientists seeking to measure temperature and relative humidity in a forest by deploying sensors. Rather than requiring a cellular data plan for each sensor or the scientists to visit each node periodically, we imagine a system where hikers traveling on well-defined trails can provide connectivity for these sensors. As a hiker walks by a sensor, the sensor will attempt to use the hiker's mobile phone as a gateway. Because the sensors conform to a common architecture, a hiker would not need to download any software to connect to the sensors. The phone, which may be disconnected from a data network, could hold the data for some time before forwarding it. Hikers may be interested in being a courier for the data because of its scientific nature [2], or because the scientists will compensate them [14].

This method of data retrieval can extend to other applications as well. Sensors installed in buildings, particularly older buildings with challenging RF characteristics, could use the daily occupants of that building to relay their data. In this case, the occupants may be incentivized by obtaining controls for temperature and lighting on their smartphones in exchange for forwarding sensor data.

2.2 Cross Platform Connectivity

Some newer wearable devices are limited by the model of smartphone to which they are capable of connecting. For example, the upcoming Apple Watch will only be able to pair with a recent iOS device to obtain network connectivity. Other smartwatches, like those from Motorola and Samsung, follow a similar model even though they all use BLE communication. This closed, siloed approach is detrimental to the growth and usefulness of this class of devices.

With an open gateway architecture, any smartwatch could ask any smartphone it encounters to agree to act as a gateway. The phone could then provide a connection for any low-bandwidth Internet applications running on the device. Certain applications which are highly user specific, such as notifications on the smartphone, may still require a specific smartphone or app running on the phone.

2.3 Masking Smartphone Failures

Requiring a BLE peripheral or wearable device to link to exactly one smartphone inserts an unnecessary failure point for these devices. If the paired smartphone is not present or is discharged, the otherwise functional tethered device loses its ability to send or receive data. An open gateway model would allow devices to use any nearby smartphones to forward or receive data. In certain situations, such as when using a fitness monitor at the gym or after a smartphone's battery has depleted, it would be preferable not to lose functionality because a specific phone is unavailable, as many do today.

(a) IoT Devices   (b) IoT Gateways   (c) BLE Apps on a smartphone

Figure 2: Currently, each of the peripherals in (a) requires its own gateway as shown in (b) and/or an application like those shown on the smartphone in (c) in order to function. Each gateway in (b) and each application in (c) does not support more than a single type of peripheral. Each gateway in (b) connects directly to the Internet through either a computer, Wi-Fi, or wired Ethernet connection.

3. PROPOSED ARCHITECTURE

To provide Internet connectivity for resource-constrained devices, we propose a smartphone-centric approach. Smartphones can act as a useful gateway due to their near-constant Internet connection, mobility, and ubiquity, but they also dictate what wireless protocol IoT devices must use based on what is commonly available on the phones. Although Wi-Fi is ubiquitous in many parts of the world, and is presently implemented in many IoT devices, its large power requirements make it unsuitable for low-power applications. While some low-power links, like IEEE 802.15.4, provide features that would be useful in this regime, their lack of smartphone support make them unattractive. Instead, we argue that Bluetooth Low Energy (BLE) is the most promising protocol for connecting IoT devices. Its widespread deployment in smartphones and suitably low-power draw make it an attractive solution.

BLE is a link-based, point-to-point protocol between two devices, one in peripheral (slave) mode and the other in central (master) mode. In our architecture, the smartphone remains in central mode while all IoT devices behave as peripherals. Peripheral nodes transmit periodic beacons, termed advertisement packets, to notify nearby central nodes of their presence. Once a central device hears an advertisement, it can establish a connection between the two devices to transfer information. This connection process is standardized by the BLE specification. How and which information is transferred between the device and smartphone is specific to each application, however. To allow the phone to behave as a generic gateway, our architecture focuses on the specification of two general and reusable approaches to transferring data that many applications could use. An overview of the architecture is shown in Figure 3.

3.1 IPv6 Routing

The first data transport mechanism between BLE peripherals and smartphones in our architecture is a raw IPv6 packet transfer over BLE. This would allow each IoT device to behave as any other IP end host and to take advantage of the flexibility of working at the network layer. The peripheral must be capable of running an IPv6 stack, which is feasible as demonstrated by the IPv6 stacks running on sensor motes [11, 20]. The phone must act as an IPv6 router between its Internet connection and the peripheral. The mechanisms for building this IP network on a BLE link are currently being formalized by the IETF and BLE SIG [5, 15, 16].

The primary challenge to using this data transport is the complexity of communicating at the IP layer. All resource-constrained peripherals should not be expected to support a full IP stack. Further, this class of sensor can benefit from offloading work to a more capable device. While the flexibility of providing an IP layer is extremely beneficial for supporting a wide variety of applications, we propose an additional data transport that offers less flexibility but is better optimized for immediate use with the BLE specification and contemporary IoT device applications.

3.2 BLE Profile Proxy

The second data transport mechanism operates by using the smartphone gateway as a proxy for the information contained in the BLE data structures on the peripheral. At a high level, the gateway relays the services, characteristics, and attributes shared with it from the BLE peripheral to a remote server. This more naturally aligns with existing BLE devices, as the data organization between the peripheral and central node in existing, application-specific BLE interactions does not fundamentally change.

3.2.1 Gateway Configuration

To support this proxy architecture, IoT peripherals must extend the data they send to the phone with meta information that dictates how the phone should proxy the BLE profile data. This configuration meta information will be contained in the peripheral's broadcasted advertisements, to which the gateways will have access without requiring a connection with the peripheral.

Data Flow. As part of the meta information advertised, the peripheral must indicate data flow parameters like the content, type, destination and rate of the data to be forwarded. We imagine that, once received on the gateway, the data would be bundled and sent as an HTTP POST request to the specified destination.

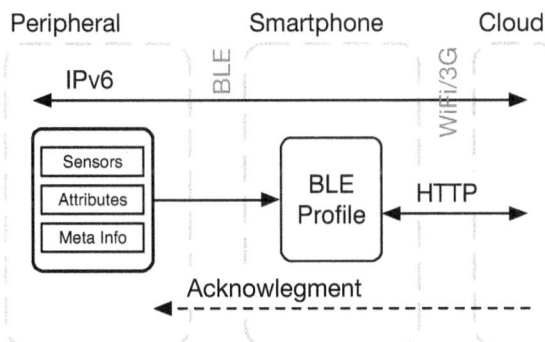

Figure 3: Proposed Architecture. Our approach consists of two data transmission mechanisms: (1) via IPv6, using the smartphone as a temporary IPv6 router and treating the peripheral as an IP-connected end host, and (2) via proxy, using the smartphone to forward the peripheral's BLE profile to the cloud.

Reliability. When connecting to an unpredictable gateway for an unknown amount of time, particularly in a mobile environment, the peripheral faces a challenge to know if its data were successfully transmitted to the intended destination. To address this, a peripheral can specify the level of reliability it would like the phone to try to achieve. This reliability setting is analogous to the transport layer selection in other networking applications. The highest two levels of reliability allow for peripherals to request that a gateway device provide immediate connectivity (level 1) or eventual connectivity (level 2). Both of these levels provide the peripheral with some form of acknowledgment from the end recipient. This supports near real-time and retryable applications, and is analogous to the delivery guarantees provided by TCP. The second two levels of reliability require that the gateway either makes a best effort to forward at a later time (level 3) or a best effort to forward immediately regardless of Internet connection state (level 4). These last two specify that the peripheral is not requesting an acknowledgment. This supports near real-time and delay-tolerant applications, and is analogous to UDP.

Gateway Services. Peripherals may wish to ask the gateway to append information on their behalf to the outgoing data. For example, information about the location of the peripheral or the current global time may be difficult for an IoT device to obtain, but straightforward for a smartphone. Therefore, the gateway smartphone should provide a suite of services that can append information to the data from the peripheral, similar to the IPv6 options framework. Implemented generically, the services subsystem could be extended to other data augmentation applications and possibly offloaded to "cloudlet-style" computational services.

User Incentivization. A major hurdle in adopting this architecture is incentivizing smartphone owners to allow their devices to behave as gateways. If such schemes are created, peripherals must be able to communicate to a potential gateway that it supports a particular incentive system. The gateway would then be able to decline forwarding for that peripheral or later retrieve its compensation. Unilateral system support, like Apple Pay, could also help.

Data. Peripherals may wish to use the remaining bits of the advertisement packet to broadcast small amounts of data. This data could then be forwarded by the gateway using the meta information without forming a BLE connection with the peripheral.

3.3 Gateway Administration

Gateway owners should be able to configure how and to what extent their smartphone is utilized as a gateway. The gateway configuration settings allow owners to cap the data rate and choose which data augmentation services and incentive programs to support. Additionally, a gateway will maintain a whitelist and blacklist to enable fine-grained access control.

3.4 Application-Specific Apps

Our proposed architecture is not intended to replace all peripheral-specific apps on a smartphone. Some apps utilize or display data that is collected by the peripheral. These apps should be designed primarily to display information from the backend cloud service, and should, instead of implementing a custom siloed gateway for the peripheral, allow all forwarding data requirements to be handled by the gateway service on any nearby smartphone.

3.5 Universal Gateway

This architecture is designed to ensure that a peripheral device is not restricted to using one specific smartphone in order to connect to the Internet. That is, any peripheral should have the opportunity to connect through any smartphone, creating a universal gateway out of every smartphone.

4. RESEARCH QUESTIONS

Our proposed architecture raises many technical challenges, including determining the terms of the relationship between an arbitrary peripheral and gateway, where in the software stack the architecture should be implemented, how the gateway should forward data on behalf of a peripheral, and how to incentivize users to enable their devices as gateways. In this section we more deeply discuss many of the research questions that must be explored to realize our open gateway proposal.

4.1 Data Flow Mechanisms and Policies

Our proposed architecture requires smartphones to forward data on behalf of connected peripherals, but the specifics of this are not solidified. How should the smartphone accomplish this? Which data should it send? Should there be a data size limit? More interestingly, how does the phone relay data back to the device? If the peripheral disconnects or moves away, how should the gateway respond? Is it responsible for storing the data and attempting to forward the data later? Should the gateways notify the remote server that its response was never heard?

Forwarding data from the peripheral to the cloud is not the only avenue for data movement. One particularly important example is remote device updates. If a bug or vulnerability is discovered in a particular device, patching a device without replacing it is critical. How does the update patch get to the peripheral? Must it query for updates? If the peripheral is located such that nearby gateways do not have an Internet connection, can mobile gateways store a set of updates and apply them at a later time?

Different peripherals may have different data integrity needs. At what point can a peripheral be sure its data reached the end server? How long should a peripheral store data locally? How does a server acknowledge receipt of a range of data? On the gateway side, if the gateway does not immediately have an Internet connection, how long should it hold the data? If different gateways offload data from the same sensor, how should reordering or deduplication be handled?

Certain peripheral-gateway interactions may be fleeting. The peripheral may not know for how long it will be able to transfer data to or from the gateway. Should the peripheral be optimistic and retry later if the gateway moved away too soon? Or should the peripheral try to evaluate the bandwidth of the link by progressively increasing the amount of data it transfers?

If a gateway provides local processing, it could greatly reduce the latency and increase the reliability of returning processed data to the peripheral. This model has been demonstrated by cloudlets, which provide local computation before the cloud to mobile phones seeking to offload to the cloud [19]. If a gateway provides local processing, how should its computing services be structured and made available? Does processing on the gateway place too high of a cost on the gateway owner?

Smartphones incur a cost when acting as a gateway for a peripheral in both battery life and data communication costs. How should gateways choose when to forward data? How does the architecture ensure that peripherals are not communication starved if the gateways are selective?

4.2 Implementation Considerations

Details of how to implement our proposed architecture remain to be explored. A major question is where on smartphones the gateway logic should reside. Must the gateway functionality be in the operating system layer? Is a user-installable app sufficient? What are the limitations of the BLE APIs available in the commercial smartphone platforms? Would changes or enhancements to the available BLE APIs facilitate gateway development?

4.3 Privacy and Security

Leveraging a wide body of smartphones as gateways raises numerous privacy issues. It is conceivable that a peripheral owner can localize a gateway owner by receiving data through that gateway from peripherals at known locations. Conversely, a peripheral moving through a collection of colluding gateways could be localized. Both may be examples of privacy violations. What techniques for anonymization of forwarded data could be used to mitigate these anti-privacy effects?

Smartphones could log all traffic they forward. What encryption utilities are best suited for constrained peripherals to prevent the smartphone from snooping? Should peripherals have long-standing, symmetric key trust relationships with the cloud to facilitate encrypted communications?

4.4 User Incentives

Incentivizing users to allow their smartphones to act as gateways is critical to realizing our architecture. We imagine a scheme in which the owner of the data forwarded through a gateway rewards the owner of that gateway for the connectivity they provided. How do the data owner and gateway device agree on the transaction cost? How do data owners protect against users abusing the system?

Incentive systems for participation in crowd-sourced sensing projects have often been proposed and have seldom been implemented. Is there a solution for the gateway application? What types of incentives are most compelling? What are the risks of potential abuse for such incentivization schemes and how can they be addressed? What if an application cannot afford to incentivize users? Would incentive tiers be an effective solution?

4.5 Trustworthiness of Gateways

Allowing anyone to operate a gateway opens the possibility for gateways to be untrustworthy or actively malicious. How can peripherals detect and blacklist bad gateways, or vice versa? How can smartphones efficiently blacklist and whitelist? Is it possible for gateways to build and demonstrate reputation-based trust? How can the negative effects of bad gateways be mitigated? How can peripherals ensure their data are successfully relayed in the face of malicious gateways?

4.6 Permanent Gateways

Smartphones carried by people are not the only potential gateways for low-power peripherals. What role do dedicated gateway hardware devices play? Can they be transparently added to the network when smartphones are not sufficient? Can laptops or other computers be compatible gateways? Should dedicated gateways be identified as they may be able to transfer more data? Should there be classes of gateways in general? What is the potential of adding BLE radios to Wi-Fi routers in the future?

4.7 Industry Adoption

To realize a ubiquitous universal gateway, IoT device manufactures, app developers, and service providers need to agree upon a standardized architecture.

Each player has an incentive to support a universal gateway. IoT device manufactures would experience an increased ability to connect their devices to the Internet. A similar increase in connectivity provided by widespread Wi-Fi networks opened up large markets in laptop and tablet computing. Service providers would experience an increase in data usage and app developers would no longer have the responsibility of implementing the gateway portion of their IoT application.

Conversely, each player may be reluctant to support a universal gateway because of the financial benefits they currently receive from customers buying into a proprietary ecosystem. What entity should coordinate support for a universal gateway? What services should a universal IoT gateway offer to be attractive to industry?

5. RELATED WORK

IPv6 in BLE. The Core Bluetooth Specifications 4.1 and 4.2 contain descriptions of a new scheme that allows peripherals access to established dedicated channels in the L2CAP layer for communication over IPv6 [5, 6]. Additionally, the Internet Engineering Task Force (IETF) has prepared two draft documents that further demonstrate the push toward enabling IPv6 over BLE. The first of these documents describes techniques in 6LoWPAN that allow for IPv6 transport over BLE [15]. The second document describes a new Bluetooth Internet Protocol Support Profile which will be responsible for configuring the BLE connection and handling the data flow for IPv6 transactions [16]. The work of the IETF helps define the next steps toward connecting BLE devices to the Internet. This, along with promising implementations of some of these ideas [24], demonstrates progress toward solving the problem of how BLE-connected IoT devices can access the Internet. Still, simply enabling IPv6 connectivity alone falls short of the full set of possibilities of a true IoT gateway. But, these activities further validate the need for IPv6 routing in the emerging Internet of Things.

Delay Tolerant Networking. The use of mobile phones as gateways leads to challenges stemming from the lack of continuous network connectivity. Mobile wireless ad hoc networks allow for the continuation of previously disrupted communication when the mobile node is in range of the network. This type of routing has been demonstrated in many projects involving delay tolerant networking [9, 18]. We consider work that describes the tradeoffs of delay tolerant networks in energy, latency, and storage while moving forward in the design of our architecture [21].

Data Muling. Many projects demonstrate that data mules, mobile surrogates such as smartphone gateways that can transport data between two hosts that would otherwise be unable to communicate with one another, can provide connectivity for sensor networks [7, 13]. Additionally, data muling over Bluetooth on human-carried mobile phones has been shown to provide a reliable network, even for remote sensor deployments [17].

Existing Services for IoT Devices. Over the past couple of years, a number of companies have announced services promoting the connection of smart products. Thread, for instance, is described as a home-based mesh network capable of connecting hundreds of products within a house and enabling online control via a border router connection to Wi-Fi [22]. Helium is a platform developed for metropolitan-sized networks of low-powered connected devices using a modified 802.15.4 protocol and IPv6 addressing, but optimized for very low data transfer [10]. The AllSeen Alliance is a group of consumer brands promoting mainstream adoption of an interoperable and universal software framework for the Internet of Things based on the AllJoyn open source project [1]. Apple's Homekit is a framework available to approved application developers in iOS 8 that enables communication and control of connected products in the house which meet Apple's technical specification [3]. Apple has also introduced iBeacon, a low-powered and low-cost BLE-based proximity solution that specifies the public transmission of unique application-specific identifying information in a BLE peripheral's advertisements for which iPhones specifically scan as a background operation [4]. Detection of an application's known peripheral identifier on an iPhone can prompt various actions, enabling location-based advertisements and rough indoor navigation.

Static Gateway Solutions. One common solution for providing connectivity to IoT devices is to bundle each type of device with a custom hardware gateway. This approach leads to both a longer time to market for the manufacturer and an explosion of hardware gateways for users with many IoT devices. Intel, McAfee, and Wind River have collaborated to provide a service to help IoT manufactures design dedicated IoT hardware gateways [12]. Although this project provides tools for building gateways that can support any specific IoT application, it remains siloed and relies on the massive deployment of a new hardware ecosystem.

6. CONCLUSION

We propose a general-purpose IoT gateway on modern smartphones as a software service that provides universal and ubiquitous Internet access to BLE-connected IoT devices. This provides a scalable alternative to the narrow, application-specific gateway structure hampering the development and growth of IoT networks today. Our proposed approach utilizes the smartphone as both an IPv6 router for less resource-constrained endpoints (allowing IoT devices to communicate as IP-connected hosts) and as a BLE proxy (relaying profile data from the IoT device to the cloud).

As we begin to explore this architecture, we hope to determine the feasibility and scalability of our proposed approach—standard gateways and peripheral services—and of our methods for ensuring reliability, security, and incentives. If successfully implemented on the global smartphone infrastructure, our architecture could expedite the growth of a global, highly-connected, robust Internet of Things in a cost-effective and convenient manner. However, even if our vision of *any* IoT device connecting to *any* smartphone proves too radical a departure from the status quo, the basic ideas could still be deployed in more constrained administrative domains, like a home, office, or university campus. This approach would provide most of the benefits we seek while relaxing the more challenging aspects of security, privacy, and trust in the network, opening the door to a post-MANET for the post-mobile era.

7. ACKNOWLEDGMENTS

We wish to thank our shepherd, Matt Welsh, and the anonymous reviewers for their detailed comments and feedback. This work was supported in part by the TerraSwarm Research Center, one of six centers supported by the STARnet phase of the Focus Center Research Program (FCRP), a Semiconductor Research Corporation program sponsored by MARCO and DARPA. This material is based upon work partially supported by the National Science Foundation under grants CNS-1111541, CNS-1239031 and CNS-1350967, and generous gifts from Intel, Qualcomm, and Texas Instruments.

8. REFERENCES

[1] AllSeen Alliance. Open source IoT to advance the Internet of Everything. https://allseenalliance.org.

[2] D. P. Anderson, J. Cobb, E. Korpela, M. Lebofsky, and D. Werthimer. SETI@Home: An experiment in public-resource computing. *Commun. ACM*, 45(11):56–61, Nov. 2002.

[3] Apple Inc. HomeKit. http://developer.apple.com/homekit.

[4] Apple Inc. iBeacon for developers. http://developer.apple.com/ibeacon.

[5] Bluetooth Special Interest Group. Bluetooth core specification 4.1. https://www.bluetooth.org/en-us/specification/adopted-specifications, 2013.

[6] Bluetooth Special Interest Group. Bluetooth core specification 4.2. https://www.bluetooth.org/en-us/specification/adopted-specifications, 2014.

[7] A. Chakrabarti, A. Sabharwal, and B. Aazhang. Using predictable observer mobility for power efficient design of sensor networks. pages 129–145. ISPN, 2003.

[8] Fitbit Inc. Fitbit. http://fitbit.com.

[9] M. Grossglauser and M. Vetterli. Locating nodes with EASE: Last encounter routing in ad hoc networks through mobility diffusion. In *INFOCOM 2003. Twenty-Second Annual Joint Conference of the IEEE Computer and Communications. IEEE Societies*, volume 3, pages 1954–1964 vol.3, March 2003.

[10] Helium Systems Inc. Helium. http://helium.co.

[11] J. W. Hui and D. E. Culler. IP is dead, long live IP for wireless sensor networks. In *Proceedings of the 6th ACM Conference on Embedded Network Sensor Systems*, SenSys '08, pages 15–28, 2008.

[12] Intel Corporation. Developing solutions for the Internet of Things White Paper. http://www.intel.com/content/dam/www/public/us/en/documents/white-papers/developing-solutions-for-iot.pdf, 2014.

[13] S. Jain, R. C. Shah, W. Brunette, G. Borrello, and S. Roy. Exploiting mobility of energy efficient data collection in wireless sensor networks. pages 327–339. Mobile Networks and Applications, 2006.

[14] A. Kittur, E. H. Chi, and B. Suh. Crowdsourcing user studies with Mechanical Turk. In *Proceedings of the SIGCHI Conference on Human Factors in Computing Systems*, CHI '08, pages 453–456, New York, NY, USA, 2008. ACM.

[15] J. Nieminen, T. Savolaienen, M. Isomaki, B. Patil, Z. Shelby, and C. Gomez. Transmission of IPv6 packets over Bluetooth low energy "draft-ietf-6lo-btle-03", 2014.

[16] J. Nieminen, T. Savolaienen, M. Isomaki, B. Patil, Z. Shelby, and C. Gomez. Transmission of IPv6 packets over Bluetooth low energy "draft-ietf-6lo-btle-04", 2014.

[17] U. Park and J. Heidemann. Data muling with mobile phones for sensornets. In *Proceedings of the 9th ACM Conference on Embedded Networked Sensor Systems*, SenSys '11, pages 162–175, New York, NY, USA, 2011. ACM.

[18] C. Perkins and E. Royer. Ad-hoc on-demand distance vector routing. In *Mobile Computing Systems and Applications, 1999. Proceedings. WMCSA '99. Second IEEE Workshop on*, pages 90–100, Feb 1999.

[19] M. Satyanarayanan, P. Bahl, R. Caceres, and N. Davies. The case for VM-based cloudlets in mobile computing. *Pervasive Computing, IEEE*, 8(4):14–23, Oct 2009.

[20] T. Savolainen and M. Xi. IPv6 over Bluetooth low-energy prototype. In *Aalto University Workshop on Wireless Sensor Systems, Aalto, Finland*, 2012.

[21] T. Small and Z. J. Haas. Resource and performance tradeoffs in delay-tolerant wireless networks. In *Proceedings of the 2005 ACM SIGCOMM Workshop on Delay-tolerant Networking*, WDTN '05, pages 260–267, New York, NY, USA, 2005. ACM.

[22] Thread Group. Thread. http://threadgroup.org.

[23] Tile Inc. Tile. http://thetileapp.com.

[24] H. Wang, M. Xi, J. Liu, and C. Chen. Transmitting IPv6 packets over Bluetooth low energy based on BlueZ. In *Advanced Communication Technology (ICACT), 2013 15th International Conference on*, pages 72–77, Jan 2013.

Reducing Energy Consumption of Alarm-induced Wake-ups on Android Smartphones

Sewook Park, Dongwon Kim, Hojung Cha
Department of Computer Science
Yonsei University
Seoul, Korea
{swpark,dwkim,hjcha}@cs.yonsei.ac.kr

ABSTRACT

Alarms are often used to set smartphones to perform tasks at scheduled times. Many applications use alarm functionality, and devices consequently experience frequent wake-ups and waste energy. In this paper, we analyze alarm-induced wake-ups in the Android platforms in terms of energy consumption. We propose a "Time Critical Alarm", in which alarms necessarily accompany wake-ups. We then propose, AlarmScope, a scheme to reduce non-critical alarms and thus minimize energy waste. Our evaluation of widely-used applications on Android smartphones shows that the proposed scheme would save between 2.6% and 12.5% of energy use.

Categories and Subject Descriptors

D.2.11 **[Software Engineering]**: Software Architectures; D.2.8 **[Software Engineering]**: Metrics—Performance Measures

General Terms

Design, Experimentation, Measurement

Keywords

Smartphones, Mobile, Energy, Alarm, Wake-up

1. INTRODUCTION

As the number of applications installed on smartphones increases, energy waste can become significant due to the inefficient operations of these applications. Recently, active work has been conducted to deal with this issue. Pathak et al. [1] analyzed various types of energy bugs arising in smartphone applications, and Ma et al. [2], using eDoctor, examined the causes of the abnormal draining of smartphone batteries. Zhang et al. [3] conducted a comparative analysis of energy bugs on various smartphone platforms. Oliner et al. [4] identified the types of energy anomalies with massive amounts of user data via Carat and proposed a method with which to address energy anomalies.

Among the approaches to reducing energy inefficiency in mobile devices, sleep functionality has, in particular, been treated as an important issue when dealing with energy waste. Sleep is generally defined as a state in which the smartphone OS freezes the system to save energy. Many works have addressed the energy bug, which refers to a state in which the system refuses to enter sleep mode or energy is constantly drained even in sleep mode. Prior works [5, 6] have proposed ways of locating no-sleep bugs at the source-code level during compile time based on static code analysis. Kim et al. [7] dynamically analyzed no-sleep bugs that were undetected during compile time, with no modification to the system. Liu et al. [8] addressed the issue of energy inefficiency caused by the abnormal behavior of sensors while in sleep mode. A method [9] was proposed for detecting a condition in which the smartphone is unable to enter the suspend mode at the device-driver level. Studies of the no-sleep bug analyzed the causes that prevent devices from entering into sleep mode, suggesting methods of detecting conditions that give rise to no-sleep bugs. In summary, the works published so far have focused on the phenomenon in which the system does not enter *sleep from wake-up* mode. However, no previous work has addressed the issue of the inefficiency of the transition from *sleep to wake-up* mode.

A smartphone generally wakes from sleep upon user input, such as pressing the power button. The smartphone may also wake up via network requests, and more explicitly, applications activate alarms via Alarm Manager. Here, unnecessary wake-ups induced by alarms may occur when an alarm type has been incorrectly assigned or alarms are used excessively. When many applications are installed on a device, wake-ups can be called frequently, resulting in an increased chance of creating unnecessary alarms. In order to manage energy efficiently on smartphones, a policy is therefore needed to address the inadequate use of alarms caused by developers.

In this paper, we propose a method, named AlarmScope, that prevents nonessential wake-ups. We first analyze the internal behavior of each alarm, as well as the applications, when a wake-up occurs via an alarm. We then investigate the energy cost for wake-ups and decide whether this cost could be reduced. We define a term, Time Critical Alarm (TCA), in order to identify and exclude alarms that are not critical to the operation of applications. AlarmScope converts non-deferrable alarm judged as non-critical to deferrable. With its implementation on the Android smartphone, we validate the effectiveness of the proposed method and demonstrate that our method is practical in terms of saving energy.

2. BACKGROUND AND MOTIVATION

We briefly explain the internal mechanism of an alarm on the Android platform. We then discuss the issues caused by the inefficient use of alarms triggered by applications.

2.1 Android AlarmManager

An application is allowed to schedule a task at a desired time through Alarm. In order for the device to exit sleep mode, AlarmManager must be used. When an application registers an alarm on the Android platform, the type of alarm and the alarm

HotMobile '15, February 12 - 13 2015, Santa Fe, NM, USA
Copyright 2015 ACM 978-1-4503-3391-7/15/02 $15.00
http://dx.doi.org/10.1145/2699343.2699346

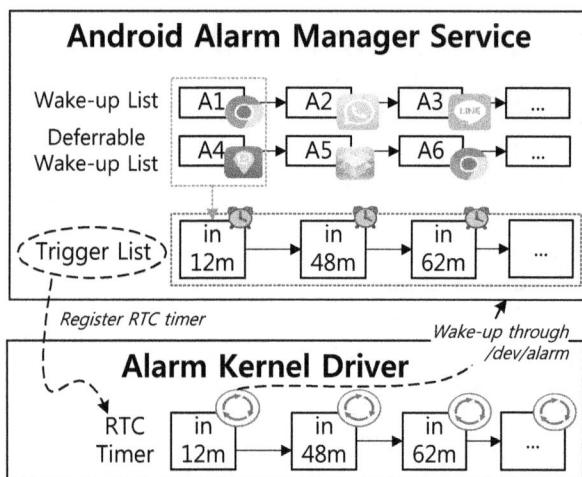

Figure 1. Android AlarmManager architecture

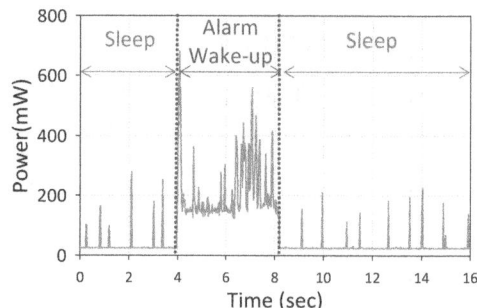

Figure 2. Power trace when an alarm wake-up occurs

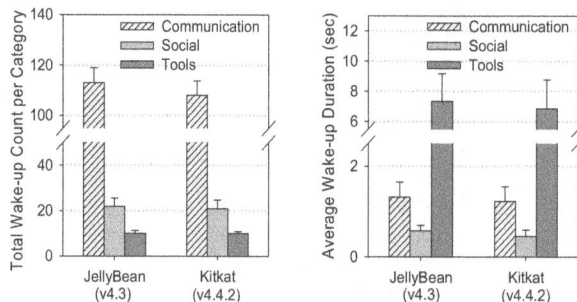

(a) Wake-up count in 1 hour (b) Average wake-up duration

Figure 3. Alarm wake-ups for 15 Apps in three categories

time are registered. Two types of alarms exist: non-deferrable alarms, which should run at the specified time, and deferrable alarms. When an alarm is registered, as shown in Figure 1, AlarmManager Service composes a list of alarms to be executed, and it registers the time points on the hardware RTC, so that the device can wake up from sleep via the kernel timer in the alarm driver. At the set time, the alarm driver writes the relevant data into /dev/alarm; the alarm library detects this and relays the data to the alarm handler in AlarmManager Service.

This mechanism does not, however, consider the energy cost of using alarms. KitKat (Android 4.4) has newly introduced the concept of Alarm Batch to improve the energy efficiency of the system. When multiple alarms are set within a close time range, they are processed in a batch at their set times.[1] This removes the need for unnecessarily frequent wake-ups in the native Android framework, but we assume it still has energy inefficiency.

2.2 Preliminary Experiment

We conducted an experiment to measure the energy consumption caused by alarms in commercial applications. The smartphone device selected was the Nexus 4 running Android 4.3 JellyBean and 4.4.2 KitKat, with 15 commercial applications installed. Among the free applications available in Google Play, we chose the ones that make frequent use of wake-up alarms. These were selected from three categories: Communication (Line, Kakao Talk, MyPeople, WeChat, KeeChat), Social (Naver Band, Naver Blog, Naver Café, Tumblr, Between), and Tools (Dodol Phone, Memoy Booster, Battery Doctor, Clean Master, Osmino WiFi). The experiment was conducted while the screen was turned off and the applications were running in the background.

Figure 2 shows the power trace before and after the smartphone enters the wake-up mode from sleep. The device used 26 (±7) mW in sleep and 209 (±100) mW during wake-up. During a wake-up induced by an alarm, the smartphone consumes 8 times more energy than in sleep mode, and frequent wake-ups significantly worsen battery efficiency.

---

[1] A similar method called 'timer coalescing' has been used to reduce energy consumption in a general-purpose OS. In the Linux kernel, the concept of a deferrable timer is used to keep the CPU idle as much as possible. In Microsoft Windows 7 and Mac OS X Mavericks, timers are put in groups to save energy on portable computers [10].

In our experiment, we counted the instances of wake-ups for an hour and measured their durations. The alarm option in dumpsys, provided in the Android platform, was used for this measurement. Energy consumption was measured with the Monsoon Power Monitor.

The number of wake-ups caused by alarms was 145 (±9) on JellyBean and 139 (±10) on KitKat. Figure 3(a) shows the number of alarm-induced wake-ups for each application category. Communication applications produced the highest number of alarms, while applications in the Social and Tools categories invoked alarms relatively less frequently. Figure 3(b) illustrates the fact that the average wake-up duration was longest for applications in the Tools category. The energy consumed on Nexus 4 with JellyBean was 196,000 (±15,000) mJ before the 15 applications were installed, and 266,400 (±16,000) mJ after installation, which is greater by 35.9%.

Our experiment backs up the claim that in order to reduce energy waste, the system should play an active role in managing alarms, instead of giving full permission to developers to use alarms.

3. ALARMSCOPE

To efficiently reduce the energy cost caused by alarm-induced wake-ups, each non-deferrable alarm must be examined to determine whether it can be made deferrable. Unfortunately, it is not an easy task to determine whether an alarm can be converted from non-deferrable to deferrable. In order to decide if the type of a given alarm was intended by the developer or assigned by mistake, a well-designed strategy is required. We have taken an intuitive approach to devise such a method.

3.1 Time Critical Alarm

We define a Time Critical Alarm (TCA) as a type of an alarm that must be activated exactly at the designated time. The following factors are considered when determining whether an alarm is a TCA: whether UI updates are involved and whether data transmission takes place after the alarm is invoked. Also, the

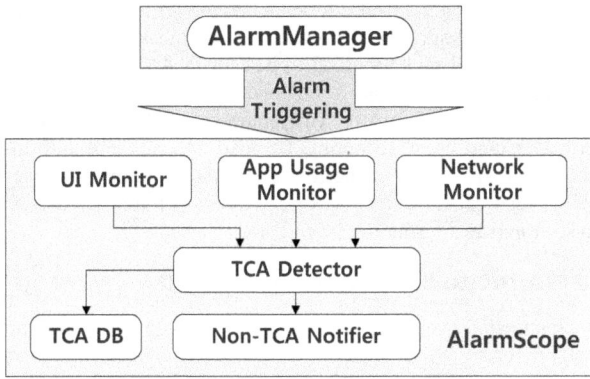

Figure 4. AlarmScope architecture

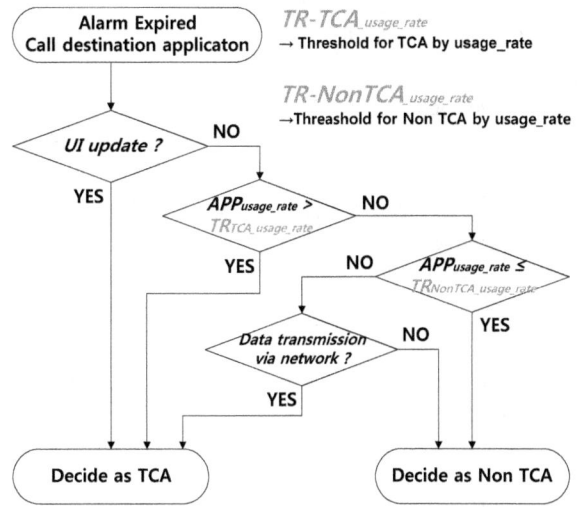

Figure 5. TCA Decision Flow

frequency of application use is given extra weight in the decision. Conditions of this kind are time-sensitive and may affect the exact operation of applications. We assume that the remainder of the alarms, which are not TCAs, are not problematic, even though there is a slight delay in their execution. The criteria for determining whether an alarm is a TCA — especially for UI updates and data transmissions — are based upon our analysis of the Android source code. This is explained in detail in Section 4.

3.2 AlarmScope Architecture

To categorize an alarm as a TCA, we developed an alarm monitoring system and named it AlarmScope. Figure 4 illustrates how the system operates on the Android platform.

AlarmScope consists of the following components: UI Monitor, App Usage Monitor, Network Monitor, TCA Detector, TCA DB, and Non-TCA Notifier. AlarmScope is activated when an alarm set in AlarmManager is triggered and relayed to an application. UI Monitor determines whether the screen is updated in any application, and App Usage Monitor keeps track of the foreground usage time for each application. Network Monitor determines whether data are transmitted from applications via the network. Based on application behavior data collected with UI Monitor, App Usage Monitor, and Network Monitor, TCA Detector decides whether a given alarm is a TCA, in which case the data are stored in TCA DB. If the alarm is a non-TCA, the data are sent to AlarmManager via Notifier.

3.3 TCA Decision Procedure

Figure 5 illustrates the procedure that determines whether an alarm is a TCA.

(1) When an application begins to run after an alarm expires, the UI update of the application is inspected via Activity. If updated, the alarm is determined to be a TCA because an immediate response to user action is required.

(2) If there is no UI update, the application usage time is considered in the TCA decision. The application usage rate is calculated using the following equation for each application. Note that the Launcher application is not considered here.

$$\text{App\_usage\_rate} = \frac{\text{Usage time length of App}}{\text{Sum of usage time length of each app}}$$

(3) TR-TCA_usage_rate is a threshold of critical application usage rate. If the App_usage_rate is greater than the TR-TCA_usage_rate, the alarm is a TCA. If the usage rate is less

---

Algorithm 1 Decide TR-TCA_usage_rate

Input : Application List sorted by usage_rate in ascending order
Output : TR-TCA_usage_rate

Initial_value ← average(App $_{\text{usage\_rate}}$)

App$_i$ ← First App whose usage_rate is larger than Initial_value
while App remains in the list **then**
  if (App$_{i+1 \text{ usage\_rate}}$ - App$_{i \text{ usage\_rate}}$) $> \sum_{i=0}^{n}$ App$_{i \text{ usage\_rate}}$
    return App$_{i \text{ usage\_rate}}$
  else
    increase i
  endif
endwhile
return App$_{i \text{ usage\_rate}}$

---

than the TR-TCA_usage_rate and also less than the TR-NonTCA_usage_rate, the alarm is a non-TCA.

(4) If the value of App_usage_rate lies between the TR-TCA_usage_rate and the TR-NonTCA_usage_rate, whether data transmission in involved is determined. The TR-NonTCA_usage_rate is used for applications that are rarely run in the foreground. An application with an App_usage_rate value lower than this threshold typically has significantly less usage time compared to other applications. The alarms in applications with less TR-NonTCA_usage_rate are negligible to the user experience. We set the value for the TR-Non-TCA_usage_rate at 0.1% after a series of extensive experiments. Eight smartphone users were polled regarding application usage, and about 20% of their applications fell within this category. On the other hand, TR-TCA_usage_rate is used for frequently-used applications, and when to apply this threshold is determined by Algorithm 1.

Algorithm 1 decides what rate to apply to the TR-TCA_usage_rate for a given application based on how frequently the application is used. Applications sorted by usage rate are considered in ascending order during the TCA decision. If the difference between the App$_i$_usage_rate and the App$_{i+1}$_usage_rate is greater than the sum of usage rates considered up to the current application, the TR-TCA_usage_rate is used for the next application.

The logic is based on the idea that the usage time differs greatly between those applications that are frequently used and those that are not. The actual frequency of application usage is reflected in the TCA decision, so the algorithm becomes effective.

4. IMPLEMENTATION ON ANDROID

Note that the newly introduced Alarm Batch functionality in KitKat does not guarantee the exact start time of the alarm. If an alarm must be executed at a precise point in time, the setExact() API must be called. We looked at the modules that use alarms in the open source code of Android and sought out where the setExact() API was called; from this information, we were able to infer which alarms were time critical.

Only five modules call setExact(): SyncManager, TwilightService, WifiStateMachine, Calendar and DeskClock. All of them perform time-critical tasks; however, the cases directly affected by applications occur when data are transmitted from an application, such as data sync, and when the screen is updated, for example, in Calendar or DeskClock. Among the many alarms used in Android open source applications, setExact() is not called except in the above five cases. We thus conclude that postponing alarms would not necessarily produce problems. Our implementation was based on this definition of TCA.

4.1 Platform Modification

When activating an alarm in AlarmManager, the relevant data registered in the alarm are verified and relayed to their destination application. An alarm contains this data internally in the PendingIntent class. We made modifications so that our defined Intent is broadcast when the send() method in the AlarmManagerService is called to relay data to an application. The AlarmScope Service receives this Intent and processes it.

The three criteria for a TCA decision are (1) UI update, (2) application usage, and (3) data transmission. We determined the criteria as follows. When the UI is updated, the finishDrawing() method in the ViewRootImpl class is called, which sends data to the WindowManager to refresh the screen. We used the UsageStatService for Application usage. The UsageStatService class keeps track of the time spent in foreground applications, and this record is stored when the application is paused. When data are transmitted, a few methods are called in classes related to socket implementation. At these points, we made code modifications which broadcast Intents to signal these conditions, which are defined separately.

If the alarm is determined to be a non-TCA event, the AlarmScope Service notifies the AlarmManager about non-TCA alarms with an Intent. When non-TCA alarm data are sent from the AlarmScope Service, the AlarmManager stores the data in memory. When a non-deferrable alarm that belongs to the non-TCA set is registered, the alarm is converted into the deferrable type. In detail, AlarmScope considers the alarms called by all APIs in AlarmManager (i.e., set(), setRepeat(), setExact(), etc.). We converted non-deferrable alarms with RTC_WAKEUP and ELAPSED_REALTIME_WAKEUP into RTC and ELAPSED_REALTIME, respectively.

4.2 AlarmScope Service

AlarmScope Service manages alarm data, which are sent from AlarmManager in the form of a list. After receiving additional Intent, AlarmScope checks whether the UI is updated or data is transmitted during a specific time. When the UI is not updated or data are not transmitted until timeout occurs, the alarm is removed from the list and is determined to be non-TCA. In this case, the application data are stored in DB and relayed to AlarmManager via Notifier. The content in AlarmScope DB is sent to AlarmManager upon rebooting so that the data are not lost. Labeling an alarm TCA is performed for each Action. In order to support such calls, each TCA is treated on a per-Action basis and is also stored as an Action.

4.3 Implementation using Xposed

As explained above, modifications must be made on the platform level in order to implement AlarmScope. Additionally, an AlarmScope service application is needed to process the relevant data during runtime. Altering the platform is time-consuming because it requires changes to the open source and generating images. To apply the modifications easily, we used Xposed [11] for implementation. On the Android platform, Xposed hooks into method calls and makes it possible to control pre- and post-method calls. Through the Xposed module, we made implementations of Intent transmission in the PendingIntent class, ViewRootImpl class, UsageStatsService class, and other socket-implementation-related classes.

Xposed runs only on rooted devices, and it is not possible to install AlarmScope on non-rooted devices. However, Xposed allows us to apply the functionality directly, without modifying the system platform, and this enables the smooth implementation of our prototype. Xposed resides on the Android Dalvik layer; thus, there is a challenge in that data transmission via socket using the native library is not detectable. Fortunately, however, we could verify that data were transmitted via the Java socket class during our preliminary experiment.

5. EVALUATION

We evaluated AlarmScope to validate its implementation and effectiveness for saving energy. We tested our implementation on Nexus 4 smartphones running Android 4.3 Jelly Bean and 4.4.2 KitKat.

5.1 Validation

We first tested whether an alarm worked correctly with AlarmScope. The test application generates non-deferrable alarms. It also periodically generates non-TCA alarms, in which neither UI updates nor data transmission via the network takes place. Then, wake-ups were traced for evaluation. In our experiment, we configured the system so that only user-installed applications were affected by AlarmScope, not the default applications shipped with the Android system.

Figure 6(a) shows the example of non-deferrable alarms delayed by AlarmScope with an interval of 30 seconds. Figure 6(b) shows the alarms and wake-ups after AlarmScope has been applied. It shows that non-TCA alarms are determined to be deferrable and hence are executed when wake-up takes place at a later point. AlarmScope gains energy benefit with the aggregated alarms due to the delay (e.g., 136 seconds and 170 seconds in Figure 6(b)). An examination of the validation data reveals that the average delay is nine seconds. The TCA-type alarms after which critical operations take place were determined to be non-deferrable and were processed at the set time. Note that the alarms generated by the Android platform and the wake-ups by network push are not delayed, and the wake-up time of alarms are not exactly the same in Android. The number of aggregated alarms is not restricted, and multiple alarms are cascaded till the next wake-up. However,

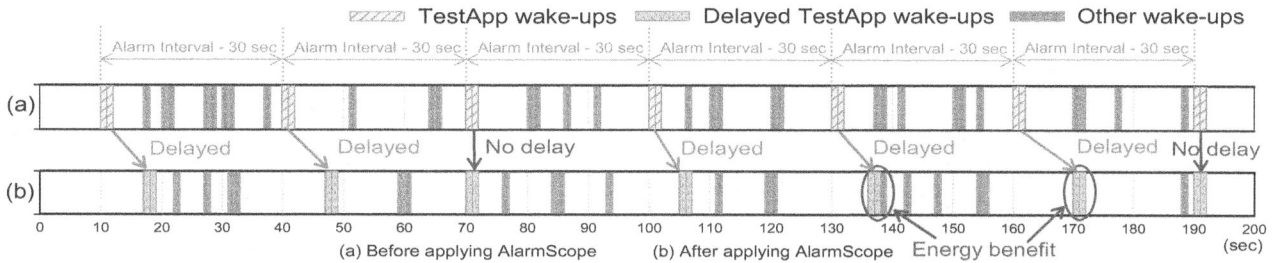

Figure 6. Trace results for Alarm-induced wake-ups

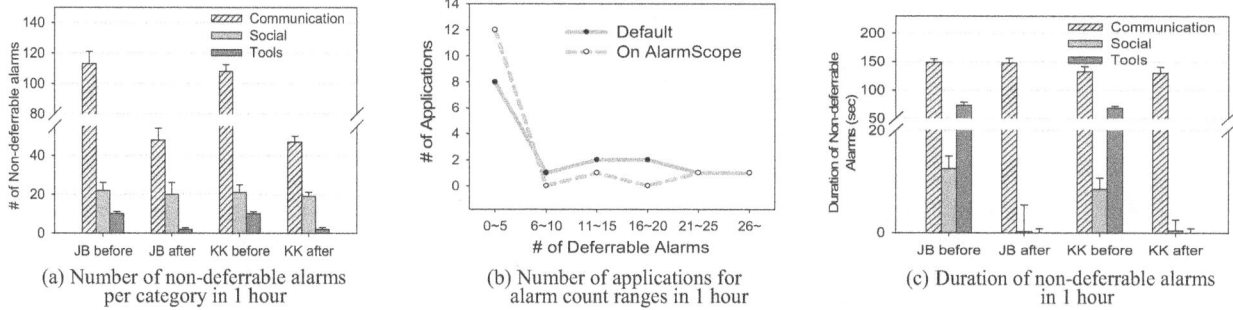

(a) Number of non-deferrable alarms per category in 1 hour

(b) Number of applications for alarm count ranges in 1 hour

(c) Duration of non-deferrable alarms in 1 hour

Figure 7. Effectiveness of AlarmScope

the maximum delay of a non-TCA alarm is about 60 seconds because the Android AlarmManager generates wake-up every minute.

5.2 Effectiveness

We investigated the effectiveness of AlarmScope using Xposed, both before and after applying AlarmScope. As in the preliminary experiment, 15 identical applications were installed, and wake-ups were counted for each category. Measurements of the entire wake-up duration of the device, as well as power consumption, were taken. As shown in Figure 7(a), the number of non-deferrable alarms decreased from 145(±9) to 67(±5) on JellyBean, and it dropped from 139(±10) down to 64(±5) on KitKat. Overall, the number of non-deferrable alarms was reduced by more than 50%. Figure 7(b) shows the number of applications for various alarm count ranges after AlarmScope was applied. The overall non-deferrable alarm counts were reduced, and most applications induced fewer than five alarm wake-ups in one hour. In Figure 7(c), the wake-up duration of non-deferrable alarm for each category is charted. The applications in the Communication category did not show any significant decrease, but those in the Social and Tools categories had meaningful reductions in their wake-up durations. This is due to the fact that the average wake-up duration is very short for non-TCA alarms generated by an application in the Communication category; thus, the reduction in this category is very small. On the other hand, the applications in the Social and Tools categories had much reduced wake-up durations because their non-TCA alarm-induced wake-up

durations are relatively longer, despite a lesser degree of reduction in alarm counts.

Figure 8(a) shows the sum of the wake-up durations caused by alarms in one hour. For our experiment, we recorded the timestamps in log files when the device woke up from sleep mode. We could observe that the total wake-up time is reduced by approximately 25%. The device does not wake up when it is time to process deferrable-type alarms. Rather, it waits until the system wakes up because a non-deferrable alarm or some other triggering event induces a wake-up, at which point the deferred alarm is processed. As shown in Figure 8(b), the energy consumed in an hour was reduced by 12.5% in JellyBean and by 7.2% in KitKat. The energy reduction comes from the increased number of grouped alarms in AlarmScope. The number of grouped alarms with AlarmScope is 1.78(±0.17) in JellyBean and 2.21(±0.20) in KitKat, while the default Android shows 1.53(±0.12) and 2.03(±0.14) grouped alarms in JellyBean and KitKat, respectively.

5.3 User Experiment

We conducted an additional experiment to measure how effective AlarmScope is in practical use. Three participants were chosen in our laboratory based on the number of applications installed. We reproduced the user environments on our test smartphone and installed AlarmScope on it to measure wake-up duration and energy consumption. KitKat was installed on the test device, and we made measurements for an hour. The numbers of applications installed on the phones were 23, 60, and 110, respectively. The numbers of applications that used wake-up alarm were three, seven, and 10 for each.

The measurements derived from the test are shown in Figure 9. The reductions in total wake-up time were 2.5%, 9.4%, and 19.3% for User1, User2, and User3, respectively. The reductions in energy consumption were 2.6%, 3.5%, and 13.3%, respectively. The reason for the significant savings in User3's device is that the amount of energy consumption at wake-up is quite large and the alarms with longer average wake-up durations were converted into the deferrable type, resulting in a large savings. We verified that AlarmScope tends to function more efficiently when the number of installed applications is large.

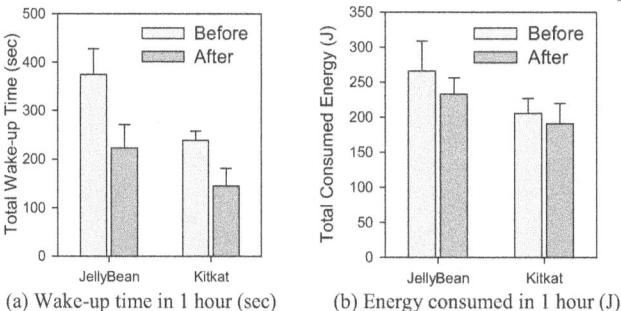

(a) Wake-up time in 1 hour (sec)

(b) Energy consumed in 1 hour (J)

Figure 8. Wake-up time and consumed energy in 1 hour

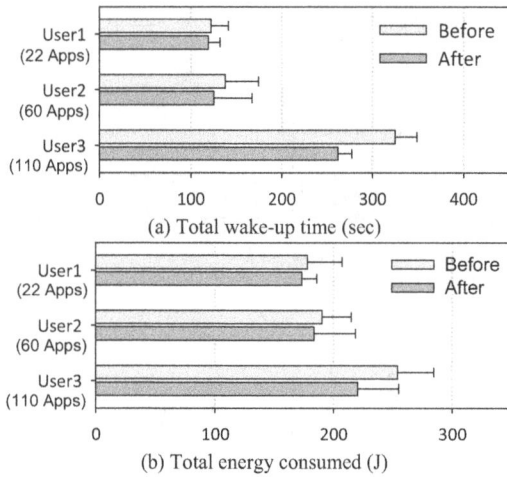
Figure 9. User experiment

Table 1. Alarm-related operations

Category	Alarm-related operations	Example applications
Communication	Communication with server Registration of push service	Kakao Talk
Social	Check version upgrade Delete cache	Naver Blog Memory Booster Tumblr
Tools	Update data Download data from server	Dodol phone Osmino WiFi

5.4 Effects of Delayed Alarms

To investigate the side-effects of AlarmScope, we analyzed the alarm-related operations in 15 applications used in the preliminary experiments. We decompiled the apk file by dex2jar [12] and JD-GUI [13] to analyze the applications in code level. Table 1 summarizes the alarm-related operations according to the application type. In communication app types (e.g., Kakao Talk), the application used wake-up alarms to communicate with a server, to run specific services, or to register push services of applications. In social app types (e.g., Naver Band, Between, Tumblr), the alarm is used for checking the application version or deleting cache information. In tool app types (e.g., Dodol phone, Memory Booster, or Osmino WiFi), the wake-up alarms update the data, clean-up memory, or download data from server.

Based on the code analysis, we found that most alarms in deployed applications are not time-critical. The alarm-related operations are possibly categorized into (1) stand-alone operation (without server), and (2) communication operation with a server. In the case of stand-alone operation, the side-effect of a deferred alarm is trivial. For example, MemoryBooster cleans up cache information every two hours. Delaying such operations by several seconds has negligible effect on the user experience. In the case of communication operations with a server, the side-effect is also negligible, since the maximum delay time of an alarm is about 60 seconds as described in Section 5.1. In fact, no applications used the setExact() function provided by the Android AlarmManager in the latest version. We further investigated 30 most-popular applications in Google Play, and found that only one application used the setExact() function. In summary, we expect that delaying an alarm would not be critical to the user experience in a practical sense; hence its side-effects are minimal.

6. CONCLUSION AND FUTURE WORK

In this paper, we proposed AlarmScope, with which we detected unnecessary alarm-induced wake-ups on the Android smartphone and converted the alarms into deferrable types to reduce energy waste. According to [14], the average number of applications installed by a given user on a smartphone is about 26 (year 2013), and this number is increasing. Our user study suggests that applying the proposed system would reduce the energy consumption and extend the average usage time of a mobile device between charging periods.

Our method is a viable solution to manage wake-ups caused by the inefficient use of alarms, but we plan to consolidate our work

further. One feasible approach is tracing the actions that follow the triggered alarms thoroughly. For example, if the final actions are checked by taint-tracking alarms, as in TaintDroid [15], the TCA decision could be further refined. The issue of false positives and false negatives will certainly be addressed in our future work. False positives, which call-out a non-time critical alarm as a TCA, need to be minimized although these would not induce system malfunctions. False negatives, which are time critical alarms that are labeled as non-TCAs, may cause system malfunctions, but AlarmScope can ignore the alarms called by time-critical function, such as the setExact() function in Android, for preventing false negative cases.

7. ACKNOWLEDGEMENTS

This work was supported by the National Research Foundation of Korea grant funded by the Korean government, Ministry of Education, Science and Technology (No. 2014-R1A2A1A1-1049979).

8. REFERENCES

[1] A. Pathak, Y. C. Hu, and M. Zhang. Bootstrapping energy debugging on smartphones: A first look at energy bugs in mobile devices. In *Proc. of HotNets '11*, ACM Press (2011), p. 5.

[2] X. Ma, P. Huang, X. Jin, P. Wang, S. Park, D. Shen, Y. Zhou, L. K. Saul, and G. M. Voelker. eDoctor: Automatically diagnosing abnormal battery drain issues on smartphones. In *Proc. of NSDI '13*, USENIX (2013), pp. 57-70.

[3] Zhang, J., Musa, A., Le, W., 2013, A Comparison of Energy Bugs for Smartphone Platforms, In *Proc. of ICSE '13*, IEEE (2013), pp. 25-30.

[4] A. J. Oliner, A. Iyer, E. Lagerspetz, S. Tarkoma, and I. Stoica. Collaborative energy debugging for mobile devices. In *Proc. of HotDep '12*, USENIX (2012), p 6-6.

[5] A. Pathak, A. Jindal, Y. Charlie Hu, and S. P. Midkiff. What is keeping my phone awake?: Characterizing and detecting no-sleep energy bugs in smartphone apps. In *Proc. of MobiSys '12*, ACM Press (2012), pp. 267-280.

[6] P. Vekris, R. Jhala, S. Lerner, Y. Agarwal, Towards Verifying Android Apps for the Absence of No-Sleep Energy Bugs. In *Proc. of HotPower '12*, USENIX (2012), p. 3-3.

[7] K. Kim and H. Cha. WakeScope: Runtime WakeLock anomaly management scheme for Android platform. In *Proc. of EMSOFT '13*, IEEE (2013), p. 27.

[8] Y. Liu, C. Xu, and S. Cheung. Where has my battery gone? Finding sensor related energy black holes in smartphone applications. In *Proc. of PerCom '13*, IEEE(2013), pp. 2–10.

[9] A. Jindal, A. Pathak, Y. C. Hu, and S. Midkiff. Hypnos: Understanding and treating sleep conflicts in smartphones. In *Proc. of EuroSys '13*, ACM Press (2013), pp. 253-266.

[10] Timer coalescing, http://en.wikipedia.org/wiki/Timer_coalescing

[11] Xposed, http://repo.xposed.info/

[12] dex2jar, http://code.google.com/p/dex2jar/

[13] JD-GUI, http://jd.benow.ca/

[14] The Average Smartphone User Has Installed 26 Apps, http://www.statista.com/chart/1435/top-10-countries-by-app-usage/

[15] W. Enck, P. Gilbert, B.-G. Chun, L. P. Cox, J. Jung, P. McDaniel, and A. N. Sheth. TaintDroid: An Information-Flow Tracking System for Realtime Privacy Monitoring on Smartphones. In *Proc. of OSDI '10*, USENIX (2010), pp. 1-6.

Energy-Efficiency Comparison of Mobile Platforms and Applications: A Quantitative Approach

Grace Metri
Wayne Satate University
gmetri@wayne.edu

Weisong Shi
Wayne Satate University
weisong@wayne.edu

Monica Brockmeyer
Wayne Satate University
mbrockmeyer@wayne.edu

ABSTRACT

Given the number of platforms and apps with similar functionalities, this paper describes the challenges and identifies the gaps toward comparing mobile platforms and apps for energy efficiency. In addition, based on case studies that focus on energy efficiency comparison of different app categories on the most popular platforms, the paper discusses insights related to the major platform providers, energy-efficient app design, and app developers common practices.

1. INTRODUCTION

Today's mobile users face choices of platforms and apps with similar functionalities. Therefore, it is important to understand their relative energy efficiencies. However, comparing platforms and apps from an energy efficiency perspective is a challenging task given the lack of appropriate tools and technologies, possible measurement errors, and designing sound case studies. Despite the challenges, we collected power related metrics on different mobile platforms in order to achieve the following: 1) to quantify the energy efficiency gain of native apps vs. their web counterparts. 2) to quantify the difference in energy efficiency of same app categories on different platforms. The contributions of this paper are:

- We discussed the challenges and identified gaps toward comparing the energy efficiency of platforms and apps.

- Using case studies which focused on energy efficiency comparison of different app categories on the most popular platforms, we derived a list of insights related to the major platform providers, energy-efficient app design, and common practices of app developers.

The paper is organized as follows. We first discuss the challenges toward comparing platforms and apps for energy efficiency in Section 2. We present our experimental approach in Section 3 followed by detailed case studies in Section 4 and a list of insights in Section 5. Next, we present some related work in Section 6 and conclude in Section 7.

2. CHALLENGES

Given the large number of choices available for users in terms of platforms and apps, then comparing and ranking the energy efficiency of both can create some sort of competitive advantage. However, such a comparison is not a straight forward task. It is very challenging at best due but not limited to the following:

- Purely comparing the energy efficiency of different platforms is a hard task due to the fact that each platform requires different tools each of which can have distinct capabilities, different accuracy rates, and introduces varying energy consumption overhead. Given the tools' limitation, we do not directly compare the energy efficiency of platforms. Instead, we select a set of apps for each platform and then compare their relative energy efficiency.

- The test environment, if not kept constant, may impact the accuracy of the data. For instance, some devices utilize ambient light sensors that adjust the display backlight based on the surrounding light. As a result, during our data collection, we strived at keeping the lighting consistent across all scenarios. Another factor which can impact the accuracy is the Wi-Fi signal strength. Therefore, we made an effort to perform all tests at consistent Wi-Fi signal strength.

- Eliminating activities of background apps and services was challenging as well. For instance, even after killing Spotify from *Task Manager* on Android, we still periodically observed some related running processes. As a result, we uninstalled from the platform under test all apps that were not installed by default. Despite all our efforts, there were still some services that we were not able to stop. For instance, on Android, we failed at stopping the activities of *Search Application Provider* and *Google Account Manager*. Similarly, on Windows, we were not able to stop many system processes. On the other hand, on iOS, we were unable to identify background processes, not because they did not exist, but because we didn't have the appropriate tools.

- The energy efficiency of an app with dynamic content may significantly differ from one experiment to another. For example, since the energy consumption of *Facebook* depends on the number of status updates of *friends*, then login into an *uncontrolled* account may introduce measurement errors based on inconsistent activities during the experiment. As a result, for our case studies, we created an account which was *controlled* and used solely for the experiment purpose where friends posted identical updates during the experiment.

- Many apps have logic in the cloud which may impact their power consumption. Since our testing model cannot enable us to compare platforms and apps fairly if they use

Table 1: List of devices

Device	OS	Processor	Memory	Storage
Nexus 7	Android 4.3	Qualcomm Snap-dragon S4	1 GB	16 GB
iPad Air	iOS 7.0.6	A7 chip with 64-bit	1 GB	16 GB
Surface 2 Pro	Windows 8.1	Intel(R) i5-4200U	4 GB	64 GB

the cloud, we refrained from comparing such scenarios. For example, the latest Chrome browser for Android and iOS can significantly reduce cellular data usage by using proxy servers hosted at Google to optimize website content [1]. For the purpose of our experiments, we did not enable this feature. Another example is streaming music using iTunes. At various time intervals, iTunes stops streaming music for commercials which are accompanied by graphical updates. When we encountered this case, we discarded the results.

Based on the above list of challenges, it is evident that comparing the energy-efficiency of mobile platforms/apps is a useful but challenging task. Therefore, new cross platform tools are needed in order to increase the accuracy of such comparison. In addition, an exhaustive list of rules for accurate data collection and procedure for energy-efficiency comparison is needed in order to avoid measurement errors.

3. EXPERIMENTAL APPROACH

Toward achieving our goal of comparing the energy efficiency of platforms and apps, we employ devices of various form factors from all three major mobile platforms, namely, Windows, iOS, and Windows, for energy characterization as shown in Table 1. This section summaries the tools we use for energy characterization for these devices.

3.1 Windows

We used Intel SoC Watch for Windows [2]. We collected the following: 1) CPU idle sleep states for the package and cores. 2) CPU frequency. 3) Number of wakeups. 4) Timer resolution intervals. 5) Number of threads per application.

EnergyMeter: An Energy Profiling Tool for Windows. We developed *EnergyMeter* which takes as an input the test duration and outputs the energy consumed by the platform, package, cores, and GPU in joules. For platform energy consumption, we relied on Windows API to get a handler to the battery in order to collect the delta of the battery capacity changes for the test duration.
In order to collect package, core, and GPU energy consumption, we relied on hardware counters. The processor supports four Machine Specific Registers (MSRs) for Running Average Power Limit [3]. *RAPL_POWER_UNIT* reports power, energy status, and time units. *PKG_ENERGY_STATUS*, *PP0_ENERGY_STATUS*, and *PP1_ENERGY_STATUS*, report package, core, and graphics energy consumption. In order to calculate the energy used by each component, we calculate the ΔE_{MSR} and multiply it by the energy unit obtained from *RAPL_POWER_UNIT*.

3.2 Android

In order to power profile our Android device, we used the Trepn profiler [4]. We were able to collect the following metrics: 1) CPU utilization per app. 2) Average power consumption and 3) virtual memory utilization per app. 4) Number of wakelocks, wifilocks, and threads per app. Due to the extensive overhead of Trepn, we used *SoftPowerMon* [5] to collect the CPU's idle sleep states and frequency. Please note that the overhead observed by Trepn did not impact the above metrics because the data collected are per app.

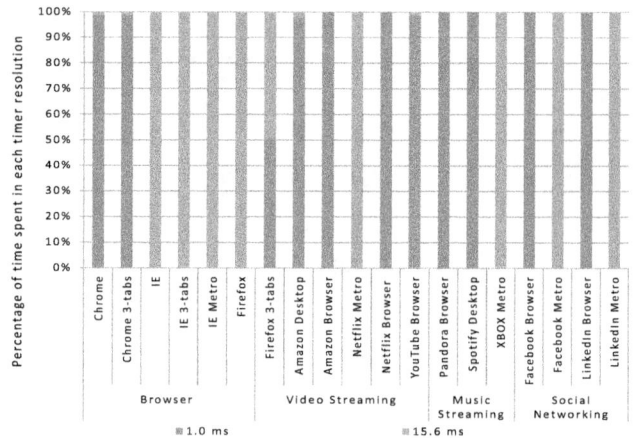

Figure 1: Timer resolution on Surface 2 Pro.

3.3 iOS

We used the *Energy Profiler Instrument* tool provided by Apple [6] and collected the following: 1) Energy consumption on an ascending scale from 0 to 20. 2) CPU utilization. 3) GPU utilization. 4) Total number of packets sent and received along with the total size in bytes for all packets.

Despite the fact that the above presented tools were capable of collecting some common metrics, however, each had different capabilities. SoC Watch and Trepn are capable of collecting a comprehensive list of metrics with fine grain precision. They are both capable of reporting per app values for several metrics such as CPU utilization. On the other hand, SoftPowerMon and the Energy Profiler Instrument are only capable of collecting a limited number of metrics with high coarse grain precision. They are also both incapable of reporting per app values for all of their metrics. Moreover, in terms of overhead, SoC Watch introduces 2% overhead which can reach up to 5% when the platform is highly active. Likewise, SoftPowerMon introduces 1-2% overhead. On the other hand, Trepen introduces ∼40% overhead even with small subset of metrics. Unfortunately, we were not able to measure the overhead introduced by Energy Instrument.

4. CASE STUDIES

Because comparing platforms and apps for energy efficiency in general is hard, if possible at all, we chose to use case studies as the first step to gain insights into comparing their relative energy efficiency. We selected four app categories and the corresponding list of most popular apps for each platform as shown in Table 2. Where applicable, we profiled the native and web-based app (Chrome was used for all web-based apps due to its availability on all three).

4.1 Browsers Scenario

We started profiling along a 3-minute timer, launched the browser (set to default webpage). Then upon the timer expiration, we stopped profiling and saved the results.

4.1.1 Surface 2 Pro Browsers

We profiled Chrome (1 and 3 tabs), IE (metro, 1 and 3 tabs), and Firefox (1 and 3 tabs) and ranked them as follows: Chrome, Chrome 3-tabs, IE, Firefox, IE 3-tabs, Firefox 3-tabs, IE Metro. *Firefox 3-tabs vs Chrome (Case*

Table 2: List of apps and corresponding version.

Scenario	Platform	App	Version
Browsers	Surface 2 Pro	Chrome	33.0.1750.146
		Internet Explorer 11	11.0.9600.16518
		Mozilla Firefox	24.0
	iPad Air	Chrome	32.1700.20
		Bing	2.0.2
		Safari	7.0.6
	Nexus 7	Chrome	33.0.1750.136
		Bing	4.2.3.20140303
		Mozilla Firefox	27.0
Video Streaming	Surface 2 Pro	Amazon Ubox Video	2.2.0.153
		Amazon (browser)	Feb 8, 14
		Netflix	2.3.0.12
		Netflix (browser)	Feb 8, 14
		YouTube (browser)	Feb 8, 14
	iPad Air	Amazon Instant Video	2.4
		Netflix	5.1.2
		YouTube	2.2.0
		YouTube (browser)	Feb 8, 14
	Nexus 7	YouTube	5.3.32
		YouTube (browser)	Feb 8, 14
		Netflix	3.2.1 build 1346
Music Streaming	Surface 2 Pro	Pandora (browser)	Feb 9, 14
		Spotify	0.9.7.16.g4b197456
		XBOX Music	2.2.444.0
	iPad Air	Spotify	0.9.3
		iTunes	7.0.6
		Pandora	5.2
	Nexus 7	Spotify	0.7.6.357
		Pandora	5.2
		Xbox Music	2.0.40226
Social Networking	Surface 2 Pro	LinkedIn HD	1.0.0.0
		LinkedIn (browser)	Feb 15, 14[1]
		Facebook	1.2.0.12
		Facebook (browser)	Feb 15, 14[2]
	iPad Air	LinkedIn	86
		LinkedIn (browser)	Feb 15, 14[3]
		Facebook	7.0
		Facebook (browser)	Feb 15, 14[4]
	Nexus 7	Facebook	6.0.0.28.28
		Facebook (browser)	Feb 15, 14[5]
		LinkedIn	3.3.1
		LinkedIn (browser)	Feb 15, 14

Table 3: Energy in joules on Surface Pro 2

Scenario	Application	Platform	Package	Core	GPU
Browsers	Chrome	734	148	22	0.69
	Chrome 3-tabs	763	165	34	1.2
	IE	824	177	36	4
	IE 3-tabs	853	247	111	0.89
	IE Metro	882	548	279	5.28
	Firefox	828	181	32	7.77
	Firefox 3-tabs	878	532	280	7.31
Video Streaming	Amazon Desk.	2023	635	135	39.83
	Amazon Browser	3063	1873	866	225.82
	Netflix Metro	1836	589	147	29.72
	Netflix Browser	3009	1493	496	259.14
	YouTube Browser	2476	1290	487	130.93
Music Streaming	Pandora Browser	1757	650	149	31.98
	Spotify Desk.	1598	404	65	0.3
	XBOX Metro	1465	332	57	3.5
Social Networking	Facebook Browser	853	165	23	1.37
	Facebook Metro	770	201	59	2.35
	LinkedIn Browser	799	160	32	1.17
	LinkedIn Metro	745	149	26	2.26

Table 4: Metrics collected on Surface Pro 2.

Scenario	Application	Active Duration in ms.	Average Package Wakeups	Average Core Wakeups
Browsers	Chome	6,371	1015	1507
	Chrome 3-tabs	10,736	1061	1595
	IE	15,786	208	754
	IE 3-tabs	5,386	145	363
	IE Metro	10,647	316	1319
	Firefox	7,996	118	457
	Firefox 3-tabs	6,260	600	1141
Video Streaming	Amazon Desktop	75,638	1,094	1,900
	Amazon Browser	379,754	575	2,648
	Netflix Metro	28,750	393	1,019
	Netflix Browser	346,010	611	2,019
	YouTube Browser	361,663	622	1,628
Music Streaming	Pandora Browser	111,995	1,079	1,956
	Spotify Desktop	24,633	1,287	1,892
	XBOX Metro	18,774	286	567
Social Networking	Facebook Browser	9098	1,011	1,451
	Facebook Metro	19,618	260	551
	LinkedIn Browser	10,911	1,067	1,584
	LinkedIn Metro	15,420	232	569

Table 5: Metrics collected on Nexus 7.

Scenario	App Name	Ave. Power in mW	Ave. CPU Percent	Ave. Virtual Memory	Thread Count	Total wake-locks
Browsers	Chrome	237	0.68	2966.63	88	1171
	Chrome 3-tabs	374	1.99	1989	66	1401
	Bing	745	7.04	912	20	0
	Firefox	235	0.09	1943	53	0
	Firefox 3-tabs	221	0.31	1955	52	0
Video Streaming	YouTube App	1,280	1.91	1003.22	65	0
	YouTube Browser	1,468	1.17	2146	77	1515
	Netflix App	1,387	3.04	1023.78	65	0
Music Streaming	Pandora	705	0.59	973.38	42	1714
	Spotify	683	4.01	1860.03	107	1646
	XBOX	483	2.08	981.23	45	1550
Social Networking	Facebook App	1,211	1.74	1817.81	49	4
	Facebook Browser	965	1.35	2089.94	72	1023
	LinkedIn App	426	0.04	946.38	31	0
	LinkedIn Browser	640	0.55	2131.36	70	1024

1): Chrome spent 99.8% in 1 ms timer resolution as shown in figure 1 significantly higher than Firefox 3-tabs causing the highest percentage of wakeups while having the same active duration as shown in Table 2. However, Chrome (1 and 3 tabs) still had a lower percentage of active cores and package compared to Firefox 3-tabs as shown in Figure 2. Thus, it was much more energy efficient. These counter intuitive results were justified once we examined the number of threads. Chrome had distributed its activities to seven threads, whereas Firefox only had one thread. As a result, Chrome took advantage of concurrency, which enabled both cores to go to sleep for longer duration and thus enabled the package to remain in idle sleep states for a long duration.

4.1.2 iPad Air Browsers

We profiled Chrome (1 and 3 tabs), Bing, Safari (1 and 3 tabs). The average energy levels are 3.87, 6.27, 2.65, 1.22, and 1.29 and CPU activities are 3.16, 3.38, 7.55, 2.94, and 3.29% for Chrome, Chrome 3-tabs, Bing, Safari, and Safari 3-tabs, respectively. They rank as follows: Safari, Safari 3-tabs, Bing, Chrome, and Chrome 3-tabs. One noteworthy observation is that Chrome consumed 62% more energy when we added two extra tabs, whereas Safari only consumed 5% more. *Bing vs Chrome (Case 2):* Bing had the highest CPU utilization even though it is the second most efficient. By examining the network activities, we noticed the differences in communication patterns. In particular, Chrome received and sent large network packets after launching the browser 11,790.31, 4.91, and 12.18 KB in and 885.49, 3.23, and 3.56 KB out. Then, it sent and received small 80 bytes packets at an approximate 30-second intervals. On the other hand, Bing sent and received relatively smaller packets after launching the browser 260.9, 194.7, and 90.19 KB in and 11.79, 16.38, and 11.02 KB out. Then, received 60 bytes packets at an approximate 2-second interval. This example is counter intuitive because we expect that frequent communication reduces the energy efficiency of the platform. Unfortunately, the tool did not offer extra details in order to explain our observation.

4.1.3 Nexus 7 Browsers

We profiled Chrome, Chrome 3-tabs, Bing, Firefox, and Firefox 3-tabs. We can rank them as follows: Firefox 3-tabs, Firefox, Chrome, Chrome 3-tabs, and Bing. *Firefox 3-tabs vs Firefox 1-tab (Case 3):* It is odd to encounter this case where Firefox 3-tabs is more energy-efficient than 1-tab. One possible explanation is that the average CPU utilization

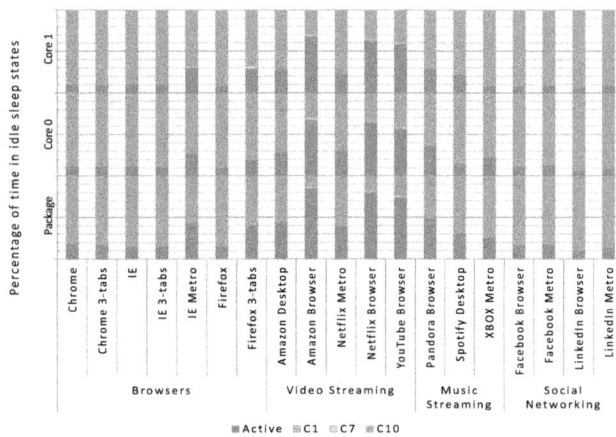

Figure 2: CPU idle sleep states on Surface 2 Pro.

increased in the case of 3-tabs as shown in Table 5, leading to an increase in CPU frequency as shown in Figure 5 which lead to an increase in performance, which was translated to less core active duration as shown in Figure 4. *Chrome vs Bing (Case 4):* Bing consumed more than triple the amount of power than Chrome as shown in Table 5. It may be attributed to the fact that Chrome has a higher multi-threading index than Bing.

4.2 Video Streaming Scenario

We started profiling along a 5-minute timer then played the video in full-screen mode until the timer expired. For the web-based case, we launched the browser and typed the credentials. Then, started profiling along a 5-minute timer. Next, we launched the browser and signed in. Then, we played the video in full-screen until the timer expired.

4.2.1 iPad Air Video Streaming

We profiled Amazon instant movies, Netflix, and YouTube (app and browser). The average energy levels are 10.73, 10.38, 10.47, and 10.71 for Amazon, Netflix, YouTube app, and YouTube browser, respectively. They rank as follows: Netflix, YouTube app, YouTube browser, and Amazon. *YouTube app vs browser (Case 5):* Even though streaming the same video using the app was more energy-efficient, however, using a browser had less percentage of CPU and graphics utilization. By examining the network activities, we noticed that YouTube app was constantly receiving packets. On the other hand, using a browser, led to much larger size of packets received at the beginning of the run (due to large buffering of the video), then throughout the test, there were long duration of 0 packet transmissions (20 seconds) followed by 5 seconds of activities. In theory, this method should enable the Wi-Fi radio to go to low-power states for an extended duration, thus reducing the energy consumption of the platform. However, buffering a large size of data led to more memory utilization, which nullified the savings from the sleep states of Wi-Fi radio and instead lead to an increase in energy consumption of the platform.

4.3 Music Streaming Scenario

We started streaming using an app (or browser). Then, we started the profiling tool with a 5-minute timer. Next, we relaunched the app (or browser) until the timer expired.

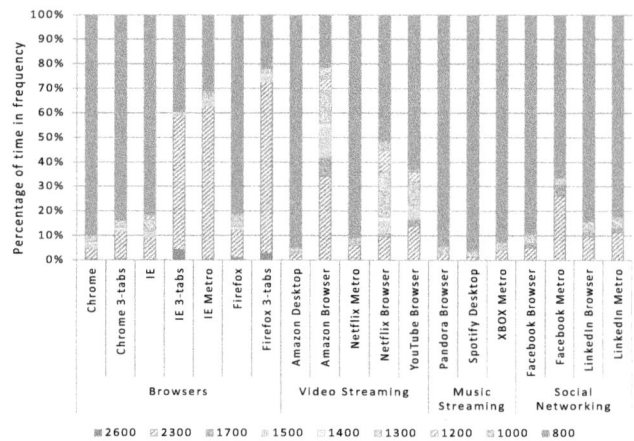

Figure 3: CPU frequency in MHz on Surface 2 Pro.

4.3.1 iPad Air Music Streaming

We profiled Spotify, iTunes, and Pandora and ranked them as iTunes, Spotify, and Pandora because the average energy levels are 5.35, 3.50, and 8.77 for Spotify, iTunes, and Pandora respectively. *Pandora vs iTunes (Case 6):* We noticed a reverse order of CPU utilization compared to the app energy-efficiency where the least energy-efficient app (Pandora) had the least CPU utilization, whereas, the most energy-efficient app (iTunes) had the most CPU utilization. Examining the network activity revealed that iTunes had sent and received during long time intervals large packets while at 2-second intervals received a small packet of 60 bytes. On the other hand, Pandora, sent out at regular 1-second intervals 166 bytes while sending and receiving during long time intervals large packets. Therefore, we can conclude that Pandora consumed more energy than iTunes because it kept the Wi-Fi radio at high power state for most of the test duration.

4.3.2 Nexus 7 Music Streaming

We profiled Pandora, Spotify, and XBOX music. *XBOX vs Spotify (Case 7):* XBOX was the most energy-efficient but music streaming had many interrupts due to poor buffering. Therefore, XBOX sacrificed the user experience either to optimize the energy efficiency or due to poor app design.

4.4 Social Networking Scenario

We started profiling with a 3-minute timer. Launched the app. Upon the timer expiration, we stopped the collection. For the web-based app, we launched the browser and typed the credentials. Then, we started profiling along a 3-minutes timer. Next, we launched the browser and signed in. Upon the expiration of the timer, we stopped the collection.

4.4.1 Surface 2 Pro Social Networking

We profiled Facebook (browser and Metro), and LinkedIn (browser and Metro) and ranked them as follows: LinkedIn Metro, Facebook Metro, LinkedIn browser, and Facebook browser. *Facebook Metro vs browser (Case 8):* The web-based version was slightly less active than the Metro version as shown in Figure 2 consuming less package and core energy as shown in Table 3. The platform energy consumption contradicted with package and core because the timer resolution was changed to 1 ms in the web based as shown in Figure 1. Thus, the average number of wakeups

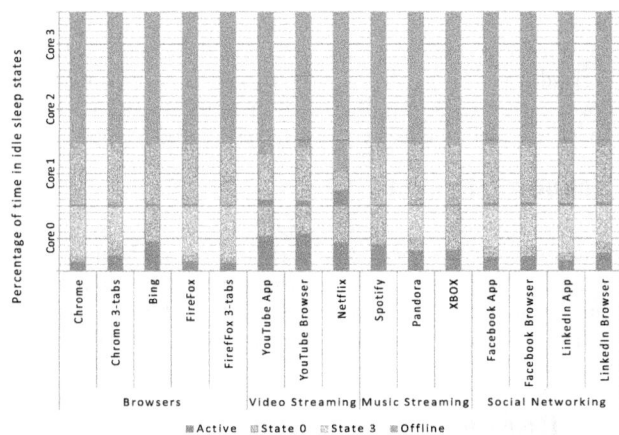

Figure 4: CPU idle sleep states on Nexus 7.

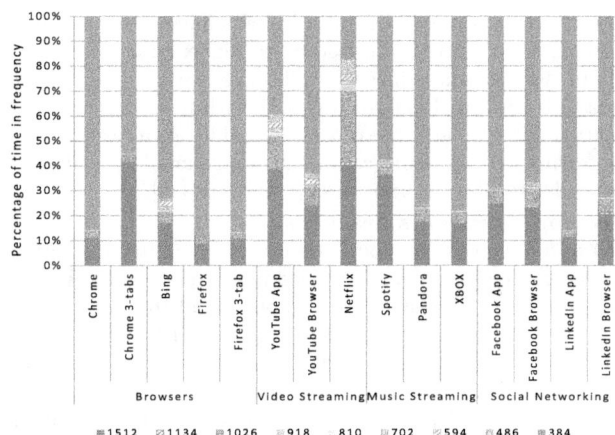

Figure 5: CPU frequency in MHz on Nexus 7.

was much larger than to Metro case as shown in Table 2. In addition, since the web-based version had lower resolution, the site got updated more frequently which kept the Wi-Fi radio active for longer duration and consumed more energy.

4.4.2 Nexus 7 Social Networking

We profiled Facebook (app and browser), and LinkedIn (app and browser) and ranked them as follows: LinkedIn app, LinkedIn browser, Facebook browser, and Facebook app. *Facebook App vs browser (Case 9):* Unlike previous observations comparing app vs web-based, the app consumed 25.5% more power than the web-based version as shown in Table 5. The possible cause may be attributed to the fact that the app had a sophisticated interface leading to 17% more GPU utilization than the web-based version.

5. INSIGHTS

Based on our analysis of the results, we deduced a list of insights and grouped them into the following four categories:

1- Power profiling mobile platforms and apps.
Designing and performing energy-efficiency comparison of platforms and apps are challenging tasks.

- Based on Section 2, new tools are needed in order to increase the accuracy of energy efficiency comparison of mobile platforms and apps. In addition, an exhaustive list of rules for accurate data collection and defined procedure are needed in order to avoid measurement errors.

- Debugging the energy efficiency of mobile platforms/apps is a complicated process where a particular power metric in a specific context can have a different meaning in another one. For instance, the higher the average wakeups value, the lower the energy-efficiency. However, that is not particularly true in the case where the average wakeups value is low but the percentage of CPU active duration is high. Therefore, creating a relationship model for correlating different metrics can significantly improve the debugging process.

2- The major three platform providers.
We observed that the three major platforms favor different tradeoffs between performance and energy efficiency.

- We noticed that apps released by Apple are more energy efficient compared to third party apps of the same category. One possible reason is that Apple's Energy Instrument had the least precise data collection options compared to other tools available on other platforms. As a result, we recommend enhancing the power profiling tool to collect additional power metrics with greater precision.

- We noticed that apps released by Google disregarded some of the energy-efficient principles in favor of performance. For example, Chrome browser on Windows changed the timer resolution to 1ms causing higher wakeups as shown in Case 1. In addition, Chrome browser on Android acquired high number of wakelocks as shown in Table 5.

- Based on our experiments, it seems that apps released by Microsoft were more concerned with energy efficiency than performance as shown in Case 8.

3- Energy-efficient app design.
We observed some app design strategies which are more energy-efficient than others.

- In general, native apps consume less energy than the web-based version as shown in Cases 5 and 8 reaching up to ~11% in Case 8. Based on our data, we attribute the cause to the fact that native apps tend to have higher CPU utilization and lower memory utilization compared to the web-based counterpart. Charland *et al.* [7] discussed the strength and weaknesses of adopting both models. Combining their findings with the information presented in this paper can further help companies make educated decisions on the model to adopt. Moreover, based on our results, it seems that Google Chrome platform may be inherently at a disadvantage since it relies on web apps. Therefore, further related research is strongly needed.

- Despite the fact that buffering large data at a time can enable the Wi-Fi radio to go to an idle state, but it can also result in an increase of the power consumption as shown in Cases 2, 4 and 5. As a result, the size of the buffer needs to be balanced between the energy savings from enabling the Wi-Fi radio to go to an idle sleep state and the extra energy consumption due to the increase in memory usage.

- Multi threading increases the energy efficiency of an app if the execution is balanced across cores as shown in Cases 1 and 4. Sabharwal *et al.* [8] showed that if an app is multi threaded and balanced across the cores, then it enables the cores to work hard for a short duration, then enter a sleep state leading to improvement of energy efficiency. In addition, Carroll *et al.* [9] investigated how core offlining and DVFS can be used together in order to reduce energy consumption and developed Medusa, an offline-aware governor.

- Apps with low resource utilization (e.g., CPU utilization) but with high average wakeups can negatively impact the energy-efficiency of the platform as shown in Cases 6 and 8. High average wakeups of the platform's idle components

43

(e.g., CPU or Wi-Fi) results in switching the component from idle to active state leading to higher power consumption. For instance, in Case 6, iTunes average energy level was 3.5 whereas Pandora was 8.77 with network communication pattern being the obvious variable. As a result, timed interrupts and network communication should be coalescent in order to prevent unnecessary wakeups [10].

4- App developers practices.
Despite the vast number of tools and literature focusing on energy efficiency, we identified potential energy-efficiency improvements of some popular apps on all three platforms.

- We noticed that apps with the same functionality that are running on the same platform can vary vastly in terms of energy consumption (more than 50% in some cases as shown in Case 4). There are already several tools available for developers in order to power profile their apps. For instance, Kansal *et al.* [11] introduced an energy profiler which lets developers make power-aware design choices and trade off between energy consumption and performance of their apps. Another example is WattsOn [12] that estimates an app's energy consumption on the basis of empirically derived power models made available by either the smartphone manufacturer or mobile OS platform developers. These types of tools are very useful but there is also a need for power benchmark for each category of apps to be used as a baseline to compare the power consumption of apps instead of simply using the device's idle power consumption as the baseline.

- Changing the timer on Windows and holding wakelocks on Android seems to be common practices due to either lack of awareness of their power consumption overhead or a conscious decision to sacrifice efficiency in favor of performance.

The above list of insights summarizes our observations from comparing the energy efficiency of our categorized apps on all three platforms.

6. RELATED WORK

Jindal *et al.* [13] developed a taxonomy of sleep bugs in Android smartphones and categorized their root causes. Then, they used their model in order to evaluate 3596 APIs used in a set of 889 apps. Chen *et al.* [14] measured the energy drainage of the top 100 free apss in Google Play in order to determine the energy savings from prefetching ads. Wang *et al.* [15] used a collaborative approach to estimate the power consumption of mobile apps. They collected data from 120,000 Android users. Then, they used the data to build their power estimation model for mobile apps. These work focused on evaluating multiple single apps in order to energy profile them. We used the knowledge provided by their work in order to compare the relative energy-efficiency of apps belonging to the same category on multiple platforms. We also presented the challenges of such a comparison and showed that despite the research focusing on energy efficiency, still some of the popular apps on the three most popular platforms did not take full advantage of the available resources to improve the energy efficiency of their apps.

7. CONCLUSION

Energy efficiency comparison of mobile platforms and apps is a hard task due to possible measurement errors and challenges in designing case studies. Despite of the challenges, we compared the energy efficiency of four app categories:

browsers, video and music streaming, and social networking on Windows, iOS, and Android. Based on the results, we derived a list of insights. In the future, we are planning on developing a power profiling analytical framework for developers in order to effectively power profile their apps.

Acknowledgment

This work is in part supported by NSF grant CNS-1205338. This material is based upon work supporting while serving at the National Science Foundation. We would like to thank our shepherd, Dr. Lin Zhong, for his constructive comments and suggestions in the preparation of the final version of this paper.

8. REFERENCES

[1] Google, "Data compression proxy," https://developer. chrome.com/multidevice/data-compression.

[2] Intel, "Intel SoC Watch for Windows," https://software.intel.com/sites/default/files/ managed/aa/4a/socwatch_windows.pdf.

[3] Intel, "Intel 64 and IA-32 architectures software developers manual combined volumes: 1, 2A, 2B, 2C, 3A, 3B and 3C," http://www.intel.com/content/dam/ www/public/us/en/documents/manuals/ 64-ia-32-architectures-software-developer-manual-325462. pdf.

[4] Qualcomm, "Trepn profiler," https: //developer.qualcomm.com/mobile-development/ increase-app-performance/trepn-profiler.

[5] G. Metri, A. Agrawal, R. Peri, M. Brockmeyer, and W. Shi, "A simplistic way for power profiling of mobile devices," in Proc. IEEE ICEAC, 2012.

[6] Apple, "About instruments," https://developer.apple.com/library/mac/ documentation/developertools/conceptual/ instrumentsuserguide/Introduction/Introduction.html.

[7] A. Charland and B. Leroux, "Mobile application development: web vs. native," Communications of the ACM, vol. 54, no. 5, 2011.

[8] M. Sabharwal, A. Agrawal, and G. Metri, "Enabling green IT through energy-aware software," IT Professional, 2013.

[9] A. Carroll and G. Heiser, "Mobile multicores: use them or waste them," in Proc. HotPower, 2013.

[10] B. Steigerwald and A. Agrawal, "Developing green software," Intel White Paper, 2011.

[11] A. Kansal and F. Zhao, "Fine-grained energy profiling for power-aware application design," ACM SIGMETRICS Performance Evaluation Review, vol. 36, no. 2, 2008.

[12] R. Mittal, A. Kansal, and R. Chandra, "Empowering developers to estimate app energy consumption," in Proc. ACM MobiCom, 2012.

[13] A. Jindal, A. Pathak, Y. C. Hu, and S. Midkiff, "On death, taxes, and sleep disorder bugs in smartphones," in Proc. HotPower, 2013.

[14] X. Chen, A. Jindal, and Y. C. Hu, "How much energy can we save from prefetching ads?: energy drain analysis of top 100 apps," in Proc. HotPower, 2013.

[15] C. Wang, F. Yan, Y. Guo, and X. Chen, "Power estimation for mobile applications with profile-driven battery traces," in Proc. IEEE/ACM ISLPED, 2013.

CQIC: Revisiting Cross-Layer Congestion Control for Cellular Networks

Feng Lu[†§], Hao Du[§], Ankur Jain[§], Geoffrey M. Voelker[†], Alex C. Snoeren[†], and Andreas Terzis[§]

† UC San Diego   § Google Inc.

Abstract

With the advent of high-speed cellular access and the overwhelming popularity of smartphones, a large percent of today's Internet content is being delivered via cellular links. Due to the nature of long-range wireless signal propagation, the capacity of the last hop cellular link can vary by orders of magnitude within a short period of time (e.g., a few seconds). Unfortunately, TCP does not perform well in such fast-changing environments, potentially leading to poor spectrum utilization and high end-to-end packet delay.

In this paper we revisit seminal work in cross-layer optimization in the context of 4G cellular networks. Specifically, we leverage the rich physical layer information exchanged between base stations (NodeB) and mobile phones (UE) to predict the capacity of the underlying cellular link, and propose CQIC, a cross-layer congestion control design. Experiments on real cellular networks confirm that our capacity estimation method is both accurate and precise. A CQIC sender uses these capacity estimates to adjust its packet sending behavior. Our preliminary evaluation reveals that CQIC improves throughput over TCP by 1.08–2.89× for small and medium flows. For large flows, CQIC attains throughput comparable to TCP while reducing the average RTT by 2.38–2.65×.

Categories and Subject Descriptors

C.2.1 [**Computer Communication Networks**]: Network Architecture and Design

General Terms

Algorithms, Design, Experimentation, Measurement, Performance

Keywords

Congestion Control; Cellular Networks; HSPA+; Cross-Layer

1. INTRODUCTION

Smartphones and other hand-held wireless devices are increasingly popular platforms for all types of network applications. Fueled by attractive pricing models for cellular data access, mobile

HotMobile'15, February 12–13, 2015, Santa Fe, New Mexico, USA.
ACM 978-1-4503-3391-7/15/02.
http://dx.doi.org/10.1145/2699343.2699345.

data traffic is increasing at an explosive rate, with 10× growth predicted in the next five years [12]. To meet this unprecedented demand, cellular carriers have actively bid for additional spectrum, deployed more cellular towers and base stations, and upgraded to the latest cellular technologies such as HSPA+ [1] and LTE Advanced [2]. These efforts lead to a tremendous cost increment in both CAPEX and OPEX. These investments are not currently being fully exploited, however: cellular operators report that their precious resources are often under-utilized. In a recent measurement study, Huang *et al.* found that, on average, TCP flows use less than 50% of the available bandwidth in deployed LTE networks due to poor protocol interactions [16].

TCP, like any congestion control protocol, strives to match a sender's packet transmission rate with the available bottleneck bandwidth. We observe that for a large fraction of mobile data traffic, the bottleneck is the last hop cellular link. In particular, over 38% of all traffic flows[1] on smartphones originate from large CDNs [11], which are increasingly locating their servers inside the networks of mobile operators to decrease latency and improve user experience. Hence, the performance of this significant portion of the (high-volume) flows in a mobile environment depends upon an accurate estimate of the last hop cellular link capacity.

Given that the capacity of a cellular link fluctuates rapidly over time, prior approaches [10, 20, 23] use per-packet signaling, such as ACKs (losses) and inter-packet spacing, and employ various models to infer the capacity of the underlying cellular channel. Unfortunately, these models are necessarily tied to specific network types and locations. In contrast, we observe that high-fidelity information about the cellular channel is readily available from the radio-layer signaling protocols employed by high-speed cellular networks (e.g., HSPA+ and LTE). Therefore, we propose to dispense with modeling the channel entirely, and instead utilize the existing physical-layer control information—in particular the channel quality indicator (CQI) and discontinuous transmission ratio (DTX)—to predict instantaneous cellular bandwidth. As a proof of concept, we design CQIC a congestion control protocol that employs physical-layer information to control its sending rate. While the benefit of using cross-layer techniques for congestion control in wireless networks has been argued multiple times in seminal papers, including [4, 6, 9], CQIC revisits this approach and suggests that the ever richer physical layer information could potentially change the way how we design congestion control protocols for cellular networks.

Our experiments indicate that CQIC can accurately and precisely estimate the capacity of a cellular link, where the average estimation error is only 8% and the 80th-percentile error is less than 20%. We implement CQIC in Google's QUIC framework [15] and com-

---

[1]The percentage is even higher for medium and large flows.

pare the download performance of CQIC with TCP on real workloads as a preliminary evaluation. CQIC attains nearly 100% of the available bandwidth while keeping the average RTT very close to the target value for all flow sizes. Specifically, for small and medium flows, CQIC outperforms TCP by 1.08–2.89× in terms of throughput while attaining similar RTT. CQIC yields similar (or slightly better) throughput performance on large flows, while reducing the average RTT by 2.38–2.65×. These results augur well for the use of physical-layer information in cellular congestion control protocols.

2. BACKGROUND

The challenges of TCP over wireless links are well-known problems, having been studied for almost twenty years [6, 7]. Much of the early work focused on avoiding misinterpretation of link-layer packet losses by means of explicit packet marking [18] or local retransmission [6]. Today's cellular data technologies conceal link-layer losses from transport protocols by deploying ARQ and error correction techniques, potentially at the cost of large variations in packet delay [10]. Furthermore, due to the nature of wireless signal propagation and channel-state-based scheduling [8], users experience a significant degree of variation in link-layer data rates. This combined delay and rate variability leads to undesirable interactions with TCP (e.g., spurious timeouts, bufferbloat, etc.) and poor bandwidth utilization.

Recent research efforts focus on understanding the impact of delay/rate variability on TCP performance [13] and improving congestion-control protocols in the face of large variations [10, 17, 20, 23]. Khafizov et al. [13] study the performance of TCP over IS-2000 networks and find that bandwidth oscillation significantly degrades TCP throughput. Assuming that TCP cannot adapt quickly enough to the delay and bandwidth fluctuations of cellular links, others try to model the variations, either deterministically [10] or dynamically based on stochastic control theory [20] and statistical methods [23]. To shorten the feedback latency, estimated bandwidth is often conveyed back to the sender via side channels such as the receiver window field in the TCP header [20] or custom control protocols [23].

CQIC differs from the aforementioned approaches—and most previous cross-layer designs[2]—by extracting capacity information directly from the physical layer. In general, the existing literature continues to rely on TCP to probe the underlying bandwidth (employing a wide variety of mechanisms to mitigate wireless-link side effects); CQIC forgoes the entire AIMD-style congestion avoidance process and directly obtains bottleneck bandwidth information from the physical layer signaling between the UE and the base station. The benefits are manifold. First, CQIC eliminates the need for a model and the associated uncertainty which degrades protocol performance. For example, model inaccuracies force Sprout to trade throughput for low end-to-end delay, sacrificing 30% or more bandwidth utilization to remain interactive [23]. Second, CQIC does not rely on packet loss signals to adjust its bandwidth estimation and avoids the bufferbloat effect prevalent in TCP-style protocols. Furthermore, the high fidelity of information at the physical layer allows CQIC to closely track the fast-changing cellular bandwidth. Finally, CQIC does not send probe traffic nor does it need a slow-start phase.

Clearly, this approach is only viable when an accurate bandwidth estimate is available from the physical layer and the band-

---

[2]Both Srivastava et al. [21] and Shakkottai et al. [22] provide excellent summaries of this topic.

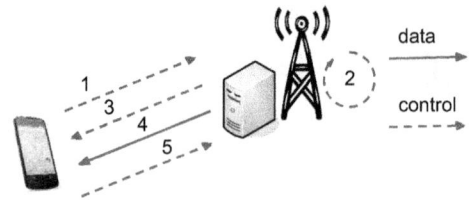

Figure 1: HSPA+ downlink data transmission.

width value is sufficient for end-to-end congestion control, i.e., the cellular link is the bottleneck. Fortunately, cellular technology advancements and shorter connection hop-count are both the prevailing technological trends.

Tight cellular control loop. The recent dramatic increase in cellular data rates is due to a combination of sophisticated new communication techniques and wider frequency spectrum [3]. In particular, advanced link technologies, such as MIMO, antenna arrays, etc., require tight control interactions between the base station and the UE. Such interactions often happen on the scale of milliseconds and a wide variety of channel information is exchanged between the two entities [1, 2]. As a result, a modern UE continuously reports the current channel quality, even when there is no network data activity. The rich information contained within these control channel messages allows CQIC to directly compute the cellular channel capacity (as we describe in the following section). Furthermore, these control messages are part of the cellular standards (e.g., HSPA+ and LTE), and readily available from the physical layer. Last but not least, CQIC does not require any changes in existing network infrastructure. Only the UE's radio firmware needs to be updated to expose control information to the upper layers.

Server proximity. The effectiveness of a congestion control protocol depends on how well it tracks the bottleneck bandwidth. Even if CQIC can accurately track available capacity on the wireless hop, end-to-end throughput might be constrained by other bottlenecks in the network. Fortunately, CDNs customarily place their servers inside the networks of mobile operators to improve application quality of experience (QoE). In general, the average distance between a UE and a CDN server is significantly shorter than between standard Internet hosts.[3] Given that medium and large flows, such as video streaming and software updates, are likely to be served by CDNs (which also constitute the majority of mobile traffic in terms of volume [11]), we believe that the end-to-end bandwidth for most cellular connections is bottlenecked by the cellular last hop. For this reason, CQIC focuses on estimating the cellular link capacity without worrying about bottlenecks elsewhere in the network.

3. CELLULAR CAPACITY ESTIMATION

In this section, we start by explaining the preliminaries of data and control exchange between base stations and mobile terminals in current cellular networks. With a basic understanding of this process, we then illustrate how CQIC leverages existing control information to estimate channel capacity. Finally, we evaluate the accuracy of CQIC's capacity estimation mechanism based on real network measurements.

3.1 HSPA+ Basics

We focus our discussion on HSPA+ networks due to their widespread availability. The control sequences described here are similar to the ones in LTE networks. In addition, we focus on downlink transmissions as cellular traffic is heavily skewed towards

---

[3]See, e.g., http://www.akamai.com/hdwp p.3.

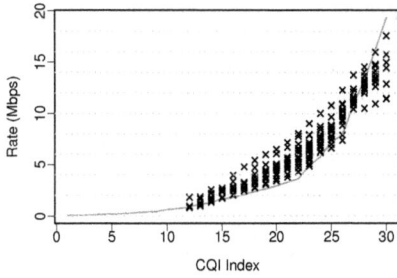

Figure 2: Actual mapping between CQI and data rate (solid line represents the CQI-Rate mapping defined by the HSPA+ specification).

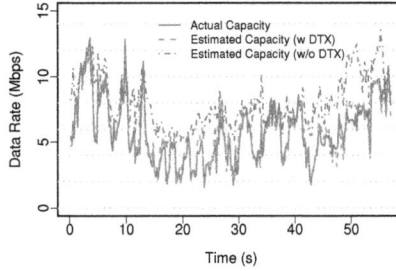

Figure 3: Capacity estimation based on CQI alone (estimated capacity w/o DTX), and based on both CQI and DTX (estimated capacity w/ DTX).

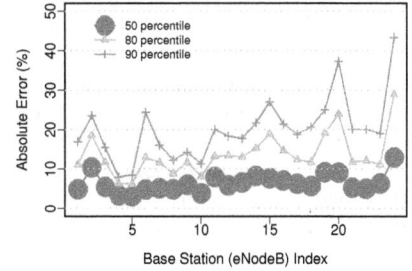

Figure 4: The 50-, 80-, and 90-th percentile of estimation error with 200 ms window size across the 24 experiment instances.

downlink; uplink estimation is straightforward as the transmission rates are known by the UE itself.

Figure 1 illustrates the sequence of control and data messages that the UE exchanges with the base station, once activated. In particular, each UE reports the channel quality (CQI) on the control channel (1); after collecting all such CQI reports from UEs, the base station determines which set of UEs will be served (2); and informs the UEs about its decision (3). The base station then delivers the next frame, which lasts for 2 ms[4] (4). Finally, the UE sends feedback (ACK/NACK) to the base station for the data block just received (5). These messages are continuously exchanged in a pipeline fashion. Even when there is no data transmission, the UE reports CQI to the base station every 2 ms as long as it remains active.

3.2 CQI-to-Rate Mapping

As defined by the HSPA+ specification [1], the base station exclusively relies on CQI to decide the data block size delivered to UEs (step 4 in Figure 1). Specifically, CQI ranges from 0 (worst) to 30 (best) according to the current downlink channel quality. In addition, there exists a one-to-one mapping, known as the CQI mapping table, between CQI and the data block size in the HSPA+ specification. For example, when CQI is 20, the NodeB will send 5,896 bits in the 2-ms data slot, which translates to a rate of 2.95 Mbps.

We validate the conformance of real-world base stations to the official CQI-to-rate mapping table through network measurement. Our validation experiment setup consists of a UDP server (which is located next to a packet gateway inside the cellular carrier's network), a mobile phone, and a host laptop. The mobile phone is connected via USB to the host laptop on which we run Qualcomm's QXDM software [19]. The QXDM tool allows us to capture radio-layer traces including the control messages mentioned in Section 3.1. We let the server send UDP packets to the mobile phone as fast as possible so the base station always has traffic for the phone. For each experiment, we recorded at least 60 seconds of trace data. All together we conducted 24 experiments: 12 static, 8 moving at walking speed, and 4 driving.

Figure 2 shows the actual mapping obtained between CQI and data rate from the 24 experiment instances. We average the number of bits sent by the same base station for a particular CQI value for each experiment, which leads to a single CQI-Rate point shown in Figure 2.[5]

We first observe that most of the mapped rates deviate from the standard data rates as defined by the HSPA+ specification. Base station vendors often choose to implement their own CQI rate mapping table and the specification is merely a recommendation. In addition, we notice that there are variations in terms of mapped data rates for the same CQI across different base stations, although the majority of these data rates are centered around some value for a given CQI (except 29 and 30). We suspect that base stations tend to be more conservative in the high-CQI region (28, 29 and 30), and may select data rates from a wide range that is below the rates defined by the specification. Overall, our results indicate that most of the base stations we measure share similar CQI-to-rate mappings.

Since base station vendors appear to implement their own CQI-to-rate mappings, it is likely that one might encounter base stations with CQI-to-rate mappings that are different from the HSPA+ specification or the ones we have profiled thus far. We foresee a number of ways to handle mapping variations. For example, one could build a large (perhaps cloud-based) key-value store where the key is the base station id and profile all base stations with crowdsourcing. In CQIC, we start with the default CQI-Rate mapping defined in the HSPA+ specification and gradually update the mapping table with each additional observed data rate.

While one can derive a mapping between base station and its CQI-to-rate table, it is not clear that mapping persists over time. Therefore, we repeat the same UDP blasting experiment described earlier at a single base station, which covers a mixture of residential and business areas, during different times of the day and under various mobility patterns. Our experimental results indicate that, at least for the base station we studied, the CQI-rate mapping is consistent and does not change with respect to time (at least over the course of a few days) and mobility variations.

3.3 Link-Capacity Estimation

CQIC employs a simple method to estimate cellular link capacity. At a high level, it uses information about previous data rates to predict the future at sub-second time scales. More specifically, we divide time into T-ms-long windows and collect CQI values (one CQI reading every 2 ms) that fall into the current observation window, i.e., $[0, T]$. For each CQI observed, we obtain the corresponding data rate based on the CQI-to-rate mapping (of the current base station). The average of these rates is then used to predict the link capacity for time $[T, 2T]$. Although CQI (capacity) fluctuates rapidly due to small-scale fading, the average rate is still dominated by large-scale fading effects, which vary less frequently at sub-second time scales. Therefore, with a time window T that captures the large-scale variation, we should be able to estimate capacity effectively.

Figure 3 shows the actual and estimated link capacity based on the CQI-driven mechanism we just described (labeled "estimated

---

[4]In some versions of HSPA, the time slot could be 10 ms as well.
[5]Not all CQI values are observed in our trace dataset.

capacity w/o DTX"). There is an evident discrepancy between the actual and estimated capacities. The reason is that as cell load increases, independent data channels are quickly exhausted and UEs have to share the same data channel in a TDMA manner.

In other words, during certain time slots, the base station may choose not to serve a particular UE even though there is pending traffic for that UE, which is known as discontinuous transmission (DTX). Hence, when estimating the cellular link capacity, both CQI and DTX should be included in the final estimate. Specifically, the DTX ratio for time window $[0, T]$ is computed based on base station scheduling information (i.e., step 3 in Figure 1), and the final link capacity estimate is the product of the CQI-based rate estimation and the DTX ratio.

Figure 4 depicts the 50-, 80- and 90th-percentile CQIC's estimation error across the 24 experiments. For each experiment, we divide the trace into 200 ms intervals and predict the cellular capacity for each interval based on the previous 200 ms interval. The overall capacity estimation accuracy across the entire trace is consistently within 8% for all 24 experiments. In addition, most of the 50- (80-, 90-th) percentile errors are within 10 (20, 30)% of the actual data rate. Although our estimation method could keep up with most of the large-scale fading trends, abrupt channel changes (CQI or DTX ratio) do happen due to nearby interference, surrounding objects, etc., leading to relatively large inaccuracy for some estimation results. Overall, CQIC's estimation method accurately and precisely predicts the downlink cellular link capacity. The estimation results are similar for 100- and 500-ms time windows.

4. CQIC DESIGN & IMPLEMENTATION

Given the ability to accurately estimate channel capacity directly from the cellular network, we now describe how the CQIC congestion control design incorporates it. In CQIC, the receiver directly estimates the underlying link capacity from physical layer information and sends the capacity as the estimated end-to-end bandwidth to the CQIC sender. On receiving the estimated bandwidth, the sender adjusts its congestion window accordingly.

We build upon Google's QUIC [15] framework, which is a new transport protocol based on UDP, to implement a CQIC prototype. In particular, we reuse the RTT estimation and reliable packet delivery modules in QUIC. We implement the CQIC receiver as a native application running on a Google Nexus 5 smartphone running Android 4.3 as modifications to QUIC. We include the CQIC sender as a new QUIC congestion control module on one of Google's experimental servers.

4.1 CQIC Sender

The CQIC sender combines rate-based and window-based congestion control. Specifically, the rate-limiting element decides the inter-packet interval T_p, given the predicted bandwidth B received from the CQIC receiver:

$$T_p = P/B$$

where P is the packet size. When the predicted bandwidth is accurate, the sender simply injects one packet every T_p seconds. In reality, as we show in Section 3, the predicted link capacity could deviate from the actual capacity. Overestimating available bandwidth fills up the buffer at the base station, leading to bufferbloat and packet losses. To prevent this problem, we complement the rate limit with a congestion window that bounds the total number of un-acked bytes the sender can send. Then, a CQIC sender operates in either the rate-limited or the window-limited mode. When the number of un-acked bytes is smaller than the congestion window size, the CQIC sender stays in the rate-limited mode and sends

a packet every T_p seconds. Otherwise, the sender injects a packet when it receives an acknowledgment.

Ideally, we want to set the congestion window as small as possible yet large enough to fill up the network pipe, i.e., we want to set the congestion window to the product of the minimum round trip time (RTT_{min}) and the end-to-end bandwidth. We reuse the RTT estimation module contained in QUIC to obtain RTT_{min}. In contrast to TCP, the CQIC sender does not probe the available bandwidth following the AIMD mechanism. Rather, it directly obtains the bandwidth estimation from the CQIC receiver. To accommodate bandwidth estimation errors, we currently set the congestion window size to the product of the predicted bandwidth and twice the RTT_{min}, i.e., $CW = B * 2RTT_{min}$ (this threshold has worked well with our experiments so far, but remains a point of continued investigation). Finally, we employ a token-bucket approach to approximate the ideal rate-limiting value in our implementation.

4.2 CQIC Receiver

The CQIC receiver continuously updates its estimation of the current cellular bandwidth, as described in Section 3.3, and sends the estimated bandwidth to the CQIC sender. Although both CQI and DTX are part of the HSPA+ specification, they are not currently exposed to the operating system of commodity smartphones.

In our prototype implementation we use Qualcomm's QXDM software [19] to obtain the CQI and DTX information from the UE. We configure the UE in diagnostic mode, and the QXDM tool continuously queries and collects various radio and chip-level information. In particular, we use the `HS-DPCCH-INFO` and `HS-DECODE-STATUS` log packets to retrieve the CQI and DTX information, respectively. The QXDM tool reports the `HS-DPCCH-INFO` and `HS-DECODE-STATUS` values every 8 ms and 2 ms, respectively, which enables the CQIC receiver to estimate the cellular bandwidth in real time. In our prototype, the CQIC receiver currently predicts the bandwidth for the next 500 ms time interval (a latency artifact of our current prototype setup), and reports its bandwidth estimate to the sender every 500 ms as well.

5. EVALUATION

We evaluate the throughput and delay benefits of CQIC using the Google Nexus device to download content from a Google server via a popular cellular network provider. Reflecting a common CDN scenario, this server is located near the network of the mobile carrier such that the cellular channel is the bottleneck link.

We compare the download performance of CQIC and TCP (CUBIC)[6] in terms of throughput and RTT experienced in deployed settings. As a first step and proof of concept, similar to Sprout [23], we only consider a single flow. By varying the retrieved object size from 0.1 to 20 MB, we simulate small, medium, and large flows. We repeat our experiments in static and mobile environments (driving around a local community) to create different channel dynamics. The evaluation helps us understand the effectiveness of CQIC in terms of bandwidth utilization and reaction to channel dynamics. The measured round trip time (RTT) of the underlying path between the UE and the server is about 70 ms.

For each object size, we use CQIC and TCP back-to-back to download an object in the hope that the channel conditions are similar for the two congestion control mechanisms. We then calculate the throughput and mean RTT for that flow. Altogether, we conduct 15 such experiments (CQI range: 6-27) for the static environment, and 10 for the mobile driving environment (CQI range: 1-30). Fig-

---

[6]TCP (CUBIC) yields higher throughput than Sprout [23].

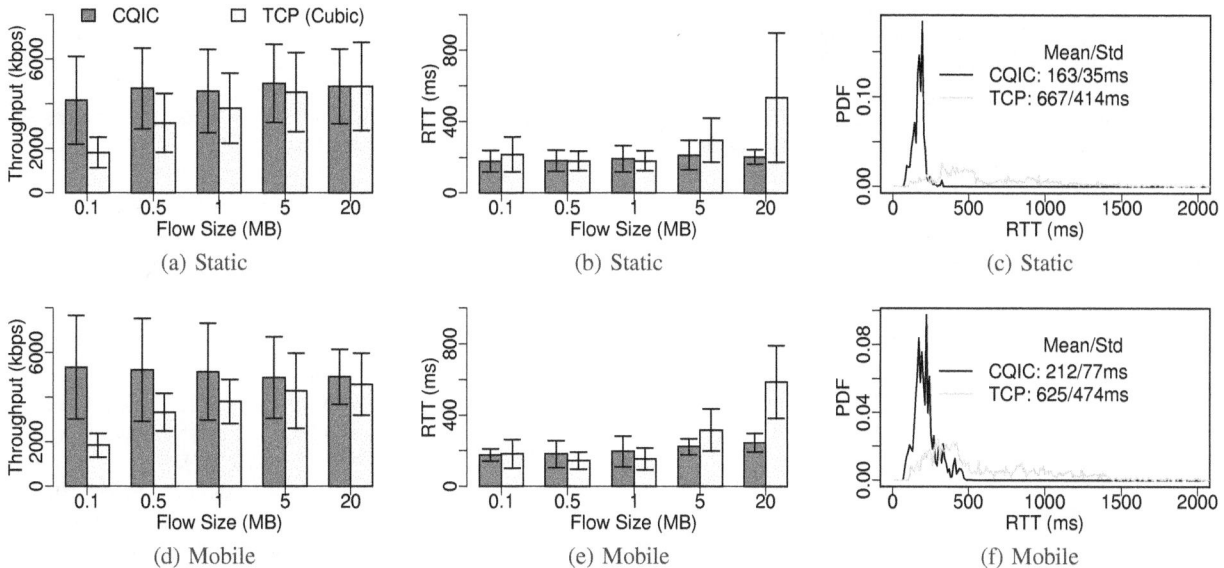

Figure 5: Performance of CQIC and TCP under static (mobile) channel conditions in terms of throughput and average RTT. The results are the average of 15 (10) experiment runs and the error bars show the standard deviations. Also shown are PDFs of the RTTs observed for a randomly chosen large flow.

ure 5 presents the average throughput, RTT, throughput breakdown, and the probability distribution function (PDF) of RTT experienced by a random large flow, under CQIC and TCP, respectively. The overall trends are very similar for both static and mobile cases.

Throughput. As shown in Figures 5(a) and 5(d), given that CQIC estimates the cellular bandwidth directly from the physical layer when the connection opens, the average throughput for small flows (i.e., less than 1MB) under CQIC is 1.5–2.9× larger than that of TCP, which initially spends time in the slow start phase. As flow size increases (e.g., 1 or 5MB), the TCP congestion window ramps up and the impact of slow start fades away. As a result, the throughput of CQIC is only marginally better than TCP (1.1–1.4×). Finally, for large flows (e.g., 20MB) CQIC and TCP attain almost identical throughput. Using `getsockopt()`, we observe that the TCP congestion window rarely decreases for the entire flow duration across all experiments in the static setting, which suggests that there are very few packet losses due to the relatively stable channel conditions and large buffer at the base station. Under the mobile setting, the throughput of CQIC is slightly higher than that of TCP for large flows. We observed that there are more packet losses in the mobile environment due to channel dynamics. These packet losses cause TCP to reduce its congestion window, even potentially time out, slightly reducing effective throughput.

Note that the large standard deviations in throughput in Figures 5(a) and 5(d) are due to different channel configurations (i.e., single vs. dual channels) experienced while conducting the experiments; downloading a 5-MB object in one run might primarily just use a single channel, while in another run it might use two. If we separate the large flows based on the number of channels used, the standard deviation is reduced substantially.

Delay. Precisely because of the large buffer deployed inside the base station, TCP attains similar throughput performance compared to CQIC for large flows. However, TCP's throughput is at the expense of high RTT as shown in Figures 5(b) and 5(e). As flow size decreases, especially for small flows (e.g., 0.1/0.5MB) where

the buffer is not completely filled, the RTT reduces accordingly.[7] In contrast, the RTT experienced by CQIC is roughly consistent across all flow sizes. Unlike TCP where the congestion window is a function of (the absence of) packet losses, CQIC sets its congestion window based on bandwidth estimates directly obtained from the physical layer. Hence, CQIC does not induce large buffers in a search for additional capacity, demonstrating another benefit of CQIC's cross-layer design.

Figures 5(c) and 5(f) show the PDF of RTTs experienced by all the packets in a randomly picked large flow under TCP and CQIC in the static and mobile cases, respectively. Since CQIC sets its congestion window to the product of the estimated bandwidth and twice RTT_{min}, it is not surprising to see that the majority of the RTTs are centered around $2 \times RTT_{min}$ (140 ms in our environment). Further, the worst-case bandwidth estimation error is also bounded as the PDF drops to zero after 500 ms, limiting the bufferbloat effect in CQIC. Finally, Figures 5(c) and 5(f) also illustrate the bufferbloat effect in large TCP flows, reflected in the long tail after 500 ms.

Deployment. Obviously, deploying CQIC requires changes to both the sender and receiver. Although both CQI and DTX are part of HSPA+ and LTE specifications, they are not currently visible to higher layers on most popular UEs. The UE radio firmware needs to be updated—possibly through an over-the-air (OTA) programming update with support from mobile chip makers and operators—to expose this information. In contrast, the server side changes of CQIC are straightforward as it only involves a software upgrade.

Fairness. It is important to recall that cellular base stations decide how to share the wireless channel among UEs (mobile devices). Transport protocols like CQIC can only control how each UE individually uses its own allocation. Moreover, CQIC assumes that the server is close to the radio access network and that the end-to-end connection is bottlenecked by the last-hop cellular link. In such a scenario, CQIC tries to match the the achievable bandwidth

---

[7]We note that the RTT for 0.1MB flows is larger than for larger size flows (e.g., 0.5 or 1MB). This behavior is due to radio state transition delays.

with the channel capacity offered by the cellular base station for the UE. In other words, the fairness among CQIC and TCP flows to different UEs are provided by the underlying scheduling algorithm implemented at the base station. For multiple flows destined to the same UE, we envision something like Congestion Manager [5] or SST [14] to manage fair bandwidth allocation among these flows. When congestion happens elsewhere in the network, CQIC needs to deploy additional mechanisms, for example falling back to TCP-style congestion control, to be TCP-friendly.

Summary. By directly estimating the underlying capacity from the physical layer, CQIC does not need to probe for available resources and thus eliminates the slow start phase completely. Furthermore, CQIC does not rely on packet-loss signals to adjust its capacity estimation and avoids the bufferbloat issue with TCP-like congestion control mechanisms. Finally, the high fidelity of CQI/DTX information at ms granularity, readily available from the physical layer, allows CQIC to closely track radio channel dynamics and promptly adjust its congestion window in response.

6. CONCLUSION

Revisiting cross-layer concepts that were explored at the dawn of mobile computing, we propose CQIC, a cross-layer congestion control design for cellular networks. CQIC directly estimates the channel capacity based on physical layer information (i.e., CQI and DTX) which are part of the HSPA+ and LTE specifications. Further, CQI and DTX information are readily available from the radio, simplifying CQIC deployment. Our preliminary evaluation, focusing on download performance in cellular networks, shows that when the last hop cellular link is the bottleneck, CQIC can outperform TCP in terms of throughput under both static and mobile environments. Moreover, CQIC attains consistently low RTT values across a range of flow sizes, avoiding the high end-to-end delay that large TCP flows experience. These initial results motivate the further exploration of congestion-control techniques that leverage physical-layer channel capacity estimates. Moving forward, we plan to study CQIC's performance under a much wider range of conditions, including interactive and streaming workloads, multiple flows, and a wider variety of network conditions. In particular, it will be critical to identify flows with bottlenecks elsewhere in the network and fall back to more traditional approaches.

Acknowledgement

We would like to thank Suman Banerjee, our shepherd, and the anonymous reviewers for their detailed feedback.

7. REFERENCES

[1] 3GPP. High Speed Packet Data Access.

[2] 3GPP. LTE Advanced.

[3] ASTELY, A., DAHLMAN, E., FURUSKAR, A., JADING, Y., LINDSTROM, M., AND PARKVALL, S. LTE: the Evolution of Mobile Broadband. *IEEE Communications Magazine 47*, 4 (2009), 44–51.

[4] BAKRE, A., AND BADRINATH, B. I-TCP: Indirect TCP for Mobile Hosts. In *Proceedings of ICDCS* (1995).

[5] BALAKRISHNAN, H., RAHUL, H. S., AND SESHAN, S. An Integrated Congestion Management Architecture for Internet Hosts. In *Proceedings of ACM SIGCOMM* (1999).

[6] BALAKRISHNAN, H., SESHAN, S., AMIR, E., AND KATZ, R. H. Improving tci/ip performance over wireless networks. In *Proceedings of ACM MobiCom* (1995).

[7] BALAKRISHNAN, HARI AND PADMANABHAN, VENKATA N. AND SESHAN, SRINIVASAN AND KATZ, RANDY H. A Comparison of Mechanisms for Improving TCP Performance over Wireless Links. *IEEE/ACM Transactions on Networking 5*, 6 (1997), 756–769.

[8] BENDER, P., BLACK, P., GROB, M., PADOVANI, R., SINDHUSHAYANA, N., AND VITERBI, A. CDMA/HDR: a Bandwidth-Efficient High Speed Wireless Data Service for Nomadic Users. *IEEE Communications Magazine 38*, 7 (2000), 70–77.

[9] BROWN, K., AND SINGH, S. M-TCP: TCP for Mobile Cellular Networks. *SIGCOMM Computer Communication Review 27*, 5 (1997), 19–43.

[10] CHAN, M. C., AND RAMJEE, R. TCP/IP Performance over 3G Wireless Links with Rate and Delay Variation. In *Proceedings of ACM MobiCom* (2002).

[11] CHEN, X., JIN, R., SUH, K., WANG, B., AND WEI, W. Network Performance of Smart Mobile Handhelds in a University Campus WiFi Network. In *Proceedings of ACM IMC* (2012).

[12] ERICSSON. Ericsson Mobility Report. http://www.ericsson.com/res/docs/2014/ericsson-mobility-report-june-2014.pdf.

[13] FARID KHAFIZOV AND MEHMET YAVUZ. Running TCP over IS-2000. In *Proceedings of IEEE ICC* (2002).

[14] FORD, B. Structured Streams: A New Transport Abstraction. In *Proceedings of ACM SIGCOMM* (2007).

[15] GOOGLE. Quick UDP Internet Connections. https://docs.google.com/document/d/1RNHkx_VvKWyWg6Lr8SZ-saqsQx7rFV-ev2jRFUoVD34.

[16] HUANG, J., QIAN, F., GUO, Y., ZHOU, Y., XU, Q., MAO, Z. M., SEN, S., AND SPATSCHECK, O. An In-depth Study of LTE: Effect of Network Protocol and Application Behavior on Performance. In *Proceedings of ACM SIGCOMM* (2013).

[17] JIANG, H., WANG, Y., LEE, K., AND RHEE, I. Tackling Bufferbloat in 3G/4G Networks. In *Proceedings of ACM IMC* (2012).

[18] KUNNIYUR, S., AND SRIKANT, R. End-to-End Congestion Control Schemes: Utility Functions, Random Losses and ECN Marks. In *Proceedings of IEEE INFOCOM* (2000).

[19] QUALCOMM. QXDM Professional Qualcomm eXtensible Diagnostic Monitor. http://goo.gl/ibV7g1.

[20] REN, F., AND LIN, C. Modeling and Improving TCP Performance over Cellular Link with Variable Bandwidth. *IEEE Transactions on Mobile Computing 10*, 8 (2011).

[21] SHAKKOTTAII, S., AND KARLSSON, P. C. Cross-Layer Design for Wireless Networks. *IEEE Communications Magazine 41*, 10 (2003), 74–80.

[22] SRIVASTAVA, V., AND MOTANI, M. Cross-layer Design: A Survey and the Road Ahead. *IEEE Communications Magazine 43*, 12 (2005), 112–119.

[23] WINSTEIN, K., SIVARAMAN, A., AND BALAKRISHNAN, H. Stochastic Forecasts Achieve High Throughput and Low Delay over Cellular Networks. In *Proceedings of USENIX NSDI* (2013).

The Case for Offload Shaping

Wenlu Hu, Brandon Amos, Zhuo Chen, Kiryong Ha, Wolfgang Richter,

Padmanabhan Pillai[†], Benjamin Gilbert, Jan Harkes, Mahadev Satyanarayanan

Carnegie Mellon University and [†]Intel Labs

ABSTRACT

When offloading computation from a mobile device, we show that it can pay to perform additional on-device work in order to reduce the offloading workload. We call this *offload shaping,* and demonstrate its application at many different levels of abstraction using a variety of techniques. We show that offload shaping can produce significant reduction in resource demand, with little loss of application-level fidelity.

1. Introduction

Offloading computation from a mobile device to the cloud or a cloudlet is a well-known technique for improving performance and extending battery life [5, 6, 9, 16]. This includes optimal partitioning of a computational pipeline into early stages that are executed locally, and later stages that are executed remotely. The partitioning may vary dynamically, depending on the supply and demand of resources such as network bandwidth, energy, and cache space [3, 7, 8].

In this paper, we show that it is sometimes valuable to perform *additional* cheap computation, not part of the original pipeline, on the mobile device in order to modify the offloading workload. We call this *offload shaping.* We show that offload shaping can be applied at many different levels of abstraction using a variety of techniques, and that it can produce significant reduction in resource demand with little loss of application-level fidelity or responsiveness.

We begin in Sections 2 and 3 by suppressing transmission of blurry images in video streams. In later sections, we advance to more sophisticated techniques. We conclude by motivating an API through which a cloud service can communicate application-specific offload shaping information to a mobile device.

2. Example: Blurry Video

Object recognition within frames in a live video stream is an example of a computationally expensive task that benefits greatly from offloading [11]. Unfortunately, some video frames may be blurry due to user movement, poor camera fo-

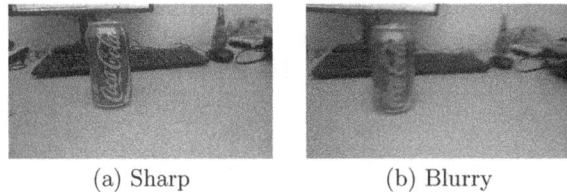

(a) Sharp   (b) Blurry

Figure 1: Sharp and blurry frames of same scene

Coke Can	Frames Judged by User 1		Frames Judged by User 2	
	Sharp	Blurry	Sharp	Blurry
Detected	161	5	166	0
Not detected	2	91	4	89

Figure 2: Impact of blurry frames on accuracy

cus, moisture on the camera lens, or other reasons. Figure 1 shows two frames of the same scene: image (a) is sharp and image (b) is blurred by camera motion. Blurry images can adversely affect the accuracy of computer vision algorithms.

Figure 2 shows the measured accuracy of object recognition (specifically, the red Coke can seen in Figure 1), using the MOPED algorithm for object detection [4]. Each of the 259 frames in the test video, captured using a Google Glass device at 640x360, contains one instance of the object. Hence, an ideal recognizer would find exactly one object in each frame. However, due to head movement during video capture, some of the frames are blurry. On the 163 frames judged to be sharp by User 1, there were only two objects missed by MOPED (false negatives). However, on the 96 frames judged to be blurry by User 1, there were 91 objects missed by MOPED. User 2 produces similar results. Clearly, recognition accuracy suffers when a frame is blurry. We expect other first-person videos taken with head-mounted cameras to also have considerable numbers of blurry frames.

It is a waste of wireless bandwidth and mobile device energy to transmit blurry frames to the offload engine, and to wait for a response that is likely not meaningful. If a mobile

	Send all	Drop blurry
Bytes transferred	0.51M	0.34M
Glass energy (J)	429(2)	292(3)
Server CPU usage (normalized)	1.00(0.01)	0.81(0.01)

Numbers in parentheses are standard deviations from 4 runs. H.264 encoding is used.

Figure 3: Benefits of dropping blurry frames

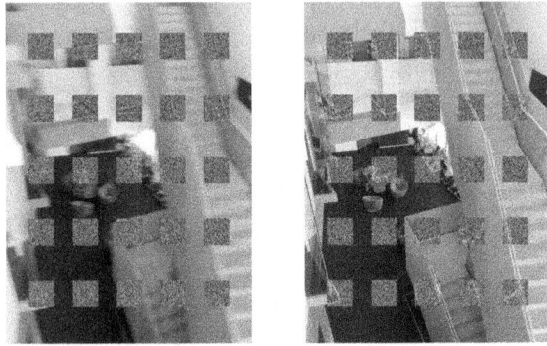

(a) Blurry   (b) Sharp

We apply a Sobel filter to 25 patches. Here, the resulting gradients are shown overlaid on the original image.

Figure 4: Blur detection by Sobel filter

		Detected by Sobel Filter	
		Blurry	Sharp
Ground Truth	Blurry	74	22
	Sharp	6	157

Figure 5: Accuracy of Sobel blur detection

device could cheaply and reliably detect blurry frames, it could suppress transmission of those frames with hardly any loss of accuracy. In the example video above, over a third of the frames can be dropped safely at the device, significantly reducing bandwidth and energy consumed. Figure 3 summarizes the measured benefits of dropping the blurry frames at the Google Glass device. In the next section, we explore a number of ways of cheaply detecting blurry frames.

3. Cheap Blur Detection

3.1 Using Image Content

Detecting blur is a well-studied problem in image processing [19]. Intuitively, image gradients will be more gradual when an image is blurry because the edges in the image are less sharp. We use a Sobel operator [18] to compute image intensity gradients. To keep computational costs low on mobile devices, our implementation samples 25 patches distributed over the image. If the gradient at any of the samples exceeds a threshold, we deem the image to be sharp. Only if the gradient is below the threshold in all samples do we deem it to be blurry. Figure 4 shows the results of this technique applied to two similar images that differ in sharpness. We verify this approach on the video used in Figure 1, comparing its results against the ground truth as judged by User 1. Despite its simplicity, this method matches human-judged blurriness with high accuracy, as shown in Figure 5.

We implement an offload-shaping *filter* on Google Glass by using a Sobel operator to drop blurry frames before transmission to a remote MOPED object detection service. We measure the effects on energy, bandwidth, and latency. In these experiments, frames transmitted from Glass are encoded in H.264 with B-frames disabled to satisfy low latency requirements of real-time applications. They are sent to a remote MOPED object detection service. This service runs on a *cloudlet* [17], a server-class machine running a cloud software stack and connected to the same LAN as the WiFi base station. We use a dedicated WiFi access point to re-

	No shaping	Drop blurry	Improvement
Bytes transferred	0.51M	0.37M	27%
Frames recognized	$171_{(2)}$	$162_{(1)}$	-5%
E2E latency (ms)	$920_{(8)}$	$859_{(14)}$	7%
Glass power (W)	$1.82_{(0.01)}$	$1.82_{(0.02)}$	0%
Glass energy (J/frame)	$1.66_{(0.01)}$	$1.51_{(0.02)}$	9%
Server CPU usage (normalized)	$1.00_{(0.01)}$	$0.84_{(0.02)}$	16%

Figure 6: Blur detection with Sobel filter

duce interference and maximize bandwidth, thus favoring offload without shaping. To stabilize Glass performance, ice packs are used to cool the device externally [10], and a Bluetooth connection is established between Glass and a phone but not used for data transmission [2]. The Glass screen is kept off as it is not useful for this type of application. We repeat each experiment 4 times, and report both mean and standard deviations (in parentheses). As MOPED is nondeterministic, accuracy results have some variability even on the same input. Unless noted otherwise, all experiments in this paper use this experimental setup.

Figure 6 shows that dropping blurry frames results in significant reductions in the bytes transferred (27%) and processing cycles used on the server (16%), as well as a modest reduction in the average end-to-end processing latency per frame (7%). The mean latency improves because results for dropped frames are known quickly. Because frames are processed sequentially after the results of the prior ones are returned, this also results in an increase in the processing rate. So although Glass power is unaffected, the average energy consumed per frame improves by 9%. All of these improvements come at a slight 5% reduction in the object detection accuracy. We note that even with "perfect" blurry-frame dropping (i.e., using User 1's labels from Figure 2), we would have a similar 5% reduction in MOPED accuracy.

3.2 Using On-Board Sensors

Mobile devices such as smartphones and Google Glass devices have on-board sensors such as accelerometers and gyroscopes. These sensors are attached to the same rigid object as the camera, so their readings are correlated with camera motion and any resulting image quality degradation.

At first glance, the accelerometer seems to be an obvious sensor for detecting blur. However, our experiments show otherwise. This is because blur is correlated with camera velocity, but the accelerometer measures the derivative of velocity (i.e., acceleration). In movements such as shaking one's head when wearing Google Glass, acceleration tends to peak when linear velocity is low. Integrating acceleration readings to yield velocity does not work well either, because large errors quickly accumulate.

Fortunately, gyroscopes are increasingly common in mobile devices and turn out to be effective at predicting blur. Gyroscopes emit angular velocity in *radians/s*. Figure 7 shows a strong correlation between gyroscope readings and blurriness ground truth, i.e. User 1's label in our test video from Figures 1 and 2.

We conclude a frame is blurry when its corresponding gyroscope reading exceeds a threshold. Figure 8 shows the trade-off between frames dropped and accuracy as this threshold is changed. Curve (a) is based on the video used above,

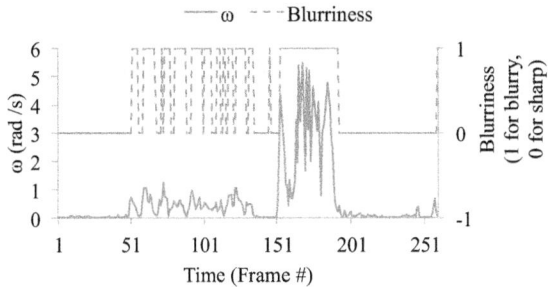

Figure 7: Correlation between blurriness and gyroscope readings ω

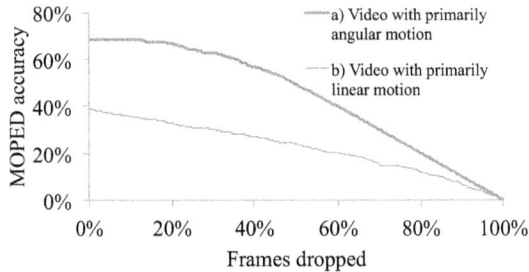

Figure 8: Frames dropped vs. MOPED accuracy while gyroscope threshold changes

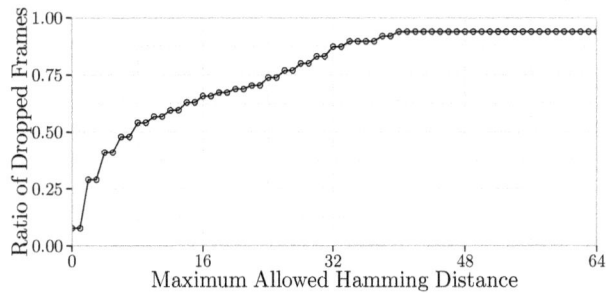

(a) Frames Dropped

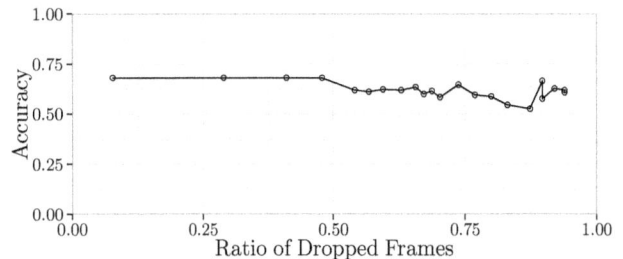

(b) MOPED Accuracy vs. Dropped Ratio

Figure 10: Effects of similarity filter

where blurriness is caused by head movement. In this case, motion is primarily angular and readily detected by the gyroscope. Here, the strategy is effective at selecting the right frames to drop, so many can be dropped before significantly affecting accuracy. We also test on a second video primarily containing linear motion. In this curve (b), gyro readings are not helpful in selecting the right frames to drop, so accuracy suffers immediately with any dropped frames. In practice, angular movements have a greater effect on blurriness, since they affect the entire scene, while effects of linear movement drop off rapidly with distance.

Using the methodology from Section 3.1 and a threshold of $0.5 rad/s$, we test the effectiveness of a filter that uses the gyroscope to predict blurriness. The results in Figure 9 show significant reductions in bytes transferred, average processing latency, and server load. Although power increases slightly on Glass, the improvement in throughput leads to better energy efficiency and the energy per frame improves significantly (20%). Once again, these improvements are achieved with only a small reduction in accuracy (8%).

4. Exploiting Inter-Frame Similarity

In live video streamed from a mobile device, the scene does not often change appreciably between consecutive frames.

	No shaping	Drop blurry	Improvement
Bytes transferred	0.51M	0.37M	27%
Frames recognized	171(2)	157(1)	-8%
E2E latency (ms)	920(8)	750(3)	18%
Glass power (W)	1.82(0.01)	1.87(0.01)	-3%
Glass energy (J/frame)	1.66(0.01)	1.33(0.01)	20%
Server CPU usage (normalized)	1.00(0.01)	0.84(0.00)	16%

Figure 9: Blur detection with gyroscope filter

The results of many computer vision algorithms will likely remain constant when applied to sequences of nearly identical frames. Hence, sufficiently similar frames can be safely discarded to conserve bandwidth and energy.

How can we determine whether a frame is very similar to the preceding one? This is much harder than it appears at first glance. Directly comparing pixel values of adjacent frames is not effective. Semantically insignificant changes (e.g., minor camera movement, or fluorescent light flicker) can cause a huge number of pixels to differ and result in a large computed distance between frames, while meaningful changes (e.g., objects moved within a scene) may not affect many pixels and will result in a small computed distance.

Fortunately, the problem of image similarity has been well studied in the literature. A family of techniques called *perceptual hashing* has been developed to encode visual properties of images into bit strings [14, 15]. Importantly, distance metrics between these image "hashes" do correspond to perceived similarity between the source images, and are robust to semantically insignificant changes.

We implement a perceptual hashing [20] filter based on a 64-bit discrete cosine transform and a simple Hamming-distance metric to determine similarity between frames. If a frame is sufficiently similar to the last transmitted frame, it is dropped, and the output of downstream processing is assumed to remain constant. We compare a frame to the last transmitted frame and not just to the previous frame; otherwise, sequences of significant but slowly-accumulated changes may be dropped entirely. We also force transmission of a frame after 15 consecutive frames have been dropped. This approach is better than a naive sampling of frames, as it can respond immediately to sudden changes in the scene, without waiting for the next sampling interval.

Figure 10 shows the filter's impact on MOPED accuracy on the video used in Figure 1. On a Google Glass device, the hash and distance metrics can be computed in about 20 ms. Figure 10(a) shows that the hashes in our experi-

	No shaping	Drop similar	Improvement
Bytes transferred	0.51M	0.23M	55%
Frames recognized	171(2)	189(1)	11%
Glass power (W)	1.82(0.01)	1.83(0.01)	-1%
E2E latency (ms)	920(8)	393(2)	57%
Glass energy (J/frame)	1.66(0.01)	0.72(0.01)	57%
Server CPU usage (normalized)	1.00(0.01)	0.27(0.01)	73%

Figure 11: Similarity filter performance

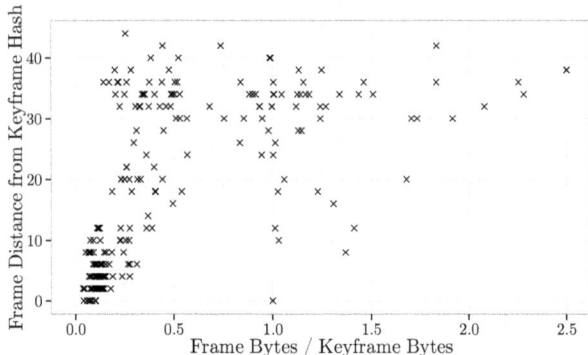

Figure 12: Similarity vs. H.264 encoded frame size (normalized)

ment never differ by more than 40 bits with the keyframe hash. Figure 10(b) shows the trade-off between dropping more frames and the MOPED accuracy. Unlike in the previous sections, where dropped frames are interpreted as detection failures, we report the detector output from the last transmitted frame for dropped frames. As a result, the relationship between accuracy and dropped frames is complex, and can vary depending on the subset of frames sent.

Figure 11 shows the reduction in energy and bytes transferred with the test video. We are sending fewer than half the bytes. As explained in Section 3.1 and 3.2, even though Glass power increases by 1%, as frames are processed at twice the original rate, energy consumed for each frame on Glass is less than half its original value. The server CPU usage also drops to almost one fourth its original value. Here, we again see significant reduction in cost, with little difference in fidelity.

Since video encoding algorithms are based on encoding differences between frames, can we use the size of an encoded frame to estimate its similarity to the preceding one? With H.264 encoding, we did not find a clear relationship with the size of the compressed frame, but did find a statistical correlation between similarity and data size when normalized to the preceding keyframe size (Figure 12). Here, the encoding was based on GOP (interval between keyframes) of 10, used an x264 "medium" preset with a "zero-latency" tuning option, and omitted B-frames. The correlation is very noisy, and whether normalized encoded frame size is useful for predicting similarity is left for future research. Furthermore, given the vast literature on video indexing and key frame selection [12], there may be other encoding techniques that provide a better correlation with similarity that can be leveraged for offload shaping.

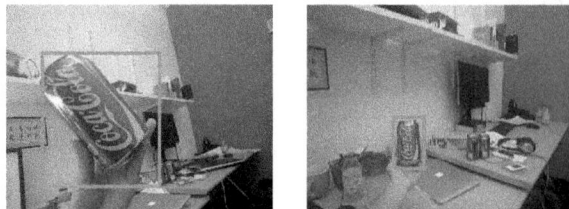

(a) Video with a large Coke can (446 frames)

(b) Video with a normal-size Coke can (510 frames)

Figure 13: Example frames for red filter

	No shaping	Send red only	Improvement
Bytes transferred	8.6M	2.8M	67%
Frames recognized	396(3)	380(5)	-4%
E2E latency (ms)	471(12)	153(2)	68%
Glass power (W)	1.80(0.01)	1.99(0.02)	-11%
Glass energy (J/frame)	0.84(0.01)	0.28(0.01)	67%

MJPEG encoding is used to deal with varying frame size.

Figure 14: Red filter with MOPED server

5. Context-sensitive Offload Shaping

Blurriness and inter-frame similarity are broadly applicable mechanisms for offload shaping, regardless of the application context. In this section, we show that strategies tailored specifically to particular application contexts can also reduce mobile resource usage. For example, every image that contains the Coke can shown in Figure 1 will have a patch of red in it. Hence, any frame lacking a red patch cannot contain a Coke can. Discarding such frames achieves effective offload shaping specific to the context of Coke-can detection. However, this specialized filter will not be useful in other contexts, such as finding blue cars.

Depending on the context, in addition to dropping unnecessary frames, it may be possible to crop the useful frames to remove unneeded background. For example, for a face recognition application, only faces are interesting. If we can use a low-cost method to detect and crop the faces on the mobile device, most of the pixels do not need to be transmitted to the back-end recognition service.

5.1 Example: Color Filter

We first use color to perform offload shaping for Coke-can detection. To select useful patches, we implement a simple red color filter using Android OpenCV. We convert frames to the HSV color space and use a simple distance threshold to find pixels close to the desired color. We crop a rectangular region that encloses the largest connected component of the desired color, with a narrow, fixed-width margin. Only this cropped region is sent to the server.

We use a mostly-sharp video, shown in Figure 13(a), to test the color filter. The green box shows the region that is cropped out and sent to the server. Results in Figure 14 show significant reduction (around two thirds) in bytes transferred and average latency. As explained in Sections 3.1 and 3.2, although the Glass power increases slightly, the energy consumed per frame drops to one third of the original. All of these benefits are achieved with only a small reduction in MOPED accuracy (4%). The benefits in this case are limited by the large size of the Coke can in the frames. For the video in Figure 13(b), where Coke can sizes are smaller

Video description	Whole frames (MB)	Faces only (MB)	Savings
One face, still	53.8	3.7	93%
Two faces, still	65.0	6.0	91%
Two faces, moving	65.8	4.9	92%

Each video is around one minute.

Figure 15: Face detection on Bosch cameras

and more realistic, only one tenth of the bytes are sent after applying the red filter and one fourth of time is needed to process each frame. Note that the video resolution here is 360x240. Our filters will make an even larger difference for videos with higher resolutions, as they make greater demands on network bandwidth.

5.2 Leveraging Hardware Accelerators

Many cameras and devices such as Google Glass now include features such as hardware accelerated face detection. Face detection in hardware helps consumer-grade cameras efficiently focus on what is commonly the most important part of any frame. Many expensive cameras and an increasing number of smartphones now also stabilize images actively. They move the lens in real-time to counter the effect of camera movement. This can be viewed as hardware accelerated blur correction. In addition, a wide range of surveillance cameras have on-board computer vision programs to generate abstract information about surveilled scenes. These programs can be re-purposed for offload shaping. For common tasks, hardware acceleration will be both quicker and more efficient than software targeting a general-purpose processor. Offload shaping can therefore leverage hardware-based as well as software-based filtering.

To explore this possibility we experimented with a Bosch surveillance camera, the Dinion HD 1080p HDR. For applications that are only interested in human faces, such as mood or face recognition, this camera's cheap, built-in face detection functionality is helpful. We built a face filter, based on the Dinion's on-board face detection, that simply crops and transmits only the faces in each frame. Figure 15 shows significant savings in bytes transferred.

6. Offload Shaping API

We have shown that offload shaping can help improve bandwidth use, response time, and energy efficiency of offloaded tasks. In addition, the best strategies for offload shaping are often context- and application-specific. In order to handle the diverse needs of different applications, the mobile device should have a simple API for dynamic specification of offload shaping. With this API, the applications can dynamically specify and adjust the shaping they want according to the context. Although we have been focusing on individual shaping techniques so far, it would also be useful to combine multiple techniques. Thus, the API should support composing components. Finally, we would like the system to be extensible, so new offload-shaping filters can easily be added to the system.

Rather than design such an API from scratch, we observe that many existing software libraries and frameworks have similar requirements and have already-established APIs to satisfy them. In particular, the GStreamer API [1] seems to fit our needs well. It was designed as a pluggable system to compose multimedia transcoding pipelines, but can be easily

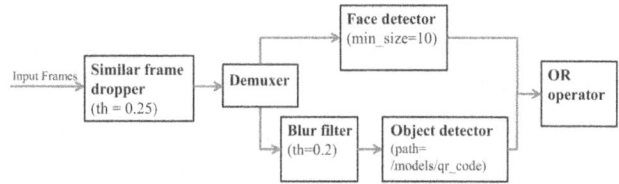

gst-launch input ! similar_frame_dropper th=0.25 ! demuxer name=dmx ! face_detector min_size=10
! or_operator name=or
dmx. ! blur_filter th=0.2 ! object_detector path=/models/qr_code ! or.

(a) Relatively sequential

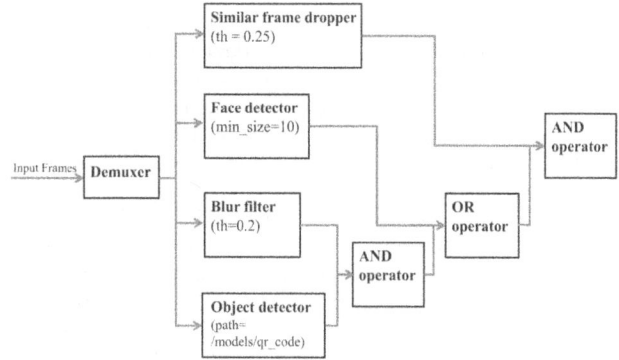

gst-launch input ! demuxer name=dmx ! similar_frame_dropper th=0.25 ! and_operator name=and2
dmx. ! face_detector min_size=10 ! or_operator name=or ! and2.
dmx. ! blur_filter th=0.2 ! and_operator name=and1 ! or.
dmx. ! object_detector path=/models/qr_code ! and1.

(b) Fully parallel

Figure 16: Example of declarative APIs and corresponding diagrams

adapted for specifying complex offload shaping policies. In addition to a programmatic interface, it has a declarative, text-based configuration language that lets us launch a set of components, express a graph of how they connect, and provide configuration strings for individual components if desired. Finally, the GStreamer framework is supported on all major operating systems, including Android and iOS.

Figure 16(a) shows an example of a complex offload-shaping strategy expressed with the GStreamer framework. Here, frames are first filtered based on similarity, and of those that pass, only frames with faces or non-blurry QR codes are ultimately transmitted from the device. To accomplish this, we need to create a library of new GStreamer components that implement the individual offload-shaping algorithms. We also need to implement logical AND / OR filters, as GStreamer has no such concepts. In addition, to keep the branches of a pipeline in sync, we replace dropped frames with small placeholders. The example also shows how components can be configured, using simple short strings. For more complex configuration, such as object models, we rely on configuring with paths or URLs to the needed data.

This declarative API is also quite flexible. Figure 16(b) shows how to express the same policy in a more parallel fashion. On a mobile device that has multiple cores or parallel sets of hardware accelerators, this version could be executed with lower latency, as the main tasks are run in parallel. Of course, this results in additional processing for frames that would have been dropped early in the sequential pipeline. The trade-off between response time and mobile resource use can be tailored to each specific application.

The GStreamer API helps us compose multiple filters in a configurable way. Such filters might be thin wrappers around existing libraries or more complicated context-specific filters implemented as custom code. Applications can distribute these filters as dynamic libraries, and could upload them to a central archive for downloading, much as multimedia CODECs are handled today. We also imagine that the most commonly-used filters will be pre-installed on mobile devices in the future and ready to use for offload shaping.

7. Conclusion

Offload shaping demonstrates that judicious use of additional computation on a mobile device can significantly improve resource usage in an offload system. Offload shaping improves cloud offloading by combining the use of hints to speed up computations with the concept of early discard [13]. The on-board sensors and computing power of mobile devices make it possible to achieve accurate early discard. In this paper, we explore various approaches to dropping low-value input data without sacrificing application fidelity. Such approaches can save significant resources on mobile devices, including processing time, network bandwidth, and energy. They also improve scalability of the back-end server, reducing inbound traffic and workload.

Offload shaping is generally valuable to a wide range of applications. Our proposed API allows individual applications to tailor a shaping strategy to their specific needs. We will explore how various applications benefit from this API in future work. This API is extensible, allowing applications to incorporate new sources of hints such as GPS coordinates, barometric pressure readings, and camera metadata. As mobile platforms become more capable, with additional sensors and hardware-accelerated processing, offload shaping will become an increasingly powerful tool enabling energy-efficient cloud and cloudlet offload.

Acknowledgements

We wish to thank Rahul Sukthankar and Rajen Bhatt for their insights and guidance on various aspects of this research. This research was supported by the National Science Foundation (NSF) under grant number IIS-1065336, by an Intel Science and Technology Center grant, by DARPA Contract No. FA8650-11-C-7190, and by the Department of Defense (DoD) under Contract No. FA8721-05-C-0003 for the operation of the Software Engineering Institute (SEI), a federally funded research and development center. This material has been approved for public release and unlimited distribution (DM-0000276). Additional support was provided by IBM, Google, Bosch, Vodafone, and the Conklin Kistler family fund. Any opinions, findings, conclusions or recommendations expressed in this material are those of the authors and should not be attributed to their employers or funding sources.

8. REFERENCES

[1] GStreamer: open source multimedia framework. http://gstreamer.freedesktop.org/, 2014.

[2] Issue 512: Bluetooth connection interfering with TCP Traffic on WiFi. https://code.google.com/p/google-glass-api/issues/detail?id=512, May 2014.

[3] R. Balan, M. Satyanarayanan, T. Okoshi, and S. Park. Tactics-based Remote Execution for Mobile Computing. In *Proceedings of the 1st International Conference on Mobile Systems, Applications and Services*, San Francisco, CA, May 2003.

[4] A. Collet, M. Martinez, and S. S. Srinivasa. The MOPED framework: Object Recognition and Pose Estimation for Manipulation. *The International Journal of Robotics Research*, 2011.

[5] E. Cuervo, A. Balasubramanian, D.-k. Cho, A. Wolman, S. Saroiu, R. Chandra, and P. Bahl. MAUI: Making Smartphones Last Longer with Code Offload. In *Proceedings of the 8th International Conference on Mobile Systems, Applications, and Services*, San Francisco, CA, June 2010.

[6] J. Flinn. *Cyber Foraging: Bridging Mobile and Cloud Computing via Opportunistic Offload*. Morgan & Claypool Publishers, 2012.

[7] J. Flinn, D. Narayanan, and M. Satyanarayanan. Self-Tuned Remote Execution for Pervasive Computing. In *Proceedings of the 8th IEEE Workshop on Hot Topics in Operating Systems*, Schloss Elmau, Germany, May 2001.

[8] J. Flinn, S. Park, and M. Satyanarayanan. Balancing Performance, Energy Conservation and Application Quality in Pervasive Computing. In *Proceedings of the 22nd International Conference on Distributed Computing Systems*, Vienna, Austria, July 2002.

[9] M. S. Gordon, D. A. Jamshidi, S. Mahlke, Z. M. Mao, and X. Chen. COMET: Code Offload by Migrating Execution Transparently. In *10th USENIX Symposium on Operating Systems Design and Implementation (OSDI 12)*, Hollywood, CA, October 2012.

[10] K. Ha, Z. Chen, W. Hu, W. Richter, P. Pillai, and M. Satyanarayanan. Towards wearable cognitive assistance. In *Proceedings of the 12th annual international conference on Mobile systems, applications, and services*, Bretton Woods, NH, June 2014.

[11] K. Ha, P. Pillai, G. Lewis, S. Simanta, S. Clinch, N. Davies, and M. Satyanarayanan. The Impact of Mobile Multimedia Applications on Data Center Consolidation. In *Proceedings of the IEEE International Conference on Cloud Engineering*, San Francisco, CA, March 2013.

[12] W. Hu, N. Xie, L. Li, X. Zeng, and S. Maybank. A survey on visual content-based video indexing and retrieval. *Systems, Man, and Cybernetics, Part C: Applications and Reviews, IEEE Transactions on*, 41(6):797–819, 2011.

[13] L. Huston, R. Sukthankar, R. Wickremesinghe, M. Satyanarayanan, G. R. Ganger, E. Riedel, and A. Ailamaki. Diamond: A storage architecture for early discard in interactive search. In *Proceedings of the 3rd USENIX Conference on File and Storage Technologies*, San Francisco, CA, March 2004.

[14] S. S. Kozat, R. Venkatesan, and M. K. Mihçak. Robust perceptual image hashing via matrix invariants. In *Image Processing, 2004. ICIP'04. 2004 International Conference on*, volume 5, pages 3443–3446. IEEE, 2004.

[15] V. Monga and B. L. Evans. Perceptual image hashing via feature points: performance evaluation and tradeoffs. *Image Processing, IEEE Transactions on*, 15(11):3452–3465, 2006.

[16] M. Satyanarayanan. Pervasive Computing: Vision and Challenges. *IEEE Personal Communications*, 8(4), 2001.

[17] M. Satyanarayanan, P. Bahl, R. Caceres, and N. Davies. The Case for VM-Based Cloudlets in Mobile Computing. *IEEE Pervasive Computing*, 8(4):3 (Sidebar: "Help for the Mentally Challenged"), October-December 2009.

[18] I. Sobel and G. Feldman. A 3x3 isotropic gradient operator for image processing. A talk at the Stanford Artificial Intelligence Project, 1968.

[19] R. Szeliski. *Computer Vision: Algorithms and Applications*. Springer, 2010.

[20] C. Zauner. *Implementation and benchmarking of perceptual image hash functions*. PhD thesis, University of Applied Sciences Hagenberg, Austria, 2010.

Can Accurate Predictions Improve Video Streaming in Cellular Networks?

Xuan Kelvin Zou[1], Jeffrey Erman[2], Vijay Gopalakrishnan[2], Emir Halepovic[2], Rittwik Jana[2], Xin Jin[1], Jennifer Rexford[1], and Rakesh K. Sinha[2]

[1] Department of Computer Science, Princeton University, Princeton, NJ
[2] AT&T Labs – Research, Bedminster, NJ
[1]{xuanz, xinjin, jrex}@cs.princeton.edu
[2]{erman, gvijay, emir, rjana, sinha}@research.att.com

ABSTRACT

Existing video streaming algorithms use various estimation approaches to infer the inherently variable bandwidth in cellular networks, which often leads to reduced quality of experience (QoE). We ask the question: "If accurate bandwidth prediction were possible in a cellular network, how much can we improve video QoE?". Assuming we know the bandwidth for the entire video session, we show that existing streaming algorithms only achieve between 69%-86% of optimal quality. Since such knowledge may be impractical, we study algorithms that know the available bandwidth for a few seconds into the future. We observe that prediction alone is not sufficient and can in fact lead to degraded QoE. However, when combined with rate stabilization functions, prediction outperforms existing algorithms and reduces the gap with optimal to 4%. Our results lead us to believe that cellular operators and content providers can tremendously improve video QoE by predicting available bandwidth and sharing it through APIs.

Categories and Subject Descriptors

C.2.4 [**Computer-Communication Networks**]: Distributed systems-Distributed applications; C.4 [**Performance of Systems**]: Modeling techniques-Measurement techniques

Keywords

Video streaming; HTTP; DASH; Adaptation; Algorithm; Design; Performance; Prediction; Cellular

1. INTRODUCTION

Video streaming accounted for 66% of total Internet traffic [5] and accounts for over 40% of cellular traffic [7]. This demand has forced cellular providers to deploy significant capacity to support high quality video streaming. Yet, despite these efforts, achieving reliable video streaming over cellular networks has proven to be difficult. For example, it is reported that the fraction of stalled videos increases with video quality, with 10.5% of 240p videos stalling while 45.7% of 720p videos experiencing a stall [6].

Most content providers today use adaptive-bit-rate (ABR) streaming where the goal is to match the delivery rate of "chunks" of the video to available end-to-end bandwidth. While simple in principle, practical implementations have to *infer* the available bandwidth and adjust rates for chunks while balancing metrics like quality, interruptions, number of rate switches (i.e., rate stability). State-of-the-art algorithms differ in how they infer available bandwidth; while some use historical throughput [10, 12], others use buffer occupancy [8] or traffic shaping [4].

Accurate inference of available bandwidth is non-trivial in part due to varying link capacities, congestion, and other factors. This task is particularly challenging in cellular networks due to the inherent variability in signal strength, interference, noise, and user mobility — all of which cause the bandwidth to vary widely over time. Consequently, there is a significant mismatch between estimates used by existing algorithms and the actual available network bandwidth, which results in low quality of experience (QoE) over cellular networks. However, recent works open a promising possibility to accurately predict available bandwidth at short and medium time scales [14, 11].

In this paper, we focus on the following question: *If accurate bandwidth prediction were possible in a cellular network, how much can we improve video QoE?* We consider cellular networks because they present both a challenge and an opportunity. While it is challenging due to the high link variability, the cellular radio link is carefully scheduled. A base station tracks multiple network metrics (routinely used in the scheduling process) that can be used to predict available bandwidth in near future (several seconds). In addition, the architecture of the network allows an operator to have a view of all devices, their link statistics, radio spectrum availability and instantaneous traffic demand. Our goal is to exploit this network information to derive available bandwidth and expose it to content providers through APIs. We further focus on video durations on the order of several minutes, which is most common in cellular networks [7].

To that end, we first identify the gap between existing algorithms (e.g., FESTIVE [10], BBA [8]) and the optimal by formulating a Mixed Integer Linear Program (MILP).

Since existing algorithms are not designed to use bandwidth predictions, we develop a class of Prediction-Based Adaptation (PBA) algorithms that use the predicted bandwidth.

Our key findings can be summarized as follows:

- Existing algorithms fail to fully utilize available bandwidth, achieving only 69%-86% of optimal quality. The performance gap is pronounced during startup where existing algorithms achieve only 15%-20% of optimal in the first 32 seconds, and 22%-38% of optimal in the first 64 seconds.

- Naive algorithms that utilize *only* predicted bandwidth for chunk rate selection do not work well and cause numerous and erratic quality switches.

- PBA that combines short-term predictions (e.g., one chunk duration) with buffer occupancy and/or rate stability function outperforms existing algorithms, achieving nearly 96% of optimal quality during startup and over the entire video, thereby outperforming existing algorithms by up to ~40%.

- PBA algorithms with different stability functions can trade off stalls and stability while maintaining much improved average quality.

Our results lead us to believe that there is tremendous improvement to be had in video QoE by accurately predicting available bandwidth and exposing them to content providers through APIs.

2. BACKGROUND AND MOTIVATION

The available bandwidth in both wired and wireless networks varies over time. To overcome this variability, the industry has shifted towards ABR streaming to deliver videos over the Internet. ABR streaming is a client-driven approach in which a video client tries to match the delivery rate of the video to that of the available end-to-end bandwidth. To make this feasible, ABR streaming breaks videos into "chunks" of a few seconds (typically 2-10 sec) and encodes each chunk at multiple bit rates, representing different levels of quality. Multiple encoding bit rates also directly correlate to PSNR levels resulting from compressing the video signal [3]. The client's task is to choose chunks of the "correct" encoding rate.

Depending on the perceived network conditions, playout buffer or other criteria, clients attempt to optimize various metrics that comprise users' QoE, including quality, interruptions and stability. For example, a client can switch to a low-quality version of the video to avoid buffer underflow during temporary network congestion, and switch back to higher quality after network conditions improve. Variants of this technology have been widely deployed in commercial systems, including Netflix, Microsoft Smooth Streaming, Apple HTTP Live Streaming (HLS) and Dynamic Adaptive Streaming over HTTP (DASH).

While simple in principle, practical client implementations of ABR streaming have to *infer* the available bandwidth and adjust chunk encoding rates accordingly. State-of-the-art approaches typically use past observations to estimate available bandwidth. One representative is FESTIVE [10], an adaptation algorithm that includes features

Table 1: Optimization variables and parameters

Symbol	Meaning
Q	number of video quality levels (play bit rates)
R_i^q	size of the i-th chunk at the q-th quality level
x_i^q	binary variable indicating selection of R_i^q
C_i	predicted bandwidth for the i-th chunk duration
L_i^j	portion of i-th chunk downloaded in duration j
M	maximum buffer size (in multiples of D)

designed to provide fair and stable performance even when multiple ABR video players compete for bandwidth. Among other features, FESTIVE uses harmonic mean of previous chunk throughputs and includes a stability function that delays video rate updates to minimize rate switches.

In contrast, Buffer-Based Adaptation (BBA) [8] is proposed to dispense with historical averaging and solely use buffer level to drive selection of video rates. The rationale is that buffer level indirectly reflects the historical throughput, which obviates a need for direct measurement and estimation. However, the authors concede that when the buffer is empty or very low, such as during the startup phase, historical bandwidth estimation is necessary. Prior work compares buffer-based and rate-based streaming algorithms to suggest that bandwidth prediction may be beneficial [15].

We contend that the *inference* of available bandwidth leads to innacurate estimates of actual bandwidth, resulting in low video QoE over cellular networks. Compared to prior work that used synthetic traces and lacked prediction-based adaptation [15], we design prediction-based class of algorithms and use real traces. We study the benefits of bandwidth prediction for potentialy complementing or even replacing existing algorithms to improve video QoE.

3. UPPER BOUND ON QUALITY

We divide the video session into time intervals of length equal to chunk duration and assume knowledge of the available average bandwidth during each chunk duration.

We seek to understand the highest possible quality for this session such that we have no interruptions. While this is clearly an idealized and impractical setting, it gives us an upper bound on the video quality possible and allows us to quantify how well existing adaptation algorithms are doing.

We formulate this optimal rate selection as a Mixed Integer Linear Program (MILP). Table 1 lists the variables and parameters used in our formulation.

For the i-th video chunk, the optimization selects exactly one quality for playback. In other words, the indicator variable x_i^q is one for exactly one quality level q and the chunk size is given by

$$ChunkSize(i) = \sum_{q=1}^{Q} R_i^q * x_i^q.$$

For each video chunk i, the optimization needs to find its quality level (x_i^q) and the goal is to maximize

$$\sum_i ChunkSize(i) = \sum_{i,q} R_i^q * x_i^q,$$

subject to constraints defined below.

3.1 Constraints

Unique quality: We pick exactly one quality for each chunk:

$$\forall i, \sum_{q=1}^{Q} x_i^q = 1.$$

No stalls: To avoid interruptions, the i-th chunk needs to finish downloading by the end of chunk duration i to be played out in chunk duration $i + 1$. In other words, we can not download any portion of the i-th chunk in any chunk duration indexed higher than i:

$$\forall i, j > i, L_i^j = 0.$$

Limited buffer: We do not want to download too many chunks ahead of their play time because, in case of abandonment, these chunks represent wasted network bandwidth. For this reason, most practical implementations have a limited buffer size. We capture this by restricting that a chunk can *not* get downloaded M chunk durations ahead of its play time:

$$\forall i, j \leq i - M, L_i^j = 0.$$

Bandwidth availability: The predicted bandwidth in the j-th chunk duration, C_j, should be sufficient to download all (portions of) chunks downloaded in the j-th duration:

$$\forall j, \sum_i L_i^j \leq C_j.$$

Download consistency: Portions of i-th chunk downloaded in various chunk durations has to sum up to the size of the i-th chunk:

$$\forall i, \sum_j L_i^j \geq \sum_{i,q} R_i^q * x_i^q.$$

We note that we do not have any constraints to force download of chunks in order and the solution may interleave the downloading of video chunks (e.g., download chunks 1 and 3 in the 1st chunk duration and then download chunk 2 in the 2nd chunk duration). We can prove (omitted for brevity) that given such a schedule, we can transform it into a sensible schedule where chunks are downloaded in sequence without violating any of the constraints.

3.2 Data and Evaluation

We compare state of the art adaptation algorithms to the MILP using 20 4G/LTE cellular traces that we collected from several large US cellular providers. Each trace provides the per-second available bandwidth over 360 seconds. To accurately represent some of the more challenging conditions to deliver ABR video, the traces were obtained from various locations with different terrains (highways, local roads, etc.) and represent situations where bandwidth is more constrained and fluctuating quickly due to changing cellular conditions. The average bandwidth across traces is 6.5 Mbps.

We assume that each chunk is 4 seconds long and a maximum buffer of 64 seconds (or equivalently, 16 chunks). We take 10 different video encoding rates from one major content provider: 235, 375, 560, 750, 1050, 1750, 2350, 3000, 3850, and 4300 Kbps [8] and assume constant bit rate for each chunk. The selected chunk duration and buffer size approximate common settings of several content providers for wired and wireless environments. A few traces could not

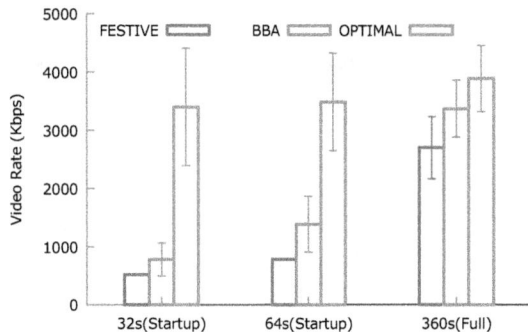

Figure 1: FESTIVE and BBA fall significantly short of optimal video quality.

satisfy MILP's strict no-stall constraint. We solved MILP on the remaining traces using a commercial solver and compared the average bit rate to those of FESTIVE and BBA[1].

Over the full traces of 360 sec (90 chunks), on average, FESTIVE and BBA achieve 68.6% and 85.7% of optimal, respectively (Figure 1). Using a re-run of MILP to maximize the rate during short and long start-up phases of 32 and 64 seconds, we find that the achievable gains obtained by MILP are significantly higher. FESTIVE and BBA reach only 15.0% and 20.1% of optimal for 32 sec, and 21.8% and 33.4% for 64 sec, respectively. These results clearly show that significant benefits can be gained by prediction, especially during startup.

4. PREDICTION-BASED ADAPTATION

In this section, we develop online versions of PBA by relaxing the assumption of perfect bandwidth knowledge for the entire session duration to shorter prediction horizons. We first highlight a naive PBA which selects the next chunk's quality based only on predicted bandwidth. This turns out to have unintended consequences.

Then, we develop a more sophisticated online PBA algorithm that obtains significant improvements in quality by combining available bandwidth prediction for only the next few seconds (e.g., one chunk duration) with buffer occupancy or rate stability function.

4.1 Naive PBA

We motivate our algorithm with a naive solution: choose the highest bit rate that is less than the predicted bandwidth. The prediction horizons are short (1 chunk duration of 4 seconds), medium (5 chunks), and long (10 chunks). The client obtains a prediction just before each chunk download. We assume that the future available bandwidth is known for a fixed time period and represented by a single average value.

Evaluation: Figures 2-4 show the three behaviors for three prediction horizons. The video rate selection based on 1-chunk horizon closely follows predicted bandwidth, leading to numerous (39) and erratic quality switches (Figure 2). This greedy rate selection is clearly reflected in very slow buffer filling, and no use of the buffer to stabilize quality.

---

[1]We implement full FESTIVE with recommended stability parameters [10] and BBA-2 variant [8].

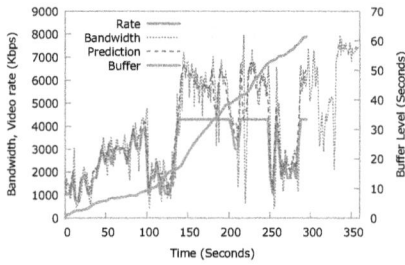

Figure 2: 1-chunk lookahead causes numerous and erratic rate switches.

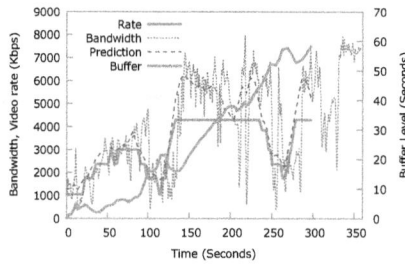

Figure 3: 5-chunk lookahead has fewer rate switches but exhibits poor buffer usage.

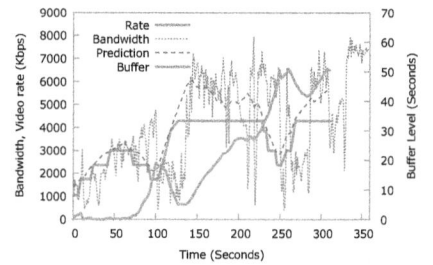

Figure 4: 10-chunk lookahead does not consider variability and leads to stalls.

Figure 3 shows a 5-chunk horizon (20 seconds), which stabilizes quality (18 switches) by averaging predicted bandwidth over a longer period, and leads to better buffer use. However, in some instances, the buffer is not appropriately used, i.e. it is refilled while bandwidth has dropped (around 120 s), and drained while bandwidth is increasing (around 40 seconds).

Finally, Figure 4 shows another extreme by taking a 10-chunk horizon (40 seconds), further stabilizing quality to 14 switches. However, this causes stalls (a cumulative stall time of 7.2 sec), because the long-term average does not include information about bandwidth variability and outages within the prediction horizon. In addition, buffer level is not considered during startup to recognize the danger of underflow due to high bandwidth variability.

While the average quality between three scenarios is similar (3.05 to 3.34 Mbps), the QoE differs significantly. There are several shortcomings of the sole use of prediction to determine quality: (i) stability is heavily impacted by highly fluctuating bandwidth, (ii) buffer fills slowly risking underflow because most of the bandwidth is used to maximize quality, and (iii) even when buffer level is high, it may not be used appropriately with respect to bandwidth fluctuations.

We take these shortcomings as takeaways to drive the design of prediction-based adaptation algorithm that improves video QoE, by considering stability, stalls, and buffer occupancy.

4.2 PBA

Since existing adaptation algorithms are not designed to use prediction, we first design a new PBA algorithm. Our PBA uses prediction, explicitly considers buffer occupancy and aggressively tries to stabilize rate selection.

We divide the buffer into three zones – *safe*, *transient*, and *risky* – based on two buffer occupancy thresholds, B_{safe} and B_{risky}. We set the safe and risky thresholds to 90% and 30% of buffer size B_{max}, respectively. A decision on the video rate for the next chunk, R_{next}, is made differently depending on the zone in which the current buffer occupancy B is, predicted available bandwidth C, and last video rate downloaded R_{last}. Algorithm 1 provides the pseudo-code.

The algorithm starts by checking the buffer occupancy against the target maximum B_{max}, and waits in case there is not enough space to store the next chunk of duration D, thereby protecting from buffer overrun. Once buffer space is available, the first step is to select a reference video rate,

---

Algorithm 1: PBA Rate Selection

Input: B: Buffer occupancy
C: Predicted available bandwidth
R_{last}: Last downloaded video rate, initialized to the highest rate

Output: R_{next}: Video rate for next chunk

if $B > B_{max} - D$ then
  | Sleep for $B + D - B_{max}$ seconds
$ref = \max\{i : R_i \leq C\}$
if $B \leq B_{risky}$ then
  | $ref = \max\{ref - 1, 1\}$
  | if $R_{ref} < R_{last}$ then
    | $R_{next} = \max\left(\{R : \frac{B}{D} + \frac{C}{R} - 1 > 2\} \cup \{R_1\}\right)$
  | else
    | $R_{next} = R_{ref}$
else if $B \geq B_{safe}$ then
  | $R_{next} = \max\{R_{ref}, R_{last}\}$
else
  | if $R_{ref} \leq R_{last}$ then
    | $R_{next} = R_{last}$
  | else
    | $\Delta B = D * (C/R_{ref} - 1)$
    | $B_{empty} = B_{max} - B$
    | if $\Delta B > 0.15 * B_{empty}$ then
      | $R_{next} = R_{ref}$
    | else
      | $R_{next} = R_{ref-1}$

R_{ref}, to be the highest available rate below predicted bandwidth C.

In the risky zone, a conservative approach is used to prevent stalls and replenish the buffer, by first reducing R_{ref} by one level. If R_{ref} is higher than the rate of last chunk, R_{last}, we upswitch to R_{ref}. However, if R_{ref} is lower than R_{last}, this means that the reduction is recommended. To avoid sudden quality drop to R_{ref}, we pick the highest rate R without draining the buffer to less than two chunks, which performs better than one chunk when variable chunk sizes are used. B/D is the number of chunks in the buffer before requesting next chunk, C/R is the additional number of chunks that will be downloaded, while -1 represents one chunk that is expected to be played from the buffer while the next chunk is retrieved. During startup, with $B = 0$, this constraint selects the rate of the first chunk equal to 1/3rd of the predicted bandwidth. If such a rate cannot be found, the only decision that can be made is to select the lowest rate R_1.

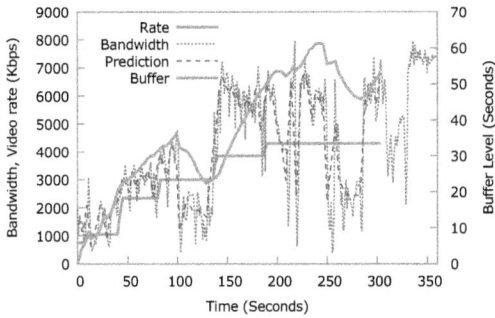

Figure 5: PBA with 1-chunk lookahead is stable and stall-free while offering high video quality.

Table 2: PBA achieves near-optimal quality.

	%Avg.rate 360 s	%Avg.rate 32 s	Number of stalls	%Rate switches
Optimal	100%	100%	0	100%
FESTIVE	68.6%	15.0%	34	101.3%
BBA	85.7%	20.1%	17	93.3%
PBA-BB	95.8%	84.8%	31	43.0%
PBA-DU	91.4%	95.8%	23	181.2%

In the safe zone, the algorithm aggressively selects the larger of R_{ref} and R_{last} to maintain stability and ride out short-term bandwidth variations.

In the transient zone, various approaches can be taken to balance the buffer occupancy, high quality, stability, and other objectives. In this implementation, we take a more aggressive approach. When R_{ref} is lower than R_{last}, we stick to R_{last} with the expectation that bandwidth will recover. If R_{ref} is higher than R_{last}, we want to grow the buffer. The algorithm will select rate R_{ref} if downloading at R_{ref} will allow at least 15% of the empty buffer space to be filled. Otherwise, we reduce by one rate and select R_{ref-1}.

Evaluation: Figure 5 shows for a specific trace how PBA behaves when buffer level is taken into consideration. Compared to naive PBA, the buffer is filled faster during startup, which is desirable. When the buffer level is moderate to high, it is aggressively exploited to ride out short fade durations and maintain high quality (100-140 seconds and 260-280 seconds). The average rate over 360 sec is 3.15 Mbps with no stalls and only 6 rate switches. Therefore, average quality is similar to naive PBA, but with significantly improved stability and appropriate buffer usage.

Next, we compare PBA to state-of-the-art proposals, FESTIVE and BBA. In addition to our PBA algorithm, we also implement an alternative using a known stability function employed by FESTIVE, called "delayed update". Using the aforementioned data set, we run simulations to investigate how close to optimal each adaptation algorithm gets. Table 2 lists algorithms and the percentage of optimal (MILP) they can achieve using a 64-second buffer. Recall that over the entire trace durations, FESTIVE and BBA come within 68.6% and 85.7% of optimal, respectively. PBA with buffer-based stability function (PBA-BB) reaches 95.8% of optimal quality, representing a relative improvement of ∼40% over FESTIVE. PBA with delayed update (PBA-DU) is within 91.4% of optimal quality. During startup phase (32 s), the value of prediction becomes abundantly clear, with up to 95.8% of optimal quality, while FESTIVE and BBA remain extremely sub-optimal.

Comparing metrics other than video quality shows a slight advantage of BBA because of fewer stalls. This is not surprising given that BBA is designed specifically to avoid stalls, unlike PBA and FESTIVE. While FESTIVE and BBA are nearly as stable as optimal, PBA-BB registers the best stability, and PBA-DU reduces stalls by decreasing stability, which is a very desirable trade-off [2]. PBA algorithms with

different stability functions can trade off stalls and stability while maintaining much improved average quality.

We finally seek to quantify the benefit of prediction, i.e. to show that the benefits come from prediction and not from other parts of the adaptation algorithm. This is not a straight-forward task, since every algorithm is designed to work best with a specific bandwidth estimate. Nevertheless, we design a basic benchmark using our adaptation algorithm with two stability functions and swap predicted bandwidth with output of other heuristics. This approach maintains the while adaptation process the same except how reference rate is computed. We use harmonic mean of last 10 chunks and last chunk throughput as the two heuristics, and 4-second (1 chunk) look-ahead for PBA. Harmonic mean is the core feature of FESTIVE and last chunk throughput is used by BBA during startup.

Table 3 shows the relative improvement that prediction (PBA) offers compared to other heuristics for a given stability function. We make several interesting observations. First, when looking at the average bit rates over the entire trace of 360 sec, all algorithms do well. Prediction provides up to 4.8% improvement on average quality while maintaining overall better number of stalls and switching statistics. Second, during the "startup" phase, prediction offers nearly 18% improvement in video rate compared to harmonic mean. Finally, out of the three, last chunk strategy performs the worst in terms of stall and switch statistics. On the other hand, harmonic-based strategy has commensurate stall and switching statistics.

With "delayed update", prediction outperforms others by a similar margin during startup phase. Prediction offers significant reduction in the number of stalls and the cumulative time stalled. However, this comes at the expense of an increased number of switches. Reducing the number of stalls is a desirable feature in terms of customer engagement [2]. Finally, PBA is stall-free in 6 more traces than harmonic (a 25% improvement).

5. OPEN CHALLENGES

While our results show that accurate predictions of available network bandwidth improve the quality of video over cellular networks, generating accurate predictions is non-trivial. We discuss some of the challenges in generating bandwidth predictions in real time and conveying them at scale.

Generating accurate predictions: The cellular radio link is carefully scheduled. A base station tracks multiple network metrics and uses them in the scheduling process. In addition, the architecture of the network allows an operator to have a view of all devices, their link statistics, radio spectrum availability, mobility patterns, and instantaneous traffic demand. Moreover, recent work [14] shows that it is possible to get very accurate predictions (98% accuracy) for

Table 3: PBA improvement over heuristics based on Harmonic mean and Last chunk throughput.

Stability function	Avg. rate, 360 s		Avg. rate, 32 s		Avg. rate, 64 s		Time stalled		Number of stalls		Rate switches	
	Last	Har	Last	Har	Last	Har	Last	Har	Last	Har	Last	Har
Buffer-based	0.4%	4.8%	10.0%	17.9%	4.6%	13.8%	35.2%	-12.3%	22.6%	0.0%	34.8%	-11.9%
Delayed update	-1.7%	0.0%	11.3%	17.3%	4.3%	11.8%	132.9%	184.5%	69.6%	139.1%	10.0%	-63.6%

short time periods (500 msec) just by observing network performance at a stationary client device. There is also evidence that we can obtain good mobility models [13] and generate feasible throughput predictions [11] over short time periods (5 seconds) even when users are mobile. These results lead us to believe that it is feasible for cellular operators to predict available bandwidth accurately.

However, the exact mechanisms, data and algorithms that need to be combined to generate accurate, real-time predictions of available bandwidth are still unknown. Further, it would be desirable to have long term predictions (e.g., MILP is able to significantly increase quality), and have multiple predictions (a very accurate short term prediction and an indicative long term prediction) or even a distribution of bandwidth over the predicted period. We are pursuing these questions as part of our ongoing work.

Exposing computed predictions: Assuming these predictions can be computed, exposing them to client applications in a timely manner poses interesting systems and protocol challenges. One proposal considers a throughput guidance protocol where bandwidth information is embedded in TCP headers [1]. This approach makes the information available to TCP stacks of senders, to be potentially used by all applications. The evaluation based on simulation suggests benefits for video streaming similar to our results presented in this paper.

We envision that the cellular provider can expose bandwidth predictions through an API that applications query each time they start downloading a video chunk. An approach using an API-based architecture for cooperation between network operators and content providers has been recently proposed [9]. Collecting and analyzing various network information including user mobility, channel quality for millions of users and generating predictions in real time to be useful for video rate selection (and other possible applications) is a significant challenge. In order to scale, we envision that a practical system will have to partition the network into small areas and independently compute predictions for each area. However, this brings with it interesting protocol challenges in terms of localization and routing of requests to the appropriate area.

6. CONCLUSION

A cellular operator typically has access to a range of in-network measurements that can be potentially used for making short to mid-term bandwidth predictions. We show that when designing video adaptation algorithms, leveraging bandwidth predictions can significantly improve video QoE. We show that during startup, the proposed PBA algorithm promises to deliver more than 4x better video quality compared to heuristic-based algorithms. This is important since it has been shown that users typically abandon in the first few minutes of the video if the picture quality suffers. We also showed that a naive algorithm that solely uses prediction does not do well and that a combination of prediction

with buffer occupancy and/or stability function is needed to extract the maximum benefit. Finally, we show that PBA algorithms with different stability functions can trade off stalls and stability while maintaining much improved average quality. For future work, we continue to address some of the open challenges in generating bandwidth predictions in real time and conveying them at scale.

7. REFERENCES

[1] Mobile throughput guidance signaling protocol. https://tools.ietf.org/id/draft-flinck-mobile-throughput-guidance-00.txt.

[2] A. Balachandran, V. Sekar, A. Akella, S. Seshan et al. Developing a predictive model of quality of experience for internet video. In *Proceedings of ACM SIGCOMM*, 2013.

[3] J. Chen, A. Ghosh, J. Magutt, and M. Chiang. QAVA: Quota Aware Video Adaptation. In *Proceedings of ACM CoNEXT*, 2012.

[4] J. Chen, R. Mahindra, M. A. Khojastepour, S. Rangarajan, and M. Chiang. A Scheduling Framework for Adaptive Video Delivery over Cellular Networks. In *Proceedings of ACM MobiCom*, 2013.

[5] Cisco. Cisco visual networking index: Forecast and methodology, 2013–2018, 2014. http://tinyurl.com/mev32z8.

[6] Citrix. Mobile analytics report, 2014. http://tinyurl.com/n4qvgnf.

[7] J. Erman, A. Gerber, K. K. Ramakrishnan, S. Sen, and O. Spatscheck. Over the Top Video: The Gorilla in Cellular Networks. In *Proceedings of ACM IMC*, 2011.

[8] T.-Y. Huang, R. Johari, N. McKeown, M. Trunnell, and M. Watson. A Buffer-Based Approach to Rate Adaptation: Evidence from a Large Video Streaming Service. In *Proceedings of ACM SIGCOMM*, 2014.

[9] J. Jiang, X. Liu, V. Sekar, I. Stoica, and H. Zhang. EONA: Experience-oriented network architecture. In *Proceedings ACM HotNets*, 2014.

[10] J. Jiang, V. Sekar, and H. Zhang. Improving Fairness, Efficiency, and Stability in HTTP-based Adaptive Video Streaming with FESTIVE. In *Proceedings of ACM CoNEXT*, 2012.

[11] R. Margolies, A. Sridharan, V. Aggarwal, R. Jana et al. Exploiting mobility in proportional fair cellular scheduling: Measurements and algorithms. In *Proceedings of IEEE INFOCOM*, 2014.

[12] R. K. P. Mok, X. Luo, E. W. W. Chan, and R. K. C. Chang. QDASH: A QoE-aware DASH System. In *Proceedings of ACM MMSys*, 2012.

[13] A. J. Nicholson and B. D. Noble. Breadcrumbs: Forecasting mobile connectivity. In *Proceedings of ACM MobiCom*, 2008.

[14] Q. Xu, S. Mehrotra, Z. Mao, and J. Li. Proteus: Network performance forecast for real-time, interactive mobile applications. In *Proceeding of ACM MobiSys*, 2013.

[15] X. Yin, V. Sekar, and B. Sinopoli. Toward a principled framework to design dynamic adaptive streaming algorithms over http. In *Proceedings ACM HotNets*, 2014.

CrowdREM: Harnessing the Power of the Mobile Crowd for Flexible Wireless Network Monitoring

Andreas Achtzehn, Janne Riihijärvi, Irving Antonio Barría Castillo,
Marina Petrova, Petri Mähönen
Institute for Networked Systems, RWTH Aachen University
Kackertstrasse 9, D-52072 Aachen, Germany
{aac, jar, iba, mpe, pma}@inets.rwth-aachen.de

ABSTRACT

High-speed mobile broadband connections have opened exciting new opportunities to collect sensor data from thousands or even millions of distributed mobile devices for the purpose of crowdsourced decision making. In this paper, we propose *CrowdREM* (crowdsourced radio environment mapping), a framework with the specific aim of monitoring and modelling wireless cellular networks. CrowdREM enables operator-independent and highly efficient collection of network performance data along all layers of the communications protocol stack. Such extensive information on network load, spectrum usage, or local coverage can help operators to optimize their networks and service quality and enable improved consumer decision making. In this paper, we introduce the CrowdREM mobile architecture and show first results from a prototype implementation on open-source mobile phones. We demonstrate the versatility of using commodity devices for network and spectrum monitoring, and present the challenges originating from the use of uncalibrated and low-precision measurement equipment. We have acquired an extensive data set from using our prototype implementation in a 21-day measurement campaign covering more than 1 000 hours of measurement data. From this we present and discuss the potential derivation of tangible and relevant network performance and signal quality indicators, which could, e.g., be conducted by independent parties.

Categories and Subject Descriptors

C.2.3 [**Computer-Communication Networks**]: [Network monitoring]; C.4 [**Performance of Systems**]: Measurement techniques

General Terms

Measurement; Performance; Reliability

Keywords

Crowdsourcing; Mobile; Drive Testing; Cellular Networks

1. INTRODUCTION

The densification and complexity explosion of wireless cellular networks is putting high burdens on network operators. Monitoring their networks for coverage holes or low performance becomes increasingly difficult, if not impossible. Traditional approaches of carrying out extensive drive testing campaigns with expensive personnel and equipment are reaching their limits, and it has become obvious that the "intelligence of the crowd" will need to be employed in order to manage networking complexities. LTE release 10 [8] has therefore foreseen a possibility to collect network performance statistics from user equipment (UE). A significant limitation of a proposed minimization of drive testing (MDT) is its focus on a single network and few user link performance aspects. For establish a truly comprehensive view of wireless network operations, extended means of collecting performance statistics from UEs will need to be employed.

Several projects already gather performance data on cellular networks for this purpose, see [7]. NetRadar [2] collects traces from mobile devices to acquire localized link throughput statistics; OpenCellID [5] collects cell tower information and correlates them with user locations to establish network density and coverage maps; and finally, OpenSignal [12] measures the signal strength of cell towers to estimate achievable throughputs. However, none of the current approaches yet takes a holistic view *along all operators and protocol levels* to enable advanced modelling, e.g. through spatial statistics and machine learning based filtering methods, to build highly relevant coverage and performance estimates.

In this paper, we present *CrowdREM*, a framework for collecting spectrum usage and protocol data with sensor fusion capabilities. CrowdREM's uniqueness comes from its capability to jointly collect spectrum and performance data from several local network operators; both, at the level of pure signal level measurements as well as through monitoring of relevant control traffic. Such extensive data, if combined and cross-correlated with local information [3] and other higher layer performance metrics, can yield an enhanced understanding of the current state of the radio environment [14, 6]. This will help operators to conduct terminal-centric network tuning, and allows users to adapt their download schedules to reduce radio activity overheads [4]. Further, CrowdREM may be maintained, e.g., by a third party to offer real-time, independent information for consumers and local regulators.

To demonstrate its feasibility, we have implemented a proof-of-concept CrowdREM on an open-source mobile phone platform. We present the challenges of distributed spectrum sensing with inexpensive hardware such as the signal degra-

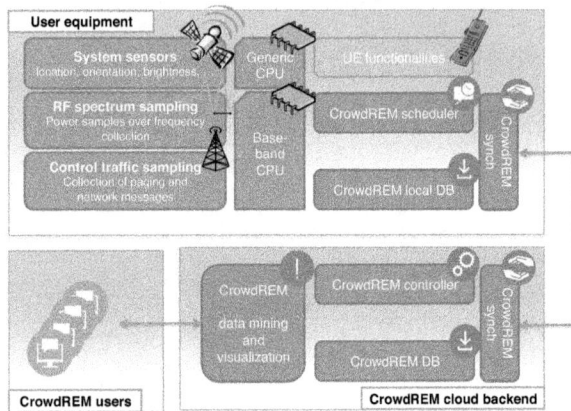

Figure 1: The CrowdREM architecture.

dation due to non-uniform antenna patterns, uncertainties on phone placement, and packet-loss induced statistical bias that need to be considered and compensated for. Our work thereby goes beyond earlier works, e.g. [9], that require complex signal processing on non-commodity hardware, and do not lend themselves for application in crowdsourcing. We have extensively tested our design with data from approximately 13 000 measurement sessions, which constitute more than 1 000 hours of monitoring data. We present both findings from calibrating the hardware and results on the signal stability over several days of measurements in stationary setups. Further, we provide initial results from the data mining of the approximately 70 million samples of control traffic messages, which underlines the benefit of crowdsourced collection to generate more precise network load estimates.

The rest of this paper is organized as follows: In Section 2 we present the CrowdREM architecture and its prototype implementation. In Section 3 we discuss, through examples of calibration measurements with our own base station and a comparison study in a fixed location, the limitations of single-device measurements. Section 4 further analyzes censoring methods for network measurements in low signal level environments, and the benefits of data fusion at a central coordinating entity for deriving tangible data on network performance indicators such as paging rate and immediate channel assignments. Section 5 concludes this paper.

2. CROWDREM ARCHITECTURE

In the following we provide a brief overview of the envisioned CrowdREM architecture. CrowdREM differs from approaches such as [9] as it is designed to operate on regular UEs, e.g. smartphones, tablets, or laptops with wireless connections. Fig. 1 shows that its design is divided between *local data collection*, *cloud data processing*, and *storage*.

At the core of the UE components, a CrowdREM scheduler manages the collection of radio environment and system data. Its main purpose is to balance the requirements of data storage and sampling costs in terms of energy consumption and service level, with the purpose of minimizing the impact of CrowdREM on the UEs regular operations and battery lifetime. As noted by Lane et al. [10], advanced prediction-based schedulers for smartphone crowdsourcing can reduce energy consumption by up to 90% depending on the scenario. For this purpose, the scheduler runs a dynamic

collection policy, which can be adapted if, e.g., more extensive data collection becomes necessary. The CrowdREM scheduler furthermore monitors user behavior, in order to preempt collection tasks when user interactions take place. The power of a policy-based data collection lies in the flexibility of defining rules for the collection process. It constantly monitors relevant system sensors such as the brightness sensor or the gyroscope to determine where the UE is currently located, and whether deviations from the regular collection schedule are necessary.

Our architectures separates pure RF spectrum sampling from the collection of control traffic data. RF sampling comprises sweeps over the various frequency bands to determine power levels according to a scheduler-defined frequency plan and bandwidth selection. The scheduler needs to take particular care that this will not disrupt ongoing transmissions. In contrast, control traffic collection may be carried asynchronously and even while user interactions take place. While normally UEs discard control traffic not intended for their own operations, for CrowdREM the baseband system needs to pass through all messages. Further, the CrowdREM scheduler needs to enforce a channel sequence to be monitored and a dwell time for the collection of control messages. We find that control traffic information is well suited to determine network load, because it alleviates the hidden node problem pure power sampling approaches as used e.g. in [4] face. The extra power required for control traffic sampling itself is minimal, since the UE constantly needs to monitor broadcast transmissions anyways; any overheads thus originate from storing and processing steps. The collected measurements are augmented with regular system sensor information to determine, e.g. the relative orientation of the UE towards the serving cell tower. They are stored in a local database, which is synchronized asynchronously and depending on bandwidth availability with the cloud-based part of the CrowdREM architecture.

All heavy processing tasks of CrowdREM have been designed to operate in the cloud to provide better battery lifetime of the UEs, maximize the crowdsourcing benefits, and minimize maintenance overheads. A central CrowdREM controller manages the integrated UEs by distributing the high-level collection policy. The controller uses the available data in the CrowdREM data mining backend. For example, it would increase the sampling cycle for UEs located in regions of high network load volatility or limited sampling device density. The CrowdREM controller would then adapt the policy of a selection of UEs to create more fine-grained sampling results. As the CrowdREM controller has a global view of the radio environment, its decision making is drawing directly from the distributed nature of the crowdsourcing approach. Several data views can be defined to study the various performance aspects of the network. Thereby, different stakeholders can review the CrowdREM data according to their analysis needs.

2.1 Prototype Implementation

We have implemented a fully functional prototype of the CrowdREM architecture on the OpenMoko platform. OpenMoko [11] is an open-source project that offers smartphones with fully disclosed hard- and software. The architecture is similar to that of commercial devices as it offloads signal processing into a baseband processor. Applications and management run in a separate embedded processor. Although the used APIs are OpenMoko-specific, their capabilities are implemented in every mobile phones. We presume that vendors may disclose their APIs given the benefits, based also on more recent discussions in the 3GPP MDT context.

After installing a modified Linux on the phone, the baseband processor firmware was replaced by OsmocomBB [13], a software suite which provides layer 1 to 3 functionalities with a fully open API. We have designed a wrapper to control OsmocomBB, collect data, and store it in the local data repository. We note that, while these steps are necessary for this particular platform, commercial smartphones may expose the same API without firmware modification. The required sniffing and power measurement components are necessarily implemented in any mobile phone, thus we consider exposing them e.g. to an Android/iOS app would be reasonable given the benefits for the various stakeholders.

We have conducted an extensive measurement campaign with the prototype in the mid-sized city of Aachen, Germany. To gather network statistics, we distributed identically configured OpenMoko phones to university students. The campaign lasted for 21 days, from which we acquired approximately 13,000 measurement session sets. We manually selected a simplified collection policy that allowed for a particularly broad data set to be generated at the cost of shorter battery lifetime. Each measurement session consisted of an initial phase in which the UE[1] scanned across all physical E-GSM channels (ARFCNs) to yield power levels and network/cell identification information. In the city area, four different network operators are active, thus we selected for each of them the strongest ARFCN for collecting control traffic. The individual per ARFCN dwell time was set to 45 seconds and all decodable messages in the logical broadcast and common control channels (BCCH and CCCH) were stored along with additional system level sensor information.

3. CELLULAR NETWORK RADIO ENVIRONMENT ANALYSIS

Using examples from our prototype implementation we will in the following show the challenges and opportunities in crowdsourced measurement setups. In this section, we focus on those physical layer measurements that are used to determine the radio environment of a UE.

3.1 Determining UE Orientation

No UE antenna is perfectly omnidirectional, thus signal strength variations may be observed even if the position of the UE remains unchanged. This defines an initial requirement for a crowdsourced measurement approach, which is to implement means to determine the relative orientation of the UE to the monitored network infrastructure, e.g. by integrating gyroscope measurements. In order to illustrate the need for this additional information, we have carried out calibration measurement through running an open-source GSM-BS (OpenBTS) [1] with the popular USRP platform acting as a radio frontend. We mounted the UE to a tripod and took measurements while rotating the phone along its x, y, and z axis. Note that the UE antenna is located in the bottom part of the phone. Figure 2 shows that the measured signal strength varies by 4.4 dB when the UE is rolled (rotating the y axis), which can be considered minor and is

---

[1]In the following we refer to the GSM mobile station (MS) as UE for the sake of conformity.

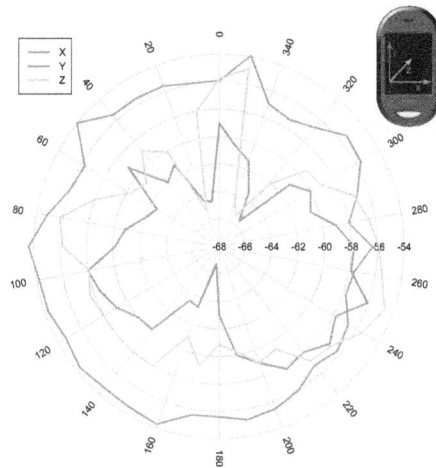

Figure 2: Reported signal strength (in dBm) of the CrowdREM prototype with respect to its orientation towards the BS.

within the measurement precision requirements of a GSM phone. While this is an expected outcome due to the geometry of the device, larger deviations could be observed when the z axis of the UE was rotated. Here, an up to 10.7 dB difference in signal strength could be observed depending on whether the bottom of the UE was pointing towards the BS or away from it. Similar observations could be made when the phone was rotated while standing upright, i.e. the phone is considerably more sensitive from the back than from the front, which is a common antenna design for smartphones. This highlights the necessity to integrate this sensory data in the data collection process and compensate for resulting uncertainties in the analysis.

3.2 UE Localization

The second challenge in crowdsourced measurements arises from imprecisions in the localization process. Small deviations in the position of a UE can yield significantly different measurements, particularly when measurements are taken in complex indoor radio environments. This is especially challenging since traditional localization methods using GPS generally fail to work in such locations. A crowdsourced measurement setup such as CrowdREM must therefore collect auxiliary information from the UE sensors to augment GPS position estimates, e.g. through Wi-Fi fingerprinting.

In the following we illustrate how extensive these measurement deviations can become in a single UE scenario with GPS-only positioning. For this, we selected the data from a UE that was often located in the same building during our measurement campaign. In total, 14 distinct measurement periods (comprised of consecutive measurement sessions) could be identified where the phone reported to be placed in an area of approximately 40 m in or around the building. A sensible assumption is that all these measurements were taken inside the user's apartment.

In Fig. 3 we show the mean measured signal strength on the 4 strongest ARFCNs for all measurement periods. Through readings from the control traffic analysis (see Section 4) we found that these ARFCN measurements always map to the same BSs. Up to 8 dB of relative deviation in

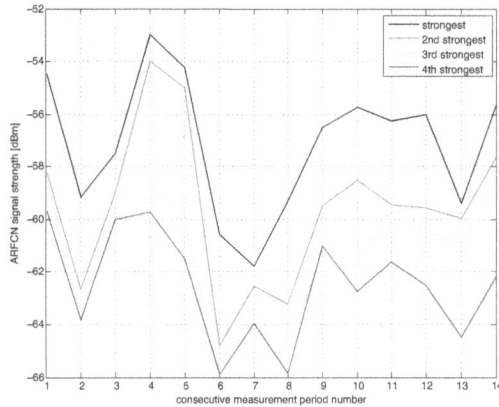

Figure 3: Observed signal strength of the strongest ARFCNs for different consecutive measurement periods. Each period is comprised of several measurement sessions, for which we report the mean signal strength value.

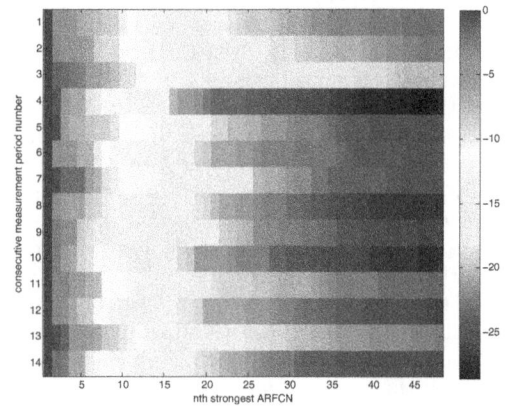

Figure 4: Deviation from strongest mean ARFCN signal strength for different consecutive measurement periods.

the measurements between consecutive periods are reported, and only for period numbers 9 to 12 more stable results are found. However, as we can see from the relative values in the figure, there is an apparent correlation between signal strength values of the different ARFCNs. We can thus conclude that despite lower localization precision, it is possible to at least establish *relative* signal strength distributions for various operators and BSs.

An example of how CrowdREM's cross-operator view of spectrum usage is beneficial is depicted in Fig. 4. Here, we have normalized the signal strength values of the 48 strongest ARFCNs to the value of the strongest ARFCN. We see in this figure the similarities between different measurement periods, e.g. 3, 5, 7, 11, and 13. We assume that the UE was located in the same place when these measurements were taken, because such result would generally only be observed with the same overall spatial geometry. By comparing these results to the absolute signal strength values of Fig. 3, we see that all values lie within the precision limits of the device. The CrowdREM architecture is thus capable of improving sensing *consistency* by taking the overall geometry of the radio environment into account.

4. CONTROL TRAFFIC ANALYSIS

While signal strength measurements yield an estimate of the physical characteristics of the radio environment, a detailed analysis of the control traffic enables us to derive relevant statistics on the performance and load of different network operators. To the best of our knowledge, CrowdREM is the first framework that explicitly uses control traffic data for such an extensive performance analysis. In the following we first discuss the issue of message losses and how it affects the monitoring accuracy, before providing example statistics on relevant network operations parameters.

4.1 Limitations of Single UE Traffic Measurements

Monitoring control traffic requires the UE to tune to the broadcasting channel(s) of the BS(s) and collect *all* decod-

able messages intended for *all* other UEs within the same location area or cell. Such collection does not require for the UE to be part of the operator network, because control traffic is generally sent through unencrypted broadcasting channels. However, since the UE itself may be located in a location with adverse signal conditions (low signal strength or high interference from other cells), not all messages can be necessarily decoded. Monitoring-derived statistics from single UEs may thus underestimate loads in cellular networks.

To illustrate the significance of this limitation we have conducted a small-scale measurement campaign with two CrowdREM devices. The first device was placed nearby a known GSM BS and set to permanently collect this BS's control traffic. The other UE was moved to the fixed locations depicted in Fig. 5b which are within the decodability-determined cell range of approximately 1.3 km. At each location, control traffic was collected for 1 minute from which we derived the message loss rate by comparing the captured messages to those from the stationary device.

Our comparison of the fractional message loss and the received signal strength of the messages in Fig. 5a indicates that if the signal strength value drops below approximately -60 dBm, the mobile UE is no longer able to decode all messages. The message loss becomes more severe when the signal strength is further lowered, e.g. if the signal strength is at on average -90 dBm, only 50% of the messages are still retrieved. Near the overall decodability threshold, virtually all messages are lost. We can see from the plot that there is a region between approximately -60 and -75 dBm where there is a clear relationship between the received signal strength and fraction of lost messages. This relationship can be used to compensate for the naturally occurring censoring bias in the data, and improve the quality of our estimates of network load provided that sufficient calibration information is available. Gathering of such calibration information is enabled through a crowdsourced architecture such as CrowdREM, which allows to cross-correlate message rates at various monitoring UEs. For lower signal strengths no clear relationship to the fractional message loss is observed, i.e. there are further deviations in reception quality not sufficiently captured by the signal strength value.

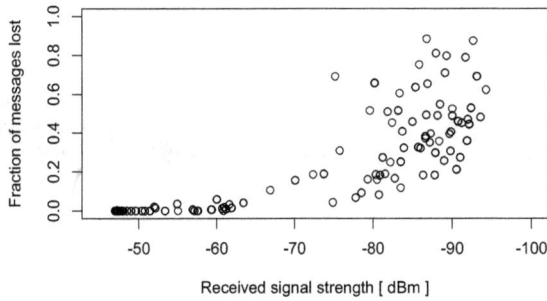

(a) Fractional message loss vs. received signal strength.

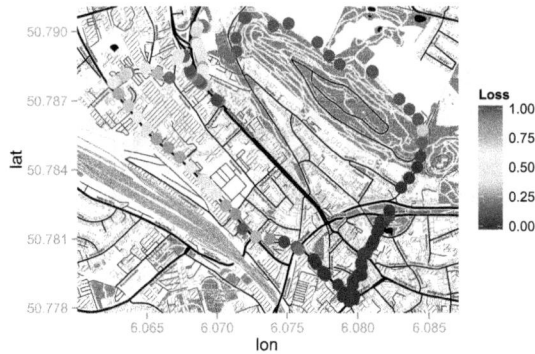

(b) Fractional message loss map.

Figure 5: Two UE measurement comparison. Fig. 5a shows the fractional loss of messages compared to the average RSSI value of the received messages. In Fig. 5b the spatial distribution of the loss rate is depicted.

4.2 Crowdsourced Network Load Estimation

A further benefit of using multiple coordinated UEs to collect control traffic is that message loss and limited UE availability do not affect the overall collection capability of the crowdsourced data mining architecture in CrowdREM. Since only a smaller number of devices are needed if good reception quality is experienced, one may extend the battery lifetime of the crowdsourcing UEs by scheduling less frequent data collection. In the following, we discuss relevant network load indicators that can be easily derived thereby. The results are illustrative for an advanced data mining that is enabled by using the CrowdREM architecture.

In our first analysis example we study the network load by means of quantifying the *paging load* observed for a single operator. In the GSM system architecture, paging messages are used to request channel reservations for UEs, e.g. to initiate a network-initiated voice call. In Fig. 6a we plot the rate of different paging messages for the location area of a single operator as measured by various UEs over 17 days in our campaign. We see that paging messages are dominated by type 1 requests, which are messages sent to up to 2 devices. Other paging messages for more than two devices (type 2 and type 3) do not contribute to the overall paging rate. Surprisingly, there is no apparent correlation between the time of day and the paging rate, which would have been expected from increased day-time user ac-

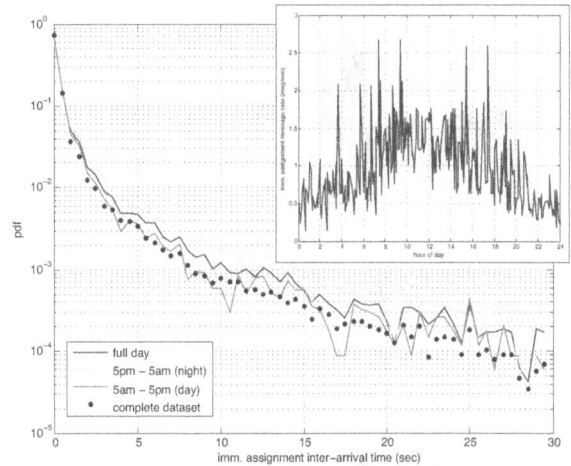

Figure 7: Probability density function of the inter-arrival times of immediate assignment messages for channel allocation.

tivity. Occasionally, higher paging rates can be observed during the night, which seems counter-intuitive. On deeper inspection we found that the operators intentionally insert blank paging messages, presumably to allow UEs to synch more frequently, which also explains the relative steadiness of ARFCN measurements (see Section 3.2) over time. Thus, we conclude that paging messages are a weak indicator of network load.

A better indicator for network activity is the number of individual UEs queried in paging messages. Fig. 6b exhibits the expected day-time dependency of network load. Furthermore, we can observe that during weekends the number of paged UEs drops, as seems intuitive. Through comparison of the different days we can make further derivations on the user behavior, e.g. increased activity is observed on Monday mornings, whereas the network load steadily drops already on Friday afternoons.

The time of day dependency can also be found in an analysis of the immediate assignment message rates of a single BS. These messages are sent to allocate channels to UEs within the cell, thus they are only observable by a smaller group of monitoring UEs in nearby locations. We take the example of a single cell that was monitored by a single CrowdREM UE. We note that such analysis is only possible if the UE is not moved during the day, and when beneficial signal quality levels are observed. For lower signal levels, means of message loss compensation as discussed in Section 4.1 need to be applied. A plot of the probability density function of the inter-arrival rate in Fig. 7 shows that during night times the inter-arrival time increases, i.e. fewer requests are made per unit time, while it noticeably decreases starting at around 5am in the morning. We can further observe lower rates during lunch time, when supposedly less calls are made. Such figures allow for the derivation of tangible load models for application in network traffic modelling as we, e.g., can already infer from the data set used to create Fig. 7 that heavy-tailed distributions are more appropriate to model the observed time variability.

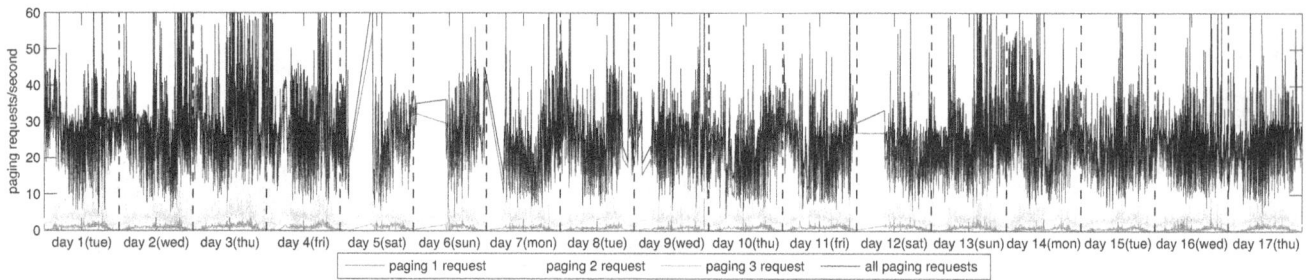

(a) Paging messages.

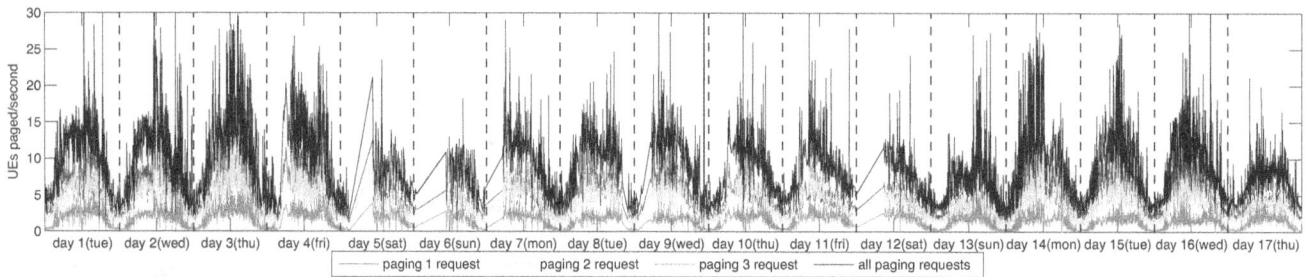

(b) Number of UEs paged.

Figure 6: Paging message rates and number of individual paged UEs per second over a period of 17 days for a single location area (LA). Rates depicted here are calculated individually for each 45-second measurement session.

5. CONCLUSIONS

In this paper, we have presented CrowdREM, a framework for the crowdsourced monitoring of cellular networks. CrowdREM enables the distributed collection of spectrum usage and network information from inexpensive mobile terminals to build a comprehensive and holistic view of the structure and use of wireless networks. Contrary to earlier works, CrowdREM is not limited to a single operator or networking aspect, but it provides means to independently derive performance statistics relevant to network operators, customers, and regulators.

Our practical analysis with a prototype implementation has showcased the benefits of using a crowdsourced data mining, where limitations in positioning accuracy, orientation, and message loss experienced for individual measurements can be compensated for through combined sampling from multiple sensor entities. We have furthermore used results from an extensive measurement campaign covering more than 1,000 hours of measurement data on live cellular networks to demonstrate the derivation of relevant network performance indicators such as the paging rate, number of active users, and the time dependency of network load. While our proof-of-concept implementation runs only on 2G networks, the principal idea of CrowdREM extends also to more current network generations.

In the future we plan to fully integrate and port CrowdREM to other platforms and 3G/4G networks to enable more extensive data collection, whereby we are also interested in other cross-layer metrics such as browser performance. Further, we are interested in studying social and economic incentives for participating in a crowdsourced data collection, e.g. through more precision localization from extended environment fingerprinting.

6. REFERENCES

[1] OpenBTS. www.openbts.org.
[2] Aalto University. NetRadar. www.netradar.org.
[3] I. Carreras et al. Crowd-sensing: Why context matters. In *Proc. IEEE PERCOM Workshops*, pages 368–371, March 2013.
[4] A. Chakraborty et al. Coordinating cellular background transfers using LoadSense. In *Proc. ACM Mobicom*, September 2013.
[5] ENAiKOON. OpenCellID. www.opencellid.org.
[6] A. Galindo-Serrano et al. Harvesting MDT data: Radio environment maps for coverage analysis in cellular networks. In *Proc. CROWNCOM*, pages 37–42, July 2013.
[7] U. Goel et al. Survey of end-to-end mobile network measurement testbeds. 2014. arXiv:1411.5003 [cs.NI].
[8] W. Hapsari et al. Minimization of drive tests solution in 3GPP. *IEEE Communications Magazine*, 50(6):28–36, June 2012.
[9] S. Kumar et al. LTE radio analytics made easy and accessible. In *Proc. ACM SIGCOMM*, pages 211–222, 2014.
[10] N. D. Lane et al. Piggyback crowdsensing (PCS): Energy efficient crowdsourcing of mobile sensor data by exploiting smartphone app opportunities. In *Proc. SenSys*, pages 7:1–7:14, 2013.
[11] OpenMoko project. OpenMoko. www.openmoko.org.
[12] OpenSignal, Inc. OpenSignal. www.opensignal.com.
[13] OsmocomBB project. OsmocomBB. bb.osmocom.org.
[14] J. van de Beek et al. How a layered REM architecture brings cognition to today's mobile networks. *IEEE Wireless Communications*, 19(4):17–24, August 2012.

A Wireless Spectrum Analyzer in Your Pocket

Tan Zhang[#], Ashish Patro[#], Ning Leng[$], Suman Banerjee[#]
Department of Computer Sciences[#], Department of Statistics[$]
University of Wisconsin-Madison, USA
{tzhang, patro, suman}@cs.wisc.edu[#], leng@stat.wisc.edu[$]

ABSTRACT

We propose Snoopy, a system that can translate one's mobile phone or tablet into a low-cost, yet effective RF spectrum analyzer. Since typical spectrum analyzers are specialized hardware that is both expensive to acquire and cumbersome to carry around, they are rarely available for quick-and-easy spectrum sensing while on the go. To address this challenge, Snoopy augments popular mobile devices with a small attachable hardware unit (RF frequency translator) that can provide a reasonable view of the wireless spectrum across different frequency bands. It achieves this by leveraging the spectral scan functionality available in certain 802.11 NICs (e.g., the Atheros 9280 family of chipsets), which provides an unique lens towards the WiFi spectrum (2.4 GHz). Through the use of suitable frequency translators, such a view can be flexibly shifted to other spectrum bands. Although such a construction might not match the precision of the most sophisticated but expensive spectrum analyzers, we show that by leveraging some carefully designed spectral features, Snoopy can achieve decent accuracy in determining TV whitespaces (512 − 698 MHz) – it can detect primary signals at up to - 90dBm with an error rate of <15%, while achieving a median error of < 4dB in estimating the power of these signals. These promising results suggest that Snoopy is an intriguing option in bringing the ability of spectrum sensing to the masses, thereby truly enabling crowdsourcing options in this domain.

Categories and Subject Descriptors

C.4 [**Performance of Systems**]: Measurement techniques; C.2.1 [**Network Architecture and Design**]: Wireless communication

Keywords

Spectrum sensing; Crowdsourcing; Smartphone; TV whitespaces

1. INTRODUCTION

Smartphones and tablets are among the most common devices that are carried around by individuals today. As the number of such devices exceed the count of the worldwide human population, a service that is enabled in these devices can truly achieve global reach.

This has led to mushrooming of many data-aggregation services implemented on them that take advantage of its scale and penetration. In this paper, we consider the possibility of implementing a low-cost RF spectrum sensing capability on this common platform, thereby unlocking significant new opportunities for citizen-contributed analytics of the RF spectrum.

Current RF spectrum sensing approaches: The ability to efficiently sense and infer spectrum occupancy is an important need in the evolving debate of spectrum availability. Many use cases exist today. Regulatory bodies across the world, such as FCC in the US and Ofcom in the UK, are exploring new policy regimes where dynamic spectrum sharing will play an increasingly central role. To ensure such decisions are grounded in reality, these organizations need widespread data to determine the efficacy of spectrum utilization. Similarly, if one is curious to learn whether prohibited wireless transmitters are operating in a certain region (for example, cellphones not in the airplane mode in a flying aircraft or in a sensitive facility), spectrum sensing can provide the answer. In particular, any kind of spectrum transmission policy enforcement rely on effective spectrum sensing at its core.

RF spectrum sensing has traditionally been done following a "cathedral" model, by using sophisticated and specialized hardware, e.g., high-end spectrum analyzers. This type of hardware is both expensive and cumbersome, and can only be operated by a few experts. Using such hardware, a few concerted efforts from researchers have led to significant spectrum measurements. Notable among them are the efforts of SharedSpectrum [14], the Spectrum Observatory project [8], and SpecNet [3]. While these measurement efforts can provide high quality and actionable data, the cost of hardware and training effort for operating these systems have limited their deployment to a selected few sites and locations.

Proposed approach in Snoopy: In this work, we envision an alternative solution where the capability of RF spectrum sensing is embedded in some popular off-the-shelf mobile devices, thus bringing spectrum sensing to the "bazaar" and opening it up to the masses. Such a solution can truly enable the creation of a widespread real-time spectrum observatory. In particular, we propose a measurement system called *Snoopy* (Spectrum knowledge out of pocket), which can turn those off-the-shelf smartphone devices into spectrum sensors to effectively perform spectrum monitoring functions.

The advantage of this bazaar-style spectrum sensing is obvious — many more users can easily deploy this service, thus allowing a greater reach of spectrum sensing activities. To realize this goal, our proposed solution - Snoopy utilizes emerging features that are available in many common WiFi NICs to collect energy samples for each WiFi subcarrier at a fine timescale (often referred to as WiFi spectrum scan). Drivers capable of exposing such spectral data exists for the Intel 5300 cards [5]. In addition, we have recently released an analogous driver for the Atheros 92xx and 93xx chipsets [19]. By attaching a RF frequency translator to this type of WiFi NICs, it is possible to turn this WiFi spectral scan feature into a wide-band spectrum sensing functionality (the exact bands that can be scanned depends on the precise frequency translator used). For our initial prototype, we use a slightly expensive RF frequency translator from prior work [13, 16]. Nevertheless, in discussion with various hardware vendors, it appears that relatively low-cost versions (< $50 [9] and likely far cheaper) are possible, especially if the focus is purely for receiving spectrum data, and not for transmitting.

While extolling the virtues of Snoopy, we hasten to add that such low cost hardware is not likely to achieve the same level of accuracy compared to those sophisticated spectrum analyzers. High-end spectrum analyzers like ThinkRF analyzer [17] usually have a much higher sampling rate (125MHz), thereby achieving a finer frequency granularity (< 1 KHz). Compared to the spectrum granularity of WiFi spectral scan in Snoopy ($\sim$ 312.5 KHz), the former can potentially achieve greater accuracy for detecting signal activity when combined with some well-known feature based detection algorithms [3, 11, 15]. Nevertheless, we show that some carefully designed statistics on the low-resolution spectrum can indeed be helpful in improving detection accuracy. These statistical features are widely present in many types of signals (e.g., TV, microphone, WiFi, WiMax) and thus generally applicable to feature detection techniques. In addition, we believe that the affordability of such hardware along with the simplicity of the mobile platform's software can make it a compelling sensing device, at least for researchers and hobbyists, thus leading to its wide adoption as a "quick-and-dirty" tool. This makes combining data from many diverse sources possible to ultimately achieve a significantly higher measurement accuracy.

Before delving into the design of Snoopy, we would like to point out that one recent effort [2] has also proposed the use of mobile devices for RF spectrum sensing. The solution is based on a different architecture that uses a RTL-SDR hardware (essentially a TV-dongle) to directly capture measurements at specific parts of a frequency band. While retaining many benefits of Snoopy, we believe that the granularity of WiFi spectral data available from common WiFi NICs are finer and richer than those available from common TV dongles, ultimately enabling Snoopy to achieve higher accuracy in estimating signal power and detecting different types of signals from spectrum measurements (e.g., TV broadcasts and microphones in the TV band in our experiment). Furthermore, a frequency translator can flexibly sense a wider band (30 MHz - 7.5GHz) than RTL-SDR (52 MHz - 2.2 GHz). Nevertheless, Snoopy suffers from a current limitation that it only works with WiFi radios based on above chipsets, which could either be built into smartphone devices or attached externally through their MicroUSB port. Unfortunately, none of them have exposed an external RF connector to interface with our frequency translator. Thus, in our proof-of-the-concept implementation, we use an OpenWrt router hosting a Atheros 9280 card to serve as mobile devices, which is connected to our translator via a RF cable (Figure 1).

Key Contributions: We had to address a number of technical challenges that form the key contributions of this work:

- We have designed and implemented a mobile device based spectrum sensing system – Snoopy. Snoopy leverages the spectrum sensing capabilities of off-the-shelf WiFi cards (Atheros chipsets 9280, 9271, etc.), while attaching them with a frequency translator to achieve a wide sensing range from 30 MHz - 7.5 GHz (§2).

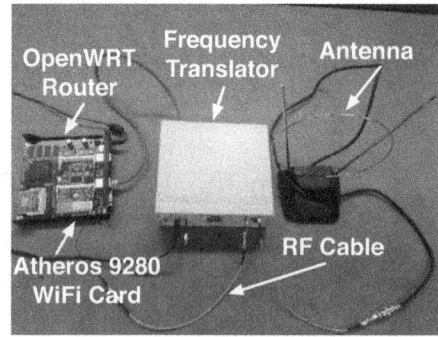

Figure 1: Snoopy sensing prototype.

- We have developed specific techniques that take the sub-carrier spectrum scan data from the WiFi cards to detect signals at low-power (up to -90dBm). Our experiments on the UHF television band show that Snoopy can detect primary signals (i.e., TV and microphone) at a wide range of power with an error rate of <15%. In addition, it can measure the power of TV channels with a median error of < 4dB in most cases (§3).
- We have ported the software module of Snoopy to an Android application that is readily available for Nexus Android tablets and phones to perform spectrum sensing in the 2.4 GHz WiFi band [20]. We have also released an open-source version of the WiFi spectral scan feature for the Android platform that can be utilized by the community [19]. We are currently working on the last hurdle of building a compatible hardware connector for our frequency translator to connect to off-the-shelf mobile devices, which will be discussed in §5.

2. SNOOPY DESIGN

In this section, we first highlight the major challenges in designing a low-cost mobile sensing platform. We then present Snoopy and its key techniques to overcome these challenges.

Design challenges: We have identified three major challenges in designing a mobile sensing platform for satisfying various aspects of performance requirement, i.e., delay, frequency range, and detection sensitivity.

- *Low-latency:* Snoopy aims to perform real-time spectrum analysis with a low latency on the order of milliseconds. This rules out many software based FFT options.
- *Frequency range:* Snoopy should be flexible enough to monitor a wide frequency range spanning UHF, cellular, ISM bands.
- *Detection sensitivity:* Prior work Airshark [12] focused on interference scenarios and is capable of detecting both WiFi and Non-WiFi interference signals at a relatively high power (> -80 dBm). In contrast, Snoopy aims to determine spectrum availability, thus having to use the same WiFi scanner in Airshark to detect primary signals (e.g., TV and microphones in the TV band) at a much lower power (up to -90dBm).

Snoopy consists of three major components — a) a frequency translator that translates incoming signals from any frequency band to the 2.4GHz WiFi band, b) a WiFi based mobile device that uses its built-in WiFi radio to collect spectrum samples (FFTs) of the translated signal, c) a software module that performs an enhanced signal detection algorithm on the spectrum scan data to detect different types of signals and measure their power. Figure 1 shows our sensing prototype, which uses a OpenWRT based router controlling an Atheros AR9280 card as the mobile device to conduct spectrum sensing.

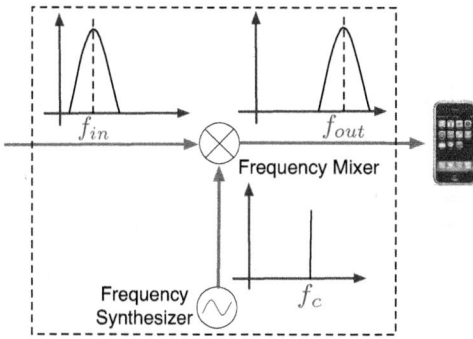

Figure 2: Simplified diagram of a RF frequency translator.

Operation	Latency
Capturing 20MHz spectrum by a WiFi radio	120us
Switching frequency bands by a translator	1ms
Signal detection for each TV channel by a router	10ms

Table 1: Approximate latency of different operations in Snoopy.

Signal Types	Spectrum Features
TV v.s. Noise	Power, Fourier Transformation coefficients
Microphone v.s. Noise	Power, 75th quartile FFT, Fourier Transformation coefficients
TV v.s. Microphone	75th quartile FFT

Table 2: Features used by Snoopy to classify different types of signals in the TV band.

Frequency translator: Figure 2 shows a simplified diagram to illustrate the operation of a RF frequency translator. A translator leverages two major hardware components for frequency translation, i.e., frequency synthesizer and frequency mixer. The frequency synthesizer is able to generate a carrier signal (sine waves) at any specified frequency f_c. This signal is taken by the frequency mixer, which combines it with the input RF signal at f_{in} to generate an output signal at a center frequency of f_{out}. Here $f_{out} = f_{in} + f_c$. By tuning f_c, we can convert signals from any target band to the WiFi band (f_{out} = 2.4 GHz), thereby allowing the WiFi radio of a mobile device to collect spectrum data of these signals after frequency conversion [1].

In our current implementation, we use the *Wide Band Digital Radio* (WDR) to perform the frequency translation function. This platform has been used in prior work [13, 16] to translate 2.4 GHz WiFi signals to the 600 MHz television band to enable TV whitespace communications. Similar platforms have been reported in prior work such as WhiteFi [4]. There are two unique advantages of our translator platform. First, it can translate signals from a wide frequency range of 30MHz – 7.5GHz, thus allowing Snoopy to monitor a variety of licensed and unlicensed bands including land mobile, radio navigation, television, cellular, satellite, and so on. In addition, its frequency synthesizer incurs very low latency ($\approx$1ms) in switching across frequencies (f_c), thus allowing Snoopy to fast sweep across a wide range of spectrum. The WDR uses an Ethernet connection to receive configuration information about f_c, and leverages RF cables to send and receive wireless signals.

Spectrum sensing on WiFi cards: After translating a target frequency band to the WiFi band, Snoopy leverages the off-the-shelf WiFi radio of mobile devices to generate its spectrum. Our current prototype is built on Atheros AR9280 AGN cards and leverages the driver module developed in prior work Airshark [12] to extract spectrum samples. Each spectrum sample comprises the power of 64 sub-carriers (FFTs) over a 20MHz WiFi channel, with each FFT representing the power over a 312.5KHz band (20MHz/64). Since these FFT samples are generated by the WiFi hardware, it incurs a very low latency (120us) for producing a 20MHz spectrum. Nevertheless, we find it can take much longer time ($\approx$20ms) to switch to a different WiFi channel. Given the much lower latency (1ms) of the translator in switching frequencies, we decide to fixed the operating channel of the WiFi card (at 2437MHz), but only changing the carrier frequency f_c of the translator. Table 1 summarizes the latency of different operations performed by Snoopy.

Using WiFi cards to determine TV whitespaces: Prior work such as Airshark [12] has used the aforementioned WiFi radio ca-

pabilities to detect non-WiFi activity. In this paper, we motivate the use of these capabilities for determining spectrum availability, with TV whitespaces as an example. Compared to detecting non-WiFi activity, this task is much more challenging due to the need to detect weak primary signals.

To demonstrate this challenge, we used Snoopy and a high-end spectrum analyzer [17] to capture the spectrum of a digital TV signal and a microphone signal at two different powers. We will give more details about this spectrum analyzer in Section 3. Figure 3 shows that the spectra captured by these devices have a similar shape for each signal type. Nevertheless, the spectrum collected by Snoopy is much more coarse-grained, with a noisy and fluctuating power distribution in most of its FFT bins. This is because its wider FFT bins can aggregate more noise and the frequency translator also introduces non-negligible distortion. This jagged spectrum leads to far less distinguishable peak features (i.e., TV pilot and microphone tones), which in turn cause higher errors of state-of-the-art feature detection algorithms [7, 11, 15] (Section 3). To improve the accuracy of primary signal detection, we have developed an enhanced feature detection algorithm that leverages some statistical feature inherent in the low resolution spectrum as described next.

Signal detection based on statistical spectrum features: Our proposed detection algorithm leverages two statistics of the low-resolution spectrum as additional features to improve detection accuracy. These statistics are 1) 75th quartile of FFTs, 2) coefficients of Discrete Fourier Transformation performed on the collected spectrum (FFT over FFT). These features are motivated by the distinct power distribution in the spectrum of primary signals from that of noise. Specifically, Feature 1 is based on the fact that a microphone signal has most of its power concentrated on its audio tones (2 – 3 FFT bins), whereas a TV signal and noise have a relatively even power distribution across the entire 6MHz TV channel (Figure 3(b) 3(d)). Thus, the 75th quartile of FFTs for a microphone signal is much *higher* than TV and noise, thus serving an effective feature to detect microphone signals.

The motivation behind Feature 2 is that the envelop of a spectrum can be represented by the sum of sinusoid waves at different frequencies, by *performing Discrete Fourier Transformation again*. The coefficients of Fourier Transformation are the weights used to combine different sinusoid waves to reconstruct the original spectral shape. Thus, the distribution of these coefficients can comprehensively capture all the shape related features, including the bandwidth and peak features used in prior approaches [7, 11, 15], along with many subtle ones such as the notch in the center of a WiFi spectrum. To make best of this generalized shape feature, we leverage some state-of-the-art classifiers to assign different weights on

---

[1]A typical RF translator can convert signals in both directions, even though we use it for reception alone.

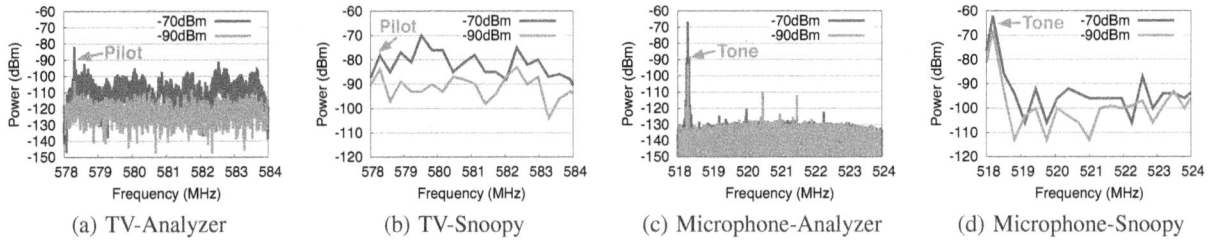

Figure 3: Spectrum of primary signals captured at different powers by a high-end spectrum analyzer (at 0.238KHz resolution) and Snoopy (at 312.5KHz resolution). The left 2 graphs show the TV spectrum and the right 2 graphs show the microphone spectrum.

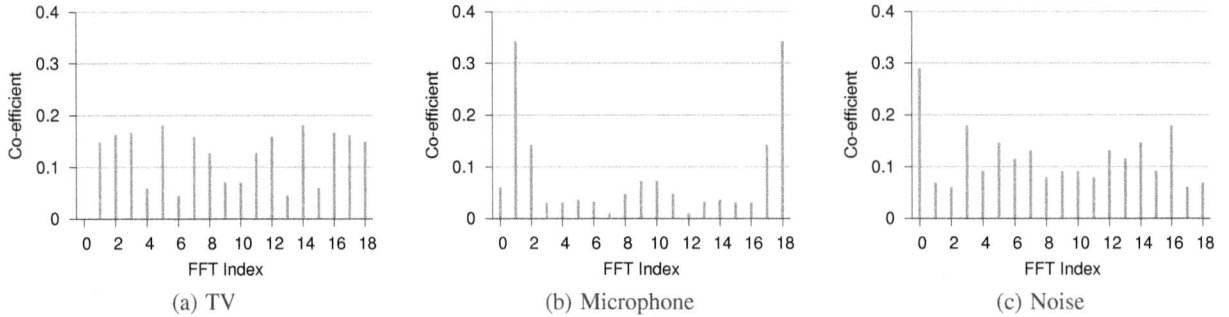

Figure 4: Coefficients of Discrete Fourier Transformation applied to the spectrum of different types of signals.

these coefficients, thereby relying more on those distinct features for signal classification.

To demonstrate the efficacy of this statistical feature, Figure 4 shows the co-efficient values after applying Fourier Transformation on the spectrum of different signals captured by Snoopy as shown in Figure 3(b) 3(d). For each spectrum, we have normalized the spectral FFTs to their median value before applying Fourier Transformation to make these coefficients invariant to the signal power. The x axis shows the index of coefficients and a higher order index indicates a sine wave at higher frequency. We note the distribution of co-coefficients differ for each type of signals. The microphone signal has a large high-order coefficient due to its narrow tone. In contrast, the noise has a larger zero-order coefficient because it has a random fluctuating pattern. Finally, a TV signal has similar co-efficients because of its trapezoid spectrum with jagged envelop. These distinct distributions suggest that the coefficients of Fourier Transformation applied to the spectrum envelop can indeed be a useful feature for classifying different types of signals.

Putting it all together, our detection procedure proceeds as follows. a) We start by using Airshark module to collect spectrum from 20 MHz spectral blocks in the UHF band. The collected spectrum is divided according to 6MHz TV channels. b) We then scale these FFTs by their median value to gather spectral features that are invariant of signal power. c) The 75th quartile of the scaled FFTs is calculated. d) We also apply Fourier Transformation on these FFTs to obtain their transformation coefficients. d) We feed these spectral statistics along with channel power to a classifier for determining the type of signals in each TV channel (i.e., TV, MIC). We have experimented with two state-of-the-art classifiers, i.e., support vector machine (SVM) and multinomial logistic regression. Their performance is compared in Section 3. Table 2 summarizes the useful features for classifying different types of signals.

Implementation: Since existing smartphones do not expose any RF connector of their WiFi radios, our proof-of-the-concept imple-

mentation uses a Alix3D2 router board equipped with an Atheros 9280 AGN card as the mobile device. The WiFi card is connected to a WDR radio via a RF cable as shown in Figure 1. The router uses an Ethernet connection to configure the WDR to measure a specific frequency band. It receives spectrum samples from the WiFi card to detect primary signals (e.g., TV and microphone) while measuring their power. The entire sensing procedure is implemented in $\approx$1000 lines of Python code. It incurs a low latency of about 10ms for processing each 6MHz TV channel. We have also released a smartphone based platform [20] that can provide spectrum sensing capabilities for the WiFi band.

3. EVALUATION

In this section, we evaluate the performance of Snoopy in performing two popular spectrum sensing functions in the UHF television band — a) detecting primary signals, b) measuring channel power. We perform a head-to-head comparison between Snoopy and a high-end spectrum analyzer to understand the performance limitation of our platform. Overall, we find Snoopy has a reasonably low error rate of <15% in detecting different types of primary signals at up to -90dBm, which is <10% higher than the spectrum analyzer. In addition, it achieves a median error of < 4dB in measuring the power for most of the TV channels.

Dataset: We collected two datasets of spectrum measurements from the Snoopy platform and a high-end spectrum analyzer from ThinkRF Inc [17]. The ThinkRF analyzer has a 8MHz capture bandwidth with 32768 FFTs, thus producing spectrums at a very fine-grained resolution of 238Hz (see Figure 3(a) 3(c)). This device was used in prior work [15] to accurately detect TV signals at up to -114dBm. Thus, we used this analyzer to establish ground-truth results by connecting both devices to a single antenna through a RF splitter. We have measured 8 UHF channels that are distributed across the entire UHF band. Using the ThinkRF analyzer, we have detected TV signals in 4 channels and microphone signals in 2 other

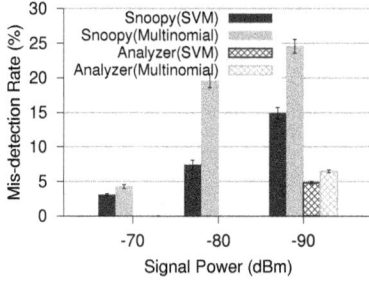

Figure 5: Error rate in detecting primary signals by Snoopy and the ThinkRF analyzer. Error bars show standard deviation.

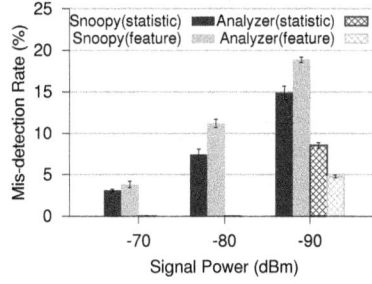

Figure 6: Error rate in detecting primary signals using different spectral features. Error bars show standard deviation.

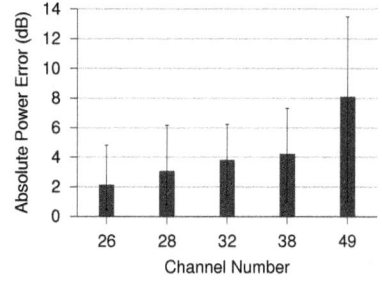

Figure 7: Median error in measuring the power of TV channels by Snoopy. Error bars show 10th and 90th quartile error.

Detected Ground truth	TV	Microphone	Noise
TV	97.7%	1.3%	1%
Microphone	8.4%	91.5%	0.1%
Noise	12.3%	0.5%	87.2%

Table 3: Accuracy of Snoopy in detecting different types of signals with a SVM classifier.

channels. We then used a RF attenuator to attenuate these primary signals (TV and MICs) for constructing spectrum traces at a wide range of power (from -90dBm to -50dBm at 10dB step).

Methodology: To evaluate the accuracy of detecting primary signals, we applied 5-fold cross validation on each dataset by using 80% spectrum samples to train different signal classifiers, and tested them on the remaining data. To quantify the performance of measuring channel power, we compared the power readings that are calculated from spectrum measurements collected by Snoopy and ThinkRF.

Metrics: We applied two metrics to evaluate Snoopy. The mis-detection rate is the ratio of the number of mis-detected spectrum measurements divided by the total number of measurements. The absolute power error is the difference in power readings between Snoopy and the ThinkRF analyzer.

Accuracy in detecting primary signals with two platforms: We start by comparing the performance of Snoopy and the ThinkRF analyzer for detecting two types of primary signals in the UHF band (i.e., TV and microphone). Figure 5 shows the error rates of detecting primary signals at various powers by the two platforms using different classifiers (i.e., support vector machine and multinomial logistic regression). We first observe that when using a SVM classifier, Snoopy can achieve low error rates of 3 – 15% for detecting primary signals at up to -90dBm. These error rates are only 3 – 10% higher than that of the commercial spectrum analyzer using the same classifier. We also note that SVM classifier performs constantly better than multinomial regression classifier for both platforms at all the signal powers. This is because multinomial regression assumes a linear trend between the classification probability and the signal power, which can be violated by these measurements. Thus, we choose SVM classifier in our final implementation. The error rates increase at a lower signal power because the weak signals have a less distinct spectral features from noise spikes. On the other hand, we have found very low error rates (<0.1%) of both platforms in detecting strong primary signals at above -70dBm. We omit this result for the sake of brevity.

Table 3 shows the error rate of Snoopy in classifying different types of signals from its entire dataset using a SVM classifier – Snoopy (SVM). We observe that most of the errors come from mis-classification between TV signals and noise because they both have a flat spectrum shape that renders the feature of 75th quartile of FFT to be less effective. In addition, the higher noise floor and distortion introduced by the Snoopy platform can lead to a jagged TV spectrum that has similar Fourier Transform coefficients to noise. We will discuss possible approaches to enhancing detection accuracy in Section 5.

Accuracy in detecting primary signals based on different features: We next quantify the performance gain of incorporating statistical features into signal detection. Figure 6 shows the mis-detection rates of the two platforms based on peak features alone and the additional use of statistical spectral features using a SVM classifier. These peak features have been used in several state-of-the-art spectrum sensing systems [11,15]. We observe that for spectrum collected by Snoopy, statistical features can reduce the error rate by 1 – 5% at different signal powers. Our further analysis shows that the 75-quartile of FFTs is effective in detecting microphone signals, while the Fourier Transform coefficients are beneficial for distinguishing both types of primary signals from noise. For the ThinkRF analyzer, however, the statistical features can introduce slightly higher errors. The reason is that the peak features in its high-resolution spectrum are clear enough for signal detection (Figure 3), and the noise fluctuation can sometimes disturb spectral statistics introducing unnecessary errors. Thus, our proposed statistical features, while beneficial for classifying coarse-grained spectrum, should be replaced with simple peak features for analyzing high-resolution spectrum. Dynamically adapting these features based on the spectral resolution is part of our future work.

Accuracy in measuring channel power: We next evaluate the accuracy of Snoopy in measuring the power of different TV channels. This function is useful for estimating the quality of an operation channel and debugging interference related issues. Figure 7 shows the median error of Snoopy in measuring the power of 4 channels with TV signals and 1 channel with noise (28). We note a low median error of <4dB and a 90th quartile error of <8dB for most of the channels except channel 49. The higher error for channel 49 comes from the significant *distortion* introduced by the frequency translator in the upper UHF band. We find this uneven frequency response is quite common for wide-band frequency translators. Fortunately, we observe all the power offsets have a low variation of < 6dB (error bar). This allows us to use the median error to effectively calibrate these power readings in Snoopy. Such a median error can be obtained by collecting a few measurements in each channel through an one-time calibration effort.

4. RELATED WORK

Spectrum utilization: Several measurement studies have identified spectrum under-utilization in different frequency bands. Authors in [18] have monitored a wide spectrum range (20MHz-6GHz) from three countries and reported that 54% of spectrum is never used and 26% is partially in use. Other work [10,21] has found substantial spectrum resources in TV whitespaces, and proposed different spectrum database designs to better predict vacant TV spectrum. Nevertheless, most of the prior work is based on measurements at a very few locations. V-Scope [15] is a recent measurement system that leverages spectrum sensors mounted on public vehicles to collect wide-area measurements for enhancing TV whitespace databases. Snoopy can significantly extend the measurement coverage of these prior systems by bringing spectrum sensing to the masses of mobile devices.

Sensing platforms: Prior measurement systems [3, 11, 15] use commercial spectrum analyzers to collect measurements, while extracting spectral features to detect different types of primary signals. Unlike these systems, Snoopy can potentially transform off-the-shelf smartphones to spectrum sensors by using a frequency translator to extend the sensing capability of their WiFi radios. While similar translation devices have been reported in prior systems [4,11], they are primarily used to enable TV whitespaces communications by translating signals of commercial WiFi radios.

A recent system [2] has explored the similar concept of spectrum sensing on smartphones by connecting them with a TV dongle (RTL-SDR). While the two systems share the same goal, their approaches differ significantly. Snoopy relies on the WiFi radio of smartphone devices to collect spectrum measurements, and leverages a frequency translator to extend its sensing range. Such an approach has a much higher sampling rate (40MHz) in the WiFi radio compared to the RTL-SDR (2.4MHz), thus providing a much wider instantaneous bandwidth (40MHz) for detecting wide-band signals. The statistical spectral features exploited by Snoopy can also be beneficial to RTL-SDR for signal detection. Nevertheless, Snoopy is not readily applicable to existing smartphone devices, which do not expose a RF connector from their WiFi radio to connect to our current translator hardware. Despite these tradeoffs, we believe the two platforms can potentially be complementary and operate together in a mobile device to meet different requirements in speed, power and accuracy in near future.

5. DISCUSSION AND FUTURE WORK

Improving measurement accuracy: Our current system relies on a single mobile device to detect primary signals. In future, we intend to enhance detection accuracy by aggregating spectrum measurements from multiple devices operating at different locations. A key challenge of this collaborative sensing is to calibrate measurement discrepancy among these sensing devices, which can be caused by hardware variation along with different position and orientation of mobile devices. We are also trying to exploit the temporal diversity of measurements collected at different time to improve accuracy. Finally, since a frequency translator can introduce varying power offset at different frequencies, it would be useful to design some self-calibration procedures to compensate this error. One possible solution is to use the WiFi radio to send a calibration signal, and measure its received power after frequency translation.

Integration with off-the-shelf mobile devices: Existing smartphones and tablets do not expose a compatible RF connector (SMA) for their built-in WiFi radio to connect to a frequency translator. To make Snoopy readily deployable, we intend to develop a new version of frequency translators that uses a MicroUSB connector to interface with smartphone devices. One alternative solution could be to attach a small WiFi repeater to the output port of the translator, which wirelessly relays the converted signals to mobile devices.

Bootstrapping users: Collecting measurements on mobile devices can reduce battery life, while uploading them to a centralized monitoring infrastructure might consume cellular data usage. To attract users to participate in this measurement campaign, we envision spectrum owners or regulation enforcement entities (e.g., whitespace spectrum database operators [6]) to purchase spectrum measurements from mobile phone users at a price based on the value of the measurements they collect. Such a business model has already been adopted in some startup companies [1] to crowd-source sensor data from mobile phones for retail store analytics and city planning.

Acknowledgments

We thank Siva Ramasubramanian and Brett Panosh for their help in data collection. We are grateful to the anonymous reviewers whose comments helped bring the paper to its final form. The authors are supported in part by the US National Science Foundation through awards CNS-1040648, CNS-0916955, CNS-0855201, CNS-0747177, CNS-1064944, CNS-1059306, CNS-1345293, CNS-1343363, CNS-1258290, and CNS-1405667.

6. REFERENCES

[1] Placemeter. http://placemeter.com/.

[2] A. Nika et al. Towards Commoditized Real-time Spectrum Monitoring. In *HotWireless*, 2014.

[3] A. P. Iyer et al. SpecNet: spectrum sensing sans frontiÃÍres. In *NSDI*, 2011.

[4] P. Bahl, R. Chandra, T. Moscibroda, R. Murty, and M. Welsh. White space networking with wi-fi like connectivity. In *SIGCOMM*, 2009.

[5] D. Halperin et al. Tool release: Gathering 802.11n traces with channel state information. *ACM SIGCOMM CCR*, Jan. 2011.

[6] FCC. Unlicensed operation in the TV Broadcast Bands, Second Memorandum Opinion and Order, 2010.

[7] H. Kim and K. G. Shin. In-band spectrum sensing in cognitive radio networks: energy detection or feature detection? In *MobiCom*, 2008.

[8] Microsoft. Spectrum Observatory. http://observatory.microsoftspectrum.com/.

[9] Mini-Circuits, Inc. Datasheet of ZX05-U432H Frequency Translator. http://www.minicircuits.com/pdfs/ZX05-U432H+.pdf.

[10] R. Murty et al. SenseLess: A Database-Driven White Spaces Network. *IEEE Transactions on Mobile Computing*, 2012.

[11] S. Narlanka et al. A Hardware Platform for Utilizing TV Bands With a Wi-Fi Radio. In *LANMAN*, 2007.

[12] S. Rayanchu et al. Airshark: Detecting non-WiFi RF Devices Using Commodity WiFi Hardware. In *IMC*, 2011.

[13] S. Sen et al. A Dual Technology Femto Cell Architecture for Robust Communication using Whitespaces. In *DySpan*, 2012.

[14] Shared Spectrum Company. Spectrum Sensing Toolbox. http://observatory.microsoftspectrum.com/.

[15] T. Zhang et al. A Vehicle-based Measurement Framework for Enhancing Whitespace Spectrum Databases. In *MobiCom*, 2014.

[16] T. Zhang et al. Enhancing Vehicular Internet Connectivity Using Whitespaces, Heterogeneity, and a Scouting Radio. In *MobiSys*, 2014.

[17] ThinkRF. The ThinkRF Wireless Signals Intelligence Platform. http://www.thinkrf.com/.

[18] V. Kone. On the Feasibility of Effective Opportunistic Spectrum Access. In *IMC*, 2010.

[19] WiNGS Lab. Spectral Scan Patches. http://comments.gmane.org/gmane.linux.kernel.wireless.general/122777.

[20] WiNGS Lab. WiSense - Realtime Wireless Diagnostic Tool in Your Pocket. http://research.cs.wisc.edu/wings/projects/wisense/.

[21] X. Ying, J. Zhang, L. Yan, G. Zhang, M. Chen, and R. Chandra. Exploring indoor white spaces in metropolises. In *MobiCom*, 2013.

60GHz Mobile Imaging Radar

Yibo Zhu, Yanzi Zhu, Zengbin Zhang, Ben Y. Zhao, Haitao Zheng
University of California, Santa Barbara, CA 93106, USA
{yibo, yanzi, zengbin, ravenben, htzheng}@cs.ucsb.edu

Keywords

60GHz wireless, imaging, mobile system

1. INTRODUCTION

Mobile computing is undergoing a significant shift right before our eyes. In the past, the user was the center of the mobile network, and her movements determined the operational properties of the mobile network. But this is changing with the arrival of autonomous mobile agents for a variety of applications. Today, semi-autonomous drones are carrying out military missions in lieu of manned-flights, while vacuum robots search for dirt in our homes. In the near future, intelligent cars will be fully in control of delivering us to our destinations, and first responder robots will be first on scene to find and rescue victims in disasters [15].

One of the critical challenges limiting the growth of these autonomous devices is the lack of accurate sensing systems, *e.g.* a mobile imaging radar system that captures the position, shape and surface material of nearby objects. These devices often operate in less than ideal sensing environments: at night or in dark rooms, or while moving at moderate speeds. Yet the desired level of accuracy is very high, and errors in sensing can produce dire consequences. For example, Google's self-driving cars are reported to use maps with inch-level precisions [18], while devices that assist the visually impaired must have errors smaller than 10cm [5, 11].

These constraints dramatically reduce the set of possible solutions. Traditional imaging systems rely on visible light imaging using cameras and object recognition. Unfortunately, they perform poorly in dark or low-light conditions, and lack the precision desired by these applications. Another approach relies on specialized hardware such as large lens radar for accurate signal detection and processing. But these devices are neither portable nor cost-effective for commodity devices. Finally, acoustic solutions have been used successfully for sensing over very short distances [24], but are easily disrupted by background noise and fail over longer distances.

60GHz Imaging Radar. An intriguing and still unexplored solution is a digital imaging radar system using reflective properties of narrow beamforming wireless links. A radar system using high frequency RF signals (e.g. 60GHz) has a number of key advantages over existing alternatives. First, 60GHz links are directional and highly focused, making them relatively immune to interference from environmental factors. Second, 60GHz beams exhibit good reflective properties, and work reliably regardless of lighting conditions under most indoor or outdoor conditions. Finally, 60GHz radios are relatively inexpensive, and small enough to be included in today's smartphones and tablets.

In this paper, we present early results in our efforts to design and evaluate a digital imaging radar system using reflections from 60GHz wireless beams. Such a system faces a fundamental challenge, that it is technically infeasible to build an accurate imaging radar using wireless hardware on a static mobile device. A simple rule from imaging radar theory [7], defined by eq.(1), holds for accuracy (radar resolution) and antenna size (aperture). For smartphone-sized antennas, even the most high frequency radios (5-120GHz) can produce resolutions no better than 1 meter, clearly insufficient for our needs.

$$Resolution = wavelength \times distance/aperture \quad (1)$$

Virtual Antenna Arrays. We take an alternative approach, by using user mobility to emulate a virtual antenna array with large aperture. Our design includes the user's mobile device as a receiver, with a decoupled transmitter either embedded in the infrastructure or "deployed" on-demand by the user (*e.g.* dropped by a drone). By taking measurements of the same reflected signal at multiple locations, we can emulate the signals received by different elements of a large antenna array. In addition, we can further improve the resolution of our "virtual antenna" using 60GHz transmissions. Since 60GHz has a carrier wavelength of 5mm (12x shorter than WiFi and cellular), using 60GHz links means a user can obtain fine-grain resolution with just small movements in the measurement area.

In the remainder of this paper, we present Nightcrawler, a 60GHz-based mobile radar system that leverages user mobility to emulate a large-aperture antenna array. We describe details of our design, including mechanisms for object detection, object imaging, and controlling precision. We present experimental results on a real 60GHz testbed, and show that we can achieve high precision (~1 cm) imaging with as little user movement as half a meter.

Our work is a promising first step in the development of high precision, wireless imaging radar systems. Initial results show promising accuracy, as well as added potential for using loss profiles to infer the *surface material* on detected objects. Ongoing work focuses on tolerating location errors for the transmitter, as well as extending imaging to multiple objects.

2. CONVENTIONAL VS. MOBILE RADAR

Before presenting our design of a high precision radar system, we need to first describe the principle and hardware requirements behind conventional imaging radars. We will then explain the differences between personal mobile radar systems and conventional imaging radar systems, and the challenges that arise as a result.

Traditional Radar Imaging. Imaging radars detect the presence, position, and shape of an object by emitting directional RF signals and capturing/analyzing the portion of signal reflected by the object. Specifically, a radar estimates its distance to the object by measuring the round trip time of the reflected signal, either directly using a highly precise clock, or indirectly by transmitting frequency modulation (FM) pulses and measuring the frequency offset of the reflected signal [7]. The radar also uses highly directional RF signals to "scan" the object. Because the signals reflected from the object and its nearby spaces carry different signal strengths, the radar can identify the object's position and shape with high precision. Finally, high-end radars can identify object material using dispersion analysis, where they emit RF signals at various carrier frequencies and collect reflection results. Since different materials have different reflection profiles across frequencies, one can estimate material type by analyzing reflection results.

Overall, traditional imaging radars have strong requirements on radio hardware, *e.g.* they require specialized FM circuits and highly directional dish antennas. These are easily met for applications where radar size and cost are not an issue, such as military radar systems or radio telescopes for use in astronomy.

Why Mobile Radar Imaging is Hard. Our goal in this paper is to design radar imaging systems to enable commodity mobile devices to recognize their surrounding environments. This is highly challenging, due to tight constraints on radio size, functionality and cost. *First*, the small form factor of mobile devices puts a hard limit on both antenna size (which determines aperture) and signal directionality. As shown by the Radar Theory in eq. (1), the small antenna size severely limits the maximum imaging resolution. For smartphone-sized antennas ($2.5cm$ aperture), the maximum imaging resolution for an object of $10m$ away is $1m$ using $120GHz$ transmissions or $24m$ at $5GHz$. *Second,* today's mobile devices are not equipped with FM pulse circuits, which are required for distance estimation by traditional radar imaging. Adding such circuits would significantly increase costs for budget-conscious mobile radio chipsets. Similar cost constraints prohibit the inclusion of hardware solutions to perform dispersion analysis for material detection or clock-based distance computation[1].

3. 60GHZ IMAGING RADAR

To overcome challenges of size and cost in mobile devices, we propose to leverage human mobility to extend the reach of a single mobile antenna. We proposes *Nightcrawler*, a mobile radar imaging system using commodity 60GHz networking chipsets[2]. Using commodity chipsets, Nightcrawler performs object imaging using just signal measurements, and improves imaging resolution far beyond the theoretical limit defined by eq. (1). It achieves this by leveraging *user mobility* and unique RF propagation properties of *60GHz transmissions*. This section describes our core ideas and sets the context for details of our prototype in §4.

Leveraging 60GHz. Today's mobile devices are equipped with multiple wireless interfaces, *e.g.* cellular, WiFi, Bluetooth, and 60GHz radio [22]. We implement Nightcrawler using 60GHz radios because its unique propagation properties present three significant advantages for our application.

- 60GHz has a carrier wavelength of 5mm, more than 12x shorter than WiFi and cellular. According to eq. (1), the required antenna aperture for 60GHz is at least 12x smaller than WiFi/cellular for the same imaging resolution.

- 60GHz's short wavelength also makes its propagation much more stable/predictable. With minimum multi-path effects, signal strength remains stable over time, and is strongly correlated with propagation distance. This increases the robustness of our imaging design. For example, our imaging system can easily distinguish between a line-of-sight signal and a reflected signal that traveled over a longer distance, and use this fact to detect the presence of objects in local neighborhood.

- The object reflection profile is more stable at 60GHz. For example, the signal reflection loss has strong correlation with the object material. This enables Nightcrawler to narrow down the material type using signal strength measurements.

Mobility enabled virtual antenna array. Nightcrawler exploits the fact that as a user moves, her mobile device can take signal measurements at multiple locations, emulating a virtual antenna array whose antenna aperture is significantly larger[3]. This enables highly directional signal reception by a mobile device similar to those required by conventional radar imaging, and overcomes the limitation imposed by the size of mobile devices.

User mobility also increases the system's detection range and ability to detect surface curvature of objects. Surfaces with different curvatures reflect the signal to different directions in the space. Measuring reflections from different locations helps the radar capture the curvature of each of the object's multiple faces.

Decoupling transmitter and receiver. Given the small size of mobile devices, any mobile radar system cannot rely on just a single device to serve as both transmitter and receiver. Our design for a mobile radar system involves the primary mobile device, which acts as a receiver, and a decoupled transmitter, which can be either infrastructure-based, or a separate mobile device.

For example, an imaging system to assist the visually impaired may include an app on the user's smartphone, which coordinates with one or more transmitters embedded in the walls or ceiling. In contrast, an autonomous device (e.g. first responder robots) can "deploy" a secondary transmitter device.

Once deployed (or periodically for infrastructure devices), the transmitter (TX) sends 60GHz beacons that reflect off of nearby objects[4]. Each beacon includes the angle of transmission, and if possible the transmitter's location. Users hold a mobile device equipped with a 60GHz receiver (RX), and move in pedestrian speeds. Each RX periodically scans[5] and records signal strengths for beacons across different directions. Nightcrawler processes these data on the fly to identify, locate and image objects in the local area.

4. Nightcrawler: A FIRST LOOK

We now describe our initial design. Seen in Figure 1, a primary device (RX) and decoupled transmitter (TX) start from "sensing" mode to identify the presence of any object. Upon detection, they switch to "imaging" mode to build a physical map of the object(s). We assume that the RX knows its relative position from the TX.

4.1 Object Sensing

Nightcrawler devices sense objects using the bootstrapping procedure defined by IEEE 802.11ad, the standard for 60GHz trans-

---

[1]To measure round trip time accurately, *i.e.* with $1cm$ accuracy, the clock precision must be at least $0.033ns$, which is extremely hard to realize on smartphones and laptops.

[2]Low-cost 60GHz chipsets are available today on the mass market, *e.g.* WiloCity chipsets cost $37.5 and has a $23m$ range [22, 26].

[3]Aperture of virtual array is equal to distance traveled by the user.
[4]The beacon transmitters rotate their beam direction periodically to cover multiple objects or larger objects.
[5]Today's 60GHz antenna arrays can adjust beam direction every $50us$. So each RX can scan multiple directions in real time.

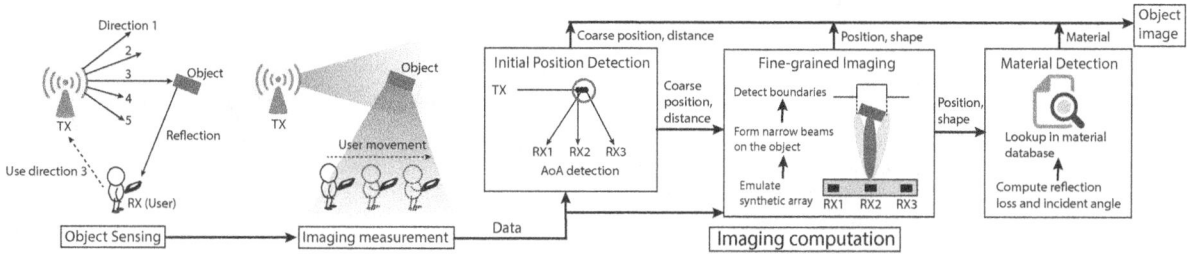

Figure 1: The high-level overview of the Nightcrawler radar imaging system.

missions [2]. The TX operates in the directional mode, steers its beam to different directions, *e.g.* in sectors of $3°$ in width, and embeds the direction in the signal. Operating in the omni-directional mode, the RX measures RSS and reports a list of TX beam directions where RSS exceeds the noise level[6]. The RX then identifies and removes from the list the set of TX beam directions whose transmissions did not experience any reflection. The remaining list of directions, if any, are those where the transmission was reflected, implying that at least one object exists in the local neighborhood.

To identify TX beam directions that did not experience reflection, the RX uses simple geometry to locate a set of candidate LoS beam directions based on the relative position of TX and RX and their antenna radiation patterns. It then validates each candidate direction by comparing its RSS to the model-predicted value without any reflection. If a direction gets (partially) reflected, its RSS will be lower than the model-predicted value due to longer propagation path and possible reflection loss.

4.2 Object Imaging

After detecting the presence of objects, Nightcrawler devices enter the "imaging" mode. Intuitively, Nightcrawler should use the above collection of "reflected TX beam directions" to drive imaging. That is, the TX focuses its transmissions on these directions (by rotating its beam repeatedly across them in a round-robin fashion) while the RX locates and images object(s) in each direction. To improve imaging efficiency, it is desirable to identify a subset of the directions that cover all the potential objects. In our preliminary work, we leave this optimization to future work and simply assume that the reflected direction set only has a single direction.

With this in mind, our following description on Nightcrawler assumes that during imaging, the TX focuses its beam on the targeted direction and transmits the same beacon signal repeatedly. The RX, while moving, operates in the directional mode and steers its beam around to capture signals at each measurement location. This is done using the *antenna alignment* procedure defined by 802.11ad – the RX steers its beam across various directions and reports the direction with the strongest RSS. Once the movement distance is sufficient, the RX executes the imaging algorithm on the measurement data to locate and image the object.

The Nightcrawler imaging algorithm includes three steps: (1) *coarse position estimation*, (2) *fine-grained imaging*, and (3) *material detection*. We now describe them in more details.

4.2.1 Coarse Position Estimation

Nightcrawler first estimates the object's relative position and distance to the RX. This narrows down the search space for the next step, which applies a more sophisticated approach to perform detailed imaging. The RX estimates the object position by extracting the angle of arrival (AoA) of the beacon signal. At each measure-

---

[6]This step is slightly different from 802.11ad where the RX only reports the direction with the strongest RSS.

ment location, Nightcrawler derives the AoA as the strongest receive beam direction. Since the TX embeds the beam direction in each beacon signal, the RX can estimate the object position as the intersection of the TX beam direction and the AoA.

Ideally, Nightcrawler should identify object position reliably from measurements at a single location. In practice, AoA detection can be noisy due to hardware artifacts, imperfect reflection from uneven surface, and the fact that each TX beam is not narrow enough. For example, our testbed results show that when using a TX beam of $10°$ beamwidth, the noise in AoA estimation can lead to up to $1m$ position error when the object is $6m$ away from the RX.

Nightcrawler overcomes this challenge by performing "majority vote" on measurements collected at multiple locations. Specifically, Nightcrawler considers data from N locations, each producing an estimated object position. It then identifies a cluster of $[N/2] + 1$ positions with the minimum MSE among themselves, and computes the center of the cluster, *i.e.* the position with the minimum MSE to all the positions, as the final object position. This solution, while simple, can effectively improve the positioning accuracy. Our testbed results in §5 show that with $N=9$, the position error in the above example reduces from $1m$ to below $10cm$.

4.2.2 Fine-grained Imaging

This step derives the precise position and shape of the object by implementing a large aperture virtual antenna array from aggregating signal measurements at different locations. Specifically, Nightcrawler identifies the object shape by detecting its boundaries as well as surface curvature, *i.e.* flat, convex or concave.

Detecting Object Boundaries. Inspired by airplane radars that implement synthetic aperture radar (SAR) to detect object size [7], Nightcrawler uses a small and moving RX antenna to emulate elements of a large array. The resulting synthetic array has a very narrow beam pattern and can identify signals at fine-grained directions. Thus the RX can observe a sharp decrease in RSS along the object boundaries, and locate these boundaries with errors bounded by the (very narrow) beamwidth of the synthetic array.

A key component of our design is how to aggregate measured signals across locations to emulate the large array. This is done by "reverse-engineering" the process of a phased array focusing its beam. Specifically, let the estimated object position in the previous step be X_0. Nightcrawler picks a set of reflection "focus points" near X_0 as the potential boundary positions. Given a target image resolution r, any two neighboring focus points should be within a distance of $r/2$. For each focus point, Nightcrawler applies a *focus* process to derive the RSS of signals reflected by the small area of width r around the given focus point. This is done by first shifting the phase of signals collected at each measurement location by its distance to the focus point and then summing up all the signals across locations. After applying this on all the focus points, the RX obtains a reflected RSS map along the object itself. The object boundaries are the two focus points where the RSS drops sharply.

Note that Nightcrawler emulates the large array without synchronizing TX and RX. This is because all the measurements are done by a single receiver RX. As long as the TX sends the same beacon signal (per TX beam direction) during imaging, the RX can eliminate any phase offset caused by differences in measurement time.

Inferring Surface Curvature. Nightcrawler recognizes the object's surface curvature based on a simple intuition – signals reflected by a flat surface display a standard sector shape that can be reconstructed based on the antenna pattern and the signal propagation distance, while signals reflected by a convex (concave) surface display a wider (narrower) sector shape. Driven by this intuition, Nightcrawler infers the surface curvature by the RX constructing the beam pattern of the received signal. Specifically, as the RX moves, it measures the RSS at different segment of the signal beam and aggregates them to build the received beam pattern.

While our first design of Nightcrawler identifies the type of surface curvature (flat/convex/concave), our ultimate goal is to discover detailed surface feature such as the curvature radius. This requires more sophisticated models on 60GHz signal reflection, which we leave to future work.

4.2.3 Material Detection

Finally, Nightcrawler infers the object material based on the RSS loss due to reflection. At 60GHz, the reflection loss correlates strongly with the material type and the incident angle. Existing measurements have built a comprehensive database on 60GHz reflection loss, covering 38 common materials and different incident angles [14]. Our own measurements on five different materials also align with existing findings.

The key element is to accurately determine the amount of RSS loss due to reflection and the reflection incident angle. To derive the reflection loss, Nightcrawler first computes the signal propagation distance (TX → object → RX) and applies the Friis free-space model to derive RSS without any reflection loss (RSS^*). It then subtracts from RSS^* the measured RSS value to derive the reflection loss. Computing the signal incident angle is easy given the relative position between TX and RX.

4.3 Imaging Overhead vs. Precision

Nightcrawler's imaging computation overhead is low. Our MATLAB implementation finishes in less than $15ms$ for all test cases. We expect that a good native C implementation on mobile devices should be comparable if not faster. Therefore, Nightcrawler's overall overhead and delay are dominated by its signal measurements.

Nightcrawler's measurement delay depends on user walking distance. The further the user walks, the larger the imaging delay. But user walking distance also directly affects the size (or aperture) of the synthetic array and thus imaging resolution. So there exists a tradeoff between imaging response time and resolution.

We should also pay attention to measurement frequency, *i.e.* the number of measurement locations for a given walk distance. Ideally we should minimize measurement frequency to save energy. However, since the number of measurement locations maps to the number of elements in the synthetic array, we need sufficient number of measurements to remove array artifacts such as side lobes. Our initial analysis suggests that for pedestrian speeds up to $1m/s$, the measurement frequency of 1 per $40ms$ (or 1 per $4cm$ movement) is sufficient to produce a high-quality synthetic array.

5. INITIAL FEASIBILITY STUDY

We perform initial evaluation on Nightcrawler using both testbed measurements and system simulations. We use commercial off-the-shelf 60GHz radios to conduct microbenchmark experiments on

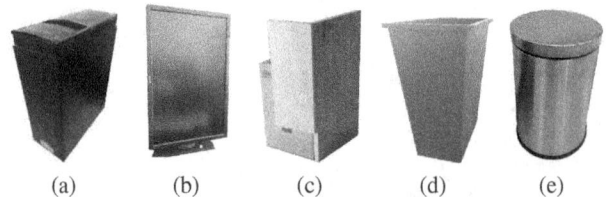

Figure 2: 5 different objects used in our testbed measurements.

Nightcrawler, and to evaluate its end-to-end imaging performance under simple scenarios. We also run simulations to identify potential performance of Nightcrawler under general scenarios.

5.1 Testbed Measurements

Our testbed consists of two HXI Gigalink 6451 60GHz radios, one as the transmitter (TX) and the other as the mobile receiver (RX). Compared with an ideal Nightcrawler system, the testbed has two hardware limitations. *First*, since there is no suitable 60GHz steerable antenna array on the market, we emulate beam steering by setting a horn antenna on a mechanical rotator and adjusting its beam direction in units of $0.5°$. This can provide accurate results because 60GHz signal strength is largely determined by directionality and signal patterns of the main beam lobe, and our horn antenna's main lobe pattern closely aligns with that of a 10x10 array [26]. Since 60GHz propagation is stable over time (verified by others [12, 25] and our own measurements), at each location the RX can accurately measure RSS across different directions despite its slower beam steering speed. *Second*, the HXI radio reports RSS without any phase information, so in the computation we set the phase of signals measured at all RX locations to the same value. This makes it difficult to perfectly focus the beam during boundary detection, and can potentially degrade the imaging performance.

Our experiments consider a simple scenario of object recognition. We place an object in the middle of a room. The TX is $2m$ away from the object and emits a fixed beam towards the object. The RX starts from an arbitrary location in the room, and as she walks around, Nightcrawler identifies the object position and shape. We test five objects with different size and surface curvature, shown in Figure 2. We also experiment with pedestrian users as objects. By default, the user walks $45cm$ and performs one RSS measurements every $1cm$. As mentioned earlier, we assume the RX knows her relative position to the TX.

Position & Distance Accuracy. We first examine the accuracy of the coarse position detection described in §4.2.1 with $N = 9$. Table 1 lists errors in estimated position, distance and surface orientation when the RX is $3m$ away from the object. Across the five different objects, the position offset ranges between $1.7cm$ and $12cm$ while the distance offset is even smaller ($< 0.4cm$)[7]. This translates into less than $1°$ orientation error. Furthermore, we observe that the accuracy is higher for objects with planar surfaces, compared to those with convex surfaces. This is because signals reflected by convex surfaces become more scattered compared with planar surfaces, leading to larger variance in estimated reflection points. We also repeat the experiments by varying the RX to object distance between $2m$ and $6m$ and obtain similar results. Overall, Nightcrawler achieves an 10cm-level accuracy which should be sufficient for most mobile applications.

Boundary Detection Performance. Table 2 lists the performance of Nightcrawler's boundary detection in terms of the off-

---

[7]The distance offset is the projection of the position offset along the line of object→RX.

Objects in Figure 2	Position offset	Distance offset	Orientation error
(a) Desktop (Metal)	1.7cm	0.1cm	0.2°
(b) Monitor (Plastic)	6.9cm	0.1cm	0.6°
(c) Board (Wood)	5.5cm	0.1cm	0.5°
(d) Convex Box (Plastic)	12.3cm	0.4cm	1.0°
(e) Cylinder (Metal)	10.4cm	0.3cm	/

Table 1: Performance of Nightcrawler's Position Estimation.

Object Width (Material)	Object-RX distance		
	3.5m	4.8m	6m
24.5cm (Metal)	1.5cm	3.0cm	3.0cm
26cm (Plastic)	4.0cm	5.0cm	4.5cm
22cm (Wood)	4.0cm	4.0cm	4.5cm

Table 2: Accuracy of Nightcrawler's boundary detection, in terms of the offset in detected object width.

set in object width. Here we compare three objects of similar size but different materials. Despite the lack of phase information, Nightcrawler already achieves $5cm$ and less error in object width estimation. Later in §5.2 our simulation result confirms that when phase information is available, the error in width detection is cut in half. In addition, we also observe that the width accuracy for the metal object is slightly better than those of the plastic and wooden objects. This is mostly because the smoother metal surface enables stronger signal reflection. Finally, we see that the closer the user (RX) is to the object, the more accurate the imaging. This aligns with the Radar Theory in eq.(1) as well as the common expectation on imaging – as a user gets closer, she sees the object more clearly.

End-to-end Imaging Results. By combining the results on position, boundary and surface curvature, Nightcrawler can produce a detailed map of the object surface. Figure 3 plots the imaging result of a metal object at different user-to-object distances. The thin blue dash line in Figure 3(b)(c) marks the true object shape, while the thick black line is the imaging result of a surface. We see that Nightcrawler can identify the physical surface almost perfectly. Notice that in this example the user's walking path is in parallel with the TX transmitting direction. This is not necessary. In our experiments, the walking direction does not affect the results much as long as the path is relatively straight. It is the user-to-object distance and walking distance that matter the most.

Tracking Moving Pedestrian. We also evaluate Nightcrawler when the object is a moving pedestrian traveling at 1m/s towards the RX (see Figure 4). Here the RX user travels $0.8m$ in total during imaging. In the first $0.4m$, the RX detects a human $2.3m$ away (with a $6.9cm$ offset); in the second $0.4m$, the human is $1.5m$ away and the position offset reduces to $0.27cm$. This preliminary result shows that Nightcrawler can potentially identify and track moving pedestrian using signal reflection.

5.2 Simulation Results

We perform simulations to examine Nightcrawler in absence of testbed artifacts. Our simulation reproduces the scenario in Figure 3(a). The metal object surface is represented by dense discrete points and does not introduce any reflection loss. The propagation follows the Friis free-space model for 60GHz transmissions.

Is phase information beneficial? Figure 5(a) compares the imaging error on object width with and without phase information. The simulation results without phase information are similar to our testbed measurements. When phase information is available, Nightcrawler's error reduces by 50%. Therefore, a practical implementation of Nightcrawler can benefit significantly from obtaining signal phase information from the underlying 60GHz chipset.

Impact of array elements. Due to cost and sizing limits, mobile 60GHz chipsets are likely to use small number of array elements, *e.g.* the Wilocity chipset has a 2×8 array, which leads to weaker directivity. We compare Nightcrawler performance using different arrays with 2×8, 6 × 6 and 10 × 10 elements, and found that they perform similarly if signal phase information is available.

Impact of object size. We examine a broad range of object sizes between $5cm$ and $1m$, and vary the user walk distance between $0.5m$ and $1m$. Our results, omitted for brevity, show that the absolute imaging error is independent of the object width, as long as the object is not too wide so that its edges fall out of the scope of a single 60GHz beam. To cover these objects, Nightcrawler needs to rotate the TX beam during the measurement process (see §4.1).

How far should users walk? Nightcrawler seeks to achieve high-resolution imaging by a user walking a short distance. Figure 5(b) plots the required walk distance vs. the resulting width error under different user-to-object distances. Since the virtual antenna aperture scales with the walk distance, it is no surprise that the further the user walks, the higher the accuracy is. A practical implementation of Nightcrawler should exploit this tradeoff to achieve robust, efficient and high responsive object imaging. Overall, the result is very encouraging – even when the user is $8m$ away from the object, traveling just $1m$ can achieve $2cm$ imaging accuracy.

6. RELATED WORK

Sonar and Radar Systems. Sonar and radar systems are deployed to detect the speed and position of moving targets, or to measure the contour of the terrain [21]. Portable radar devices are available to detect concealed weapons in airports [10]. To provide high-resolution imaging, these systems require either special hardware, *e.g.* X-Ray or lenses too large for mobile devices [23]. Different from existing works, Nightcrawler achieves high-resolution imaging using 60GHz networking chipsets that are being integrated into today's mobile devices. While our design is inspired by the SAR method used by airplane radars [7], our key contributions include the novel application of the SAR concept to mobile 60GHz scenarios and the detailed system design and experimentation.

Camera-based Systems. Many have developed image-based object recognition systems [9, 16, 17]. These methods, however, cannot accurately measure distance between user and object. Google's Project Tango [1] detects an object's position and shape using three bulky cameras, including an infrared depth camera and a fish-eye lens. Yet it only works in environments with good visibility, and cannot reliably identify object material. Nightcrawler overcomes these challenges by leveraging 60GHz networking chipsets in mobile devices. We show that reflections of 60GHz signals can reveal key physical properties of the object surface even without any light.

RF-based Systems. Recent works on WiFi-based systems [4, 3, 8, 19] target coarse-grained human or object tracking, *e.g.* detecting relative movement of human body, recognizing predefined user gestures [20], or scanning tumors or weapons on human body [6]. Nightcrawler differs from these works by performing detailed imaging on objects, including its shape, surface curvature and material. Nightcrawler chooses 60GHz as the underlying RF technology because compared with WiFi, 60GHz offers much smaller wavelength and much more stable (and predictable) signal propagation. This largely boosts the imaging performance, enabling Nightcrawler to identify, locate and image various objects with high precision.

7. OPEN CHALLENGES

We present the initial design of Nightcrawler, a 60GHz imaging radar that locates and images objects in local neighborhood.

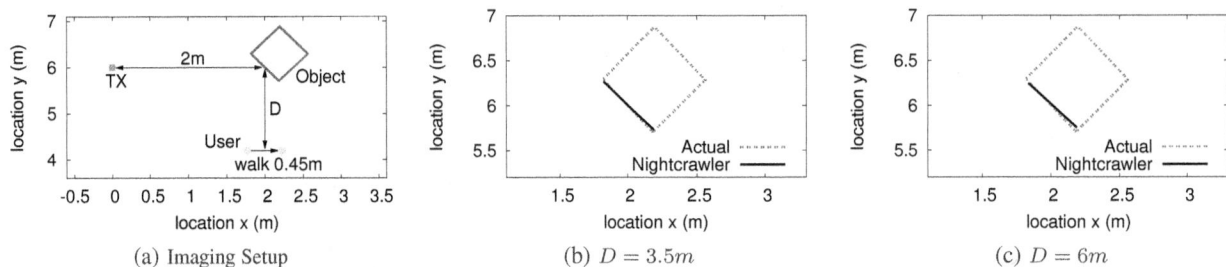

(a) Imaging Setup   (b) $D = 3.5m$ (c) $D = 6m$

Figure 3: Testbed results: Nightcrawler images a metal object when varying the user-to-object distance D.

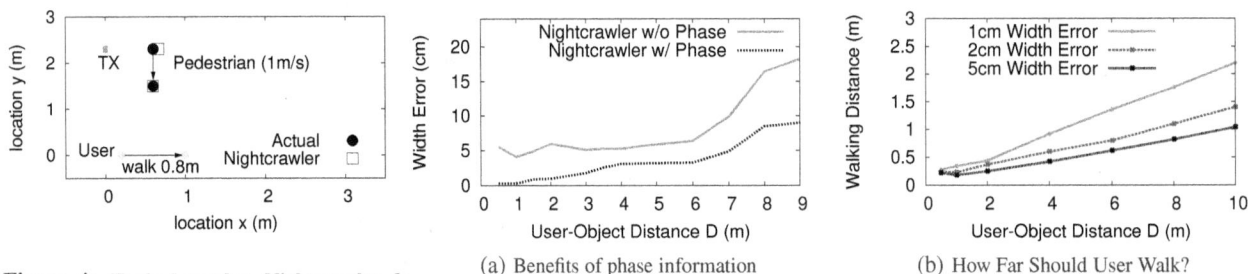

Figure 4: Testbed results: Nightcrawler detects and locates a pedestrian user.

(a) Benefits of phase information   (b) How Far Should User Walk?

Figure 5: Simulated Nightcrawler radar imaging results for a metal object.

Our initial evaluation under simple scenarios confirms the feasibility of Nightcrawler in performing high-resolution object imaging. As ongoing work, we seek to improve and further experiment on Nightcrawler. In particular, we consider the following directions.

Handling device positioning errors. Our basic design assumes the RX knows her position to the TX and tracks her position precisely when walking. In practice, any positioning error translates into inaccurate phase shifts during boundary detection (see §4.2.2), and can largely affect imaging performance. Addressing this challenge requires mechanisms for reliable ranging and motion tracking (*e.g.*[13]) and those for identifying and correcting phase errors.

Identifying curvature details. We take a data-driven approach to extract surface curvature details – collect a large measurement on different surfaces, identify key features and then develop efficient classification algorithms.

Imaging multiple objects. When multiple objects are in range, Nightcrawler can potentially image them simultaneously. Doing so requires the RX to first narrow down a subset of "reflected TX beam directions" that cover all the objects (see §4.2.2). The TX then beams along these subset of directions during the imaging measurement process.

8. REFERENCES

[1] https://www.google.com/atap/projecttango.
[2] IEEE 802.11 Task Group AD. http://www.ieee802.org/11/Reports/tgad_update.htm.
[3] ADIB, F., KABELAC, Z., KATABI, D., AND MILLER, R. C. 3d tracking via body radio reflections. In *Proc. of NSDI* (2014).
[4] ADIB, F., AND KATABI, D. See through walls with wi-fi! In *Proc. of SIGCOMM* (2013).
[5] AL-SALIHI, N. Precise positioning in real-time for visually impaired people using navigation satellites. *International Journal of Engineering and Technology 12*, 2 (2010), 83–89.
[6] BHARADIA, D., JOSHI, K. R., AND KATTI, S. Full duplex backscatter. In *Proc. of HotNets* (2013).
[7] CHAN, Y. K., AND KOO, V. C. An introduction to synthetic aperture radar (sar). *Progress in Electromagnetics Research B* (2008), 27–60.
[8] CHETTY, K., ET AL. Through-the-wall sensing of personnel using passive bistatic wifi radar at standoff distances. *Trans. on Geoscience and Remote Sensing 50*, 4 (2012).

[9] DAVISON, A. J., ET AL. Monoslam: Real-time single camera slam. *Trans. on Pattern Analysis and Machine Intelligence* (2007).
[10] FEDERICI, J. F., ET AL. Thz standoff detection and imaging of explosives and weapons. In *Proc. of Defense and Security* (2005).
[11] GUERRERO, L. A., VASQUEZ, F., AND OCHOA, S. F. An indoor navigation system for the visually impaired. *Sensors 12* (2012).
[12] HALPERIN, D., ET AL. Augmenting data center networks with multi-gigabit wireless links. In *Proc. of SIGCOMM* (2011).
[13] KUMAR, S., ET AL. Accurate indoor localization with zero start-up cost. In *Proc. of MobiCom* (2014).
[14] LANGEN, B., LOBER, G., AND HERZIG, W. Reflection and transmission behavior of building materials at 60ghz. In *Proc. of PIMRC* (1994).
[15] LINE, M. Robot rescue: First-responders of the future. FoxNews.com, June 2014.
[16] LOWE, D. G. Object recognition from local scale-invariant features. In *Proc. of ICCV* (1999).
[17] LOWE, D. G. Distinctive image features from scale-invariant keypoints. *International journal of computer vision 60*, 2 (2004).
[18] MADRIGAL, A. C. The trick that makes google's self-driving cars work. The Atlantic, May 2014.
[19] MOSTOFI, Y. Cooperative wireless-based obstacle/object mapping and see-through capabilities in robotic networks. *IEEE TMC* (2013).
[20] PU, Q., ET AL. Whole-home gesture recognition using wireless signals. In *Proc. of MobiCom* (2013).
[21] SCHEER, J. A., AND MELVIN, W. L. *Principles of modern radar*. The Institution of Engineering and Technology, 2013.
[22] SHANKLAND, S. Wilocity: 2015 phones getting extra-fast 802.11ad networking. CNet, February 2014.
[23] TSENG, T.-F., ET AL. High-resolution 3-dimensional radar imaging based on a few-cycle w-band photonic millimeter-wave pulse generator. In *Optical Fiber Communication Conference* (2013).
[24] ZHANG, Z., ET AL. Swordfight: Enabling a new class of phone-to-phone action games on commodity phones. In *Proc. of MobiSys* (2012).
[25] ZHOU, X., ET AL. Mirror mirror on the ceiling: Flexible wireless links for data centers. In *Proc. of SIGCOMM* (2012).
[26] ZHU, Y., ET AL. Demystifying 60ghz outdoor picocells. In *Proc. of MobiCom* (2014).

Indoor Person Identification through Footstep Induced Structural Vibration

Shijia Pan
Electrical and Computer
Engineering
Carnegie Mellon University
shijiapan@cmu.edu

Ningning Wang
Electrical and Computer
Engineering
Carnegie Mellon University
ningningwang@cmu.edu

Yuqiu Qian
Computer Science and
Technology
University of Science and
Technology of China
qyq79@mail.ustc.edu.cn

Irem Velibeyoglu
Civil and Environmental
Engineering
Carnegie Mellon University
ivelibey@andrew.cmu.edu

Hae Young Noh
Civil and Environmental
Engineering
Carnegie Mellon University
noh@cmu.edu

Pei Zhang
Electrical and Computer
Engineering
Carnegie Mellon University
peizhang@cmu.edu

ABSTRACT

Person identification is crucial in various smart building applications, including customer behavior analysis, patient monitoring, etc. Prior works on person identification mainly focused on access control related applications. They achieve identification by sensing certain biometrics with specific sensors. However, these methods and apparatuses can be intrusive and not scalable because of instrumentation and sensing limitations.

In this paper, we introduce our indoor person identification system that utilizes footstep induced structural vibration. Because structural vibration can be measured without interrupting human activities, our system is suitable for many ubiquitous sensing applications. Our system senses floor vibration and detects the signal induced by footsteps. Then the system extracts features from the signals that represent characteristics of each person's gait pattern. With the extracted features, the system conducts hierarchical classification at an individual step level and then at a trace (i.e., collection of consecutive steps) level. Our system achieves over 83% identification accuracy on average. Furthermore, when the application requires different levels of accuracy, our system can adjust confidence level threshold to discard uncertain traces. For example, at a threshold that allows only most certain 50% traces for classification, the identification accuracy increases to 96.5%.

Categories and Subject Descriptors

H.4 [**Information Systems Applications**]: General

Keywords

person identification; structural vibration; indirect sensing

1. INTRODUCTION

Many smart building applications require indoor person identification for personalized tracking/monitoring/services. For example, in nursing home, identifying monitored patients and tracking individual activity range helps nurses understand patients' conditions. Similarly, such person identification information can also be used in smart stores/malls. By identifying customers visiting different stores in a shopping mall, different purchasing patterns can be recognized for more efficient advertisement arrangements.

Various methods and apparatuses have been explored for person identification [5, 6, 7, 8, 9, 10, 11, 12, 14, 16, 17]. These methods and apparatuses specify biometrics (face, iris, finger print, hand geometry, gait, etc.) [5, 6, 7, 8, 9, 10, 11, 12, 14, 16, 17] and sensing technologies (vision, sound, force, etc.) [5, 6, 9, 7, 11, 12]. Some biometrics, such as iris [16], finger print [8] and hand geometry [14], achieve relatively high identification accuracy and are widely used for access control. However, they often require human interactions; hence, they are limited for ubiquitous smart building applications. Others, such as face [10, 17] and gait [5, 6, 7, 9, 11, 12], when used in surveillance applications, are difficult to get enough sensing resolution required for recognition from a distance [9]. Numerous sensing technologies have been explored and proven useful and efficient; nevertheless, these technologies have their limitations. Vision-based methods [9, 11] often require line-of-sight, their performance changes with lighting conditions. Also, high computational cost limits their applications. Likewise, sound-based methods [5, 7] might be limited by deployments at conversation sensitive area. Meanwhile, force-based methods [6, 12] utilize specialized floor tile sensors for footstep detection. In that sense, dense deployment and high installation cost are inevitable for such systems.

In this paper, we present a person identification system through footstep induced structural vibration. People walk differently; therefore, their footsteps result in unique structural vibrations. Our system measures such vibration, detects signals induced by footsteps, extracts features from these signals, and applies a hierarchical classifier to these features to identify each registered user. Due to better wave attenuation properties in solids, with proper amplification,

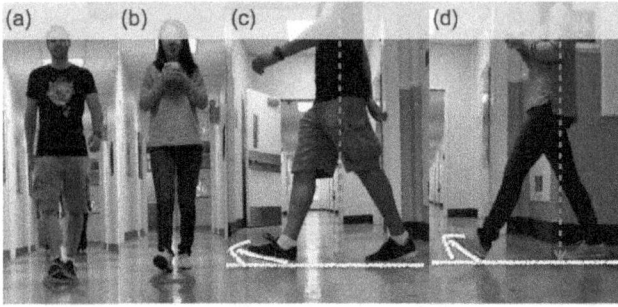

Figure 1: These photographs show two people walking with different gait patterns. (a) and (b) are their front views. They show differences in the distances between left and right feet of each person (indicated by blue double arrows). (c) and (d) are the side views of persons walking. They display the differences in the angles between the feet and the floor when the heels strike the floor (indicated by white arrows). They also show the center of gravity variation across different people (shown as green dotted arrows).

our system can detect individuals in a relatively large range. As a result, our system's sensing density is low compared to those force-based methods. Compared to vision-based and sound-based methods, our measurement suffers less interferences from obstacles that move around, since the vibration travels in structure. Furthermore, the installation of our system is non-intrusive: we deploy the geophone on the floor surface without damaging the structure. The major contributions of this work include:

- To the best of our knowledge, this is the first work that demonstrates footstep induced floor vibration can be used to identify people.

- We designed a hierarchical classification algorithm to identify people with high confidence level.

The rest of the sections in this paper is organized as following. In section 2, we first explain that people have unique footstep patterns. Then section 3 introduces our person identification system design, followed by its evaluation and results in section 4. Based on the evaluation on our current system, we analyzed the practical challenges in section 5. In the end, we provide summary and conclusions in section 6.

2. FOOTSTEP PATTERNS

Each person has a unique walking pattern due to many factors, including individual physical characteristics, the center of gravity position during the walk, the way feet contact the ground, etc. Figure 1 shows an example of how walking patterns vary across different people. The person appears in Figure 1 (a) and (c) is taller and heavier than the person in Figure 1 (b) and (d). In addition, the person in Figure 1 (a) has a narrower distance between left and right feet compared to the person in Figure 1 (b). In Figure 1 (c), the person walks with his center of gravity centered between front and back feet, while in Figure 1 (d) the person tends to lean back when she walks. Moreover, in Figure 1 (c), the person has a smaller foot-floor angle than the person in Figure 1 (d).

In this section, we discuss the uniqueness and consistency of the footstep induced floor vibration for each person. We

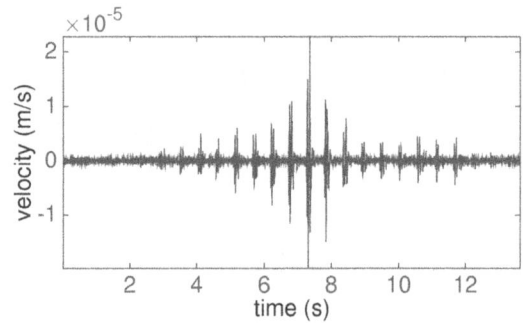

Figure 2: This plot shows floor vibration captured by a geophone when a person passes by it. The sensing range for this particular case is approximately 10m, which can be affected by various factors including floor type, shoe type, etc. Step events near the geophone have larger amplitudes and higher signal-to-noise ratios (SNR) than those further away.

define floor vibration signal induced by a footstep as a **step event (SE)**. We consider a sequence of SEs from a continuous walk as a **trace**. Figure 2 demonstrates a typical trace consisting of multiple SEs. We collected multiple traces of different people and compared their SEs.

Variation between SEs from different persons: SEs from different people show distinguishable variations in both time and frequency domains. Figure 3 shows SEs from three people. The left and right columns show corresponding time and frequency domain signals, respectively. In addition, red dotted lines and green dash-dot lines indicate locations of peaks and valleys in frequency domain respectively. As shown in Figure 3, the locations of peaks and valleys vary among different people, which can be used as features to identify them.

Consistency between SEs from the same person: On the other hand, SEs from one person bear resemblance between each other. Figure 4 shows three SEs from one trace. The left and right columns show corresponding time and frequency domain signals, respectively. Note that they span similar time duration with nearly identical velocity profiles in time domain. The frequency domain patterns (i.e., peaks and valleys, marked by dotted and dash-dot lines) are well-aligned across these three different SEs. Hence, these experiments demonstrate that a SE is a feasible metric for person identification.

3. SYSTEM DESIGN

We design our person identification system with three modules: sensing, footstep analysis, and decision making. Figure 5 displays components and relations of these modules. The sensing module monitors floor vibration induced by person walking. Then the footstep analysis module extracts SEs from sensor readings [13] and obtains features to represent characteristics of each SE. Once these features are extracted, the decision making module takes the features and runs through the hierarchical classifier, which includes step level and trace level classifications.

3.1 Sensing Hardware

The sensing module consists of three major parts: geophone, amplifier, and analog-to-digital converter (ADC). We set the geophone on the floor to capture floor vibration sig-

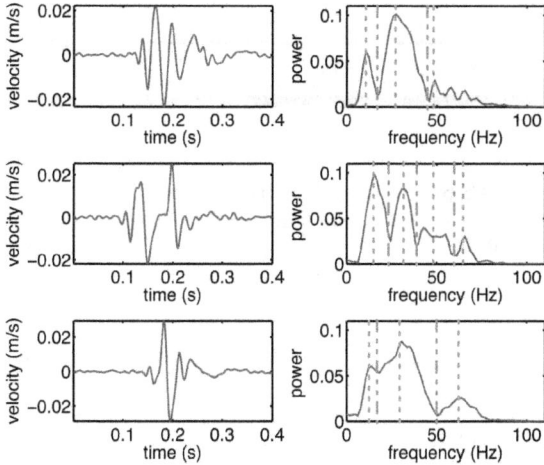

Figure 3: We compare SEs from three different people wearing soft-soled shoes. Each sub-figure in the left column displays a SE of each person in time domain, while the right column shows the corresponding frequency domain signal. Different gait patterns are illustrated as misalignment of peaks (marked by red dotted lines) and valleys (marked by green dash-dot lines) in frequency domain.

Figure 4: We compare SEs from the same person. Each sub-figure in the left column displays a SE of the person in time domain, while the right column shows the corresponding frequency domain signal. The aligned peaks (marked by red dotted lines) and valleys (marked by green dotted lines) in frequency domain indicate similarities between SEs. The waveforms in time domain also bear high resemblance.

nals. However, the raw signals are not large enough for SEs to be distinguishable from sensor noise after ADC. To improve the signal-to-noise ratio (SNR), we amplified the raw signal by connecting the geophone to an op-amp with an empirical amplification gain of 1000x, which allows approximately 10m sensing range for particular factors including floor type, shoe type, etc. We sampled at 25 kHz to capture the signal characteristics in a wide range of frequency.

3.2 Footstep Analysis

The key to person identification is to extract and analyze the characteristics of SEs. There are two major components in the footstep analysis module: 1) step extraction to obtain SEs and 2) feature extraction to characterize SEs.

3.2.1 Step Extraction

The floor vibration from one trace contains multiple SEs as shown in Figure 2. SEs contain a person's identity information, while the interval between SEs is mainly noise. Therefore, to identify people, we need to extract SEs from the entire vibration signal. We first model the noise as a Gaussian distribution and then apply an anomaly detection method to extract SEs [13]. The threshold value to detect a SE is determined by an allowable false alarm rate.

3.2.2 Feature Extraction

In order to extract features efficiently, we first select steps with high SNR in a trace, then we extract features of selected steps that represent characteristics of the footsteps.

Step Selection: The SEs in one trace have different SNR depending on the relative step location to the sensor. This leads to the variation on classification performance. In the process of data collection, we observed that on average the

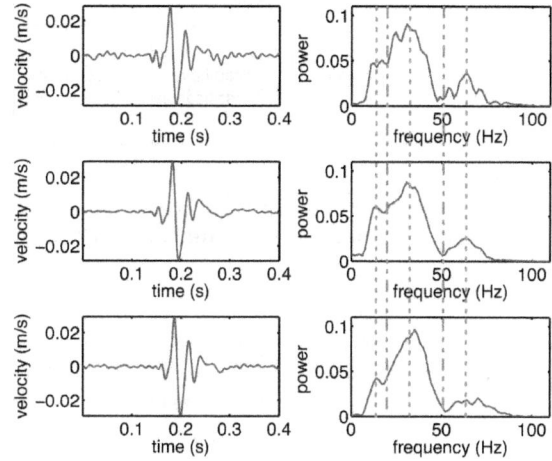

five steps closest to the sensor have highest SNR. Therefore, we extract five SEs closest to the sensor for classification.

Step Normalization: Once the SEs are selected, they are normalized to remove effects of the distance between the footstep location and the sensor. The SE closer to the sensor has a higher signal energy, which is calculated as the sum of squared signal values. Hence, we divide each SE by its signal energy to remove the distance effect, because such effect is irrelevant to the person's identity.

Step Features: After normalization, we compute features in both time and frequency domains to present different characteristics of SEs for each person. Time domain features include standard deviation, entropy, peak values, partial signal before and after the maximum peak, etc. In frequency domain, we use features including spectrum centroid, locations and amplitudes of peaks, power spectrum density, etc.

3.3 Decision Making

The person identification is modeled as a hierarchical classification problem in our system. A hierarchical classifier includes step level and trace level classifications. It increases the identification accuracy by utilizing the fact that steps from the same trace belong to the same person.

3.3.1 Step Level Classification

Each person's walking pattern is unique and consistent as discussed in Section 2. In that sense, we utilize SE features, which reflect such uniqueness, to conduct step level classification. Our system takes features of SEs from different people's traces to generate a classification model using Support Vector Machine (SVM), which maximizes the distance between data points and the separating hyper-plane [1]. The multi-class C-Support Vector Classifier (C-SVC) [2, 4] from LIBSVM library [3] is applied with the Radial

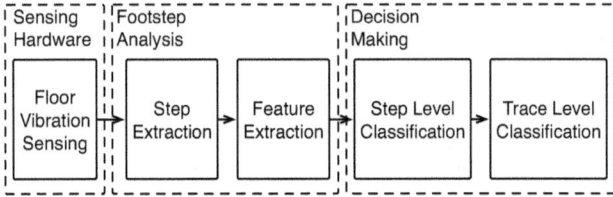

Figure 5: System overview. The system consists of three modules: sensing, footstep analysis, and decision making.

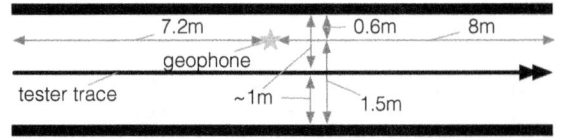

Figure 6: Experimental setup in a hallway. A geophone was installed near the wall (0.6m away), and human subjects were instructed to walk along the center line of the hallway.

Basis Function (RBF) kernel to perform the non-linear separation. The step level classification with LIBSVM gives out both the identification label and the confidence level as the result of the testing SE.

3.3.2 Trace Level Classification

We observed high resemblance on SEs from the same trace as discussed in section 3.2.1. By classifying identity at trace level, we reduce classification uncertainty by eliminating outlier SEs from the step level classification and enhance the overall identification accuracy of the system.

Remove Low Confidence Level SEs: Each SE classified by the C-SVC classifier obtains a identification label and a confidence level as the step level classification result. Since we are investigating the five steps with highest SNR from one trace (Section 3.3.1), we will have a confidence matrix $P_{s \times n}$, where n is the number of people to be classified, and s is the number of SEs selected from the trace. The identity of the SE with highest confidence level is selected to be the identity of the entire trace.

Confidence Level Threshold: Some of the applications tolerate unclassifiable (unknown) traces while requiring high accuracy for classified traces. For example, our person identification system can be deployed in the supermarket for customer behavior analysis or shelf location optimization. In such scenarios, it is acceptable that the system cannot identify some of the customers, but achieving high accuracy for the classified customers is important. In addition, when a new person's trace is detected, it is possible that SEs in the new trace are not similar to any of the footsteps in the database. In this case, the confidence levels of all steps in a trace are equally low, and the system needs to detect such situation. Therefore, we set a confidence level threshold $CL_{threshold}$ to determine whether the classification result of the trace is reliable enough for identification. We consider the trace to be identifiable when the confidence level is higher than the threshold. Otherwise, we consider the trace to be unclassifiable. The system can adjust this threshold to obtain different identification accuracy based on the application.

4. EVALUATION

In order to prove the feasibility of the methodology, we conducted an experiment on campus.

4.1 Experiment Setup

Figure 6 shows the location and setup of our experiment. The experiment is performed in a hallway at first floor of Building 19 at NASA AMES Research Park at the Carnegie Mellon University Silicon Valley campus. In the hallway we placed one geophone sensor 0.6m away from one of the wall.

An analog amplifier magnifies the signal from the geophone with an empirical gain of 1000X to improve the signal resolution as shown in Figure 7. We then recorded the data using the oscilloscope sampling at 25 kHz.

Five people with soft-soled shoes participated in data collection. During data collection, there is no noticeable noise created by other sources, such as floor vibration from other people walking, vending machine, and flushing toilets etc. Each person walked along the hallway back and forth 20 times. Each time a person walk sixteen meters with the sensor in the middle of the route. In that case, the sensor will not capture the starting and stopping steps of a person's consecutive steps in a trace. The person walking along the line displayed in Figure 6, which is approximately one meters from each sidewall of the hallway.

4.2 Result Analysis

To evaluate the performance of our method, we present the results of both step level and trace level classification. Due to the application we described earlier, we evaluate our system performance using classification accuracy, which is calculated as number of correct cases divided by number of all cases, as a gauge. We selected 80% of the data from each person as training data, and used the rest for testing. We conducted cross-validation to prevent biased results.

Figure 9 shows the step level (dotted red line) and the trace level (solid red line) classification accuracies with different $CL_{threshold}$. As the confidence level threshold increases, the accuracy approaches 100%. However, when all steps are classified, the identification accuracy is only 63%. This means that step level classification alone is not enough for our system.

The trace level classification accuracy shows a similar trend as the step level classification accuracy. However, the hierarchical classification algorithm significantly improves the accuracy to 83% when classifying all traces. The confusion matrix in Figure 8 indicates the percentage of traces of the ith person ($P_i, i = 1...5$) which are recognized as the jth person ($P_j, j = 1...5$). We can calculate the precision of each registered users from the matrix and the average is 84%.

While this may be enough for applications such as shopper identification (where coverage is more crucial than accuracy), it is not suitable for high accuracy applications (such as security related applications). In applications requiring high accuracy, the confidence level threshold needs to be raised. The solid green line with diamond markers in Figure 9 shows the classified traces (CT) percentage as the confidence level threshold increases. To illustrate the effects of thrsholding on the confidence level, we also present the classified steps (CS) percentage by thresholding on step level classification results using the dotted green line with dia-

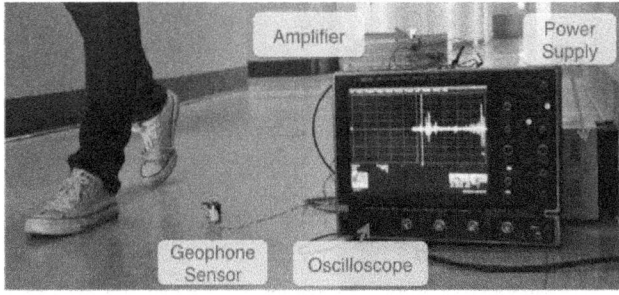

Figure 7: Data Collection Setup. The data was collected with our sensing hardware, which consists of geophone, amplifier, oscilloscope, and power supply, at the sampling rate of 25 kHz.

	P1	P2	P3	P4	P5
P1	1.00	0.00	0.00	0.00	0.00
P2	0.00	0.85	0.10	0.05	0.00
P3	0.10	0.00	0.70	0.15	0.05
P4	0.10	0.00	0.00	0.90	0.00
P5	0.05	0.05	0.20	0.00	0.70

Figure 8: The trace level classification confusion matrix indicates the percentage of traces of the ith person ($P_i, i = 1...5$, y axis) which are recognized as the jth person ($P_j, j = 1...5$, x axis) by our system.

mond markers. By comparing the CT and CS percentage, we observe similar decreasing trend. The CS percentage has steep drop between threshold 25% to 50% comparing to CT percentage, which confirms the efficiency of the trace level classification. We see that when roughly 50% percent of the traces are classified, the trace level classification accuracy is more than 96%. This suggests that the system can be tailored for various applications based on their accuracy requirements. We further observe that when the confidence level threshold increases, each person's identification accuracy increases with similar trend. This implies that the gait patterns in our database are well separable using the features and the classification method we designed.

5. PRACTICAL CHALLENGES

In this section, we analyze some of the practical challenges our system may encounter in practical scenarios. We further discuss what can be done to tackle these challenges.

5.1 Sensing Multiple People Simultaneously

In real world scenarios, more than one person may appear in the same sensing area simultaneously. The system need to count the number of people and identify each of them. Prior work has been done on determining the appearance of exactly one person or multiple people in the sensing area using neural network classifier [15]. We plan to focus on the people counting problem first. Knowing the number of people, we can apply blind source separation to separate mixed signals and then identify people from separated signals.

5.2 Increasing Number of Registered Users

When the number of registered users increases, we expect the identification accuracy to decrease because as the number of people increases, the probability of people in the database sharing similar foot-strike will increase. In addition, as the number of registered users (classes) increases, the multi-class SVM's computational complexity will also increase. In order to handle the increasing number of registered users, we plan to separate levels of features and combine other localization based information (such as stride length) to have an efficient multi-level identification method.

5.3 Impacts of Shoe Types

Different shoe types will cause floor vibrations with different signal characteristics, even if it is the same person walking with similar gaits. The signals of one person wearing different shoes need to be recognized and categorized as

the same person. This can be achieved by clustering traces with similar behavior patterns (activity range, stride length, etc.) as the same identity.

5.4 Impacts of Gait/Behavior Change

People's gaits/behaviors can be influenced by their mood, their load, and their shoe type (especially high heels). When the system handles behavior change, it can utilize space information, including a person's activity range, office seat arrangement, building floor plan, etc., to infer each person's different gait patterns.

5.5 Location-Based Characterization

By using multiple sensors to capture the same SE, the system can localize the SE. Similar to acoustic signals, the attenuation model of SE signals and the time difference of arrival (TDoA) between each sensor pair can be obtained. Once such information of SE signals is obtained, various existing localization algorithms can be applied. With SEs' location information, we can extract more features to characterize gait patterns. For example, we can infer a person's step strength from the attenuation model and use it as a feature. Furthermore, we can calculate a person's stride length and stride width, with the sequence of SE locations, which can also be used as features.

5.6 Environmental Influences

We observed that there are several noise sources in a building, which mainly fall into two categories: the appliances noise and human activities. The electrical appliances that contain motors (such as vending machine, coffee machine, and refrigerator) excite the floors of the building at certain frequencies. For example, most alternating current motors runs at 60 Hz. On the other hand, aperiodic human activities causing floor vibration include flushing toilet, shutting door, moving carts around, etc. The system should understand these noises and remove them accordingly. For example, the fixed-frequency noise can be removed by applying a band-stop filter. The system should recognize vibration signals from non-walking activities by analyzing signal envelop and frequency decomposition and then separating such signals from detected SEs.

5.7 Structural Influences

We notice that the physical floor structure around a sensor affects SE amplitude during the experiment. A sensor mounted on the floor directly above a beam detected less impulse oscillation compared to a sensor placed between two beams. Structural characteristics, such as material stiffness,

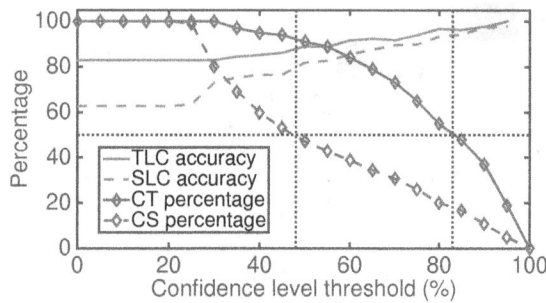

Figure 9: Person identification results under different confidence levels. We identify a person only when the predicted confidence level is over the threshold ($CL_{threshold}$). Red lines are identification accuracy. The red solid line is the trace level classification (TLC) accuracy, while the red dashed line is the step level classification (SLC) accuracy. The TLC accuracy is always higher than the SLC. The green lines with diamond markers are percentage of classified cases under the confidence level threshold. The green solid line is the classified traces (CT) percentage, while the green dashed line is the classified steps (CS) percentage. Thresholding on the confidence level improves classification accuracy by eliminating potential incorrect classification cases. The trace level classification improves from 83% to 96.5% when the system allows only 50% of the cases to be classified.

also affect vibration signals captured by the sensors. Signals captured from concrete structures are smaller than those from wood structures. Therefore, when we deploy systems at different locations or in different structures, we need to adjust the amplification level to achieve an ideal signal resolution. A form of automatic gain control can be used in our system to automatically adjust the analog amplification based on the measured signal amplitude.

6. CONCLUSION

In this work, we demonstrated the possibility to identify different people with their SEs. Our system achieves over 83% identification accuracy when identifying every trace for five people. In addition, trace level classification improves to 96.5% when the system focuses on the top 50% traces that are more confident. This adjustable confidence factor also allows the system designer to adjust our system based on the needs of the application. Our final goal is to improve the simplicity of the deploy-ability and maintainability of such systems in large-scale civil structures.

7. REFERENCES

[1] R. K. Begg, M. Palaniswami, and B. Owen. Support vector machines for automated gait classification. *Biomedical Engineering, IEEE Transactions on*, 52(5):828–838, 2005.

[2] B. E. Boser, I. M. Guyon, and V. N. Vapnik. A training algorithm for optimal margin classifiers. In *Proceedings of the fifth annual workshop on Computational learning theory*. ACM, 1992.

[3] C.-C. Chang and C.-J. Lin. Libsvm: a library for support vector machines. *ACM Transactions on Intelligent Systems and Technology (TIST)*, 2(3):27, 2011.

[4] C. Cortes and V. Vapnik. Support-vector networks. *Machine learning*, 20(3):273–297, 1995.

[5] C. DeLoney. Person identification and gender recognition from footstep sound using modulation analysis. 2008.

[6] S. Elrod and E. Shrader. Smart floor tiles/carpet for tracking movement in retail, industrial and other environments, Sept. 27 2005. US Patent App. 11/236,681.

[7] J. T. Geiger, M. Kneißl, B. W. Schuller, and G. Rigoll. Acoustic gait-based person identification using hidden markov models. In *Proceedings of the 2014 Workshop on Mapping Personality Traits Challenge and Workshop*, pages 25–30. ACM, 2014.

[8] A. K. Hrechak and J. A. McHugh. Automated fingerprint recognition using structural matching. *Pattern Recognition*, 23(8):893–904, 1990.

[9] A. Kale, A. Sundaresan, A. Rajagopalan, N. P. Cuntoor, A. K. Roy-Chowdhury, V. Kruger, and R. Chellappa. Identification of humans using gait. *Image Processing, IEEE Transactions on*, 13(9):1163–1173, 2004.

[10] A. Lanitis, C. J. Taylor, and T. F. Cootes. Automatic face identification system using flexible appearance models. *Image and vision computing*, 13(5):393–401, 1995.

[11] H. Ng, H.-L. Ton, W.-H. Tan, T. T.-V. Yap, P.-F. Chong, and J. Abdullah. Human identification based on extracted gait features. *International Journal of New Computer Architectures and their Applications (IJNCAA)*, 1(2):358–370, 2011.

[12] R. J. Orr and G. D. Abowd. The smart floor: a mechanism for natural user identification and tracking. In *CHI'00 extended abstracts on Human factors in computing systems*, pages 275–276. ACM, 2000.

[13] S. Pan, A. Bonde, J. Jing, L. Zhang, P. Zhang, and H. Y. Noh. Boes: building occupancy estimation system using sparse ambient vibration monitoring. In *SPIE Smart Structures and Materials+ Nondestructive Evaluation and Health Monitoring*, pages 90611O–90611O. International Society for Optics and Photonics, 2014.

[14] S. Pan, A. Chen, and P. Zhang. Securitas: user identification through rgb-nir camera pair on mobile devices. In *Proceedings of the Third ACM workshop on Security and privacy in smartphones & mobile devices*, pages 99–104. ACM, 2013.

[15] A. Subramanian, K. G. Mehrotra, C. K. Mohan, P. K. Varshney, and T. Damarla. Feature selection and occupancy classification using seismic sensors. In *Trends in Applied Intelligent Systems*, pages 605–614. Springer, 2010.

[16] C.-l. Tisse, L. Martin, L. Torres, et al. Person identification technique using human iris recognition. In *Proc. Vision Interface*, pages 294–299, 2002.

[17] M. A. Turk and A. P. Pentland. Face recognition using eigenfaces. In *Computer Vision and Pattern Recognition, 1991. Proceedings CVPR'91., IEEE Computer Society Conference on*, pages 586–591. IEEE, 1991.

Human Assisted Positioning Using Textual Signs

Bo Han*   Feng Qian*   Moo-Ryong Ra*
AT&T Labs – Research, Bedminster, New Jersey, USA
{bohan,fengqian,mra}@research.att.com

ABSTRACT

Location information is one of the key enablers to context-aware systems and applications for mobile devices. However, most existing location sensing techniques do not work or will be significantly slowed down without infrastructure support, which limits their applicability in several cases. In this paper, we propose a localization system that works for both indoor and outdoor environments in a completely *offline* manner. Our system leverages human users' perception of nearby textual signs, without using GPS, Wi-Fi, cellular, and Internet. It enables several important use cases, such as offline localization on wearable devices. Based on real data collected from Google Street View and OpenStreetMap, we examine the feasibility of our approach. The preliminary result was encouraging. Our system was able to achieve higher than 90% accuracy with only 4 iterations even when the speech recognition accuracy is 70%, requiring very small storage space, and consuming 44% less instantaneous power compared to GPS.

1. INTRODUCTION

Location is one of the key context information and has enabled numerous context-aware systems and applications. To determine the location, today's mobile devices use various sensors and related techniques such as GPS, Wi-Fi fingerprinting, cellular triangulation *etc.* All these approaches let the device figure out the location automatically and each of them complements one another by having distinct characteristics of availability, accuracy, infrastructure requirements, and resource consumption. However, most existing techniques rely upon the infrastructure support and/or heavy training for their proper use. For instance, on many smartphones, A-GPS (Assisted GPS) is typically used to get an initial location fix quickly. In this case, nearby cell towers or equipment directly connected to towers originate and deliver hints to smartphones so they can narrow down the search space. Without the help, it will take a long time to bootstrap the localization system. Some other localization techniques also require heavy training on the region of interest. Radio signal based fingerprinting techniques, such as ultrasound, Wi-Fi, and FM radio are representative examples.

In this paper, we propose an alternative positioning system by leveraging a human's perception of her surroundings. The loca-

---

*All authors made equal contribution.

Device name	Release	Has GPS	Has Cellular	Has Wi-Fi
Google Glass	2013/03	No*	No	Yes
Samsung Gear 2	2014/04	No	No	No
Apple Watch	2015	No	No	Partial**

* The sensor might exist but not yet accessible through the API.
** Can only communicate with its paired phone.

Table 1: Localization sensors on popular wearable devices.

Figure 1: Examples of textual Signs in outdoor environment.

tion is computed based on what the user sees and tells the system. One notable difference from prior art is that the acquisition of location information can be performed based on only local information. This is particularly useful for wearable devices. As depicted in Table 1, many such devices, including Google Glass and Apple Watch, do not have GPS, thereby the only way for them to obtain location information is to ask their paired devices, typically a smartphone. Moreover, the capability of completely local computation enables several unique use cases, which are articulated in §2.

Our localization methodology leverages *textual signs* we see every day. They include street signs, local business logos, public transportation signs, house numbers, decorative logos, *etc.* These textual signs offer several properties making them ideal as location signatures. First, they are prevalent as long as the area is reasonably populated (§5.1). Second, they are easily recognizable and readable with little ambiguity. Third, users can easily identify those spatially and temporally stable signs (Figure 1) and ignore those temporary signs that are not suitable for fingerprinting the location, such as text on a vehicle or on an advertisement banner. In contrast, automated approaches such as Optical Character Recognition (OCR) may have difficulties detecting many texts due to their diverse styles (examples in Figure 1), and OCR cannot tell which signs are stable. Another benefit of using text is the resultant signature database is small in size. As shown in Table 2, each entry corresponding to a sign takes only a few bytes. Therefore, the database of a large regional area can be stored locally. By integrating the database with offline maps, the entire positioning system can run locally without requiring GPS or Internet connectivity. The database can be constructed and updated by crowdsourcing without any domain knowledge or specialized equipment (*e.g.,* by leveraging Google Street View, see §4), making it much easier than collecting data for traditional maps [17]. For positioning, the user can, for example, read out several (*e.g.,* 3 to 5) signs nearby she sees. The text is recog-

ID	Text	Location	Tag
1	Greene St.	40.729256,-73.995753	Road
2	West 4 St.	40.729256,-73.995753	Road
3	Rocco Restaurant	40.727938,-74.000157	Restaurant
4	23 St. Station	40.745528,-73.998623	Transportation (subway)
5	Downtown Brooklyn		
6	Century 21 dept. store	40.774097,-73.982095	Shopping
7	Imagine	40.775921,-73.975867	Landmark
8	Regal	40.757065,-73.989077	Cinema
9	405	40.774135,-73.950709	House number

Table 2: Sign database for signs in Figure 1.

nized and then matched against the database to localize the user. Out scheme works in both outdoor and indoor environments.

In this paper, we make the following contributions. First, we collect real data from Google Street View and OpenStreetMap [5] and examine the feasibility of our idea. Second, we design robust algorithms to tolerate various inaccuracies and ambiguities due to human perception, the user input procedure, and the signs themselves (§3), and then perform a simulation study to demonstrate the feasibility of the proposed algorithm (§5.2). Third, in our system's regime, users can use different means to enter the text of the signs. Among others, we conducted a case study using speech recognition, which is convenient for wearable devices such as Google Glass and the result was very encouraging (§5.3). Unlike general-purpose natural language interfaces [1], our speech recognition module uses a simple language model and usually a small vocabulary consisting of words on nearby signs. Thus, the entire processing chain is able to run locally.

Note that, our goal is to build a human-assisted positioning system that achieves outdoor and indoor localization in a complete offline manner without using GPS, Wi-Fi, cellular, and Internet connectivity. We do not expect our approach to replace traditional localization methods. Instead, it provides a very useful alternative when traditional approaches cannot work due to various reasons.

2. MOTIVATION: USE CASES

We motivate our approach by discussing several use cases.

"Offline" Localization. Bob's grandmother is visiting him. Realizing she was lost in the unfamiliar city, she called her grandson. Using our system, Bob is able to quickly figure out where she is by asking her to describe her surroundings. In some cases, the same goal can be achieved by checking the street signs. However, street signs are not always nearby and not always available (e.g., in a theme park or shopping mall).

Facilitating Location Search and Recollection. Alice barely remembers the place where she met her friend last week. It was near a Starbucks and a Thai restaurant. Our system provides a way to effectively search this location based on the limited information.

Offline Localization on Wearable Devices. Many wearable devices such as Google Glass and Apple Watch do not have GPS (Table 1). Consequently, the only way for them to obtain location information is to ask their paired smartphones via Bluetooth. Therefore, if the user does not bring her smartphone, or if the phone runs out of battery, the wearable device cannot know its location. Our proposal fills this gap by requiring neither location sensor (GPS, Wi-Fi, cellular, etc.) nor Internet connectivity. It works in both outdoor and indoor environments.

Infrastructure-free Indoor Localization. Localization in indoor environments usually requires hardware beacons and/or heavy training. In our approach, location can be determined by leveraging existing textual signs such as room names and numbers. The sign database can be easily constructed by walking in the building and/or marking the locations of textual signs on the floor map.

3. LOCALIZATION SYSTEM DESIGN

Our proposed system consists of three components: the sign database, the user input module, and the localization algorithm. When a user enters a nearby textual sign, it is matched against the sign database to get a set of candidate locations. These locations then are fed into the localization algorithm to refine the user's location. The above steps are repeated until the user's actual location is pinpointed. We detail the three components below.

Challenges. At first glance, the proposed scheme looks straightforward. One key challenge, however, is to handle the inaccuracy that may appear in each step. First, the user may misread some signs. Second, the user may only enter part of the sign based on common conventions. For example, "King Harbor Seafood Restaurant" can be partly entered as "King Harbor" or "King Harbor Seafood". Third, the user input module (e.g., the speech recognition engine) may make mistakes by translating the text to something different. Fourth, the same sign (e.g., "Bank of America") may appear in multiple places thus causing ambiguities. Last but not least, a sign recognized by the user may not be in the database. We need robust algorithms to tolerate such inaccuracies. Another challenge stems from the fact that our system runs completely locally on mobile devices with limited storage, computation capability, and battery life. Therefore, it needs to be as lightweight as possible to minimize the resource consumption, but without compromising the accuracy and user experience.

3.1 The Sign Database

The sign database contains precise locations of the textual signs. It can optionally contain tags for other value-added services. Based on the original database, our system generates an auxiliary data structure called *token table* by splitting each textual sign into separate words (i.e., tokens) and constructing mappings from each token to the set of signs in which the token appears. For example, from Table 2, we have "rocco"→{3}, and "regal"→{8} where "rocco" and "regal" are two tokens, and the numbers are sign IDs. The reason for introducing tokens is to tolerate errors. As will be described in §3.2, user input is processed at the basis of each token instead of each sign as a whole. Therefore, if the user only enters part of a sign, or if there are mistakes in some words of the sign, the sign may still be identified because some tokens partially match.

3.2 User Input Interface

Our system can accommodate any input interface as long as the method let users conveniently enter the tokens. For instance, speech recognition can be used. Or if an on-screen keyboard is available, one can simply type. We mainly focus on speech recognition (SR) as our primary input interface because microphone is one of the most prevalent sensor on mobile devices and SR is particularly suitable for wearable devices. When the user reads out a nearby sign, the SR engine translates her speech back into the text, which is then processed by the localization algorithm. SR performs a series of computations to find a match between a raw voice signal with words (or sentences) in the database. Typical SR processing chain requires three models: an acoustic model, a phonetic dictionary, and a language model. The acoustic model translates continuous raw voice signal to *phones*. The phonetic dictionary enables to map the *phones* to words [1]. The language model decides legitimate sentences e.g., word A cannot appear after word B.

In our initial design, we keep our language model simple in order to make the size of local database for SR as small as possible. As a result, the user input is recognized at the basis of each word token. Our SR is thus unaware of the structure of the text on signs as it only

---

[1]"words" and "tokens" are interchangeable in this paper.

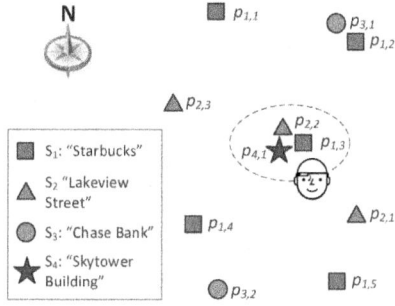

Figure 2: An example for illustrating the localization algorithm.

translates user's speech into individual tokens. Here is the high-level description of token recognition procedure. Let the input be a sequence of tokens $\{t_i\}$. Their matched signs $\{s_i\}$ can be quickly identified by looking up each t_i in the token table (§3.1). A token can match zero, one, or more signs in the token table. For each token t_i, we define its *frequency* $f(t_i)$ as the number of its unique matches (*i.e.*, signs containing t_i) divided by the total number of unique signs in the database. Tokens with high $f(t_i)$ are ignored based on a predefined threshold (*e.g.*, 0.001 based on Figure 4) because they are unlikely to have enough discrimination power.

Also, note that the phonetic dictionary and language model can be changed dynamically in our case. Specifically, in the incremental update phase (§3.3), it only contains a small subset of all tokens in the database depending on where the user is. These operations can be done locally on most mobile devices, given the fact that nowadays it is common to observe multi-core CPUs on mobile platform and we have a relatively small number of tokens *e.g.*, several thousand per city (§5.3). All those factors discussed so far *i.e.*, simple language model and dynamically generated model files, contribute to reduce the complexity of the SR engine, thereby making it feasible to run on today's mobile devices with reasonable accuracy, as to be demonstrated in §5.3.

We admit that, as a completely offline approach, our SR accuracy can be potentially inferior to those cloud-based SR systems backed by large database. Also, tokens with same or similar pronunciations make it inherently difficult to distinguish them. To mitigate this issue, we also includes a feature allowing a user to correct the SR result at a *per-token* basis. The system displays its best guess, as well as k other candidate tokens and a "not listed" option so that the user can correct the result within a time window by using either voice command or physical buttons.

3.3 The Localization Algorithm

The localization algorithm works in a continuous manner. It takes as input a stream of signs $S = \{s_i\}$. The output is either the estimated location or *unknown* indicating the location cannot be accurately determined due to a lack of input.

For each s_i, we find its entries $p_{i,j}(1 \leq j \leq k_i)$ in the database where k_i is the number of entries of s_i in the database. Assume we have m signs $s_1,...,s_m$ from the user. Some signs might be incorrect. Also some may correspond to multiple locations (*i.e.*, $k_i > 1$). In order to automatically filter out incorrect signs and locations, we leverage a key assumption that the majority of signs should have (at least) one entry appearing near the user's true location because the user can see them. That is to say, for at least m_0 signs, $\exists j'$ such that $p_{i,j'}$ is close to the true location, assuming we get $m_0 \leq m$ signs correct. Consider an example in Figure 2. The user enters four signs s_1, s_2, s_4, and something else that is mistakenly interpreted into s_3 (*e.g.*, due to inaccurate speech recognition). s_1, s_2, and s_3 appear at multiple locations in the database. Despite of these

---

Algorithm 1 Localization Algorithm
```
1:  S = {s_i}, t = 2, stop = FALSE;
2:  while (stop <> TRUE && t <= T) do
3:      found = 0;
4:      for (∀S' ⊆ S, |S'| = t) do
5:          r = centroid of S';
6:          if (∀s_i, s_j ∈ S', distance(s_i, s_j) < D ) then
7:              found++;
8:          end if
9:      end for
10:     t++;
11:     if (found == 0) then
12:         stop = TRUE; Output: unknown location;
13:     else if (found == 1) then
14:         stop = TRUE; Output: location is r;
15:     end if
16: end while
17: if (found <> 1) then
18:     Output: unknown location;
19: end if
```

noises, $p_{1,3}$, $p_{2,2}$, and $p_{4,1}$ form the largest cluster, which with high probability corresponds to the user's real location.

Following the intuition from Figure 2, we design a localization algorithm, with the high-level idea of searching for the largest cluster of signs by gradually increasing the size of the set of correct sign locations. As shown in Algorithm 1, For any subset of 2 possible locations, we measure their distance and count the number of subsets with distance smaller than D, a pre-defined threshold. If we do not find any such subset, the location is unknown. If such subset if unique, the estimated location is the centroid of this subset of locations. If there are multiple such subsets, we repeat the above procedure for any subset of 3 possible locations, 4 possible locations,.... until the subset size reaches a threshold $T \leq |S|$. We empirically found this algorithm is more robust than off-the-shelf clustering algorithms such as k-means for our problem. We evaluate its accuracy in §5.2.

Bootstrapping and incremental update are two scenarios in which the above algorithm can be applied. In the bootstrapping phase (*e.g.*, when the device is turned on), our system has no knowledge of the user's previous location. In this case, the search space in the sign database can be large (*e.g.*, at city level). Afterwards, in the incremental update phase, the system can use the user's last known location (if it is "fresh" enough) to predict the user's current coarse-grained location, which can be leveraged to significantly reduce the textual sign search space. This leads to higher accuracy for both speech recognition (as the vocabulary becomes smaller) and the localization algorithm (because a sign corresponds to fewer locations). One way to estimate the user's coarse-grained location is as follows. Let (x_0, y_0) be the user's previous location measured ΔT minutes ago. Let V and D be her maximum walking speed and her range of visibility, respectively. Assuming the user only walks, then the location of signs she currently sees, denoted as (x, y), must satisfy $(x - x_0)^2 + (y - y_0)^2 \leq (V\Delta T + D)^2$. Clearly this is the most simple and conservative estimation, which can be significantly improved by considering walking speed [11], direction [23], and other coarse-grained localization techniques by leveraging various sensors. The bootstrapping phase will be triggered manually or automatically, for example, after sensing the user has taken a vehicle or a train [12]. We demonstrate the benefits of incremental update in §5.

3.4 Discussions

In this subsection, we discuss some limitations of our system and potential user interface suitable to our system.

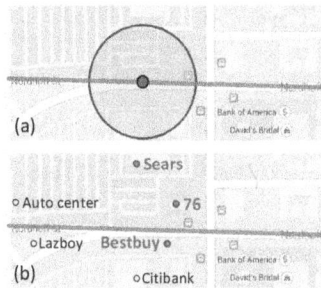

Figure 3: (a) Traditional GPS-based map. The thick blue line is the computed route. (b) Map using sign-based localization. Entered signs are highlighted. Some other signs not yet entered are also displayed to help user identify them, and enter them by selection or speech.

Comparison to Fully-Automated Approach. An inherent limitation of our approach is the localization usually takes longer, and it is difficult to derive a bound for the accuracy, because we rely on human users instead of location sensors. Therefore, our system will *not* replace automated localization methods. Instead, it provides a useful alternative when traditional approaches cannot work due to various reasons (*e.g.,* in use cases described in §2). Notably, our proposal does have one crucial advantage: by asking users to actively participate in the localization process, it can improve users' space awareness and their recollection of the environment [10].

Map User Interface. In traditional GPS-based mobile maps, the app directly shows user's location, as shown in Figure 3(a). However, our approach uses neither the distance nor the direction information of the signs so it is difficult to leverage triangulation to pinpoint the user's exact location. Instead, we propose to directly highlight the textual signs entered by the user so that she can (probably more easily) figure out her location by using the signs as references. The display is updated when the user enters the next token. Between consecutive updates, the map can move slowly based on user's walking speed and direction, in order to make the location update smoother. Signs not yet entered can also be displayed (but not highlighted) to help user identify them, and enter them by simply selecting (or reading) them. This makes sign-based navigation very convenient, as shown in Figure 3(b).

Comparison to Offline Maps. Several vendors (*e.g.,* Garmin and Baidu) provide offline maps allowing users to access them without Internet connectivity. However, users still need to use GPS or Wi-Fi fingerprinting to locate themselves on the map. Our work attempts to bridge this gap by making localization completely offline. Also, Baidu Map [2] provides a "search in view" feature allowing users to search POI (Point of Interest) names within the currently displayed area. But it only searches for one POI (*e.g.,* KFC) at a time and shows all its instances, making it not suitable for localization.

Using General Landmarks. Potentially, the landmarks can be extended from textual signs to more general objects (*e.g.,* a particular statue on a street). However, compared to textual signs, these general landmarks provide much more vague description of the location, and using them as location signatures may cause more ambiguities. We will consider this direction in future work.

4. DATA COLLECTION

To demonstrate the feasibility of our proposal, we collected data from two sources: Google street view and OpenStreetMap [5].

Google street view is a feature in Google Maps that provides panoramic views from positions along many streets in the world. We randomly picked 19 outdoor locations in the U.S., Canada, U.K., and two indoor locations. For the AT&T Building, we conducted a real walk

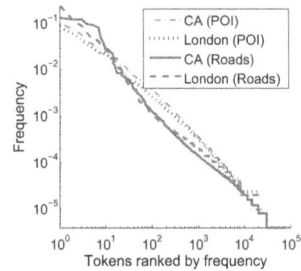

Figure 4: Ranked token frequency (both axes in log scale).

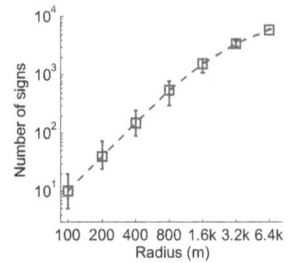

Figure 5: Number of signs within a confined area (London).

and collected the signs. For all other 20 locations, we randomly select spots with street view, "walk" in the street for a short distance (~ 0.1 mile), and manually record observed textual signs. The results are shown in Table 3. The street view approach allows us to construct high-quality signature database without physically going to the site, and is ideal for crowdsourcing. For example, an interface can be easily added for users to tag the signs in street view images. Some sign images can also be used as CAPTCHAs so that all Internet users can contribute. We do notice a limitation of using street view images from one single repository: some signs are blocked by obstacles so Table 3 only reports a subset of signs.

OpenStreetMap (OSM). We also crawled OSM to obtain names of POI (point of interest) in much larger areas. OSM [5] is a crowdsourcing-based world mapping project involving 200,000 contributors in 2011 [17]. The OSM raw data [6] employs three main data structures to represent map elements: node, way, and area. We built a custom tool that analyzes these data structures and extracts their associated names (if they exist). We assume each POI has a sign corresponding to its name on the map. For a *node*, the sign's location is the same as the node's. For an *area*, we pick a random node on its boundary as the sign's location. For *ways*, we extracted their names but the road signs' locations are difficult to estimate. One limitation of this synthetic approach is that it only produces a subset of signs whose contents and locations may also deviate from those of the real ones. However, we believe the dataset is sufficient for our feasibility study in §5, in which we study three areas: London metropolitan area (55K signs), New York City ($\sim$21K signs), and the state of California (139K signs).

5. PRELIMINARY RESULTS

Using the two data sources described in §4, we show preliminary results to demonstrate the feasibility of our proposal.

5.1 Characterizing Textual Signs

Sign Popularity. Table 3 summarizes the Google street view results. For the vast majority of the 21 locations covering diverse environments, we observed a non-trivial amount of textual signs. Generally, the signs are denser in downtown than in suburb and residential areas. However, we did not find a strong correlation between sign density and city size (except for very large cities). In indoor environments, signs mostly consist of room names and numbers. We believe our system is applicable in most places. Note that obviously temporary signs (*e.g.,* ad banners) and signs that are too general (*e.g.,* traffic signs) are not included in Table 3.

Token Distribution. Next, we characterize tokens in two locations: the state of California and the London metropolitan area. For each location, we examine tokens in POI signs and tokens in road signs, from OSM. This results in four token sets. Figure 4 shows log-log plot of the ranked frequencies of the four sets. The distributions are heavy-tailed. Although a tiny fraction of tokens, which will be ignored by the localization algorithm, are very general, the vast

Table 3: Signs collected from Google street view.

Location Type	City Name	City Population	Approximate Location	Walked Dist.	Num of Signs
Big city, downtown	New York City, NY	8.4 M*	9th Ave. / 54th St.	0.1 mile	24
Big city, residential	Queens, NY	2.2 M	37th Dr. / 108th St.	0.1 mile	12
Big city, downtown	Chicago, IL	2.7 M	State St. / Madison St.	0.1 mile	15
Big city, suburb, residential	Oak Park, IL**	51 K	S East Ave. / Randolph St.	0.2 miles	8
Big city, suburb, residential	Portland, OR	584 K	SE Mill St. / SE 11th Ave.	0.1 mile	11
Big city, suburb	St. Louis, MO	318 K	S Broadway / Stansbury St.	0.2 miles	11
Mid-sized city, downtown	Chattanooga, TN	173 K	E 8th St. / Market St.	0.1 mile	11
Mid-sized city, downtown	Salinas, CA	164 K	E Gabilan St. / Monterey St.	0.1 mile	11
Mid-sized city, suburb	Loveland, CO	70 K	N Lincoln Ave. / E 29th St.	0.1 mile	9
Mid-sized city, suburb	Aberdeen, SD	26 K	S 5th St. / SW 12th Ave.	0.2 miles	9
Mid-sized city, suburb	Fairbanks, AK	32 K	N Cushman St. / 1st Ave.	0.1 mile	9
Mid-sized city, suburb, residential	Prince Albert, SK, Canada	35 K	Bennett Dr. / 4th Ave. West	0.2 miles	12
Small city, tourism	Key West, FL	25 K	Southard St. /Duval St.	0.1 mile	22
Small city	Riverton, WY	11 K	E Park Ave. / N Broadway Ave.	0.2 miles	10
Small town, residential	Fairfield, IA	9 K	E Adams Ave. / S Main St.	0.2 miles	8
Small town	Rushville, IL	3 K	S Congress St. / W Lafayette St.	0.1 mile	13
Small town	Windermere, Cumbria, UK	8 K	Near town centre	0.1 mile	9
University campus	Ann Arbor, MI		U of Michigan north campus	0.1 mile	6
Theme park	San Diego, CA		The Seaworld theme park	0.1 mile	6
Indoor, museum	Chicago, IL		Art Institute of Chicago	0.1 mile	10+
Indoor, office building	Bedminster, NJ		AT&T Building ***	0.1 mile	10+

Notes: * Includes all five boroughs of New York City. ** Near Chicago. *** Our office building. Conducted real walk.

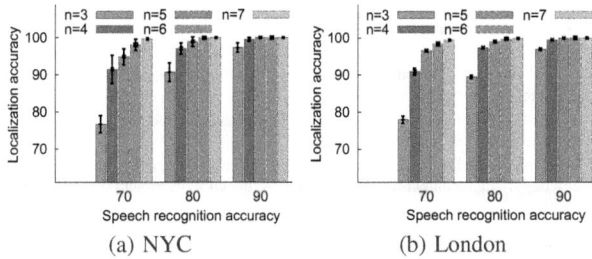

(a) NYC   (b) London

Figure 6: The accuracy of localization algorithm.

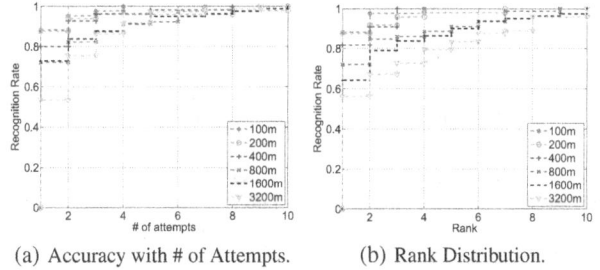

(a) Accuracy with # of Attempts.   (b) Rank Distribution.

Figure 7: SR performance: The results are potentially the worst case since the participant was a non-native speaker and we use the Sphinx software out-of-box, *i.e.*, without optimizing acoustic model, dictionary, and language model files.

majority of tokens belong to very few signs (most only one). They are therefore ideal for quickly pinpointing the user's location.

Signs in a small area. We show that if the search is confined within a small area, the number of signs decreases significantly. We randomly pick 50,000 locations in London. For each location (x_i, y_i), we count the number of signs within $(x - x_i)^2 + (y - y_i)^2 \leq R^2$ where the radius R ranges from 100m to 6.4km. Figure 5 shows that the number of signs decreases accordingly as the search area becomes smaller. Note that in the incremental update phase, which is the common usage scenario compared to the bootstrapping phase (§3.3), usually the search area is small.

5.2 Localization Algorithm

We evaluate the performance of the proposed localization algorithm for different levels of speech recognition accuracy (70%, 80% and 90%) and with difference numbers of input signs (from 3 to 5). We show the results for the New York City and London OSM data sets in Figure 6. We randomly select 5,000 user locations in London and 500 user locations in New York City (the London OSM data set is denser than NYC). Based on Table 3, we only consider user locations with more than 10 signs within 100 meters and thus we set D in Algorithm 1 to be slightly larger than 200 meters. The estimated location is considered accurate if the distance between the user location and the centroid of the selected signs is less than $D/2$. Note this does not imply the localization accuracy is $D/2$. Instead, it intuitively means the selected signs are indeed what the user sees. We run the simulation 5 times and report the average and standard deviation for $T = 4$. There are two major observations from Figure 6. First, better speech recognition can improve

the performance of localization. Second, more input signs can lead to better localization accuracy. Even when the speech recognition accuracy is 70%, the proposed algorithm works for more than 90% locations with 4 signs and more than 99% locations with 7 signs.

5.3 Speech Recognition (SR)

Methodology. We adapt one popular implementation of a SR chain called Sphinx [3]. We use its Android version (PocketSphinx) and make use of the acoustic model as it is. In the experiments, we first randomly pick a set of locations in London and NYC. Then, for each location, we collect token sets from the OSM data with different radii (100m∼6400m). Each token set has 67∼4186 tokens for London and 12∼1038 tokens for NYC. We take each token set as input and generate a dictionary and language model, which are then used by one experimental trial. In each experiment, the participant randomly takes a word from the *phones-words* dictionary and pronounces it one at a time. The software presents 10 potential candidates. If there was a correct answer, we treat it as a successful recognition. Otherwise, the participant repeats the word again. When he gets a success, we record a rank of the correct candidate suggested by the recognition system.

Results. We first take a look at the storage overhead imposed by having a phonetic dictionary and a language model and verify that it is very small. Specifically, for the NYC dataset, the dictionary has sizes 203 bytes~8 kbytes (100m, 6400m respectively) and the size of the language model is 703 bytes~15 kbytes. In case of the London dataset, the dictionary size is 701 bytes ~ 31 kbytes and the language model size lies in 1.6 kbytes ~ 63 kbytes.

We next examine the recognition performance of SR shown in Figure 7. It is worth mentioning that the results can be the worst case performance since the participant for the experiment was a non-native English speaker and we use the recognition software out-of-box *i.e.,* we did not tune the default acoustic model or the dictionary/language model generated by PocketSphinx. Overall we think the results are encouraging. Up to 400m radius, repeating once more *i.e.,* 2 trials in total, gives 95% of recognition rate. Even for all other cases, 4 trials will cover 90% of accuracy. We note that this is very preliminary result and plan to do a more comprehensive evaluation with a diverse set of participants and more optimized software settings later *e.g.,* using better trained acoustic and dictionary/language models, as well as improved feature acoustic extraction techniques [18].

We also measured the energy consumption of the SR component and compare it with that of GPS sensor. We use Monsoon Power Monitor [4] and Samsung Galaxy S4 device for the measurement. The SR component (including both microphone and SR processing) consumes ~44% less instantaneous power compared to that of GPS (369.22 mW vs. 208.48 mW), which fortifies our use of SR.

6. RELATED WORK

GPS has been used as a primary source of location information and provide accurate data in an outdoor environment. But not all mobile devices are equipped with GPS (Table 1) due to concerns such as energy consumption. Further, GPS sensing does not always provide a precise location in urban environment. It is highly susceptible to obstacles in the sky and can have errors as high as more than 100 meters [16, 21]. Recently a technique for acquiring GPS signal in indoor environment has proposed [19]. However it is not yet applicable to the off-the-shelf devices due to the use of specialized radio components and complexity of the system.

In the last decade, numerous research efforts propose localization techniques based on radio signal based fingerprinting. These include ones based on GSM signal [20], Wi-Fi signal [7], FM signal [8] *etc.* Unfortunately, some of them are based on the information that is in general not available in off-the-shelf mobile devices [20] or requires heavy training [7]. In contrast, our system uses microphone (or on-screen keyboard) as input, which is mostly available in today's mobile devices including wearables and our sign database is relatively easy to construct compared to above-mentioned techniques. A number of works aim to strategically combine multiple approaches [21, 15, 25, 14, 22]. They trade-off location accuracy with other system resources, such as energy, thereby different from our approach where the focus is to provide purely local localization systems based on human perception.

When it comes to dealing with textual signs, one intuitive approach is to use image-based positioning [24] *i.e.,* let the device see what a human sees. Although the approach is complementary to our system, it requires multi-stage CV algorithms and large databases (*e.g.,* 300K images for 50K locations at NYC [24]), making cloud the best place for performing such tasks. It thus requires Internet connectivity and brings additional concerns of delay [13], energy consumption, and cellular data usage. Light and viewing angle can significantly reduce the image matching accuracy.

Although explored in slightly different context, the idea of leveraging human assistance to determine a location had been explored and inspired our work. In the GUIDE tourist guide system [9], a visitor is shown several thumbnail images of local attractions and asked if any of them matches the visitor's surroundings. This approach is not directly applicable to a general-purpose localization system like ours due to scalability issues.

7. CONCLUSION AND FUTURE PLAN

As discussed in §6, there have been a large number of indoor and outdoor localization proposals using various sensing techniques. Instead, we provide a solution for offline localization without using GPS, Wi-Fi, cellular, or Internet connectivity, by exploiting human users' perception of nearby textual signs. It enables several important use cases, such as offline localization on wearable devices, in both outdoor and indoor environments. Currently we are working on *(i)* prototyping on Google Glass using speech recognition as the user interface, *(ii)* building a city-level sign database by tagging Google street view images using crowdsourcing, and *(iii)* improving speech recognition accuracy, before conducting field trials.

8. REFERENCES

[1] Apple Siri on iOS 7. https://www.apple.com/ios/siri/.
[2] Baidu Map. http://map.baidu.com/.
[3] Cmu sphinx: Open source toolkit for speech recognition, http://cmusphinx.sourceforge.net/.
[4] Monsoon power monitor, http://www.msoon.com/LabEquipment/PowerMonitor/.
[5] OpenStreetMap. http://www.openstreetmap.org.
[6] OpenStreetMap Data. http://wiki.openstreetmap.org/wiki/Planet.osm.
[7] P. Bahl and V. N. Padmanabhan. Radar: An in-building rf-based user location and tracking system. In *IEEE INFOCOM'00*.
[8] Y. Chen, D. Lymberopoulos, J. Liu, and B. Priyantha. Fm-based indoor localization. In *ACM MobiSys'12*, pages 169–182, 2012.
[9] K. Cheverst, N. Davies, K. Mitchell, and A. Friday. Experiences of developing and deploying a context-aware tourist guide: the GUIDE project. In *Mobicom*, 2000.
[10] J. Chung. *Mindful Navigation with Guiding Light: Design Consideration of Projector based Indoor Navigation Assistance System*. PhD thesis, MIT, 2012.
[11] J. geun Park, A. Patel, D. Curtis, S. Teller, and J. Ledlie. Online Pose Classification and Walking Speed Estimation using Handheld Devices. In *ACM Ubicomp*, 2012.
[12] S. Hemminki, P. Nurmi, and S. Tarkoma. Accelerometer-Based Transportation Mode Detection on Smartphones. In *SenSys*, 2013.
[13] J. J. Hull, X. Liu, B. Erol, J. Graham, and J. Moraleda. Mobile Image Recognition: Architectures and Tradeoffs. In *HotMobile*, 2010.
[14] M. B. Kjærgaard, J. Langdal, T. Godsk, and T. Toftkjær. EnTracked: Energy-Efficient Robust Position Tracking for Mobile Devices. In *ACM MobiSys'09*, 2009.
[15] K. Lin, A. Kansal, D. Lymberopoulos, and F. Zhao. Energy-Accuracy Trade-off for Continuous Mobile Device Location. In *ACM MobiSys'10*, 2010.
[16] M. Modsching, R. Kramer, and K. ten Hagen. Field trial on GPS Accuracy in a medium size city: The influence of builtup. In *3rd Workshop on Positioning, Navigation and Communication (WPNC)*, 2006.
[17] P. Neis and A. Zipf. Analyzing the contributor activity of a volunteered geographic information project – the case of openstreetmap. *ISPRS International Journal of Geo-Information*, 1(2):146–165, 2012.
[18] S. Nirjon, R. Dickerson, J. Stankovic, G. Shen, and X. Jiang. sMFCC: exploiting sparseness in speech for fast acoustic feature extraction on mobile devices – a feasibility study. In *HotMobile*, 2013.
[19] S. Nirjon, J. Liu, G. DeJean, B. Priyantha, Y. Jin, and T. Hart. Coin-gps: indoor localization from direct gps receiving. In *ACM MobiSys'14*.
[20] V. Otsason, A. Varshavsky, A. LaMarca, and E. De Lara. Accurate gsm indoor localization. In *UbiComp 2005: Ubiquitous Computing*, pages 141–158. Springer, 2005.
[21] J. Paek, J. Kim, and R. Govindan. Energy-Efficient Rate-Adaptive GPS-based Positioning for Smartphones. In *Mobisys*, 2010.
[22] J. Paek, K.-H. Kim, J. P. Singh, and R. Govindan. Energy-Efficient Positioning for Smartphones using Cell-ID Sequence Matching. In *Mobisys*, 2011.
[23] N. Roy, H. Wang, and R. R. Choudhury. I am a Smartphone and I can Tell my User's Walking Direction. In *ACM MobiSys*, 2014.
[24] F. X. Yu, R. Ji, and S.-F. Chang. Active Query Sensing for Mobile Location Search. In *ACM MM*, 2011.
[25] Z. Zhuang, K.-H. Kim, and J. P. Singh. Improving Energy Efficiency of Location Sensing on Smartphones. In *Mobisys*, 2010.

Step-by-step Detection of Personally Collocated Mobile Devices

Animesh Srivastava
Duke University
animeshs@cs.duke.edu

Jeremy Gummeson
HP Labs Palo Alto
jeremy.gummeson@hp.com

Mary Baker
HP Labs Palo Alto
mary.baker@hp.com

Kyu-Han Kim
HP Labs Palo Alto
kyu-han.kim@hp.com

ABSTRACT

Many people now carry multiple mobile devices on a daily basis. Wearables, smartphones, tablets, and laptops all have their different advantages, but collectively they can increase a user's device management burden. Management problems include leaving a device behind accidentally, receiving notifications on the wrong device, and failing to secure all of the devices as needed. Reducing this burden requires detecting which of a user's devices are "personally collocated" – those devices he currently wears, carries, or has under his immediate physical control. We present a lightweight method to detect personal collocation by comparing accelerometer-based footstep signatures across the devices over time. Through several experiments, we demonstrate that the technique is lower latency and lower power than state-of-the-art RSSI-based collocation techniques. We describe other advantages and limitations of our method and also provide several examples of higher-layer applications and services that can make use of personal collocation information.

Keywords

Collocation, Mobile Computing, Device Management

1. INTRODUCTION

Many current smartwatches alert their owner if he leaves his phone behind. When this popular feature works well, it helps users avoid leaving phones unattended or losing them altogether. These alerts could usefully apply to other devices as well, including tablets, phablets, and laptops. We call the set of devices currently worn, carried, or physically controlled by a user his *personally collocated* devices, and since each of these form factors has its own set of advantages, many people now use more than one of them on a daily basis. Carrying more devices increases the management burden on the user, making it easier for him to lose them or leave them unattended, but a useful alert could in-

form the user of any change in his set of personally collocated devices.

Unfortunately, the predominant methods for providing this alert are often not fast enough, and people might not receive the alert until they have strayed far away from their neglected devices. One approach determines collocation state by computing correlations across sensor data collected from different devices [7], but this approach requires *minutes* of data. Other approaches use the received signal strength (RSSI) of Bluetooth Low Energy (BLE) beacons and assume that an RSSI value below a certain threshold indicates separation of the devices [5]. RSSI values vary significantly depending on device placement around the body, so it is difficult to pick a meaningful threshold.

We illustrate the problem with the RSSI approach in Figure 1 where we plot BLE beacon RSSI values sent by a BLE system on chip (SoC) worn on the wrist and measured by a phone placed in several configurations around a user (phone in a pocket, on the table by the user, or held to his ear; wrist wearable in his lap or on the table). We see from these box plots, each of which represents one minute's worth of data, that the configuration greatly affects received signal strength, despite the devices remaining close. For comparison, we also plot the median signal strength of BLE beacon packets received by the mobile phone in a user's pocket when the user increases his distance from the beaconing BLE device. Using distance values from this plot and the RSSI values of the configurations, we would incorrectly assign separation distances of anything between 2 and 45 meters to the various configurations.

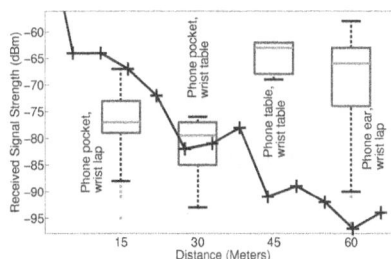

Figure 1: Signal strength of BLE beacons from a wrist wearable measured on a mobile phone. We overlay a plot of RSSI versus distance. The X axis (distance in meters) applies only to this RSSI plot.

In this paper, we describe a new lower-latency method for detecting the personal collocation of mobile devices by comparing footstep patterns detected on each device. Our method is suitable for any collection of personal devices, although we focus here on phones and smartwatches. Nearly all current types of mobile devices include a 3-axis accelerometer useful for recognizing various human activities. Accelerometers are now sufficiently low power to run continuously with minimal energy overhead [6]. We also see a trend toward using special-purpose processing cores to minimize the cost of analyzing motion data [3]. Human mobility is a natural fit to achieve detection of device separation, and its latency scales according to the speed of the given user.

While we can detect many interesting movement features from full-bandwidth accelerometer data, we only need to detect walking patterns. Since normal human movement patterns include regular footstep intervals when moving from one location to another, detecting and comparing signatures based on the timestamps of these footstep events suffices to detect personal device collocation in most cases. Since human footsteps occur at relatively low rates, processing requirements are low and can execute periodically, at a rate proportional to human mobility rates.

To avoid transmitting bulky raw accelerometer data, our mobile devices run a lightweight step detection algorithm locally and transmit the timing of step events in a single BLE packet. Since connection maintenance requires exchanging periodic radio packets anyway, exchanging step signatures consumes negligible additional energy overhead.

After comparing footstep data on a chosen device (in this case, the user's mobile phone), our technique informs personally collocated mobile devices of their status. With this method, low-latency detection implies that the devices are not yet very far apart, which is an advantage for the applications we describe in the next section. Note that by itself, our method has limitations: it is vulnerable to spoofing and does not apply to some forms of assisted mobility. Instead, it provides an early warning of device separation suitable for many applications.

2. APPLICATIONS

What are some potential applications for our collocation technique? We highlight a few below, all of which assume that a wearable device, such as a smartwatch, remains on its owner. Devices closely collocated with the smartwatch are therefore personally collocated.

Forgot my device: The more mobile devices we carry with us, the easier it is to lose one of them. We can use a wearable such as a smartwatch to alert us to separation from other devices. Low-latency detection can mean the difference between reclaiming the phone you left a couple of seats behind you, or watching the bus drive away with it. Low-latency detection also gives bad guys less time to steal or otherwise compromise the forgotten device.

Automated message responses: From the point of view of a user's phone, the sooner it knows it is no longer with its owner, the sooner it knows the owner cannot respond to calls or messages. The phone can then trigger automated responses to senders or redirect their communications toward another device known to be near the owner.

Early screen lock: Managing the security of our devices is more burdensome as the number of devices increases. Mobile phones, for example, typically use a screenlock to protect the contents of the phone after an idle period. A short idle period reduces the chance of compromise when a user leaves his phone unattended, but it can also frustrate the user who must more often unlock his phone. Our technique can lock the phone quickly if the user is not with it, which allows for longer timeout periods while the device is collocated.

3. OUR APPROACH

In this section, we explain our accelerometer-based personal collocation system. First we show how to establish and revoke a personal collocation relationship between a pair of devices based on their mobility. Next, we provide an overview of the step detection algorithm we use to identify this mobility. Finally, we describe the algorithm that compares device mobility to determine whether devices are personally collocated.

3.1 Sensing Collocation from Mobility

Personal collocation and mobility are related, but not synonymous. Two devices could be moving, but not with the same user. They could also be stationary, but physically proximate to the same user. We ask the question: *How can we use human footstep patterns detected on different devices to determine which subset of devices are currently with a given user?*

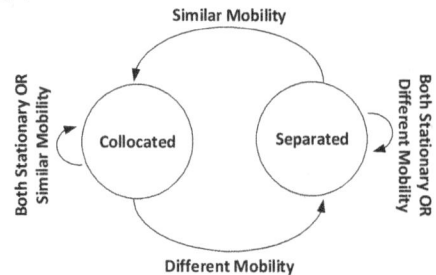

Figure 2: We model mobility-based personal collocation as transitions between two logical states.

In Figure 2, we model collocation as a state machine and show how the presence or absence of human mobility maps the devices to a *Collocated* or a *Separated* state. Initially, we have no information to determine whether two devices are together or not, and we assume they are *Separated*. Devices remain in the *Separated* state until they both move with their user, experiencing similar human mobility. After some amount of similar mobility, we consider the devices *Collocated*. If both collocated devices keep moving or stop moving together, they remain *Collocated*. If one device experiences mobility and the other does not, they transition back to the *Separated* state. Next we describe how we detect human mobility.

3.2 Detecting Human Mobility

To detect whether or not two devices are with the same user, we use a human-centric mobility detection mechanism – sensing footsteps. Mobile devices that include accelerometers that are rigidly attached to the body or loosely held in the user's hand or pocket each observe the same footstep events. To disambiguate footsteps from other movement features, we modify a well-established technique [8] to suit low-power wearable devices, as described next.

Acceleration magnitude: Depending on the orientation of a device, one of the three axes of the accelerometer registers higher variation in acceleration due to the footstep. To avoid the computation overhead of tracking device orientation or handling data from each axis separately, our version of the algorithm simply computes the magnitude of the accelerometer axis samples:

$$accelmag = \sqrt{accel_x^2 + accel_y^2 + accel_z^2}$$

Noise smoothing and activity filtering: We then filter out spurious accelerometer noise by using a moving windowed average computed across accelerometer magnitude samples. The size of the window over which we smooth the accelerometer samples depends upon the frequency of input samples. In our case we found that for an input size of 50 samples per second, a window size of four works well:

$$magnitude_t = \frac{(accelmag_t + accelmag_{t-1} + accelmag_{t-2} + accelmag_{t-3})}{4}$$

After smoothing the data, our algorithm estimates the variability of samples by measuring the difference between maximum and minimum accelerometer magnitude. We find that a magnitude greater than 0.4 g (refer to section 5) detects footsteps across various human activities, and filters out lesser motion due to activities such as typing.

Dynamic threshold step detection: Next, we compute a dynamic threshold to detect the presence of a step. We estimate this quantity, updated every second, as:

$$dyn = \frac{(max\_magnitude + min\_magnitude)}{2}$$

We detect a step if the accelerometer magnitude shows a negative slope crossing this dynamic threshold.

Frequency filter: We use one additional filter to shape the data. Large but rapid vibrations recorded by the accelerometer unrelated to walking or running may count as steps. We discard these spurious movements by constraining the frequency of step counts. We assume that humans typically can run as fast as five steps per second but will walk no slower than one step per second. Therefore the time gap between two valid steps should be in the range [0.2 sec, 1 sec]. Next, we discuss how we infer mobility pattern similarity observed by multiple devices.

3.3 Comparing Human Mobility Patterns

After detecting footsteps on each device during a given interval, we need a robust mechanism to decide whether both of the devices are in motion, both of the devices are stationary, or only one of them is in motion. Since the detection of individual footsteps on a particular device is not completely reliable, we need a method that is robust to variations in the timing of individual steps. In particular, it can be challenging to match step data for devices at different locations on the body (i.e. phone in the pocket, smart watch on the wrist). The intuition behind our technique is to filter out short-lived variations in step counts by looking for sustained periods of motion on the devices. Later in the evaluation section we show how much filtering we require for practical application scenarios.

We implement our collocation algorithm as a finite state machine that is somewhat more complex than previously illustrated, because the state transitions between *Separated* and *Collocated* require some counting. Both devices start in the state *Separated*, since we have not yet collected any motion data. During a one second interval, if both devices detect one or more footsteps, we transition to state *Maybe Collocated*. The devices will remain in this state and increment a counter, provided that both devices continue to see at least one footstep every interval. If this condition is violated, we reset the counter and we transition back to state

Separated. When the count value reaches at least threshold value x, we transition to state *Collocated*. The two devices remain in state *Collocated* until one of the two devices detects footsteps while the other does not. If that happens, we transition to the state *Maybe Separated*. For each interval in which we see activity on one of the devices and not the other, we increment a counter. We transition back to state *Separated* when the counter reaches threshold value y. We refer to the number of consecutive intervals that contain footsteps as the *consecutive interval threshold*.

4. IMPLEMENTATION

To evaluate step-based personal collocation, we use the combination of a trace-driven simulator and a hardware implementation. The trace-driven simulations consist of an offline, simulated version of our algorithm that uses acceleration data collected from a commodity smartwatch and smartphone to determine their collocation state. The advantage of this approach is that it provides access to full-bandwidth accelerometer data and allows us to tune various system parameters to understand their impact on performance. Our hardware system implementation determines collocation state in real-time and uses custom hardware – this platform enables us to understand the power profile of our algorithm, but it lacks the full bandwidth data required for tuning.

Both implementations have three main components: a *step-detection module* running on both the smartphone and wearable device, a *step-data handler* to relay the steps detected on the wearable device to the smartphone, and a *collocation-detector module* running on the smartphone.

4.1 Trace-Driven Simulations

To understand and evaluate the efficacy of our system, we need to understand the impact of various parameters on system performance. We created a trace-driven simulation framework that allows us easily to modify system parameters and compare performance. We use the MotoACTV (Android 2.1) smartwatch (`https://motoactv.com/home/page/features.html`) and a Samsung Galaxy S3 (Android 4.3) smartphone to collect acceleration data. values.

We developed an app for these devices that is configured to label a set of tasks such as sitting, walking and running. We ask users to perform a sequence of predetermined tasks and press a button when transitioning between these tasks. We use the system timestamps of these button presses as ground truth for activity timing in the evaluation. The app continuously records accelerometer values obtained from the device, as well as the signal strength of Bluetooth devices encountered during the experiment. To ensure the data from both devices is properly aligned, we synchronize them to the same Network Time Protocol (NTP) server just prior to data collection. After data collection, a set of MATLAB scripts parse through the accelerometer data and determine collocation state across the entire length of the trace. We compare the times of collocation state transitions to the labeled ground truth to determine the overall latency of collocation detection.

4.2 Hardware and Software Implementation

Wrist Wearable Device To understand the power profile of a state-of-the-art wearable device we use a development board from Nordic Semiconductor based on the nRF51822, augmented with a 3-axis accelerometer (ADXL362) for step detection. The accelerometer continuously samples acceleration values at 50 Hz and stores the data in a FIFO buffer. Once every second, the Nordic SoC reads the 50 accumulated samples and passes the data to the step-data handler service (described below) for further encoding and transmission to the smartphone over a BLE channel.

We designed the step-data handler to minimize the number of BLE packet transmissions required to relay the complete step-data from the wearable device to the smartphone. Upon receiving the step data from the step detection module, the step-data handler extracts the following information: number of steps detected N_{step}, the timestamp of the first step detected T_{first_step}, and the indices out of 50 accelerometer samples at which subsequent steps occur t_i. The BLE data packet therefore has the following structure: $<N_{step}, T_{first\_step}, t_1, t_2, ..., t_{N_{step}-1}>$. Since the device samples the accelerometer values at a uniform rate f_{sample} ($\frac{1}{50}$ in our case), we can compute t_i as:

$$t_i = T_{first\_step} + i * f_{sample}$$

N_{step} and t_i are one byte long and T_{first_step} is four bytes long. The maximum amount of data a BLE packet can hold is 27 bytes. Therefore, one BLE packet is enough to relay data for 23 steps which is more than sufficient for our purposes. The BLE packet is then immediately queued for transmission. In our solution, the wearable and phone form a connection to exchange step and collocation state packets; while BLE supports a range of different interval settings for maintaining a connection, we choose an interval identical to the data generation rate (once per second) to minimize connection overheads.

Smartphone: We use a Samsuing Galaxy S3 as the smartphone device in our hardware implementation. The step-detection module on the smartphone samples accelerometer magnitudes at 50 Hz and runs the same step detection algorithm as the smartwatch. Instead of trying to align the timestamps of individual footsteps, the collocation-detector module partitions the step data into multiple intervals (bin) of identical width for both the wearable and the phone and focuses on comparing properties of the bins such as total number of steps and amount of time between the steps. The collocation detector uses the state transition rules previously described to determine the collocation of the devices.

5. EVALUATION

In this section we evaluate our system using the implementations described in Section 4. We compare the performance of our system against RSSI-based collocation techniques and show that we provide performance improvements while operating within a minimal power budget. In each experiment, we evaluate our system by analyzing the accelerometer traces collected from a watch and smartphone for various daily activities. While this isn't an exhaustive collection of potential activities, the activities chosen are common during a typical day and represent scenarios containing minimal to severe motion. We categorize these activities as:

Steps detected on one device: *Drinking, Typing* and *Gesturing* represent scenarios where the watch accelerometer detects motion from the user's hands while the smartphone registers no activity because it is in the user's pants pocket or next to him on a table.

Dataset	mean(g)	std (g)	min (g)	max(g)
Drinking	0.94	0.08	0.75	1.70
Typing	0.93	0.04	0.53	1.21
Gesturing	0.97	0.14	0.44	1.86
Walking	1.08	0.19	0.69	1.83
Running	1.91	1.17	0.39	6.56
Stair-climbing	1.06	0.21	0.57	1.79

Table 1: Summary of wrist acceleration datasets used for evaluating collocation stability.

Steps detected on both the devices: *Walking, Running*, and *Stair-climbing* represent activities where both the devices register vibrations due to footsteps.

5.1 Stability of Collocation State

One measure of the performance of our system is its stability in the *Collocated* state under adverse conditions. For example, a user with both a smartwatch and phone walks into his office, sits down in front of his computer, puts his phone on the desk and starts working. In this scenario, both his devices will observe footsteps until he puts the phone on the desk. While the phone is on the desk, the watch may still detect arm motion, but both devices should remain in a *Collocated* state. Therefore, our algorithm should reject false-positive steps from arm motions to avoid falsely reporting device separation.

To tune the parameters of our collocation technique for stability, we look at the motion properties of the benchmark datasets shown in Table 1. We collect five example traces from the wrist of a single user, where each trace contains two minutes of activity data. We first observe that there is more variability in acceleration magnitude when the user is moving rather than when stationary. In the walking, running, and stair-climbing benchmarks, we find that the devices continue to stay in *Collocated* state, provided that we require the difference between the maximum and minimum acceleration values be more than 0.4g during each one-second interval in which we detect steps. For the stationary benchmarks, we pre-initialize both the devices to the *Collocated* state. During these experiments, we leave the phone on the table while the user performs the activities, meaning that our step detection algorithm could falsely determine the user has walked away from the phone. For *Typing* and *Drinking* we find no cases where the collocation state falsely transitions to *Separated*. However, we had more trouble in the case of *Gesturing*, since this activity involves large and rapid motion of the hands.

To reject these motions, one technique is to increase the acceleration magnitude threshold required during each interval– we find that by increasing this value to 0.5 g, we can eliminate most occurrences of the false positives. However, this threshold setting results in the step detection algorithm missing steps during walking activites. Instead, we filter these transitions by increasing the consecutive interval threshold described in section 3.3 and show the resulting impact in Figure 3(a). For evaluation, we compute a mean across all the gesture traces of the fraction of time the devices spend in the *Collocated* state – ideally this should be one. We use this performance metric, as opposed to false positive or false negative rates, since collocation state evolves continuously over time rather than being a set of discrete events. Since gesturing involves significant vertical motions of the wrist, we find that we need to increase the interval thresh-

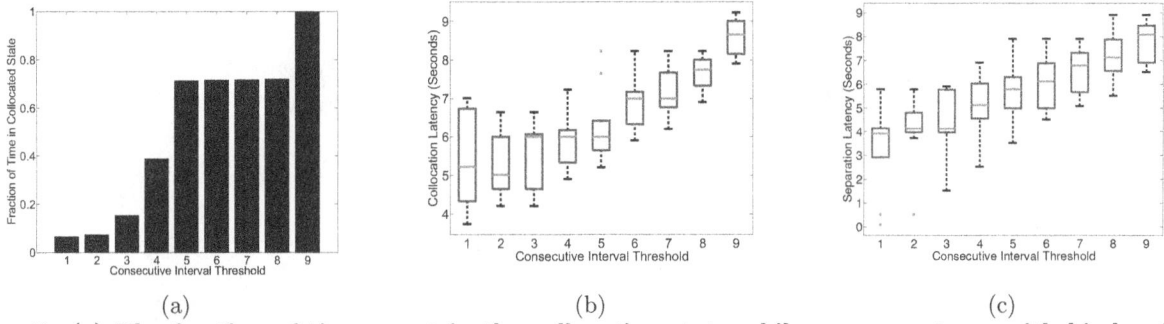

Figure 3: (a) The fraction of time spent in the collocation state while a user gestures with his hands (the most challenging of our datasets) for 2 minutes with a device on his wrist and the phone in his pants pocket. (b) Latency of establishing collocation. (c) Latency of establishing separation.

old to nine to filter these bursts of motion and remain in the *Collocated* state. The drawback of using such an agressive threshold is an increase in the latency of the detection of true separation events, as described below.

The stability of the *Separation* state is also important to the user experience, but it is unlikely that two devices will accidentally show similar enough motion to become collocated, unless the motion is injected by a malicious user (see Section 7).

5.2 Latency of Collocation Detection

Another measure of our system is how long it takes to detect transitions between personal collocation of devices and their separation. The latency of detecting these transitions is essential to the user experience for applications. To explore the latency tradeoffs, we collect data similar to that shown in Figure 4. A user wearing a smartwatch and carrying a phone in his hand walks towards a desk, sits down, leaves the phone on the desk, walks away, walks back towards the desk and then walks away with the phone and the wearable. We collected 10 instances of a user performing this series of motions. In 100% of these examples, we correctly identify the states of *Separation* and *Collocation* as compared to user-generated ground truth, but the latency of detection varies. Figures 3(b) and 3(c) show the impact of increasing the interval threshold on collocation and separation detection. A small interval threshold results in fast detection of separation and collocation but will have the aforementioned stability issues when spurious wrist motions are present. A larger interval threshold provides stability in the presence of noisy wrist data at the cost of higher detection latency. Nonetheless, even the higher-latency results compare favorably to using RSSI to detect collocation, as described next.

5.3 Comparison to RSSI based techniques

We compare the performance of step-based personal collocation to one that uses received signal strength to determine that two devices are separated. On his wrist, a user wears both a Nordic evaluation board beaconing at +4dBm every 25 ms, and a MotoACTV logging acceleration. Since the RSSI values contain a significant amount of noise, we use a 30-sample windowed average to smooth the data. The phone logs its own acceleration as well as the signal strength of the beacons transmitted by the Nordic SoC. The user leaves the phone on the table and walks away. The RSSI-based tech-

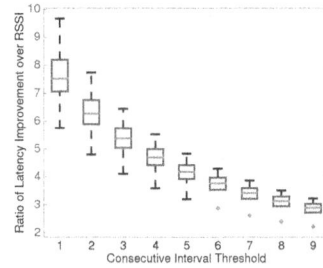

Figure 5: The latency of device separation is much lower using our step-based technique, rather than an RSSI-based technique.

nique assumes that the two devices become separated at the distance when RSSI drops below -85 dBm – we chose this threshold based on the data presented in Figure 1. We run the step-based collocation algorithm with a varying interval threshold parameter and compute the latency in seconds between when the user starts walking and when the two devices are considered separated. In Figure 5 we show the relative improvement of latency for step-based collocation as compared to the RSSI-only technique. The x-axis shows how this improvement diminishes as we increase the interval threshold to make the algorithm more robust to noise. With a interval threshold parameter of 1, step-based personal collocation achieves ~7.5x lower latency than the RSSI-based technique. In a noisier scenario, such as when the user is gesturing, we need an interval threshold of 9 as shown in Figure 3(a). Even with this aggressive setting, step-based collocation still performs ~ 3x better.

5.4 Energy Efficiency

To evaluate the energy efficiency of our solution, we measure the energy consumed by the smartwatch hardware implementation described in Section 4.2 and summarize the average power overhead imposed by our approach. When considering the CPU, accelerometer, and radio components of a wearable device, the combined costs result in only 21.4 μW of average power. To put this in perspective, our service consumes 1.94 Joules of energy per day out of the typical ~4428 Joules available on a modern wrist wearable (Samsung Gear Live used as reference platform).

The power consumption of the step detection algorithm running on the smartphone is also important. We leave a detailed power consumption analysis to future work. However, we note that modern smartphones (i.e. Motorola Moto

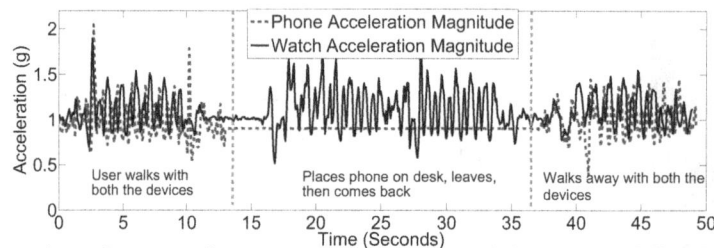

Figure 4: We detect steps based on accelerometer data collected from a mobile phone held in the hand and a smartwatch. This example shows transitions between *Collocated* and *Separated* states.

X, LG Nexus 5, Apple iPhone 5S) have dedicated coprocessors for collecting step data. Pedometer APIs in Android 4.4 enable apps to get a step count several times a second while leaving the CPU in a sleep state, which indicates our approach should have negligible impact on battery life.

6. RELATED WORK

Other work has also used motion detection to determine personal collocation of devices. One technique compares full-bandwidth accelerometer data from a set of medical sensors to determine whether they are on the same person [2]. This is a more communication intense technique than our step-based approach, and the authors use it only to establish a secure pairing for the devices' Bluetooth radios. Another technique uses the Fast Fourier Transform of accelerometer data collected from each device and a coherence matrix to determine whether a pair of devices are together [4]. This work distinguishes whether devices are collocated on a moving person, but it does not handle corner cases when there is no movement. Finally, GruMon [7] uses correlations between accelerometer, compass, and barometer sensor data from different devices to establish logical group relationships between sets of devices on different people. While useful, this technique requires minutes of sensor data to establish group relationships, which is not suitable for the use cases we describe in Section 2.

Another robust way to determine that devices are on the same person uses capacitive communication through the user's skin [1], but this technique does not work for devices in pockets or bags.

7. LIMITATIONS AND FUTURE WORK

While our step-based method for detecting personal collocation has several advantages over existing RSSI-based methods, it also has limitations. One important limitation is vulnerability to spoofing. Our method is intended to assist users with device management, but it does not protect against adversaries trying to fool the system. For example, if an adversary steals a user's device and walks alongside him, our collocation detector may say the two devices are collocated even though they are on different people. We also note that our collocation technique is limited to walking-based mobility that involves regular footsteps; it will not work for people using assitive mobility devices such as crutches or wheel chairs.

Our future work is to improve the robustness of our technique by combining it with RSSI and frequency domain techniques [4]. A decrease in signal strength may help alert us to separation of devices in the adversarial case mentioned above. The lack of a prolonged downward trend in RSSI readings may help us retain the *Collocated* state when a person is sitting and yet one device detects false positive step events. We can apply frequency domain techniques only during periods of spurious motion or transitions between *Collocated* and *Separated* states to improve detection latencies and diminish reliance on statically defined threshold values.

8. CONCLUSION

We describe a new, lightweight approach toward detecting personal collcation of devices using footstep signatures. Since the technique uses motion data directly to approximate distance between devices, it can detect collocation at lower latency than radio-based approaches that use time-varying, noisy RSSI data over distance. By leveraging low-power accelerometer hardware, our approach imposes little energy overhead beyond that required by BLE connections and pedometer-based functionality.

9. REFERENCES

[1] J. Bae, H. Cho, K. Song, H. Lee, and H.-J. Yoo. The signal transmission mechanism on the surface of human body for body channel communication. *Microwave Theory and Techniques, IEEE Transactions on*, 60(3):582–593, 2012.

[2] C. T. Cornelius and D. F. Kotz. Recognizing whether sensors are on the same body. *Pervasive and Mobile Computing*, 8(6):822–836, 2012.

[3] A. Cunningham. The iphone 5s, the moto x, and the rise of the co-processor. `http://arstechnica.com/gadgets/2013/09/the-iphone-5s-the-moto-x-and-the-rise-of-the-co-processor`, 2013.

[4] J. Lester, B. Hannaford, and G. Borriello. "Are you with me?"–using accelerometers to determine if two devices are carried by the same person. In *Pervasive computing*, pages 33–50. Springer, 2004.

[5] Bluetooth SIG. Proximity profile. `https://developer.bluetooth.org/TechnologyOverview/Pages/PXP.aspx`, 2011.

[6] B. Priyantha, D. Lymberopoulos, and J. Liu. Enabling energy efficient continuous sensing on mobile phones with littlerock. In *Proceedings of IPSN*, pages 420–421. ACM, 2010.

[7] R. Sen, Y. Lee, K. Jayarajah, A. Misra, and R. K. Balan. Grumon: Fast and accurate group monitoring for heterogeneous urban spaces. In *Proceedings of SenSys*, pages 46–60. ACM, 2014.

[8] N. Zhao. Full-featured pedometer design realized with 3-axis digital accelerometer. *Analog Dialogue*, 44(06), 2010.

The Missing Numerator: Toward a Value Measure for Smartphone Apps

Anudipa Maiti and Geoffrey Challen
Department of Computer Science and Engineering
University at Buffalo
{anudipam,challen}@buffalo.edu

ABSTRACT

While great strides have been made in measuring energy consumption, these measures alone are not sufficient to enable effective energy management on battery-constrained mobile devices. What is urgently needed is a way to put energy consumption into context by measuring the *value* delivered by mobile apps. While difficult to compute, an accurate value measure would enable cross-app comparison, app improvement, energy inefficient app detection, and effective runtime energy allocation and prioritization. Our paper motivates the problem, describes requirements for a value measure, discusses and evaluates several possible inputs to such a measure, and presents results from a preliminary (unsuccessful) attempt to formulate one.

1. INTRODUCTION

Measuring app energy consumption[1] on mobile devices is nearly a solved problem. This is due to great strides made in both generating and validating energy models that deliver accurate runtime energy consumption estimates [4, 11, 8, 7, 12] and in accurately attributing energy consumption, even for asynchronous and shared resources [10, 2]. Accurate energy models bring us closer to the goal of effective energy management on battery-constrained devices.

But accurate energy measurement alone is not enough, because even perfectly-accurate measurements of energy consumption are insufficient to answer critical energy-related questions faced by users and developers, including:

- Which of the following two apps is more energy efficient?

- Will this change to an app make it more energy efficient?

- Is a particular app an *energy virus*?

- How should the limited energy resources on a given app be prioritized?

---

[1]To avoid confusion between app and energy usage, we use *consumption* exclusively when referring to energy usage and *usage* exclusively when referring to user interaction with apps.

HotMobile'15, February 12–13, 2015, Santa Fe, NM, USA
Copyright is held by the owner/author(s). Publication rights licensed to ACM.
ACM 978-1-4503-3391-7/15/02$15.00.
`http://dx.doi.org/10.1145/2699343.2699360`

Unifying all of these questions is one missing component: a measure of app *value*, which can be used alone or combined with energy consumption to compute energy *efficiency*:

$$\frac{value}{energy}$$

Armed with a measure of value we can return to the difficult questions posed above. By computing efficiency users can perform apples-to-apples comparisons of apps in order to evaluate two video conferencing tools, web browsers, or email clients. Developers can determine whether a new feature delivers value more or less efficiently than the rest of their app and better understand the differences in energy consumption across different users. Measuring value allows a rigorous definition of an *energy virus* as an app that delivers little or no value per joule, and for systems to reward efficient apps by prioritizing limited resources based on app value or energy efficiency. After all the progress we have made in computing the denominator—energy consumption—we believe that the search for the missing numerator is the most important open challenge in energy management.

Developing such a measure, however, is difficult. To be effective it must work across almost the entire spectrum of smartphone apps, which represent an incredible diversity of different goals, interfaces, and interaction patterns. It must also work across a variety of different users with different usage patterns. It must be efficient to compute, since it should not compete for the same limited energy resources that it is intended to help manage. Ideally it should require little to no user input, since this will make it burdensome and error-prone. And to make matters worse, there is no obvious way to measure ground truth to compare against—even in a lab. Despite all these challenges, however, even a semi-accurate value measure would greatly benefit energy management on battery-constrained smartphones. With users continuing to report battery lifetime as their top concern with smartphones [9], we believe this effort is worthwhile.

In this paper we motivate the idea of a value measure and describe an early failure at developing one. We begin in Section 2 by describing how useful such a measure would be while also formulating design requirements for the value measure itself. Section 3 presents an overview of possible inputs into such a measure and discussion of how each could be measured and how useful it might be. In Section 4 we present our initial effort at formulating a value measure based on content delivered through the video display and audio output—an attempt that we consider a failure based on the result of a user survey, but a failure that we hope sheds some light on this difficult challenge.

2. USES AND REQUIREMENTS

To motivate the need for a value measure, we return to the questions posed in the introduction and explore each in more depth. These use cases also help us develop requirements for our measure, which are summarized at the end of this section. We begin by exploring the basic question at the heart of the problem: what is the value of an app?

2.1 What is App Value?

All smartphone users intuitively realize that smartphone apps differ in value—an email client, for example, is probably more valuable than a app that makes random sounds. But is it possible to quantify these subjective distinctions and produce a value measure? To argue that this is possible we present two experiments that elucidate smartphone app value in the form of both ordinal and cardinal utilities:

1. You will be required to remove some number of apps from your smartphone. Order the apps you are currently using from least important to most important. The N least important apps will be removed.

2. You will be required to create an energy budget for the apps you use on your smartphone. During any discharging cycle, once an app runs out of energy you will not be able to use it until you plug in your smartphone. Allocate battery percentages to each app you use.

We plan to engage smartphone users in studies to explore in more detail which of these approaches is more effective, comparing them by comparing users' levels of satisfaction under each scenario. In the first experiment we ask users to uninstall apps because often apps have a background component that keeps consuming energy even when the app is no longer being used. For our value measure we are hopeful that users will prove capable of assigning cardinal utilities to apps—as in the second experiment—since this matches most directly with our proposed value measure and could provide ground truth for a value measure computed automatically. The second experiment also engages users directly in the task of allocating energy, which is one way that a value measure could be used. However, if ordinal utilities prove more intuitive we can still compare the ordering generated by our measure with the ordering generated by users, although the values of the measure will still require justification.

In either case, we believe that these experiments do suggest the existence of quantifiable value for smartphone apps. We are not claiming, however, that these setups are the only way or the right way to measure value. In both cases low value measures have fairly extreme consequences—the app is actually removed or rendered unusable. This may cause users to overvalue essential tools such as communication apps and undervalue inessential apps that nevertheless provide them with a great deal of enjoyment such as games. However, given that our goal is a value measure that can be paired with and used to allocate energy, and that energy exhaustion has such severe consequences on the usability of all apps, a more extreme experimental setup may be justified.

2.2 Comparing Apps

With some confidence that smartphone app value can be quantified, we now proceed to motivate the idea of a value measure by discussing several ways in which it could be used.

The most powerful use of a value measure would be to compare apps by comparing their energy efficiency, there-fore overcoming the most critical flaw in current attempts to compare or categorize apps by their energy consumption alone [6]. Consider attempting to compare a chat client and video conferencing app by only measuring their energy consumption. Unless it is terribly written, the chat client will consume less energy. But this does not mean that it is efficient, or that the video conferencing app is not. Ultimately, all the energy consumption comparison truly reveals is that the two apps do different things—which we already knew.

Using energy consumption alone even makes apples-to-apples comparison of the same app difficult. Given an app that consumes twice as much energy on Alice's smartphone than on Bob's, the question of why is left unanswered by pure energy measures. Even if usage time can be used to normalize the comparison, power consumption alone cannot incorporate differences due to the different app features or app configurations used by Alice and Bob.

By computing value and, thus, energy efficiency, we can overcome these weaknesses. A value measure should allow us to compare the efficiency of two apps in different categories based on how efficiently they use energy to deliver user value. Comparisons within the same app category should allow users to select the most efficient email client or web browser. Aggregating results over all users, differences in app energy efficiency should reflect how well the app is written and how well it predicts and adapts to users, not just differences in the core features it provides. When comparing two users using the same app, differences in efficiency should reflect differences in app configurations or app features.

2.3 Evaluating App Changes

A second use for the value measure is helping developers improve their apps and deliver more value per joule. Today's energy profiling tools may be able to show the energy impact of adding a new feature or changing the way that a particular feature is implemented, but energy consumption alone is not sufficient to apply Amdahl's Law properly to the problem of improving app energy efficiency. Developers should strive to make the parts of their app that generate a large amount of value as energy-efficient as possible, remove parts that generate little value while consuming a great deal of energy, and defer work on everything else.

2.4 Detecting Energy Viruses

A measure of app value makes it possible to produce a rigorous definition of the term *energy virus*: an app that produces little to no value per joule. The choice of threshold will require some study, as it is probably impossible to produce a single efficiency cutoff that cleanly separates malicious apps from ones that are merely poorly-written. This definition of energy virus can also be made on a per-user basis. This is important since a non-malicious but poorly-written app that continues to consume energy even long after the user has stopped using it—and it has stopped providing value—functions as an energy virus for that user, but may not for a user that interacts with it more frequently.

2.5 Prioritizing System Resources

An app value measure should be able to be used to prioritize limited system resources, particularly energy but also storage, memory, networking bandwidth and processor time. While mechanisms differ, most previous attempts to control energy consumption rely on some form of rate control which allocates a rate to each app and enforces that rate by slowing or stopping the app when it exceeds its allocation [1, 10, 13, 3]. However, all of these previous efforts have ignored the critical question of how rates should be set. No matter how effective the enforcement mechanisms are, systems that rely on rates will fail if they provide the same rate to Skype and Snapchat, or to a very efficient app and an energy virus.

A measure of value can be used alone or in conjunction with energy consumption to help prioritize limited energy resources. The simplest approach is to attempt to enforce an energy allocation based on the relative value assigned to each app. To encourage apps to be more energy efficient, it may also be beneficial to weight allocations by their energy efficiency, providing a boost to apps that provide a larger amount of value per joule. While there are likely many ways to combine energy consumption with a value measure in order to prioritize energy consumption, it is not clear that energy consumption can be prioritized effectively without some measure of value. The same approach can also be applied to determine how much of any limited system resource to allocate to each app, Together these resource allocation measures can be designed to ensure that high-value apps run smoothly at the expense of lower-value apps.

2.6 Summary of Requirements

The use cases above give rise to a set of requirements for a possible value measurement:

- It should enable aggregate comparisons between apps across categories and users.

- It should enable comparisons between the same app across users or inputs, requiring that it be calculable given data from a single user.

- It should enable targeted development by highlighting what parts of an app generate value and what parts do not.

- It should be efficiently computable without unduly consuming the resources that it is designed to help manage.

- It should be derived with little to no input from the user.

3. VALUE MEASURE INPUTS

To continue we discuss possible inputs to a value measure and how to collect them at runtime. In each case, we also discuss how such statistics could be misleading.

3.1 Overall Usage

There are a variety of different ways to measure overall app usage that could be useful inputs to our value measure. Total foreground time is straightforward to measure, particularly on today's smartphones where one app tends to dominate the display. However, next-generation smartphone platforms that provide multiple apps with simultaneous access to the display will complicate this task by making it more difficult to determine which app the user is paying attention to. Number of starts is also a potentially-useful input, as may be the distribution of interaction times across all times that the app was brought to the foreground.

While these measures of contact time are intuitive, there are obvious cases in which they fail, particularly for apps that spend a great deal of time running in the background in order to deliver a small amount of useful foreground information—such as a pedometer app.

3.2 User Interface Statistics

Patterns of interaction may also be useful to observe, and inputs such as keystrokes and touchscreen events are simple to track. However, there is more obvious differentiation between app interaction patterns between categories—users deliver far more keystrokes to a chat client than to a video player—so interaction statistics will have to be used in conjunction with complementary value measure components that offset the differences between high-interaction and low-interaction apps. This approach also fails in the case where apps deploy confusing or unnecessary interfaces that require a great deal of unnecessary interaction to accomplish simple tasks. Clearly, such apps should not be rewarded.

3.3 Notification Click-Through Rates

Another interesting statistic that could provide insight on app value is how often users view or click through app notifications. When notifications are delivered but not viewed, then it is unclear whether the app needed to deliver them. When clickable notifications—such as those for new email—provide a way for users to immediately launch the app, the percentage of notifications that are clicked versus ignored could be used to at least evaluate how effective the notifications are, and may also reflect on overall app value.

Notification view and click-through rates also help put into context the energy used by apps when they are running in the background. Legitimate background energy consumption should be for one of two purposes: (1) to prepare the app to deliver more value the next time it is foregrounded, as is the case when music players download songs and store them locally to reduce their runtime networking usage; or (2) to deliver realtime notifications to the user. The effectiveness of background energy consumption to fill caches will be reflected in the apps overall energy usage, since retrieving local content is more energy efficient than using the network. Effectiveness of background consumption to deliver notifications may be reflected in the rate at which notifications are viewed or clicked, since a notification that is not consumed did not need to be retrieved.

However, in some cases apps may do an effective job at summarizing the event within the notification itself, providing no need for the user to bring the app to the foreground. Clearly, such apps should not be penalized.

3.4 Content Delivery

Another approach to measuring value that we feel is promising is to consider apps as content delivery agents and measure how efficiently they deliver information to and from the user. Encouragingly, multiple apps that we have previously considered can fit into this framework:

- **Chat client:** the content is the messages exchanged by users, and efficiency is determined by the amount of screen time and interaction required to retrieve and render incoming messages and generate outgoing messages as replies. Value is measured by the content of the messages. Efficient chat clients exchange many messages per joule.

- **Video player:** the content is the video delivered to the user and efficiency is determined by the amount of network bandwidth and processing needed to retrieve and render the video. Value is measured by the information delivered by the videos and efficient video players present a large amount of video content to their users per joule.

- **Pedometer:** the content is the count of the number of steps presented to the user and efficiency is determined by the accelerometer rate and any post-processing required to produce an accurate estimate. Value is measured as the ability to maintain the step count and efficient pedometers can achieve more accuracy in computing values per joule.

However, while this framework is conceptually appealing, fitting each app into it requires app-specific features that we are trying to avoid: content is measured in messages for the chat client, frames for the video player, and the step value accuracy for the pedometer. This raises the question of whether a single measure of content delivery requiring no app-specific knowledge can be utilized in all cases. We explore this question in more detail, as well as differences between the other value measure inputs we have discussed, through the experiment and results described next.

4. RESULTS

To examine the potential components of a value measure further, we utilize a large dataset of energy consumption measurements collected by an IRB-approved experiment run on the PHONELAB testbed. PHONELAB is a public smartphone platform testbed located at the University at Buffalo [5]. 220 students, faculty, and staff carry instrumented Android Nexus 5 smartphones and receive subsidized service in return for willingness to participate in experiments. PHONELAB provides access to a representative group of participants balanced between genders and across a wide variety of age brackets, making our results more representative.

Understanding fine-grained energy consumption dynamics required more information than Android normally exposes to apps. In addition, to explore components of our value measure we also wanted to capture information about app usage—including foreground and background time and use of the display and audio interface—that was not possible to measure on unmodified Android devices. So to collect our dataset we took advantage of PHONELAB's ability to modify the Android platform itself. We instrumented the `SurfaceFlinger` and `AudioFlinger` components in the Android platform to record usage of the screen and audio, and altered the ActivityManagerService package to record energy consumption at each app transition. This allows energy consumption by components such as the screen to be accurately attributed to the foreground app, a feature that Android's internal battery monitoring component (the Fuel Gauge) lacks. Changes were distributed to PHONELAB participants in November 2013 via an over-the-air (OTA) platform update. The resulting 2 month dataset of 67 GB of compressed log files represents 6806 user days during which 1328 apps were started 277,785 times, and used for a total of 15,224 hours of active use by 107 PHONELAB participants.

Our analysis begins by investigating several components of a possible value measure and shows the effect of using each to weight the overall energy consumed by each app. Next, we formulate a simple measure of content delivery by measuring usage of the screen and audio output devices and test it through a survey completed by 47 experiment participants. Unfortunately, our results are inconclusive and open to several possible interpretations which we discuss. We present our results in tabular format where for each measure we rank 10 best performing and 10 worst performing apps in descending order.

4.1 Total Energy

Clearly, ranking apps by total energy consumption computed by adding all foreground and background energy consumption over the entire study says much more about app popularity than it does about anything else. Table 1a shows the top and bottom energy-consuming apps over the entire study. As expected, popular apps such as the Android Browser, Facebook, and the Android Phone component consume the most energy, while the list of low consumers is dominated by apps with few installs. This table does serve, however, to identify the popular apps in use by PHONELAB participants, and as a point of comparison for the remainder of our results.

4.2 Power

Computing each app's power consumption by scaling their total energy usage against the total time they were running, either in the background or foreground, reveals more information, as shown in Table 1b. Our results identify Facebook Messenger, Google+, and the Super-Bright LED Flashlight as apps that rapidly-consume energy, while the Bank of America and Weather Channel apps consume energy slowly. Differences between apps in similar categories may begin to identify apps with problematic energy consumption, such as contrasting the high energy usage of Facebook Messenger with other messaging clients such as WhatsApp, Twitter, and Android Messaging.

4.3 Foreground Energy Efficiency

Isolating the foreground component of execution time provides a better measure of value, since it ignores the time that users spend ignoring apps. Table 1c shows a measure of energy efficiency computed by dividing total foreground energy consumption by total foreground time of an app. Some surprising changes from the power results can be seen. A number of apps have remained in their former categories: Bank of America, which was identified as a low-power app, is also a highly-efficient app when using foreground time as the value measure; and Facebook Messenger, which was identified as a high-power app, is also marked as inefficient. Other apps, however, have switched categories. ESPN Sportscenter and Yahoo Mail do not consume much power, but also don't spend much time in the foreground; interestingly, none of the high-power apps looked better when their foreground usage was considered.

4.4 Content Energy Efficiency

Finally, we use the data we collected by instrumenting the `SurfaceFlinger` and `AudioFlinger` components to compute a simple measure of content delivery. We measure the audio and video frame rates and combine them into a single measure by using bit-rates corresponding to a 30 fps YouTube-encoded video and 128 kbps two-channel audio, with the weights representing the fact that a single frame of video contains much more content than a single sample of audio. We use this combined metric as the value measure and again use it to weight the energy consumption of each app, with the results shown in Table 1d.

Comparing with the foreground energy efficiency again shows several interesting changes. Yahoo Mail, which foreground energy efficiency marked as inefficient, looks more efficient when content delivery is considered. While it is possible that one PHONELAB participant uses it to read email

Rank	App Name	Energy (As)	Rank	App Name	Consumption Rate (A)
1	Android Browser	41052.703	1	Facebook Messenger	0.774
2	Facebook	37268.388	2	Google+	0.614
3	Chrome Browser	22719.020	3	Super-Bright LED Flashlight	0.600
4	Android Phone	18122.433	4	UB Parking	0.598
5	Gmail	17402.896	5	Android Music	0.446
6	Android Messaging	17342.926	6	Google Search	0.428
7	WhatsApp Messenger	16467.477	7	NFL Mobile	0.386
8	Google Search	15370.252	8	Pandora	0.326
9	Candy Crush Saga	12767.649	9	Starbucks	0.282
10	Android Gallery	11050.363	10	Android News and Weather	0.254
10	Google+	586.586	10	Chrome Browser	0.099
9	Android Calculator	449.474	9	WhatsApp Messenger	0.095
8	NFL Mobile	344.492	8	Twitter	0.078
7	UB Parking	311.766	7	Yahoo Mail	0.077
6	Super-Bright LED Flashlight	218.870	6	Android Messaging	0.061
5	Starbucks	174.609	5	Skype	0.040
4	Google Keep	174.263	4	YouTube	0.036
3	Dropbox	160.939	3	ESPN SportsCenter	0.021
2	ESPN SportsCenter	108.965	2	The Weather Channel	0.019
1	Bank of America	98.007	1	Bank of America	0.011

(a) Most and Least Energy-Consuming Apps.   (b) Fastest and Slowest Energy-Consuming Apps.

Rank	App Name	Efficiency	Rank	App Name	Value
1	Bank of America	83.717	1	YouTube	18497.052
2	The Weather Channel	49.861	2	Candy Crush Saga	14051.369
3	Skype	23.779	3	Bank of America	12954.196
4	YouTube	19.880	4	Dropbox	7063.746
5	Android Messaging	12.933	5	Android Messaging	6555.140
6	Android Gallery	9.260	6	Android Gallery	5773.902
7	Android Calculator	9.189	7	Twitter	5610.394
8	Twitter	8.645	8	Android Clock	5085.873
9	Chrome Browser	8.524	9	Yahoo Mail	5083.615
10			10		
10	Yahoo Mail	3.287	10	NFL Mobile	1275.985
9	ESPN SportsCenter	3.184	9	UB Parking	1071.529
8	Google Search	1.984	8	Pandora	1049.971
7	Android Music	1.972	7	Facebook Messenger	1012.536
6	Pandora	1.779	6	Android News and Weather	990.386
5	Super-Bright LED Flashlight	1.667	5	Adobe Reader	985.680
4	UB Parking	1.507	4	Google+	898.589
3	NFL Mobile	1.437	3	Android Phone	748.077
2	Google+	1.270	2	Google Search	682.005
1	Facebook Messenger	1.199	1	The Weather Channel	571.405

(c) Apps Sorted by Foreground Energy Efficiency.   (d) Apps Sorted by Content Energy Efficiency.

Table 1: **Evaluating Components of a Value Measure.** PHONELAB data is used to weight overall app energy usage in a variety of different ways. Omitted results are caused by Android reporting energy consumption for non-apps such as the Android System.

very quickly, it may be more likely that it uses a "spinner" or other fancy UI elements that generate artificially high frame rates without delivering much information. The inability to distinguish between meaningless and meaningful video frame content is a significant weakness of this simple approach. YouTube and Candy Crush Saga both earn high marks, which is encouraging given that they are very different apps but also might be a result of overweighting screen refreshes. The Android Clock is also an unsurprising result, as it requires almost no energy to generate a relatively-large number of screen redraws in timer and stopwatch mode.

4.5 Survey Results and Discussion

To continue the evaluation of our simple content-based value measure, we prepared a survey for the 107 PHONE-LAB participants who contributed data to our experiment. Our goal was to determine if users would be more willing to remove inefficient apps, as defined using our content-based

measure. As a baseline, we also asked users about the apps that consumed the most energy. We used each participants data to generate a custom survey containing questions about 9 apps: the 3 least efficient apps as computed by our content-based value measure, the 3 apps that used the most energy on their smartphone during the experiment, and 3 apps chosen at random. For each we asked them a simple question: "If it would improve your battery life, would you uninstall or stop using this app?" To compute an aggregate score for both the content-based and usage based measures, we give each measure 1 point for a "Yes", 0.5 points for a "Maybe" and 0 points for a "No". 47 participants completed the survey, and the results are shown in Figure 1. For each user, if the score of one measure is higher than the other, it is considered a "win" for the former.

Overall the results are inconclusive, with the content-delivery measure not clearly outperforming the straw-man usage measure at predicting which apps each user would be

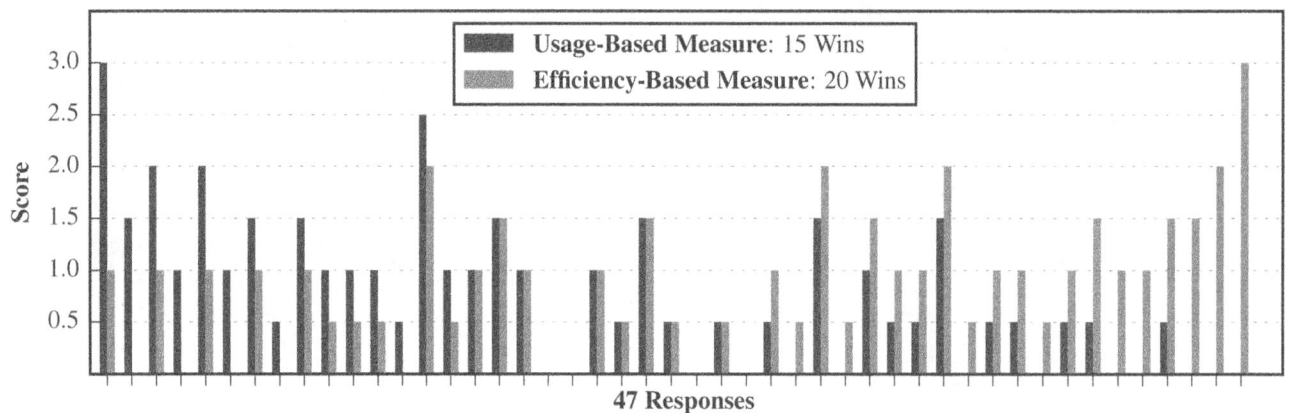

Figure 1: **Survey Results.** The height of each bar demonstrates how many of the suggested apps the user is willing to remove for better battery life, with suggestions based on overall usage or our new content-delivery efficiency measure. Our new measure does not convincingly out-perform the straw man.

willing to remove to save battery life. Given the crude nature of our metric, this is not particularly surprising, and can be interpreted as a sign that we need a more sophisticated value measure incorporating more of the potential inputs we have previously discussed. However, on one level the results are very encouraging: most users were willing to consider removing one or more apps if that app would improve their battery lifetime. Clearly, users are making this decision based on some idea of each app's value—the challenge is to replicate their choices using the information we have available to us.

5. CONCLUSIONS

To conclude, we have argued that our inability to estimate app value is a critical weakness that is threatening our successes at accurately estimating and attributing energy consumption. We have motivated the need for a value measure by describing the multiple ways in which it would aid in the management of energy and other resources on battery-powered smartphones. Using an energy consumption dataset collected on PHONELAB we have explored separately several potential inputs to a value measure and determined how they weight energy consumption. Finally, we have presented results from a failed effort to formulate an effective value measure. While this first attempt was unsuccessful, we hope to engage the mobile systems community in this effort so that more sophisticated and successful value measures can be developed.

Acknowledgments

Students and faculty working on estimating app value are supported by NSF awards 1205656 and 1423215. The authors thank the anonymous reviewers for their feedback.

6. REFERENCES

[1] FLINN, J., AND SATYANARAYANAN, M. Energy-aware adaptation for mobile applications. SIGOPS Oper. Syst. Rev. 33, 5 (1999), 48–63.

[2] FONSECA, R., DUTTA, P., LEVIS, P., AND STOICA, I. Quanto: Tracking energy in networked embedded systems. In Proceedings of the USENIX Symposium on Operating Systems Design and Implementation (OSDI) (November 2008).

[3] LORINCZ, K., RONG CHEN, B., WATERMAN, J., WERNER-ALLEN, G., AND WELSH, M. Resource aware programming in the pixie os. In Proc. 6th ACM Conference on Embedded Networked Sensor Systems (SenSys'08) (New York, NY, USA, 2008), ACM, pp. 211–224.

[4] MA, X., HUANG, P., JIN, X., WANG, P., PARK, S., SHEN, D., ZHOU, Y., SAUL, L. K., AND VOELKER, G. M. eDoctor: Automatically Diagnosing Abnormal Battery Drain Issues on Smartphones. In Proceedings of the 10th USENIX conference on Networked Systems Design and Implementation (Berkeley, CA, USA, 2013), NSDI'13, USENIX Association, pp. 57–70.

[5] NANDUGUDI, A., MAITI, A., KI, T., BULUT, F., DEMIRBAS, M., KOSAR, T., QIAO, C., KO, S. Y., AND CHALLEN, G. Phonelab: A large programmable smartphone testbed. In Proc. 1st International Workshop on Sensing and Big Data Mining (SenseMine 2013) (November 2013).

[6] OLINER, A. J., IYER, A. P., STOICA, I., LAGERSPETZ, E., AND TARKOMA, S. Carat: collaborative energy diagnosis for mobile devices. In SenSys (2013), C. Petrioli, L. P. Cox, and K. Whitehouse, Eds., ACM, p. 10.

[7] PATHAK, A., HU, Y. C., AND ZHANG, M. Where is the Energy Spent Inside My App?: Fine Grained Energy Accounting on Smartphones with Eprof. In Proceedings of the 7th ACM european conference on Computer Systems (New York, NY, USA, 2012), EuroSys '12, ACM, pp. 29–42.

[8] PATHAK, A., HU, Y. C., ZHANG, M., BAHL, P., AND WANG, Y.-M. Fine-Grained Power Modeling for Smartphones Using System Call Tracing. In Proceedings of the sixth conference on Computer systems (New York, NY, USA, 2011), EuroSys '11, ACM, pp. 153–168.

[9] PUNZALAN, R. Smartphone Battery Life a Critical Factor for Customer Satisfaction . http://www.brighthand.com/default.asp?newsID=18721.

[10] ROY, A., RUMBLE, S. M., STUTSMAN, R., LEVIS, P., MAZIÈRES, D., AND ZELDOVICH, N. Energy management in mobile devices with the cinder operating system. In Proceedings of the Sixth Conference on Computer Systems (New York, NY, USA, 2011), EuroSys '11, ACM, pp. 139–152.

[11] XU, F., LIU, Y., LI, Q., AND ZHANG, Y. V-edge: Fast self-constructive power modeling of smartphones based on battery voltage dynamics. In Proceedings of the 10th USENIX Conference on Networked Systems Design and Implementation (Berkeley, CA, USA, 2013), nsdi'13, USENIX Association, pp. 43–56.

[12] YOON, C., KIM, D., JUNG, W., KANG, C., AND CHA, H. AppScope: Application Energy Metering Framework for Android Smartphones Using Kernel Activity Monitoring. In Proceedings of the 2012 USENIX conference on Annual Technical Conference (Berkeley, CA, USA, 2012), USENIX ATC'12, USENIX Association, pp. 36–36.

[13] ZENG, H., ELLIS, C. S., LEBECK, A. R., AND VAHDAT, A. Currentcy: a unifying abstraction for expressing energy management policies. In Proceedings of the annual conference on USENIX Annual Technical Conference (Berkeley, CA, USA, 2003), USENIX Association, pp. 4–4.

maybe We Should Enable More Uncertain Mobile App Programming

Geoffrey Challen, Jerry Antony Ajay, Nick DiRienzo, Oliver Kennedy,
Anudipa Maiti, Anandatirtha Nandugudi, Sriram Shantharam,
Jinghao Shi, Guru Prasad Srinivasa, and Lukasz Ziarek

Department of Computer Science and Engineering
University at Buffalo

maybe@blue.cse.buffalo.edu

ABSTRACT

One of the reasons programming mobile systems is so hard is the wide variety of environments a typical app encounters at runtime. As a result, in many cases only post-deployment user testing can determine the right algorithm to use, the rate at which something should happen, or when an app should attempt to conserve energy. Programmers should not be forced to make these choices at development time. Unfortunately, languages leave no way for programmers to express and structure uncertainty about runtime conditions, forcing them to adopt ineffective or fragile ad-hoc solutions.

We introduce a new approach based on *structured uncertainty* through a new language construct: the maybe statement. maybe statements allow programmers to defer choices about app behavior that cannot be made at development time, while providing enough structure to allow a system to later adaptively choose from multiple alternatives. Eliminating the uncertainty introduced by maybe statements can be done in a large variety of ways: through simulation, split testing, user configuration, temporal adaptation, or machine learning techniques, depending on the type of adaptation appropriate for each situation. Our paper motivates the maybe statement, presents its syntax, and describes a complete system for testing and choosing from maybe alternatives.

1. INTRODUCTION

All programmers must deal with uncertainty about runtime environments. For example, the most appropriate algorithm for a given task may depend on inputs that are unknown when the function is written, and its performance may depend on device-specific features that are impossible for the developer to anticipate. In other cases, real-world testing may be required to choose between several approaches, which has led to the popularity of split testing.

Uncertainty is especially problematic for mobile app programmers. Specific device features, such as accurate GPS

```
if (plugged == false && batteryLevel < 10) {
  // Try to save energy
} else {
  // Don't try to save energy
}
```

Figure 1: **Typical Error-Prone Energy Adaptation.** The threshold is arbitrary and the attempt to conserve energy may succeed only at certain times, only for certain users, only on certain devices, or never.

location, may or may not be available. Networks come and go and their properties change: from fast and free Wifi links to slower metered mobile data connections. Energy may be plentiful or scarce, depending on the device's battery capacity and the user's energy consumption and charging patterns. These constantly fluctuating exogenous conditions make writing effective mobile apps particularly challenging.

Today programmers are forced to anticipate these changing conditions at development time and implement the required adaptation themselves. Figure 1 shows an example of an Android app attempting to adapt to the device's battery level by establishing regular- and low-battery code paths, with the latter attempting to save energy—possibly by utilizing a slower but more energy-efficient algorithm, computing an approximate result, or deferring the computation.

Unfortunately, this approach has several serious weaknesses. The most important is perhaps the least obvious: it is unclear that the different code paths achieve the desired result. There may be no differences between the alternatives (neither conserves energy), the alternative designed to conserve energy may actually consume more due to bugs or incorrect assumptions, or the outcome may depend on other factors not considered by the programmer, such as the type of network the device is currently using.

In addition, attempts at pre-deployment adaptation frequently produce arbitrary decision thresholds. Even if the two code paths in Figure 1 achieve the desired result, it is unclear what battery level threshold should trigger the energy-saving path, whether a single threshold will work for all users, and whether the threshold should depend on other factors such as how frequently the app is used.

Finally, the current approach to adaptation fails to support post-deployment testing. While it is possible to enable flexibility, runtime adaptation, and split testing using the languages currently used to program mobile systems, these tasks require writing large amounts of error-prone boilerplate code that retrieves settings from remote servers and adjusts values at runtime.

```
maybe {
    // Try to save energy (Alternative 1)
} or {
    // Don't to save energy (Alternative 2)
}
```

Figure 2: **Example** maybe **Statement.** The programmer provides multiple alternatives. The system determines how to choose between them.

The root of the problem is that **today's languages force programmers to be certain at a moment when they cannot be: at development time.** While this problem is endemic to existing programming languages, when developing mobile apps it is magnified by the amount of variation developers must confront. Our solution is simple: (1) provide developers with a way to express *structured uncertainty*, and (2) use the resulting flexibility to enable a large array of downstream tools for resolving uncertainty by choosing from the alternatives provided by the developer.

In this paper, we present a novel a language construct for expressing structured uncertainty: the maybe statement. Unlike previous approaches to adaptation that relied on language support, maybe does not encourage programmers to provide more information about their app to allow the compiler to improve performance or guarantee correctness. Rather, maybe allows the programmer to express and structure uncertainty by providing two or more different *alternatives* implementing multiple approaches to runtime adaptation. Together, multiple alternatives can produce the same energy-performance or energy-accuracy tradeoffs described previously. Conceptually, maybe extends the process of compilation and optimization to include post-deployment testing while also enabling flexible adaptation that may produce per-user, per-device, or time-varying decisions.

Figure 2 shows how our earlier example can be easily rewritten using a maybe statement. Unlike the previous example, maybe does not rely on the developer to implement a decision process or correctly predict the effects of each alternative. Instead, the maybe system makes runtime choices about which alternative to use by measuring the tradeoffs produced by each alternative and (in this case) activating an energy-saving alternative when appropriate. When they are unsure what to do, all developers have to do is provide alternatives; the maybe system does the rest. maybe allows developers to respond to uncertainty with flexibility, which is used to enable testing-driven adaptation.

The rest of our paper is structured as follows. We begin by providing a more complete description of the maybe statement in Section 2. Section 3 describes several techniques for transforming development-time uncertainty into runtime certainty. We continue by describing several example use cases in Section 4, discussing the implications of the maybe statement in Section 5, and presenting related work in Section 6. We conclude in Section 7.

2. MAYBE STATEMENT SEMANTICS

To begin we provide an overview of the maybe statement's semantics describing how it allows developers to structure uncertainty. We refer to each of the values or code paths a maybe statement can choose from as an *alternative*.

2.1 Setting Variables

Variables can be used to represent uncertainty. Examples include an integer storing how often a timer should trigger

```
// Setting variables
int retryInterval = maybe 1-16;
String policy = maybe "auto", "quality", "perf";

// Function alternatives
@maybe
int myFunction(int a) { /* First alternative */ }
@maybe
int myFunction(int a) { /* Second alternative */ }

// Inlining evaluation code
maybe {
    ret = fastPowerHungryAlgorithm(input);
} or {
    ret = slowPowerEfficientAlgorithm(input);
} evaluate {
    return { "repeat": false,
             "score" : nanoTime() + powerDrain() }
}
```

Figure 3: **More** maybe **Statements**

communication with a remote server, or a string containing the name of a policy used to coordinate multiple code blocks throughout the app. Figure 3 shows examples of an integer that can take on values between 1 and 16, and a string that be set to either "auto", "quality", or "perf".

2.2 Controlling Code Flow

Code flow can also represent uncertainty. Examples include using multiple algorithms to compute the same result or multiple code paths representing different tradeoffs between performance, energy, and quality. Figure 2 shows the maybe statement in its simplest form, controlling execution of multiple code blocks. If multiple alternatives are specified, the system chooses one to execute; if only one alternative is specified, the system chooses whether or not to execute it. Single-alternative maybe statements can encapsulate or reorganize logic that does not affect correctness, but may (or may not) produce some desirable outcome.

Figure 3 shows several extensions of the maybe statement providing syntactic sugar. maybe function annotations allow uncertainty to be expressed at the function level, with the alternatives consisting of multiple function definitions with identical signatures. maybe statements that require custom evaluation logic can include an **evaluate** block as shown in the final example. **evaluate** blocks provide app-specific *a posteriori* logic to evaluate the selected alternative. The **evaluate** block must return a single JSON object with two components: (1) a positive integer **score**, with smaller being better; (2) and a boolean **repeat** indicating whether the system must use the same alternative next time. Hints and custom evaluation logic can also be applied to other types of maybe statements through annotations.

While it should be possible to nest maybe statements, it may require compiler support to provide guarantees about how maybe decisions are maintained across multiple code blocks. As we gain more experience with our rewrite-based prototype, described next in Section 3, we will revisit the question of nesting in future compiler-based maybe systems.

As a final remark, note that structured uncertainty is not randomness. Randomness weights multiple options statically—there is no right or wrong decision. In contrast, the maybe statement indicates that during any given execution one alternative may better than the others. The goal of the system is to determine which one.

3. FROM UNCERTAINTY TO CERTAINTY

While `maybe` allows programmers to specify multiple alternatives, ultimately only one alternative can be executed at runtime. Either a single, globally-optimal alternative must be identified, or a deterministic decision procedure must be developed. Before discussing options for adapting an app to its runtime environment, we first explain our runtime's support for `maybe` alternatives, including *a posteriori* evaluation and data collection. Then, we discuss how `maybe` testing enables a variety of different adaptation patterns.

3.1 Evaluating Alternatives

The optional `evaluate` block of a `maybe` statement allows programmers to provide app-specific *a posteriori* evaluation logic. However, in many cases, we expect that `maybe` statements will be used to achieve common objectives such as improving performance or saving energy. To streamline application development, our current system evaluates `maybe` statements without a `evaluate` block by measuring both energy and performance. In cases where one alternative optimizes both, that alternative will be used—although the decision may still be time-varying due to dependence on time-varying factors such as network availability. When alternatives produce an energy-performance tradeoff we are exploring several options, including collapsing both metrics into a single score by computing the energy-delay product (EDP) of each alternative, or allowing users to set a per-app energy or performance preference.

`evaluate` blocks can also record other information to aid adaptation. While the `score` value is used to evaluate the alternative, the entire JSON object returned by the `evaluate` block is delivered to the developer for later analysis. This allows `maybe` statements to be connected with end-to-end app performance metrics not visible on the device. We expect that some `evaluate` blocks may need to know which alternative was executed to compute a score—for example, if the two alternatives produce different quality output. We are exploring the use of automatically-generated labels to aid this process.

If a `maybe` alternative throws an error, the system will bypass the `evaluate` block and give it the worst possible score. By integrating a form of record-and-replay [5], it may be possible to roll back the failed alternative and retry another. While `maybe` is intended to enable adaptation, not avoid errors, the existence of other alternatives provides a way to work around failures caused by uncertainty. Fault tolerance may also encourage developers to use `maybe` statements to prototype alternatives to existing well-tested code.

A final question concerns when a `maybe` alternative should be evaluated. Some alternatives may require evaluation immediately after execution. Others may require repeated execution over a longer period of time to perform a fair comparison. As described previously, `evaluate` blocks can indicate explicitly whether or not to continue evaluating the alternative, and we are determining how to make a similar choice available to `maybe` statements without `evaluate` blocks. In addition, `evaluate` blocks can store state across multiple alternative executions allowing them to evaluate not only micro- but also macro-level decisions. In both cases, however, the `maybe` system allows developers continuous per-statement control over alternative choice and evaluation as described in more detail later in this section.

3.2 `maybe` Alternative Testing

We next describe the pre- and post-deployment testing that helps developers to design an *adaptation* policy, a strategy for ultimately selecting between alternatives. While the `maybe` system automates many of the tedious tasks normally associated with large-scale testing, we still provide ways for the developer to guide and control any step in the process.

3.2.1 Runtime control

To begin, we briefly outline how our Android prototype implements the `maybe` statement. We (1) rewrite each `maybe` conditional to an `if-else` statement controlled by a call into the `maybe` system and (2) generate a similar setter for each `maybe` variable. Variable values and code branches are now all under the control of a separate `maybe` service which can be deployed as a separate app or incorporated into the Android platform. It is responsible for communicating with the global `maybe` server to retrieve adaptation parameters for all `maybe`-enabled apps on the smartphone. When possible, we avoid interprocess communication during each `maybe` decision by caching decisions in the app, with the `maybe` service delivering cache invalidation messages when particular decisions change. The `maybe` service tracks when alternative decisions change, runs `evaluate` evaluation logic when appropriate, and returns testing results to the `maybe` server.

Because unexpected runtime variable changes could cause crashes or incorrect behavior, we only alter `maybe` variables when they are (re)initialized, not at arbitrary points during execution. If the app wants to enable periodic readaptation of certain variables, such as the interval controlling a timer, it can do so by periodically resetting the value using another `maybe` statement. This ensures that `maybe` variables only change when expected.

3.2.2 Simulation or emulation

Pre-deployment simulation or emulation may provide a way to efficiently evaluate `maybe` statements without involving users. Building simulation environments that accurately reflect all of the uncertainties inherent to mobile systems programming, however, is difficult. To complicate matters, `maybe` alternatives may depend on details of user interaction that are difficult to know *a priori*, particularly when new apps or features are being developed. So in most cases we believe post-deployment testing will be required.

However, pre-deployment testing may still be a valuable approach, particularly when a large number of `maybe` statements are being used. Since this can explode the adaptation space, simulations may be able to help guide the developer's choices of which `maybe` statements may have a significant impact on performance and should be evaluated first. Other `maybe` statements can be evaluated later or eliminated.

3.2.3 Split testing

Eventually code containing a number of `maybe` statements will be deployed on thousands or millions of devices. At this point, large-scale split testing and data-driven learning can begin. If the user community is large enough, it may be possible to collect statistically-significant results even for all possible permutations of `maybe` alternatives. For apps with a small number of users, or a large number of `maybe` statements, we can collect data for variations of one or several `maybe` statements while holding the rest constant. As an adaptation policy is designed and deployed for the statement being tested, we begin to vary and measure the next group of `maybe` statements. Developers can observe and control the testing process through a web interface.

Each time a `maybe` statement is reached or `maybe` variable is set, the `maybe` system records:

- what `maybe` was reached;
- what alternative was used and why. This includes all environmental features used to make the decision, as well as any other available provenance information;
- what `evaluate` block evaluated the alternative, and the entire JSON object it returned, including the score;
- and a variety of other environmental and configuration parameters that the user permits access to: A user identifier; device and platform information; networking provider and conditions; location; battery level; and so on.

This dataset is periodically uploaded to the `maybe` server and used to drive the adaptation approaches discussed next.

3.2.4 Simultaneous split testing

While large-scale split testing is intended to provide good coverage over all possible sources of uncertainty we have discussed, it still normally requires that only one decision be made at any given time—implying that two alternatives may never be evaluated under identical conditions. For `maybe` statements, however, we are exploring the idea of performing *simultaneous* split testing. In this model the app forks at the top of the `maybe` statement, executes and scores all alternatives, and then continues with the outputs from the best alternative at the bottom of the `maybe` statement. On single-core devices this can be done in serial, while the growing number of multi-core smartphones provides the option of doing this in parallel. The benefit of this approach is that each alternative is executed under near-identical conditions. The drawbacks include the overhead of the redundant executions and the possibility for interference between alternatives executing in parallel.

3.3 `maybe` Endgames

The entire `maybe` approach is predicated on the fact that there does exist, among the alternatives, a right decision, even if it depends on many factors and uncertainties. We continue by discussing how the dataset generated by post-deployment testing can be used to determine how to correctly choose `maybe` alternatives at runtime.

3.3.1 Simple cases

In the simplest case, testing may reveal that a single alternative performs the best on all devices, for all users, at all times. In this situation, the `maybe` system may offer a way for the developer to immediately cease testing of that alternative and even automatically rewrite that portion of code to remove the `maybe` statement. However, it is also possible that the situation may change in the future when a new device, or Android version, or battery technology is introduced, and so the programmer may also choose to preserve the flexibility in case it is useful in the future.

The slightly more complicated case is when testing reveals that alternatives provide stable tradeoffs between energy and performance—one alternative always saves energy at the cost of performance. In this case the system only has to determine whether to prioritize energy or performance.

While this decision seems simple, it is itself complicated by differences in battery capacity, charging habits, mixtures of installed apps, and the importance of the app to each user. However, the stability of the alternatives' outcomes means that once an energy or performance policy decision has been made, the choice of alternative has also been made.

3.3.2 Static adaptation

In the more complicated cases, testing reveals that the choice of alternative depends on some subset of the factors driving uncertainty in mobile systems programming. We break this group into two subsets, depending on whether the adaptation is time varying (dynamic) or not (static). We begin with the second, somewhat easier case.

If the alternative is determined through static adaptation then the correct decision is a function of some unchanging (or very-slowly changing) aspect of the deployed environment. Examples include the device model, average network conditions, the other apps installed on the device, or user characteristics such as gender, age, or charging habits. In this case it is possible that the correct alternative can be determined through clustering based on these features, and once determined will remain the best choice for a long time.

3.3.3 Dynamic adaptation

If the choice of alternative depends on dynamic factors such as the accuracy of location services, the amount of energy left in the battery, or the type of network the device is currently connected to, then it is possible that no single alternative can be chosen even for a single user. Instead, the `maybe` system allows developers to evaluate one or more strategies to drive the runtime alternative selection process.

Note that `evaluate` blocks are *not* intended to accomplish this kind of adaptation. First, they run after the `maybe` statement has been executed, not before. Second, per-`maybe` strategy defeats the flexibility inherent to the `maybe` approach and would devolve into the fragile decision-making we are trying to avoid.

Instead, the `maybe` system allows developers to experiment with and evaluate a variety of different dynamic adaptation strategies deployed in a companion library, with the decision guided by post-deployment testing. For example, if the performance of an alternative is discovered to be correlated with a link providing a certain amount of bandwidth, then that adaptation strategy can be connected with that particular `maybe` statement.

Observe that in some cases of dynamic adaptation, what begins as a `maybe` statement may end as effectively `if-else` statement switching on a static threshold—the same approach we attacked to motivate our system. However, through the process of arriving at this point we have determined several things that were initially unknown: (1) what the alternatives accomplish, (2) that a single threshold works for all users, and (3) what that threshold is. And by maintaining the choice as a `maybe` statement, they can continue adaptating as devices, users, and networks change.

Another benefit of this approach is that time-varying decisions can be outsourced to developers with expertise in the particular area affecting adaptation decisions. For example, by exposing an energy-performance tradeoff through a `maybe` statement, a developer allows it to be connected to a sophisticated machine learning algorithm written by an expert in energy adaptation, instead of their own ad-hoc approach.

3.3.4 Manual adaptation

In some cases even our best efforts to automatically adapt may fail, and it may be impossible to predict which alternative is best for a particular user using a particular device at a particular time. If the differences between the alternatives are small, then it may be appropriate to simply fall back to a best-effort decision. However, if the differences between the alternatives are significant then the maybe alternatives may need to be exposed to the user through a settings menu. Fortunately, information obtained through testing can still be presented to the user to guide their decision. Note that this requires labeling alternatives in a human-readable way.

3.4 Continuous Adaptation

Finally, even once a decision process for a particular maybe alternative has been developed, it should be periodically revisited as users, devices, networks, batteries, and other factors affecting mobile apps continue to change. To enable continuous adaptation, developers can configure maybe statements to continue to periodically experiment with alternatives other than the one selected by the alternative testing process. Changes in alternative performance relative to the expectations established during the last round of alternative testing may trigger a large-scale reexamination of that maybe statement using the same process described above.

4. EXAMPLE USE CASES

The maybe system is inspired by our frustrations building smartphone apps that confront the uncertainties inherent to mobile systems programming. In this section we describe several examples of how to use the maybe statement drawn from our own experiences.

4.1 PocketParker App

PocketParker [8] estimates parking lot availability by using the smartphone's accelerometer to detect users entering and leaving parking spots. To do this is an energy-efficient manner, we initially developed a custom activity recognition algorithm that duty-cycled the accelerometer to conserve energy. Towards the end of our development, Google released their own activity recognition API as a part of their Google Play Services framework. Based on several small-scale tests there was no clear winner when comparing the two algorithms, and so we decided to use Google's implementation to offload the maintenance burden. Supporting both algorithms, switching between them at runtime, and assessing the resulting impact on a larger user population would have required a significant amount of development effort.

Such runtime decisions fit naturally into the maybe framework. Instead of having to choose based on small-scale local testing, the maybe system can manage the transition from a mature but app-specific and expensive to maintain algorithm to a potentially-immature but canonical library implementation. As the library implementation improves and begins to out-perform the hand-tuned alternative, the maybe system can conduct repeated testing and move more users over to the library implementation. For some users or on some devices, the library implementation may never outperform the app-specific algorithm, in which cases maybe allows both alternatives to coexist safely while ensuring that each user enjoys whichever approach is most effective for them.

4.2 PhoneLab Conductor

PHONELAB is a large scale smartphone platform testbed at the University at Buffalo [9]. We leverage the Android logcat subsystem as a data collection mechanism—experiments log their data into a system-wide log buffer and we collect and upload this data on their behalf.

We developed an app called the PHONELAB Conductor for this purpose which provides a good example of custom maybe evaluation logic. The goal of our app is to collect data reliably while minimizing energy consumption, storage usage, and metered data usage. With the maybe statement branching between multiple policies for uploading data—such as always waiting until the user reaches a plug, or always initiating an upload once the storage allocated is 50% full—the evaluation logic would provide the worst possible score if data had been lost, or otherwise a score combining the multiple attributes the app is trying to minimize.

Due to the uncertainties we faced during development, we implemented a configuration interface that periodically retrieves parameters from our server and uses them to reconfigure variable components of the app. This allows us to control aspects of program behavior such as the amount of storage space we use on each device for logs, how often we check for updates, and how to decide whether to upload data. Several of these features have proven essential after deployment—for example, when an upload policy that worked previously abruptly stopped working on a newer Android version. Development of this app would have been considerably easier using maybe, which could automate the process of pushing policies to clients in an energy-efficient way, and enabling per-user goal-driven adaptation.

4.3 Navjack Sensing Platform

The Navjack project is exploring hijacking in-car navigation devices built from recycled smartphones [3] and deployed in personal vehicles to enable city-scale sensing. Volunteers install a device that acts as a dedicated navigation aid and car performance monitor but also continuously collects sensor data, utilizing the car's battery for power, the car's driver for maintenance, and inexpensive machine-to-machine (M2M) data plans for telemetry.

Navjack's goal is to produce high-quality data in response to queries while minimizing cellular data usage and car battery energy consumption. Many uncertainties specific to this app complicate the process. Some car cigarette lighters and USB charging docks provide power while the vehicle is off, while some do not. Users drive their vehicles for different durations and at different frequencies. Cellular coverage varies, altering the energy-per-bit required to offload data. All of these factors complicate post-deployment adaptation.

maybe statements in Navjack can be used to control the sampling rate, the set of sensors that are used, and the conditions under which uploads are attempted. This app provides an example of an adaptation state space that can potentially get quite large, and so it may provide a good chance to evaluate both our ability to perform pre-deployment simulations to reduce the state space and the success of post-deployment clustering techniques to identify salient user differences.

5. DISCUSSION

We have yet to determine how natural programmers will find the maybe statement. Encouragingly, maybe statements are similar to the ubiquitous if-else statement, and in many cases can directly replace `if-else` statements that attempt runtime adaptation. To coordinate the adaptation of multiple code paths a single `maybe` variable can be used to control multiple `if-else` statements.

Overuse of the `maybe` statement may cause problems. If dependencies exist between `maybe` statements, the overall configuration space may expand exponentially, complicating post-deployment adaptation. Compile-time analysis may be required to detect dependencies between `maybe` statements and encourage programmers to limit their use of `maybe` to ensure that downstream optimization remains feasible.

`maybe` statements should not be used when adaptation can be refactored into a library. As an example, an app should not use `maybe` to decide which network interface to use when attempting to achieve a common objective, such as maximizing throughput. This adaptation should be refactored into a dedicated library, which might use its own `maybe` statements. Not only is the resulting codebase smaller, but the total number of `maybe` statements to test is reduced.

However, the `maybe` statement represents a fundamentally different approach to runtime adaptation than systems that rely on libraries because library development still requires development-time certainty. While library developers are more likely to be experts at the type of adaptation their library performs, we still believe that even the most skilled programmers will benefit from being able to express structured uncertainty. `maybe` allows all developers—including both app and library writers—to shed the burden of producing a single certain approach and instead write uncertain code containing the flexibility required to enable powerful data-driven approaches to post-deployment adaptation.

6. RELATED WORK

New systems such as EnFrame [12] reflect growing interest in managing uncertainty at the language level. EnFrame focuses on enabling programming with uncertain data, rather than the runtime adaptation enabled by `maybe`.

Aspect oriented programming (AOP) [6] aims to increase modularity through the separation of cross-cutting concerns. The programmer expresses cross-cutting concerns in stand alone modules, or aspects, which specify a computation to be performed as well as points in the program at which that computation should be performed. Fundamentally, the goals of AOP and the `maybe` statement differ, with AOP focusing on modularity and `maybe` focused on enabling adaptation by expressing uncertainty.

`maybe` shares similarities with language-based approaches to adapting energy consumption such as Eon [11] and Levels [7]. However, these approaches still require programmers to express certainty by associating code with energy states, rather than allowing the `maybe` system to determine which energy states are appropriate. `maybe` can also enable adaptation driven by goals other than energy management.

Attempts to enable more adaptive mobile systems date back to systems such as Odyssey [10]. However, a taxonomy of approaches to enabling adaptation on early mobile systems [1] reflects the focus of early efforts on incorporating adaptation into libraries that could be used by multiple apps. As we have pointed out previously, while adaptation libraries are useful, `maybe` statements can make them more powerful by allowing programmers to express uncertainty.

Recent approaches that allow mobile devices to effectively offload computation by automating client-cloud partitioning are also related to the `maybe` statement. Systems such as Tactics [2] and MAUI [4] used a variety of approaches to enabling this form of adaptation but are narrowly-focused on harnessing opportunities for remote execution. At present `maybe` focuses on single-device adaptation, but we are interested in exploring the ability to use uncertainty to distribute computation between multiple devices as future work.

7. CONCLUSION

To conclude, we have described the `maybe` statement: a new language construct allowing developers to express structured uncertainty at development time and for that uncertainty to be resolved through later testing and adaptation. We are in the process of building a prototype of the `maybe` system for Android smartphones.

Acknowledgments

Students and faculty working on the `maybe` project are supported by NSF awards 1205656, 1409367, and 1423215. The `maybe` team thanks the anonymous reviewers and our shepherd, Mahadev Satyanarayanan, for their feedback.

8. REFERENCES

[1] BADRINATH, B., FOX, A., KLEINROCK, L., POPEK, G., REIHER, P., AND SATYANARAYANAN, M. A conceptual framework for network and client adaptation. Mobile Networks and Applications 5, 4 (2000), 221–231.

[2] BALAN, R. K., SATYANARAYANAN, M., PARK, S. Y., AND OKOSHI, T. Tactics-based remote execution for mobile computing. In Proceedings of the 1st international conference on Mobile systems, applications and services (2003), ACM, pp. 273–286.

[3] CHALLEN, G., HASELEY, S., MAITI, A., NANDUGUDI, A., PRASAD, G., PURI, M., AND WANG, J. The Mote is Dead. Long Live the Discarded Smartphone! In Proc. 15th Workshop on Mobile Systems and Applications (ACM HotMobile 2014) (Feb. 2014).

[4] CUERVO, E., BALASUBRAMANIAN, A., CHO, D.-K., WOLMAN, A., SAROIU, S., CHANDRA, R., AND BAHL, P. Maui: making smartphones last longer with code offload. In Proceedings of the 8th international conference on Mobile systems, applications, and services (2010), ACM, pp. 49–62.

[5] GOMEZ, L., NEAMTIU, I., AZIM, T., AND MILLSTEIN, T. Reran: Timing-and touch-sensitive record and replay for android. In Software Engineering (ICSE), 2013 35th International Conference on (2013), IEEE, pp. 72–81.

[6] KICZALES, G., LAMPING, J., MENDHEKAR, A., MAEDA, C., LOPES, C., MARC LOINGTIER, J., AND IRWIN, J. Aspect-oriented programming. In ECOOP (1997), SpringerVerlag.

[7] LACHENMANN, A., MARRON, P. J., MINDER, D., AND ROTHERMEL, K. Meeting lifetime goals with energy levels. In ACM Conference on Embedded Networked Sensor Systems (SenSys'07) (November 2007).

[8] NANDUGUDI, A., KI, T., NUESSLE, C., AND CHALLEN, G. Pocketparker: Pocketsourcing parking lot availability. In Proceedings of the 2014 ACM International Joint Conference on Pervasive and Ubiquitous Computing (New York, NY, USA, 2014), UbiComp '14, ACM, pp. 963–973.

[9] NANDUGUDI, A., MAITI, A., KI, T., BULUT, F., DEMIRBAS, M., KOSAR, T., QIAO, C., KO, S. Y., AND CHALLEN, G. Phonelab: A large programmable smartphone testbed. In Proc. 1st International Workshop on Sensing and Big Data Mining (SenseMine 2013) (November 2013).

[10] NOBLE, B. D., SATYANARAYANAN, M., NARAYANAN, D., TILTON, J. E., FLINN, J., AND WALKER, K. R. Agile application-aware adaptation for mobility. In SOSP '97: Proceedings of the sixteenth ACM symposium on Operating systems principles (Saint Malo, France, 1997), pp. 276–287.

[11] SORBER, J., KOSTADINOV, A., BRENNAN, M., GARBER, M., CORNER, M., AND BERGER, E. D. Eon: A Language and Runtime System for Perpetual Systems. In ACM Conference on Embedded Networked Sensor Systems (SenSys'07) (November 2007).

[12] VAN SCHAIK, S. J., OLTEANU, D., AND FINK, R. Enframe: A platform for processing probabilistic data. arXiv preprint arXiv:1309.0373 (2013).

The Case for Operating System Management of User Attention

Kyungmin Lee, Jason Flinn, and Brian Noble
University of Michigan

ABSTRACT

From wearable displays to smart watches to in-vehicle info-tainment systems, mobile computers are increasingly integrated with our day-to-day activities. Interactions are commonly driven by applications that run in the background and notify users when their attention is needed. In this paper, we argue that existing mobile operating systems should manage user attention as a resource. In contrast to permission-based models that either allow applications to interrupt the user continuously or deny all access, the OS should instead predict the importance and complexity of new interactions and compare the demand for attention to the attention available after accounting for the user's current activities. This will allow the OS to initiate appropriate interactions at the right time using the right modality. We describe one design for such a system, and we outline key challenges that must be met to realize this vision.

1. INTRODUCTION

Mobile computing systems are increasingly integrated with our day-to-day activities. This trend will only grow with the rise of wearable computing platforms such as Google glass and smart watches, as well as with the deployment of pervasive platforms such as in-vehicle infotainment systems.

Many mobile applications help users while they perform primary tasks such as walking, driving, and interacting with other people and their environment. A user engaged in such tasks may have very limited attention to spare for the mobile application. Consequently, such applications often run in the background and try to interact with the user only when such interaction will be meaningful. This is a fundamentally different model of interaction than that used by traditional desktop systems. Instead of the user initiating the interaction at a convenient moment, e.g., by opening the application, the application now initiates the interaction, e.g., via a smartphone notification or by an audio tone from an in-vehicle system.

HotMobile'15, February 12–13, 2015, Santa Fe, New Mexico, USA.
Copyright © 2015 ACM 978-1-4503-3391-7/15/02 ...$15.00.
http://dx.doi.org/10.1145/2699343.2699362.

Consequently, mobile systems can no longer defer to the user the decision of whether to initiate a new interaction; for instance, they must decide whether or not to disturb the user by delivering an audio, visual, or haptic notification. This decision requires that they balance the anticipated importance of the interaction with the distraction caused by interrupting the user's primary activity.

We argue that the operating system should ultimately be responsible for making this decision. User attention is a limited and precious resource, and the operating system should manage how applications are allowed to consume that resource. Thinking of attention as an OS-managed resource is a valuable framework; for instance, we can draw analogies to multiprocessor scheduling and consequently leverage techniques from that domain to help manage this new resource.

Currently, most mobile operating systems use a simple, permission-based approach for managing attention. For instance, when an application is installed, the user may allow or deny permission to deliver audio or haptic notifications on a smartphone. This approach is too coarse-grained. A user may consider some notifications to be more important than others. Availability of attention varies; e.g., the user may be able to briefly interact with an in-vehicle computer when stopped at a red light, but not when driving on a crowded highway. Permission-based systems do not adjust for these factors; an "allowed" setting causes the mobile device to beep, vibrate, or otherwise disturb its user with notifications when she is not available, and a "denied" setting causes her to miss important notifications even if she has ample attention to spare.

The OS is uniquely suited to manage user attention. Determining the right time to interrupt the user requires understanding the user's current activities, which in turn requires access to raw sensor data and sensitive information such as calendars. If the computer were to delegate attention management to applications, then every application would require access to a wealth of private information; in contrast, the OS is already trusted with the privacy of this data. Additionally, since the OS is traditionally responsible for allocating limited resources to competing applications, it is the logical point at which to consider the competing demands for attention from multiple applications so as to avoid overloading the user and so as to prioritize notifications that have the highest global importance to the user. Finally, a single implementation in the OS reduces development effort compared to implementing notification management in every application.

Applications should be responsible for notifying the OS when they wish to interact with the user; they should express the possible modes of interaction and assign an application-local importance to the request. The OS should convert the application-local importance to a global scale and quantify the expected attention that the user will need to devote to the interaction. The supply and demand for attention can be decomposed into distinct elements such as audio, video, haptic, and cognitive attention—this decomposition allows for the possibility, for example, of listening to streaming music while driving a vehicle. The OS will also infer the importance and attention demanded by the user's current activities; this includes both activities external to the computer system (e.g., walking or talking) as well as internal activities (e.g., the user's interactions with other applications). If the user has attention to spare, or if the importance of the notification is judged to be high enough to interrupt the user's current activity (and thus free up sufficient attention), the OS initiates the interaction. Otherwise, the interaction is deferred for a more opportune moment. If the application presents multiple modalities of possible interaction, then the OS chooses the best one based upon its assessment of available audio, visual, haptic, and cognitive attention.

In the next section, we describe in more detail our vision for system management of attention. In particular, we draw inspiration from the scheduling of jobs on a heterogeneous multicore system and model the supply and demand of attention within a similar framework. This allows us to leverage an existing body of work on multicore scheduling. Then, Section 3 presents some ides about how the OS can estimate the supply and demand of user attention, as well as the importance of current tasks and notifications. We then discuss related work and conclude.

2. OVERVIEW

Management of user attention as a resource should be the responsibility of the operating system, but the operating system needs input from both applications and the user in order to do a good job. An application possesses a great deal of domain-specific knowledge that can be used to determine the relative importance and attention required by the interactions that the application initiates. The user can provide valuable feedback about what interactions were and were not worthwhile so that the operating system can learn models that adapt the systems interruption behavior to that user's preferences. In this section, we outline interfaces that separate these concerns among the operating system, the user, and applications.

As with most current mobile systems, we envision that an application running in the background must go through the OS to initiate a user interaction (e.g., as today's mobile phone apps must go through system software to deliver a push notification). Rather than simply apply a blanket policy to allow or deny such interactions, we propose a more nuanced approach. The application provides a numeric measure of how important it believes the interaction will be to the user. This measure is application-specific; it ranks the importance only relative to other interactions initiated by that application. The application also provides a list of the possible modalities of interaction (e.g., an e-mail application might be able to read a new e-mail aloud or display the content on a touchscreen). For each modality, the application may optionally specify a quantitative prediction of the user attention that will be consumed during the resulting interaction.

This interface requires that the system have some model for quantifying attention. While any such model will necessarily be a gross simplification, there are some properties we wish to expose. First, attention may take many forms. For instance, a driver may have the attention to listen to directions from a GPS application but not to look at the screen. This suggests that attention could be expressed as a vector over those various forms (e.g., audio, visual, haptic, cognitive, and other forms of attention). Second, paying attention can be thought of imposing a load over a given time period on each of those forms.

This leads to a very useful analogy: attention management can be modeled as a scheduling problem in which each form of attention is a separate core on a heterogeneous multiprocessor. A user interaction can be modeled as imposing load on some or all of these cores. Interactions require gang scheduling [4] since performing the task requires simultaneous consumption of audio, cognitive, etc. attention. Further, attention consumed by external tasks can be modeled as additional jobs that impose a measurable but time-varying load. Interactions have an importance, equivalent to task priority in scheduling, and pausing and resuming interactions has a non-negligible cost for context-switching. Note that the advantage of such a model is not that it is the most accurate possible model of user interaction, but rather that it is an approximation that maps the problem into a domain (multiprocessor scheduling) in which there is a large body of existing research results. This allows the OS to leverage sophisticated algorithms and apply them to a new resource.

Returning to the API, an application specifies the attention it predicts an interaction will take as a load imposed on the attention vector over a time period. As described in Section 3.2, we envision that such estimates can be calculated as a function of low level I/O interactions such as text displayed, number of buttons pressed, and so on. We also describe methods by which the operating system can provide estimates for the application by observing its past interactions and learning models that predict future attention consumed.

As described in Section 3.3, the operating system monitors the user's current activities and interactions with other applications to continually estimate the load on attention. If the new interaction would not overload any of the forms of attention, then it is allowed. If not, the operating system converts the application-local importance into a global priority as described in Section 3.1. It then considers if the priority of the interaction is greater than that of any current activity by a margin sufficient to overcome the context switch cost of interrupting the current activity. It checks if the additional attention freed by interrupting that activity is sufficient to schedule the requested interaction. If so, it allows the application to initiate the interaction (e.g., by displaying a notification, generating an audio tone, etc.). If not, the operating system defers the interaction until a more opportune time (of course, the application may cancel the interaction request before that time arises). While we have described an algorithm for only a single possible mode of interaction and a single competing activity, sophisticated scheduling algorithms can be used to schedule multiple activities and/or choose between different modalities of interaction.

Next, the user chooses whether or not to respond to the application. Note that although some attention has already been consumed, a user may always choose to ignore or delay interacting with the application — this indicates the operating system made a poor decision. Learning from such experiences is a key part of our design. Some feedback can be gathered automatically. For example, if the user does not respond to the notification (e.g., by turning on the phone screen to see the notification), then the user was likely too busy to notice or deal with any interaction. Thus, the operating system's estimate of current activity importance or load was likely too low.

Often, explicit user feedback could be quite useful. The challenge is too allow for such feedback in a non-intrusive manner. One possibility is to provide a few simple options ("not now", "not important", "great, I wanted to know that", etc.) that are easily accessible via voice recognition, swipe gestures, etc. and improve system models from such examples. We discuss this possibility in Section 3.1.

Thus, we envision the operating system having ultimate responsibility for deciding when and how new interactions take place. However, the operating system takes input from both applications and users to make such decisions. In the next section, we describe some of the more challenging subproblems in building such a system.

3. CHALLENGES

In this section, we outline three challenges that must be overcome to realize our vision, and discuss possible solutions to each.

3.1 Predicting interaction importance

Ideally, a mobile system should only interrupt the user for activities that are more important than whatever tasks the user is currently performing. Further, the difference in importance should be sufficient to make up for the context-switch overhead of pausing and resuming the current activity. For instance, a mobile device should not bother a user who is in a meeting for an advertising e-mail from a retailer, but it should likely ping the user for an urgent e-mail from his boss.

The application is in the best position to assess the importance of interactions that it initiates relative to all other interactions it initiates. For instance, current e-mail applications assess with high accuracy spam, advertising, and priority e-mails, and social applications such as Facebook can identify high-interest updates. In contrast, the OS lacks the context and visibility to make such fined-grained distinctions. Thus, we ask the application to provide a numeric ranking of importance for each proposed interaction relative to the other interactions the application initiates.

The OS can not blindly rely on the application's ranking of importance. Some applications may purposely overestimate their importance to game the system. The ability to predict importance may vary substantially from application to application; e.g., some e-mail services may do a good job of identifying spam and high priority mail, while others may not. Finally, it is difficult for an application to assess how much worth it provides to any given user. Some people are social networking addicts and others care not a whit for the latest updates from their friends.

We therefore propose that the OS learn a function that maps the local importance provided by an application to a global scale. For each interaction, the OS can gather data about whether the user found the interaction important. Given sufficient data, the OS can normalize the application predictions. Thus, an application that games the system by marking all interactions as high-priority or one that is unable to differentiate between low-importance and high-importance interactions will see its global importance fall over time, while applications that consistently provide good estimates will be more likely to interrupt the user for their high-priority interactions.

Often, the OS can gather some data by observing user behavior after it initiates each interaction. If the user receives a notification and performs the task associated with the notification, then there exists positive evidence the user found the interruption useful. In contrast, if a user dismisses or ignores the notification, then there exists evidence that the interaction may have been less important than believed.

Although a user's response time to a notification is a good indicator, the response time alone is not always conclusive. We may also need to consider the user's attention level at the time the notification was received. For instance, if a user is driving a car and receives an important e-mail, that user will likely not read the e-mail until later. Even though the notification is important, the user's response time is high due to other high-priority tasks. We can account for this by also including the importance and complexity of the user's current activities in the model.

Due to the limits of passive observation, we also want to allow users to help train a better model through explicit feedback. One possibility is to give user's simple choices to describe the quality of the interaction. Some possibilities are: "Yes, I wanted to know that", "Why didn't you tell me sooner?", "I'm too busy", "That's not important", etc. Similar to spam filtering, we can present the user with a small number of optional feedback choices during each interaction. If specifying such choices are optional and easy to accomplish (e.g., via voice recognition or a special swipe), then a user can customize their models with only a moderate amount of additional work.

Explicit feedback also helps the system to adapt to different users' behavior and preferences. For instance, some users may rarely wish to be interrupted, while others may welcome constant notifications. Further, behavior may not map directly to importance: e.g., a text from a spouse to pick up milk from the store may be dismissed quickly but it also may be of high importance.

3.2 Predicting attention demand

In addition to predicting the importance of a future interaction, the OS must also predict its complexity, i.e., the amount user attention that will be consumed by the interaction. As described in Section 2, we view attention as a vector of different forms of interaction (audio, visual, haptic, and cognitive)—a prediction should therefore map the proposed interaction onto this vector.

The approach that we plan to take for this mapping is inspired by our prior work on AMC [15]. In that work, we measured load by observing interactions with an in-vehicle touchscreen. For example, we measured button presses required to complete a task, the amount of text on the screen, the size and placement of text, the presence of animation features, and so on. For each low-level measurement, we applied a threshold to determine whether or not an application demanded too much attention to be used while driving a vehicle. A threshold was appropriate for this work since we only considered one possible foreground activity (driving).

We can broaden this approach by using quantitative functions to map low-level interactions to specific forms of attention such as audio or visual. For instance, a notification that displays text demands visual attention; a larger amount of text displayed naturally maps to a greater demand on attention. Using AMC-like tools, we can monitor how the user interacts with an application in response to a notification; e.g. through voice recognition, touchscreen events, and button presses, and we can measure the type and quantity of output produced. From low-level measures of, e.g., text displayed, buttons pressed, voice commands issued, etc., the OS can derive a quantitative measure of attention demanded during each interaction.

The simplest possible approach would be to predict that each new interaction will demand roughly the same attention required by prior interactions initiated by the same application. A more flexible approach could allow the application to also specify some local measure of complexity; e.g., an e-mail application could calculate this measure from the length of an e-mail, the presence of attachments or images, etc. Similar to the prior section, the OS could then learn a function that maps application-local complexity estimates to the global, measured complexity of the actual interaction.

An application may support multiple modes of interaction; e.g., it might read a text message aloud or display it on the screen. We envision that such applications will expose these modalities to the OS and the OS will then learn a separate model for each one. This would make it possible for the OS to realize that an incoming text could be read aloud to a walking or driving user even though the message could not be displayed on a screen.

3.3 Measuring available attention

The final major challenge is assessing the user's available attention. This is more challenging than measuring demand because it will usually involve detecting and evaluating user activities external to the computer system such as driving, walking, conversing, etc.

Further, a blanket classification of activity will be insufficient. For instance, a person driving a car on a empty, straight highway will typically have some attention to spare, e.g., to select music, whereas the same person driving at rush hour on a snowy day may have no available attention. Therefore, in order to accurately determine the available attention level, a mobile system needs to consider not only the user's current activity (or possibly multiple activities) but also user's engagement level with each activity.

Fortunately, there is a considerable body of work on activity recognition that we can use to meet this challenge. Mobile devices possess myriad of sensors (e.g., GPS, accelerometer, microphone, camera, gyroscope, etc). Usage of these sensors [14] for activity recognition has been well studied [13, 7, 18, 19, 20]. For instance, Kern et al. [13] use audio sensor data and a classification algorithm to determine whether a user is in a lecture, on the street, in a conversation, or at a restaurant. They also use body-worn accelerometers to determine whether a user is sitting, standing, walking, or running.

Thus, we could rely on these results to enable the OS to determine the activities that a user is currently engaged

Activity	Possible attention level
Sitting around	Very low - Very high
Playing with a phone	Mid - Very high
Walking	Mid - High
Having a conversation	Low - High
Writing an e-mail	Low - Mid
In a meeting	Very Low - Mid
Driving at high speed	Very Low - Mid

Table 1: Examples of activities and range of possible attention level

in performing. If the computation needed for classification is too burdensome for a mobile device, it can potentially be offloaded to a trusted remote server [6]. Note that the applications need not be entrusted with either the raw sensor data or the activity observations in this design.

Next, the OS can infer the possible range of available attention based on the recognized activity. Table 1 illustrates one hypothetical mapping between some activities and their corresponding range of attention consumption. Additional sensors can be involved at this point to narrow the range. For instance, if a user is driving a vehicle, speed and position can be read from the CAM bus and GPS unit respectively, while road conditions can often be inferred from traction control and ABS data.

Additionally, an OS can rely on supplementary data such as a user's calendar to obtain information about the environment (e.g., whether the user in a important meeting). Since different environments require different level of user engagement, a mobile OS can use user's current environment as a hint about the user's engagement level.

In addition to activity and engagement level sensing, a mobile OS can use information about user's cognitive state to make decision on whether to interrupt or not. For instance, Lu et al. [17] created a system that determines user's stress level in real-time using a mobile device's microphone. Alternatively, a user's emotional state can be important. LiKamWa et al. [16] describe a system that can determine a user's emotion based on his mobile device usage patterns. When a user is annoyed or stressed, an unwanted notification could be more annoying than usual. In our model, the context switch cost increases in such instances, which would bias the OS against interruption.

Activity and engagement sensing is an important and nascent field. Our objective is to provide a framework in which research results from this field can be used by the operating system to make better decisions about initiating user interactions. Thus, as results in this area continue to improve, our OS can do a better job of determining how and when to request its user's attention. Even with the challenges outlined in this section, we believe that OS support will do substantially better than current allow/deny permission models.

4. RELATED WORK

The detrimental effect of poorly-timed notifications in a desktop environment has been well-studied [3, 2, 11]. However, as Iqbal et al. [12] suggest, users are willing to tolerate some disruption in return for receiving valuable notifications. These results demonstrate the need for a user context-aware notification system.

Determining the best time to interrupt a user for a notification has been studied extensively [1, 8, 9, 10]. Horvitz et al. [9] developed PRIORITIES, an desktop e-mail notification system that uses a Bayesian model to infer the user's available attention level and compute the expected cost of interruption and deferring alerts. When the benefit of an alert outweighs the cost of interruption, the system delivers the notification to the user. We agree with the principles of this work, but argue that such solutions should be implemented by the OS rather than by individual applications. Further, current notification systems must deal with the complexity of mobile environments in which the user may be devoting attention to walking, driving, or other tasks.

Recently, there has been research on determining proper task break points for mobile devices. Fischer et al. [5] determined the end of mobile device interactions to deliver notifications at such instances. Okoshi et al. [18] determined accurate application-specific break points, during which the user can be interrupted while she is using an application. Ho et al. [7] determined when the user is transitioning from one physical activity to another (e.g., from sitting to walking) using body-worn accelerometers and used those moments to deliver notifications. These prior systems do not consider the importance of the notification, nor do they consider the possibility of interrupting an activity to initiate a new task. Our goal is to initiate appropriate interactions even when doing so requires the user to interrupt a current task.

Kern et al. [13] proposed a notification design that senses the user's environment and delivers socially acceptable notification modality to the user. It can sense when a user is in a lecture and knows not to disrupt the user with a loud noise. This design is the closest to our proposal, but it can only detect four environments and six user activities. Furthermore, it treats all notifications with the same importance.

Additionally, in contrast to all these prior approaches, we propose a specific framework for cooperation between applications, the user, and the OS to determine when to initiate new interactions. Thus, a major focus of our work is to determine how best to manage attention as a service provided by the mobile operating system.

5. CONCLUSION

In this paper, we argue that a mobile device's operating system should be responsible for managing user attention as a resource. With this new responsibility, a mobile OS can create a user attention-aware notification system that initiates new interactions at the right time with right modality without interrupting high-importance tasks. We have laid out a design and methodology for creating such a system, and we have identified key challenges in realizing our vision.

Acknowledgments

We thank the anonymous reviewers of this paper for their thoughtful comments. This research direction was inspired by a conversation with Venkatesh Prasad. The work was supported by a grant from Ford Motor Co. Any opinions, findings, conclusions, or recommendations expressed in this material are those of the authors and do not necessarily reflect the views of Ford or the University of Michigan.

6. REFERENCES

[1] Piotr D. Adamczyk and Brian P. Bailey. If not now, when?: The effects of interruption at different moments within task execution. In *Proceedings of the SIGCHI Conference on Human Factors in Computing Systems*, CHI '04, pages 271–278, Vienna, Austria, April 2004.

[2] Brian P. Bailey and Joseph A. Konstan. On the need for attention-aware systems: Measuring effects of interruption on task performance, error rate, and affective state. *Computers in Human Behavior*, 22(4):685–708, 2006.

[3] Mary Czerwinski, Eric Horvitz, and Susan Wilhite. A diary study of task switching and interruptions. In *Proceedings of the SIGCHI Conference on Human Factors in Computing Systems*, CHI '04, pages 175–182, Vienna, Austria, April 2004.

[4] Dror G. Feitelson and Larry Rudolph. Gang scheduling performance benefits for fine-grain synchronization. *Journal of Parallel and Distributed Computing*, 16(4), December 1992.

[5] Joel E. Fischer, Chris Greenhalgh, and Steve Benford. Investigating episodes of mobile phone activity as indicators of opportune moments to deliver notifications. In *Proceedings of the 13th International Conference on Human Computer Interaction with Mobile Devices and Services*, pages 181–190, Stockholm, Sweden, August 2011.

[6] Jason Flinn. *Cyber Foraging: Bridging Mobile and Cloud Computing*. Morgan and Claypool Publishers, September 2012.

[7] Joyce Ho and Stephen S. Intille. Using context-aware computing to reduce the perceived burden of interruptions from mobile devices. In *Proceedings of the SIGCHI Conference on Human Factors in Computing Systems*, CHI '05, pages 909–918, Portland, Oregon, April 2005.

[8] Eric Horvitz and Johnson Apacible. Learning and reasoning about interruption. In *Proceedings of the 5th International Conference on Multimodal Interfaces*, ICMI '03, pages 20–27, Vancouver, Canada, November 2003.

[9] Eric Horvitz, Andy Jacobs, and David Hovel. Attention-sensitive alerting. In *Proceedings of the Fifteenth Conference on Uncertainty in Artificial Intelligence*, UAI'99, pages 305–313, Stockholm, Sweden, July 1999.

[10] Shamsi T. Iqbal and Brian P. Bailey. Understanding and developing models for detecting and differentiating breakpoints during interactive tasks. In *Proceedings of the SIGCHI Conference on Human Factors in Computing Systems*, CHI '07, pages 697–706, San Jose, California, April 2007.

[11] Shamsi T. Iqbal and Eric Horvitz. Disruption and recovery of computing tasks: Field study, analysis, and directions. In *Proceedings of the SIGCHI Conference on Human Factors in Computing Systems*, CHI '07, pages 677–686, San Jose, California, April 2007.

[12] Shamsi T. Iqbal and Eric Horvitz. Notifications and awareness: A field study of alert usage and preferences. In *Proceedings of the 2010 ACM Conference on Computer Supported Cooperative Work*, CSCW '10, pages 27–30, Savannah, Georgia, February 2010.

[13] Nickey Kern and Bernt Schiele. Context-aware notification for wearable computing. In *Proceedings of the 7th IEEE International Symposium on Wearable Computers*, pages 223–230, Washington, DC, October 2003.

[14] N.D. Lane, E. Miluzzo, Hong Lu, D. Peebles, T. Choudhury, and AT. Campbell. A survey of mobile phone sensing. *Communications Magazine, IEEE*, 48(9):140–150, Sept 2010.

[15] Kyungmin Lee, Jason Flinn, T.J. Giuli, Brian Noble, and Christopher Peplin. Amc: Verifying user interface properties for vehicular applications. In *Proceeding of the 11th Annual International Conference on Mobile Systems, Applications, and Services*, MobiSys '13, pages 1–12, Taipei, Taiwan, June 2013.

[16] Robert LiKamWa, Yunxin Liu, Nicholas D. Lane, and Lin Zhong. Moodscope: Building a mood sensor from smartphone usage patterns. In *Proceeding of the 11th Annual International Conference on Mobile Systems, Applications, and Services*, MobiSys '13, pages 389–402, Taipei, Taiwan, June 2013.

[17] Hong Lu, Denise Frauendorfer, Mashfiqui Rabbi, Marianne Schmid Mast, Gokul T. Chittaranjan, Andrew T. Campbell, Daniel Gatica-Perez, and Tanzeem Choudhury. Stresssense: Detecting stress in unconstrained acoustic environments using smartphones. In *Proceedings of the 2012 ACM Conference on Ubiquitous Computing*, UbiComp '12, pages 351–360, Pittsburgh, Pennsylvania, September 2012.

[18] Tadashi Okoshi, Hideyuki Tokuda, and Jin Nakazawa. Attelia: Sensing user's attention status on smart phones. In *16th International Conference on Ubiquitous Computing*, pages 139–142, Seattle, Washington, September 2014.

[19] Carlos Paniagua, Huber Flores, and Satish Narayana Srirama. Mobile sensor data classification for human activity recognition using MapReduce on cloud. In *Proceedings of the 9th International Conference on Mobile Web Information System*, pages 585–592, Ontario, Canada, August 2012.

[20] Yunus Emre Ustev, Ozlem Durmaz Incel, and Cem Ersoy. User, device and orientation independent human activity recognition on mobile phones: Challenges and a proposal. In *Proceedings of the 2013 ACM Conference on Pervasive and Ubiquitous Computing Adjunct Publication*, UbiComp '13 Adjunct, pages 1427–1436, Zurich, Switzerland, September 2013.

Can Deep Learning Revolutionize Mobile Sensing?

Nicholas D. Lane
Microsoft Research

Petko Georgiev
University of Cambridge

ABSTRACT

Sensor-equipped smartphones and wearables are transforming a variety of mobile apps ranging from health monitoring to digital assistants. However, reliably inferring user behavior and context from noisy and complex sensor data collected under mobile device constraints remains an open problem, and a key bottleneck to sensor app development. In recent years, advances in the field of deep learning have resulted in nearly unprecedented gains in related inference tasks such as speech and object recognition. However, although mobile sensing shares many of the same data modeling challenges, we have yet to see deep learning be systematically studied within the sensing domain. If deep learning could lead to significantly more robust and efficient mobile sensor inference it would revolutionize the field by rapidly expanding the number of sensor apps ready for mainstream usage.

In this paper, we provide preliminary answers to this potentially game-changing question by prototyping a low-power Deep Neural Network (DNN) inference engine that exploits both the CPU and DSP of a mobile device SoC. We use this engine to study typical mobile sensing tasks (e.g., activity recognition) using DNNs, and compare results to learning techniques in more common usage. Our early findings provide illustrative examples of DNN usage that do not overburden modern mobile hardware, while also indicating how they can improve inference accuracy. Moreover, we show DNNs can gracefully scale to larger numbers of inference classes and can be flexibly partitioned across mobile and remote resources. Collectively, these results highlight the critical need for further exploration as to how the field of mobile sensing can best make use of advances in deep learning towards robust and efficient sensor inference.

Categories and Subject Descriptors: C.3 [Special-Purpose and Application-Based Systems]: Real-time and embedded systems.

General Terms: Design, Experimentation.

Keywords: Mobile Sensing, Deep Learning, Deep Neural Network, Activity Recognition.

1. INTRODUCTION

By exploiting sensors in wearables and smartphones, apps are exposing users to powerful new mobile experiences that have the potential to change the way users live and interact with each other. Advances in the area of mobile sensing en-

HotMobile'15, February 12–13, 2015, Santa Fe, NM, USA.
Copyright © 2015 ACM 978-1-4503-3391-7/15/02 ...$15.00.
http://dx.doi.org/10.1145/2699343.2699349.

able users to: quantify their sleep and exercise patterns [6], monitor personal commute behaviors [26], track their emotional state [25], or even measure how long they spend queuing in retail stores [27]. The driving force underpinning these innovations is the use of algorithms to infer behaviors and contexts from sensor data collected by mobile devices.

However, critically today inferring many important behaviors from mobile sensor data under real-world conditions remains brittle and unreliable (e.g., [6]); this in turn is acting as a bottleneck to sensor app development, preventing many apps from being ready for consumers – especially those that require more difficult (but also powerful) forms of behavior modeling. The field of mobile sensing would be transformed overnight if a breakthrough in the level of robustness and efficiency of mobile inference could be achieved – such an advance would revolutionize the sensing app landscape by broadening the number of inference categories accurate enough for mainstream use. But challenges to robust sensor inference are numerous and varied, including for example: coping with uncontrolled device positions [21] (e.g., in a pocket, in a bag); background noise (e.g., outdoors, while driving) when sampling data [23]; and adapting to the differences in data generated by a diverse user population [17] (e.g., lifestyle, demographics). Although the mobile sensing community continues to develop approaches that minimize these effects, more fundamental advances in the machine learning techniques used are also needed to close the gap between the promise and actual reality of sensing apps.

A strong candidate for such fundamental advances in how mobile sensor data is processed is *deep learning*; an emerging area of machine learning that has recently generated significant attention – enabling, for example, large leaps in the accuracy of mature domains like speech recognition, where previously only incremental improvements were seen for many years [2]. In a recent high-profile example [18], deep learning algorithms were also shown to be capable of learning complex concepts – such as the appearance of cats in videos – with incredibly little supervision (i.e., example data manually labeled for each concept of interest). More broadly, deep learning techniques are now key elements in achieving state-of-the-art inference performance in a variety of applications of learning [13] (e.g., computer vision, natural language processing). Promisingly, achieving such levels of robust inference (as seen in speech) often requires overcoming similar data modeling challenges (e.g., noisy data, intra-class diversity) to those found in mobile sensing. In addition, many of the instances where deep learning has been successful are related to inference tasks of importance to mobile sensing (e.g., emotion recognition, speaker identification).

It is somewhat surprising that deep learning has yet to have a widespread impact on mobile sensing. Only limited usage exists today coming in the form of largely cloud-based models that provide, for example, speech and object recognition within mobile commercial services [2]. Little exploration has been done into deep learning methods applied to activity, behavior and context recognition. Deep learning techniques are also absent from the vast majority of mobile sensing prototypes that are deployed and evaluated. Perhaps this is partially due to the computational overhead associated with deep learning, and the fact early mobile sensing efforts were highly computationally constrained. However, mobile architectures have advanced enormously in recent years (an iPhone 6, for instance, is a 10x computational jump over a 5-year old iPhone 3GS). Such advances are radically changing what is possible to locally perform.

What is missing today are systematic studies to understand how advances in deep learning can be applied to inference tasks relevant to mobile sensing; in addition to the development of new mobile runtimes that can perform inference using these models in an energy-efficient low-latency manner. In this paper, we begin to examine this timely issue with an exploratory study into the potential for deep learning to address a range of core challenges to robust and resource efficient mobile sensing. To better understand the interaction between modeling accuracy and system resources, we prototype a mobile Deep Neural Network (DNN) classification engine capable of a variety of sensor inference tasks. The role of the engine is to classify sensor data on the mobile device, assuming deep model training is performed in an offline manner with conventional tools. The design of the engine exploits a broad range of modern mobile hardware and executes most inference operations on the low-power DSPs present in many already available smartphones (e.g., Samsung Galaxy S5, Nexus 6). As a result, this engine achieves resource efficiencies not possible if only using a CPU.

Our study findings show, as would be expected, benefits to inference accuracy and robustness by adopting deep learning techniques. For example, we show our DNN engine can achieve comparable accuracy levels for audio sensing using significantly simpler features (a 71x reduction in features), relative to modeling techniques more typically used. We also discover a number of less expected results related to mobile resource usage. For instance, we find that DNNs can have a resource overhead close to the most simple comparison models, yet simultaneously have accuracy levels equal to any tested alternative. Moreover, our DNN implementation is able to scale gracefully to large numbers of inference categories unlike the models used today. These results indicate forms of deep learning (DNNs in this case) may also provide important improvements in the resource-efficiency of sensing algorithms on mobile devices. We anticipate this preliminary study will provide a foundation for subsequent research that explores the application of deep learning to mobile sensing. More importantly, we believe the findings of this work may even represent the start of transformative changes in how mobile inference algorithms are designed and operate – powered by concepts from deep learning.

2. DEEP LEARNING

Modeling data with neural networks is nothing new, with the underlying technique being in use since the 1940s [22]. Yet this approach, in combination with a series of radical advances (e.g., [16]) in how such networks can be utilized and trained, forms the foundation of *deep learning* [13]; a new area in machine learning that has recently revolutionized many domains of signal and information processing – not only speech and object recognition but also computer vision, natural language processing, and information retrieval.

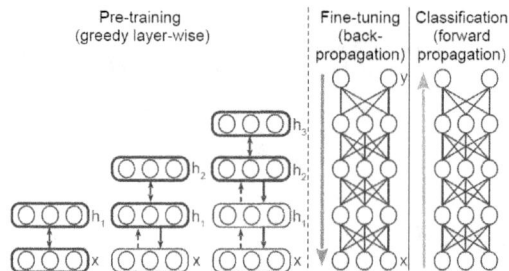

Figure 1: Example phases of building a Deep Neural Network with 3 hidden layers (h_1, h_2, and h_3), input layer x and output layer y. Shown are the pre-training, fine-tuning and classification phases of a DNN variant called a Deep Belief Network.

Deep Neural Network Primer. Many forms of deep learning have been developed with example techniques including Boltzmann Machines, Deep Belief Networks, and Deep Autoencoders (each detailed in [13]). Figure 1 illustrates a common example of deep learning; specifically a Deep Neural Network (or DNN). A DNN is a feed-forward neural network (i.e., the network does not form a cycle) that maps provided inputs (e.g., audio or accelerometer data or features derived from them) to required outputs (e.g., categories of behavior or context). The network consists of nodes organized into a series of fully connected layers; in-between the input and output layers the DNN contains additional bridging layers (called "hidden" layers). Each node uses an activation function to transform the data/state in the prior layer that in turn is exposed to the next layer. Commonly used node activation functions are drawn from the sigmoid family. A logistic sigmoid $y = \frac{1}{1+e^{-x}}$, for instance, has the property of returning values in the range $(0, 1)$ making it suitable for representing probabilities. Output nodes are an exception, these typically use a softmax function in which the final inference is determined by the node with the largest value (i.e., the conditional probability). See [13] for more.

A DNN is trained usually in two stages. First, an unsupervised process referred to as "pre-training" is applied to bootstrap hidden node and edge parameters. This stage was a significant breakthrough in deep learning, when it was discovered that this can be effectively done in a greedy layerwise fashion without labeled data – simplifying the learning when multiple hidden layers are present. Second, a supervised process occurs, referred to as "fine-tuning", that uses backpropagation algorithms to adjust the parameter values initialized in the previous stage. Parameters are adjusted to minimize a loss function that captures the difference between network inferences and ground-truth labeled data.

Of course, many variations on this training process have been proposed; and similarly DNNs themselves can be utilized in various ways to perform inference. Not only are they used simply as classifiers in isolation (as we do in our study) but they are also chained together to interpret data of differing modalities (e.g., [9]), or combined with other types of models (e.g., HMMs, GMMs) to form hybrids (e.g., [15]) or act as front-end feature selection phase (e.g., [24]). Similarly, beyond a basic DNN is a rich family of approaches and machinery such as (the aforementioned) Deep Belief Networks and Boltzmann Machines or others like Convolutional Neural Networks. However, we limit this work to a relatively simple form of deep learning (single DNNs), leaving the exploration of additional techniques for future study.

Figure 2: Qualcomm Snapdragon 800 MDP/S [1].

stand up chair	sit down chair
get up bed	lie down bed
climb stairs	descend stairs
eat meat	eat soup
drink glass	brush teeth
use phone	walk
comb hair	pour water

Table 1: Activities of daily living (ADL).

Existing Mobile Use of Deep Learning. As previously described, there are some early examples of deep learning being applied in mobile settings. For instance, the speech recognition models used by phones today exploit deep learning techniques (e.g., [2]); but crucially they operate off-device, in the cloud. Some existing application domains of deep learning (such as emotion recognition [15] and others related to audio) are very similar to requirements of mobile sensing and should be able to be adapted for sensor app purposes. Other important sensing tasks like activity recognition are largely unexplored in terms of deep learning, with only isolated examples being available (such as for feature selection [24] or non-mobile activity recognition in controlled or instrumented environments [12, 3]). These inference tasks will require more fundamental study as they lack clear analogs in the deep learning literature. Moreover, significant systems research is required to understand how the full range of deep learning techniques can be used locally on mobile devices while respecting energy and latency constraints. For example, mobile OS resource control algorithms aware of how to regulate the execution of one or more instances of deep learning inference are currently missing; as are new deep learning inference algorithms tailored to mobile SoC components like GPUs and DSPs.

3. PRELIMINARY INVESTIGATION
We now detail our initial study into the suitability and benefits of deep learning when applied to mobile sensing.

Study Aims. Three key issues are investigated:

- *Accuracy:* Are there indications that deep learning can improve inference accuracy and robustness to noisy complex environments? Especially when sensor data is limited, either by features or sampling rates. (See §4).

- *Feasibility:* How practical is it to use deep learning for commonly required sensing tasks on today's mobile devices? Can we push today's hardware to provide acceptable levels of energy efficiency and latency when compared with conventional modeling approaches? (See §5).

- *Scalability:* What are the implications for common scalability challenges to mobile sensing if deep learning is adopted? For example, how well does it perform as the number of monitored categories of activities expands? (A common bottleneck in forms of mobile sensing such as audio [20]). Moreover, how easily can deep learning inference algorithms be partitioned across computational units (i.e., cloud offloading), a frequently needed technique to manage mobile resources [11]. (Also see §5).

By examining these important first-order questions regarding deep learning in the context of mobile sensing our study highlights new directions for the community, as well as provides the foundation for follow-up investigations.

Mobile DNN Implementation. In the proceeding two sections, we report experiments performed with a working deep learning implementation developed for an Android smartphone with a Jelly Bean 4.3 OS. The implementation is targeted towards DNN models used in typical continuous sensing tasks such as keyword spotting [5] and activity recognition rather than intermittent workloads, such as speech or image recognition, which require more complex cloud-only models due to their that significant memory and compute requirements. To maximize the mobile resource efficiency, we take advantage of a low power co-processor similarly to [8]: we use the Hexagon DSP of the Qualcomm Snapdragon SoC available in off-the-shelf smartphones and wearables. This Qualcomm SoC is particularly suitable for always-on sensing tasks since the sensors can be continuously monitored at a low cost by the DSP allowing the power-hungry CPU to often remain in low-energy sleep mode. To give a perspective on the possible energy savings, we observe on average an $8\times$ to $14\times$ reduction in the energy consumption when the DNN inference algorithms run on the DSP instead of the CPU. These benefits come at the expense of several DSP limitations including: constraints on the size and complexity of the DNN (due to the small program and memory space of the DSP); as well as only the more simple inference algorithms having acceptable runtime latency (partially due to these algorithms not being fully optimized for the DSP). Naturally, well-known cloud-based models like DeepFace [7] (used by Facebook for face recognition) can not be supported locally with this prototype; rather at this point we can only use carefully constructed simple models.

The co-processor is programmable through the publicly released C/assembly Hexagon SDK but development is enabled only on special boards such as the Snapdragon 800 MDP/S (Figure 2) which we use for the classification engine implementation. We implement the sensing framework and algorithms in C: interfacing between the Android OS and the DSP is achieved through a general computational offloading mechanism (FastRPC) mediated through the Android Native Development Kit (NDK). Our DNN version for the DSP allows several key parameters to be changed, namely the number of hidden layers and their size, the number of features in the input layer, the number of classes in the output layer, as well as the node activation function. In the following sections, we tune these parameters accordingly and report smartphone results. However, the findings can be generalized to other mobile devices since the same Snapdragon architecture, featuring a DSP in addition to the CPU, is present on new consumer wearables like the Android LG G Watch with a Qualcomm Snapdragon 400 SoC.

4. INFERENCE ACCURACY
We begin by investigating the potential for more robust and accurate mobile inference by adopting techniques from deep learning. The two key results from our experiments are:

- Basic DNN techniques do well with noisy accelerometer activities: we observe a 10% accuracy gain over the next best comparison method, even when no deep learning pre-training methods are used to additionally boost the accuracy by initializing the weights of the network;

- For audio sensing (speaker and emotion recognition), a simple DNN model with a $71\times$ reduction in the number of input features provides comparable or superior accuracy against learning techniques in common usage.

Behavioral Context	Dataset Description
Activity Recognition	wrist-worn accelerometer activities [10]
Emotion Recognition	emotional prosody speech [19]
Speaker Identification	10-minute speech from 23 speakers each

Table 2: Sensing datasets overview.

Such preliminary findings are indications of the possible benefits by adopting techniques from deep learning. Here we have only applied some of the most basic DNN-related machinery. Consequently, we believe more comprehensive exploration will lead to even larger performance gains.

Experiment Setup. We examine three inference domains commonly studied within mobile sensing, one based on accelerometer data and the others using the microphone. Specifically these are: activity recognition, emotion recognition, and speaker identification. The particular classes of behavior we study appear in a wide range of proposed and existing sensor-based mobile apps, for example: mHealth [6, 25], digital assistants (e.g., Microsoft's Cortana or Apple's Siri) and life-logging [20, 21]. The complexities of recognizing the categories of behavior evaluated in the wild – using conventional modeling – are well recognized [6, 17].

Datasets. Table 2 details the three datasets we use and specifies the classes of behavior they contain. Two of the datasets are audio-based (for speaker identification and emotion recognition) provided by the authors of [25] and one is accelerometer-based [10] containing a general set of Activities of Daily Life (ADL) shown in Table 1. The ADL dataset is composed of the labeled recordings of 14 simple activities performed by 16 volunteers wearing a single tri-axial accelerometer attached to the right wrist of the volunteer and sampled at a rate of 32Hz. The emotions corpus [19] contains the emotional speech of 7 professional actors delivering a set of 14 distinct emotions grouped by Rachuri et al. [25] into 5 broad categories: happiness, sadness, fear, anger and neutral speech. The speaker data consists of 10-minute voice recordings of 23 speakers reading article excerpts. The microphone sampling rate is set to 8kHz in the datasets.

DNN Design. For the accuracy benchmarks we evaluate a DNN with fairly standard parameters that can be trained fast with a basic backpropagation algorithm. The DNN has 1 hidden layer with nodes equal to $(f + c)/2$ where f is the number of input features and c is the number of output classes. A sigmoid activation function is employed for the hidden layer and a softmax function for the output layer. In the sound processing scenarios, the traditionally adopted Gaussian Mixture Models (GMMs) [4] accept as input features a series of 32 Perceptual Linear Predictive (PLP) coefficients [25] extracted from 30ms audio frames every 10ms for a total of 5 seconds. Consequently, the emotions and speaker inferences are performed on 5-second long utterances. The DNN uses instead summary features (mean, median, std, min, max, 25 percentile, 75 percentile) derived from the original ones to succinctly represent the distribution of each of the 32 PLP coefficients over the window. Thus, the DNN uses 7×32 features in total as opposed to 500×32 which significantly reduces the descriptiveness of the acoustic observations leading to potential accuracy losses.

Benchmark Classifiers. Comparison benchmarks are provided by a set of baseline classifiers commonly adopted in mobile sensing scenarios. Gaussian Mixture Models (GMMs) with diagonal covariance matrices are often used for sound

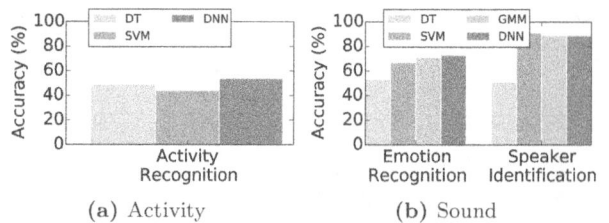

(a) Activity   (b) Sound

Figure 3: Accuracy results for several popular classifiers applied to typical mobile sensing tasks: (a) activity recognition and (b) audio sensing. For the voice-related inferences, the DNN works with much simpler features (a 71× reduction in the total number of features compared to the GMM case) while still yielding comparable or better accuracy results. This demonstrates the highly discriminative and robust nature of the DNN modeling.

processing [21, 23] which have proven particularly effective for speaker-related inferences [25, 20]. The classifier works with a maximum likelihood principle: each class to be recognized is represented by a single GMM and the classification computes the probability of each class in turn. Other techniques that generally yield good results are Support Vector Machines (SVM) [4] which have successfully been incorporated in emotion recognition systems [14]. Last, Decision Trees (DT) virtually dominate the activity recognition and transportation mode detection landscape [21, 26]. Like the DNN, for audio inference the SVM and DT operate on the summary features instead of those used by the GMM.

Experiment Results. In Figure 3a we display the various classifiers performance on the ADL dataset. We note that distinguishing between the 14 activities is a challenging task as some of them such as eating meat are fairly complex to be identified with a single accelerometer. The problem difficulty justifies the relatively low (< 60%) accuracy achieved by the classification models with default parameters; yet, the DNN outperforms the DT leader by 10%. In this case, the DNN appears capable of uncovering hidden feature dependencies not easily captured by the DT branching logic.

In Figure 3b we compare the accuracy of the DNN using the weaker summary feature set for the emotion/speech processing. Here, even with the significant loss of feature complexity, *the DNN provides superior accuracy results of 73% for the emotion recognition example and comparable 89% accuracy for the speaker identification.* We highlight that these results are obtained when the DNN is trained without a pre-training step and further accuracy improvements are likely when restricted Boltzmann machines (or similar) are used for the initialization of network weights [13].

5. RESOURCE EFFICIENCY

In our next set of results we examine energy and latency properties of DNNs applied to common behavioral inference tasks. The three key results from our experiments are:

- DNN use is feasible on the DSP and has a low energy and runtime overhead allowing complex tasks such as emotion detection or speaker identification to be performed in real time while preserving or improving the accuracy;

- DNN solutions are significantly more scalable as the number of recognized classes increase;

- Splitting models between computational units (e.g., a local device and cloud) is more flexible with a DNN that offers energy/latency trade-offs at a finer granularity.

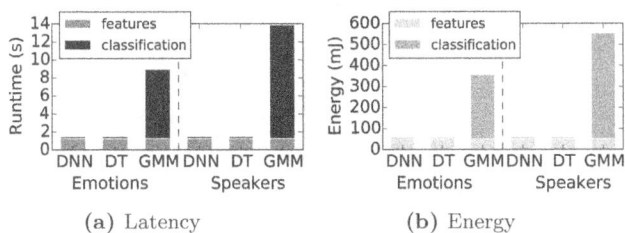

(a) Latency   (b) Energy

Figure 4: Latency and energy of the emotion recognition and speaker identification when deployed on the DSP. The example DNNs have a low latency/energy overhead similar to a DT.

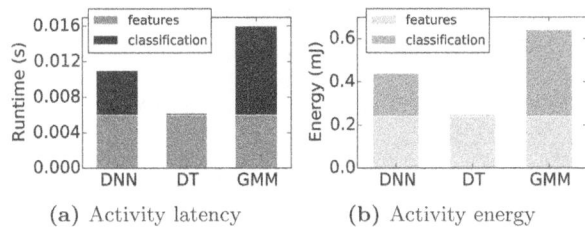

(a) Activity latency   (b) Activity energy

Figure 5: Latency and energy of the activity recognition when deployed on the DSP. The accelerometer pipelines are extremely cheap and DNNs still have a lower overhead compared to GMMs.

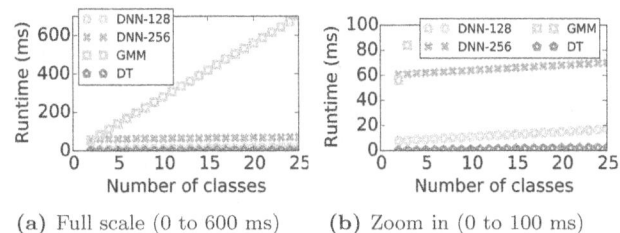

(a) Full scale (0 to 600 ms)   (b) Zoom in (0 to 100 ms)

Figure 6: DSP runtime of the inference stage of the various classifiers as a function of the number of classes. The results suggest that DNNs scale extremely well with the increase in the number of classes, in a manner similar to a DT, while often providing superior accuracy.

Our early results point to the ability of DNNs to provide energy and latency trade-offs that will be suitable for a wide-range of mobile sensing scenarios; while also having beneficial resource characteristics not found in any other commonly used model.

Experiment Setup. We use the implementation detailed in §3 to evaluate the energy and latency characteristics of the three inference domains from §4. Unless otherwise specified, the adopted default DNN parameters are 3 hidden layers, 128 nodes per layer, and a rectified linear unit (ReLU) [28] activation function. These settings closely match recently applied DNNs to speech and emotion recognition tasks [5, 15]. The DNN model is further used to implement a keyword spotting example [5] illustrating one of the key DNN approaches, namely hybridizing the classification with post-processing. The example brings to light cloud offloading benefits studied in the third of our experiments. The GMMs are set up with 128 mixture components [25]. The classification models (DT, GMM, DNN) and derived sensing applications used in the experiments are all deployed on a smartphone's DSP so that comparisons are put into a low-power context suitable for mobile sensing tasks.

Feasibility Results. In this first experiment we provide insights with respect to the DSP runtime and energy footprint of DNNs compared against other techniques (DT, GMM) widely used in the mobile sensing literature. In Figure 4 we plot the latency and energy profiles of the sound-related apps detailed in §4. The emotion recognition task with GMMs, for example, runs for approximately 9 seconds and requires 350mJ on the DSP to process 5 seconds of audio data. A most notable observation is that *the DNN classification overhead is extremely low compared to a GMM-based inference and matches the overhead of a simple Decision Tree.* We recall that both the emotion recognition and speaker identification operate on acoustic features extracted from 5 seconds of audio samples which means that *the DNN versions of the applications, unlike the GMM-based implementations, can perform complex sound-related inferences in real time with comparable or superior accuracy.* The prohibitively high GMM overhead stems from both the large amounts of features (500×32) serving as acoustic observations and the additive nature of the classification where one full GMM is required per class. In the activity recognition scenario examined in Figure 5, the results are similar: the DNN has a lower overhead compared to GMMs and inferences can be performed in real time. The runtime values for all models are reported for processing 4 seconds of accelerometer data and 24 features so that the low runtimes of barely 16ms indicate how cheap accelerometer-based sensor apps are.

Scalability Results. In this part of the analysis we shed light on how the DNN scales with the increase in the number of inferred classes. Mobile context inference tasks often require a larger number of behaviors or activities being recognized such as multiple activity categories [21] (e.g. still, running, walking with phone in pocket, backpack, or belt etc.), multiple words, emotional states or speakers [25]. In Figure 6 we plot the runtime of the classification stage of the three models (DT, GMM, DNN) as a function of the number of recognized contextual categories. Again, the DNN behaves in manner similar to a simple Decision Tree where the larger number of supported classes does not significantly affect the overall inference performance. The runtime of the feed-forward stage of a deep neural network is dominated by the propagation from the input and multiple hidden layers which are invariant to the number of classes in the output layer. The GMM-based classification computes probability scores for each class represented by an entire GMM so that an inference with 25 added categories/classes is $25\times$ more expensive than one with a single class. This justifies the more than $11\times$ slower inference compared to a 256-node DNN [15] for 25 recognized categories and an identical number ($750 = 25 \times 30$) of input features for all models.

Cloud Partitioning Results. In this experiment we investigate the benefits of DNN-based inference usage with respect to cloud offloading. To set up the experiment we consider a speech recognition scenario where a set of keywords need to be detected from voice on the mobile device. A common DNN approach adopted in speech processing [5, 15] is repeatedly invoking the DNN feed-forward stage on short segments, such as once every 10ms in a keyword spotting application [5], and then performing post-processing on the sequence of extracted DNN scores for obtaining the final inference, such as the probability of encountering a keyword. In Figure 7b we demonstrate that the high frequency of DNN propagations facilitates *cloud offloading decisions to be per-*

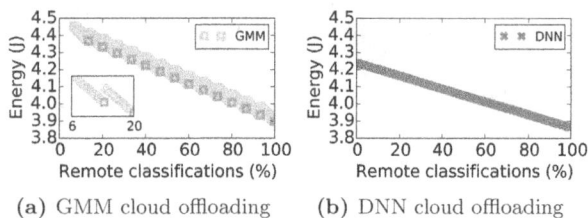

(a) GMM cloud offloading   **(b)** DNN cloud offloading

Figure 7: Energy footprint of a speech recognition inference model based on GMMs or DNNs when a proportion of the classifications are performed in the cloud. For the GMM case a zoom-in for the 6% to 20% partition range is also provided. Experiment duration is 15 seconds with a WiFi connection assumed (5Mbps uplink). DNN usage allows for a graceful reduction in the energy consumption unlike the choppy GMM offloading.

formed at a fine level of granularity with a graceful reduction in the total energy consumption when a larger proportion of the DNN inferences are performed in the cloud.

In contrast, a GMM-based approach would usually increase the total amount of time acoustic observations (features) are accumulated before resorting to an inference. This together with the overhead of evaluating the probability of multiple GMMs (e.g. one per keyword) for a single inference, lead to the much choppier falls in the energy consumption for this model when a percentage of the GMM computations are offloaded to the cloud, as illustrated in Figure 7a. This phenomenon is portrayed in Figure 7a with the saw-like shape of the energy curve. We highlight that *such a curve is harder to control to a specific energy budget.* Situations where a certain number of the per-class GMM inferences need to be performed remotely may often be encountered because of latency/resource constraints, for instance, which introduces the above mentioned local-remote split inefficiencies. The DNN energy curve with a smoother gradient is therefore largely preferable.

6. CONCLUSION

In this paper, we have investigated the potential for techniques from deep learning to address a number of critical barriers to mobile sensing surrounding inference accuracy, robustness and resource efficiency. Significantly, we performed this study by implementing a DNN inference engine by broadly using the capabilities of modern mobile SoCs, and heavily use the DSP in addition to the CPU. Our findings show likely increases to inference robustness, and acceptable levels of resource usage, when DNNs are applied to a variety of mobile sensing tasks such as activity, emotion and speaker recognition. Furthermore, we highlight beneficial resource characteristics (e.g., class scaling, cloud offloading) missing from models in common use today (e.g., GMMs).

We believe this first step in understanding how deep learning can be used in mobile contexts provides a foundation for more complete studies, and will lead to the development of important innovative classifier designs for sensing apps. Our study only scratches the surface of potentially a revolution in the widespread adoption of consumer-ready sensing apps powered by deep learning.

7. REFERENCES

[1] Qualcomm Snapdragon 800 MDP. http://goo.gl/ySfCFl.
[2] L. Deng, et al. Recent Advances in Deep Learning for Speech Research at Microsoft. In *ICASSP '13*.
[3] S. Ji, et al. 3D Convolutional Neural Networks for Human Action Recognition. *IEEE Trans. Pattern Anal. Mach. Intel*, 35(1):221–231, Jan 2013.
[4] C. M. Bishop. *Pattern Recognition and Machine Learning (Information Science and Statistics)*. Springer-Verlag New York, Inc., Secaucus, NJ, USA, 2006.
[5] G. Chen, et al. Small-footprint Keyword Spotting using Deep Neural Networks. In *ICASSP '14*.
[6] S. Consolvo, et al. Activity Sensing in the Wild: A Field Trial of UbiFit Garden. In *CHI '08*.
[7] Y. Taigman, et al. DeepFace: Closing the Gap to Human-Level Performance in Face Verification. In *CVPR '14*.
[8] P. Georgiev, et al. DSP. Ear: Leveraging Co-Processor Support for Continuous Audio Sensing on Smartphones. In *SenSys '14*.
[9] S. E. Kahou. Combining Modality Specific Deep Neural Networks for Emotion Recognition in Video. In *ICMI '13*.
[10] B. Bruno, et al. Analysis of human behavior recognition algorithms based on acceleration data. In *ICRA '13*.
[11] E. Cuervo, et al. MAUI: Making Smartphones Last Longer with Code Offload. In *MobiSys '10*.
[12] M. Zeng, et al. Convolutional Neural Networks for Human Activity Recognition using Mobile Sensors. In *MobiCASE '14*.
[13] L. Deng and D. Yu. Deep Learning: Methods and Applications. Now Publishers Inc. Jan. 2014.
[14] F. Eyben, M. Wöllmer, and B. Schuller. OpenEar – Introducing the Munich Open-source Emotion and Affect Recognition Toolkit. In *In ACII*.
[15] K. Han, D. Yu, and I. Tashev. Speech Emotion Recognition using Deep Neural Network and Extreme Learning Machine. In *Interspeech '14*.
[16] G. E. Hinton, S. Osindero, and Y.-W. Teh. A Fast Learning Algorithm for Deep Delief Nets. *Neural Comput.*, 18(7):1527–1554, July 2006.
[17] N. Lane, et al. Enabling large-scale human activity inference on smartphones using community similarity networks (CSN). In *UbiComp '11*.
[18] Q. V. Le, et al. Building high-level features using large scale unsupervised learning. In *ICML '12*.
[19] M. Liberman, et al. Emotional prosody speech and transcripts. 2002.
[20] H. Lu, et al. Speakersense: Energy efficient unobtrusive speaker identification on mobile phones. In *Pervasive '11*.
[21] H. Lu, et al. The jigsaw continuous sensing engine for mobile phone applications. In *SenSys '10*.
[22] W. S. McCulloch and W. Pitts. A Logical Calculus of the Ideas Immanent in Nervous Activity. *Bulletin of Mathematical Biology*, 5(4):115–133, Dec 1943.
[23] E. Miluzzo, et al. Darwin phones: The evolution of sensing and inference on mobile phones. In *MobiSys '10*.
[24] T. Plötz, et al. Feature learning for activity recognition in ubiquitous computing. In *IJCAI '11*.
[25] K. K. Rachuri, et al. Emotionsense: A mobile phones based adaptive platform for experimental social psychology research. In *UbiComp '10*.
[26] S. Reddy, et al. Using mobile phones to determine transportation modes. *ACM Trans. Sen. Netw.*, 6(2):13:1–13:27, Mar. 2010.
[27] Y. Wang, et al. Tracking human queues using single-point signal monitoring. In *MobiSys '14*.
[28] M. D. Zeiler, et al. On rectified linear units for speech processing. In *ICASSP '13*.

Mobile AD(D)

Estimating Mobile App Session Times for Better Ads

John P. Rula   Byungjin Jun   Fabián E. Bustamante

Northwestern University

{john.rula, byungjin.jun, fabianb}@eecs.northwestern.edu

ABSTRACT

While mobile advertisement is the dominant source of revenue for mobile apps, the usage patterns of mobile users, and thus their engagement and exposure times, may be in conflict with the effectiveness of current ads. User engagement with apps can range from a few seconds to several minutes, depending on a number of factors such as users' locations, concurrent activities and goals. Despite the wide-range of engagement times, the current format of ad auctions dictates that ads are priced, sold and configured *prior* to actual viewing, regardless of the actual ad exposure time.

We argue that the wealth of easy-to-gather contextual information on mobile devices is sufficient to allow advertisers to make better choices by *effectively predicting exposure time*. We analyze mobile device usage patterns with a detailed two-week long user study of 37 users in the US and South Korea. After characterizing application session times, we use factor analysis to derive a simple predictive model and show it is able to offer improved accuracy compared to mean session time over 90% of the time. We make the case for including predicted ad exposure duration in the price of mobile advertisements and posit that such information could significantly impact the effectiveness of mobile ads by giving publishers the ability to tune campaigns for engagement length, and enable a more efficient market for ad impressions while lowering network utilization and device power consumption.

Categories and Subject Descriptors

H.4 [**Information Systems Applications**]: Communications Applications

General Terms

Experimentation; Measurement; Performance

Keywords

Mobile; Apps; Ads; Prediction

1. INTRODUCTION

Advertisement is the dominant source of revenue for mobile apps, with nearly 90% of available apps offered for free. Mobile ad sales more than doubled between 2012 and 2013, totaling over $17.96 billion, and are projected to rise another 75% in 2014 alone [5]. Despite this impressive growth, we posit that the effectiveness of current ad campaigns may be hindered by the usage patterns of mobile users, and their engagement times.

Ad campaigns are aimed, among other goals, at improving online site traffic, creating advertising recall, brand recognition [1] and brand awareness [4]. Display ad campaigns target exposure, rather than site traffic or sales, and have traditionally used a pricing scheme based on the number of impressions delivered (measured as CPM or cost per thousand impressions). Following a model inherited from the newspaper and a mostly-static Web era [6], online display ads treat all impressions the same, independently of the total exposure time, despite the clear benefits that longer exposure has on recognition and recall [6, 7].

While user engagement with mobile apps can range widely, from seconds to several minutes, depending on factors such as users' locations, concurrent activities (e.g., running, sitting on a train) and goals (e.g., entertainment, finding direction, work), we argue that the usage patterns and wealth of easy-to-gather contextual information on mobile devices is sufficient to *effectively predicting session or exposure time*.

In mobile settings, where there is only one app in the foreground, ad exposure time is bound by application session time. Knowing either can benefit all parties in the advertisement ecosystem. Advertisers can use this information to tune campaigns for engagement length, and bid on the appropriate value of an impression. Session time information could reward publishers for engaging users, give ad networks additional freedom to optimize their selections, and reduce wasted resources on end host devices by eliminating data for ads which are never shown. Surprisingly considering its many benefits, we are not aware of any study to attempt to predict the length of a mobile application session or ad exposure times through contextual factors.

We make the case for including predicted ad exposure time in the price of mobile advertisements in current ad exchanges where impressions are auctioned at their onset. Using a detailed two-week-long user study, we analyze the mobile device usage behavior of 37 users (200,000 application sessions) in two mobile markets – the US and South Korea. We show that application session times form a long tailed power law distribution, implying a large disparity in the quality and value of mobile ad sessions. We employ factor

---

[1]*Recall* is the proportion of users who report remembering an advertising with a minimal prompt, while *recognition* uses text or images as probes.

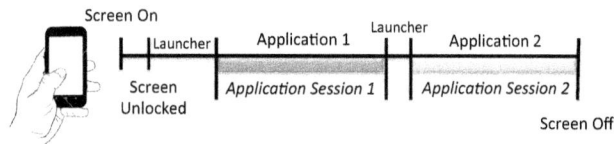

Figure 1: Diagram of actions recorded by our measurement service. We are only interested in the time a particular app is both visible and in the foreground on a user's device, indicated as *Application Session 1* and *Application Session 2* in the Figure.

analysis of device contextual components to determine dominant influences in device usage and application session time and to inform the design of our predictive models. We then show that our prediction model improves accuracy over mean session time over 90% of the time. Our preliminary results show that even a simple first-approximation model to predict session time can significantly improve over current practices of ad campaigns.

2. BACKGROUND AND MOTIVATION

There are a number of common billing models for online advertisement, including Cost Per Click (CPC), Cost Per Mille or thousand impressions (CPM), and Cost Per Action or Acquisition (CPA). Independently of the billing model, advertisers typically purchase ad space by bidding in an auction format.

Bids for impressions are based on the user target profile, which includes demographics such as gender, age and purchasing power, and mobile application category. For instance, certain (classes of) users are particularly coveted due to factors such as their interest in the advertisers' subject or their purchasing power. Ads on more popular websites or applications are also worth more, as are advertisements in more prominent locations on websites.

To the best of our knowledge *no ad auction today takes into account the (expected) time a user is engaged with an application (or advertisement)*, despite the known benefits of longer session times [6]. A simple approach to incorporate session time would be to rely on average impression times during bids. As we show in the following section, considering the high variance and expected long tail distributions of app session times, assuming average values would not be particularly useful.

We argue that, unlike their traditional online counterparts, mobile ads are well suited to include accurate temporal information in their advertisements. The constraints of mobile devices allow mobile applications to accurately measure the amount of time a user is exposed to an advertisement. For starters, in mobile setting, there is only one application that can be in the foreground at a time. This eliminates the ambiguity of having multiple windows, or browser tabs open simultaneously. Device usage is bounded by the time the screen is illuminated, and user interaction can be ensured by the progression through user identification mechanisms such as lock-screens. This ensures that a user is actively engaged with the application within a fine margin. An illustrative example of mobile device and application use flow is shown in Figure 1.

Knowing the session length of a publisher's impression can benefit all parties in the advertising ecosystem, from advertisers themselves to end users. This information could allow advertisers to actually pay for the amount of time their ads are shown. In addition, advertisers can tune their ad campaign media for the appropriate session length. Similarly, publishers with long user

Figure 2: Two snapshots of *AppT* illustrating a subset of the applications monitored, their usage time, and activity, as well as the observation intervals supported (3, 12 and 24 hours and all-time).

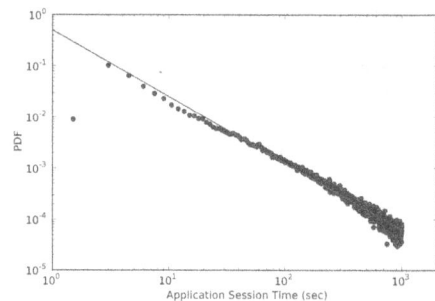

Figure 3: Distribution of application session times form a power law distribution in the form of $f(x) = 0.499x^{-1.3014}$. Average application session time from our dataset is 258 seconds.

engagement can be accordingly compensated. Knowing the session length during an ad request allows the ad network the flexibility to adjust the ordering of ads, and multiplex ad sessions if desired. Last but not least, knowing session time, allows advertising libraries to avoid wasting network resources and cap bandwidth by only downloading the ads which are needed for the allotted time [10].

While there exist many benefits to this type of mobile advertising model, however, if would require a reinvention of the existing advertising marketplace. We instead propose that the same benefits can be enjoyed by predicting the length of a mobile application session, and using this information in existing online ad auctions. Our idea leverages the rich context available mobile devices to build predictive models of application session times. Mobile devices have access to a wealth of contextual information for an app usage, including the user's location, activity, historical usage patterns, and network performance – context which is unavailable for desktop users. Given that error would be inevitable in these predictions, we formalize the cost of prediction error and calculate the cost of this error in the following section.

3. COLLECTING APP SESSION TIME

To explore the possibility of predicting app session time and determine the set of contextual factors necessary for this, we conducted a field study tracking the usage patterns of a set of real users. To this end, we developed and made available an application we call *AppT* – for *Application Time*. AppT tracks application session times, defined as the length of time a mobile app is in the foreground on the user's device (illustrated previously in Fig. 1). Figure 2 presents two screenshots of our app.

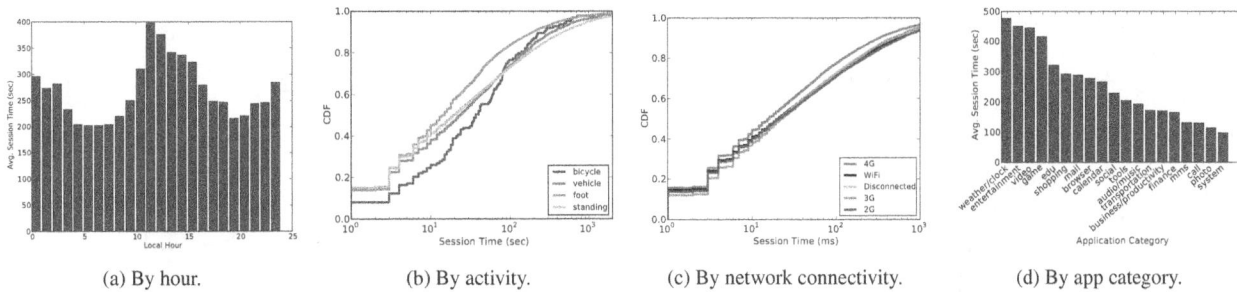

| (a) By hour. | (b) By activity. | (c) By network connectivity. | (d) By app category. |

Figure 4: Application session times for users under different contexts.

We consider each application to be the *foreground application* if it visible to the user (i.e. the screen is illuminated and not behind a lock screen), and the first ranked foreground application by the Android operating system. For the duration of screen illumination, we polled the foreground application from the operating system every 1.5 seconds. In addition to application session time, AppT records contextual information from each participant's device, including the screen illumination time, network conditions, and user activity.

For this study, we use AppT collected detailed application usage time from 35 users, in the United States and South Korea, during a two week periods in March and April 2014. Our dataset includes over 200,000 individual application sessions.

3.1 Mobile App Usage

We find application session times to follow a power law distribution. Figure 3 plots the distribution of application session time, showing that it forms a power law in the form of $f(x) = 0.499x^{-1.3014}$. A long tail distribution means a highly skewed mean session time. For instance, the average session time from our dataset was 258 seconds, however, this value represents the 90th percentile of the entire distribution.

4. CONTEXTUAL FACTOR ANALYSIS

We perform, to the best of our knowledge, the first analysis of contextual factors on mobile application session time. Using the collected dataset we explore the impact of user activity, network connectivity and performance, and temporal components on mobile application session time, and use this analysis to inform the design of our prediction models. We expect that different (types of) applications will be use and be impacted differently by the different factors we explore. Rather than assuming a model per application, we explore the use of an application name/class in our contextual analysis.

We want to identify those that are most dominant and informative for predicting application session time. To this end, we use two quantitative approaches for comparing factors: analysis of variance (ANOVA) tests for statistical independence between categories within a factor (e.g., standing, walking, bicycling, in a vehicle) and information gain analysis to measure the decrease in entropy per category.

In our context, high statistical independence between categories hint at the relative value of that contextual factor as a predictor of application session time. Similarly, high information gain (i.e. entropy reduction) indicates greater predictability of application session time based on the factor's categories. As an illustrative example, if one would like to predict the height of an Olympic athlete, a high statistical independence between each athlete's sport (e.g. between basketball and figure skating), of the height

distribution grouped by sport, would indicate that *sport*, can serve as a good predictor.

4.1 Contextual Factors

The rich information available on the context of a mobile device usage has proved valuable to make application launch prediction [12, 15, 16]. Our hypothesis is that this information can be further leverage to accurately predict application session time.

A description of the contextual factors we gathered in our study are given below.

Temporal Components. We expect temporal information, such as time of day or day of the week, to have an effect on the total usage and application session length on users' devices. To view temporal trends in application session time, we look at how app session lengths change over time. We analyze how session times change with regard to the *hour of the day* and the *day of the week*.

Figure 4a shows the average session time for our study users binned by each hour of the day. The figure shows bimodal usage peaks each day, with application session length peaking at 2 pm and 12am local time. In addition, we observed larger peaks of high session times on Saturdays and Sundays than during weekdays.

User Activity. Given the level of integration of mobile devices into our everyday lives, we also expect user activity to have a dominant role in determining application session time. For instance, an exercise tracking application might have a much higher probability of being used while the user is running or cycling, however, the total engagement time during each session might be much shorter during the activity than later, when they are reviewing their performance.

To this end, AppT records the *current user activity* as taken from the DetectedActivity intent built into Android operating system. Activities are detected in 20 second granularities, recording whether the user is walking, standing, in a vehicle, running or bicycling.

Figure 4b plots session length per activities for all users. In aggregate, walking and cycling sessions show, respectively, the shortest and longest median session times with respective values of 16 and 41 seconds. Interestingly, both stationary and vehicular sessions are similarly distributed but present significantly different average session times (262 and 175 seconds).

Network Connectivity Besides the time and current activity of a user when in an application, one would expect the quality and performance of the device's network connection to impact application session times. For instance, a messaging application such as WhatsApp would be of little use without any network connectivity, while poor network conditions tend to render a mobile web browser virtually unusable. We captured each device's current *connectivity state* (connected or disconnected) along with the current *radio interface* (e.g. WIFI, LTE, UTMS, etc) in use during a connected period.

We found individual network connectivity states to offer very similar distributions for application session time. Figure 4c plots the distribution of application session times under different connectivity conditions (e.g. 4G, 3G, WiFi, etc). The figure shows almost identical curves for all connectivity states with the exception of LTE, which shows shorter application session than each other network state.

Mobile Application Given the wide range of applications available and the different intended usage modes, we expect that either the application or its type to be key for predicting session time prediction. For our analysis, we use the application's *package name*, which uniquely identifies it within the Android ecosystem. We focus our study on the top ten most commonly used applications for users. We found this subset to be sufficient to account for most of the device utilization – indeed, we found the top 5 applications alone already account for over 80% of device usage, on average.

Application sessions also differ based on the category of application. We categorized each application package into one of 19 different categories (e.g. messaging, game, video). We found the category of mobile application to play a significant determinant of average session time. Average session times for each category are plotted in descending order in Figure 4d. The figure shows, surprisingly, that common phone utilities such as weather/clock had the highest average session times of nearly 3 minutes. Other apps such as messaging and phone contacts had some of the lowest average session times.

4.2 Analysis of Variance (ANOVA)

ANOVA tests are used to determine independence between subpopulations of a population (categories of a factor, in our context). ANOVA represents independence between categories by looking at the overlap between confidence intervals of each class. The formula shown by Equation 1 calculates the F ratio, which is then plugged into the standard F-distribution to obtain p-values for significance [8].

$$F = \frac{MS_{Treatments}}{MS_{Error}} = \frac{\frac{\sum n_j (\bar{x}_j - \bar{x})^2}{k-1}}{\frac{\sum (n_j - 1)\sigma_j^2}{n-k}} \quad (1)$$

We ran ANOVA tests, per user, for each factor described previously in Section 4.1. The significance levels are represented as p-values for each factor and shown in Figure 5. Typically p-values less than 0.05 (dash vertical line) indicate high levels of subpopulation independence, while p-values less than 0.1 (solid vertical line) indicate weak independence [8].

We use these results to determine which factors should be included within our prediction model. Those with high group independence (low p-values) mean that grouping by that category produces statistically significant differences in each subpopulation, indicating a factor will be useful for prediction.

Our results (Fig. 5) show hour of the day to have the highest group independence, followed by mobile application, user activity and day of week. Indeed, time of day shows high levels of group independence (p-values < 0.05) for over 90% of users. Mobile application showed similar independence also for over 90% of users. User activity obtained the next highest , with weak independence for nearly half of the user population, and radio type seeing independence in nearly 30% of the user population. Connectivity was the least independent of all factors, showing strong independence in only 10% of the user population and weak independence in only 20% of users. Unlike time of day (hour),

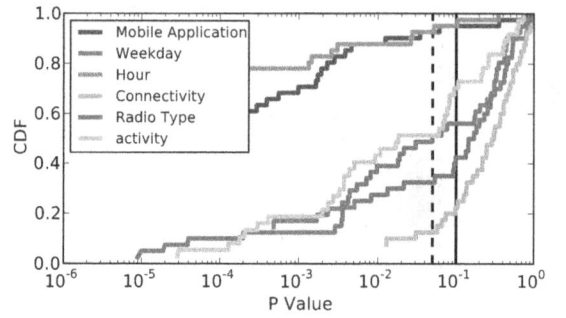

Figure 5: P-values for users for different contextual groups. P-values < 0.05 (dotted line) indicate statistical significant independence, while p-values < 0.1 (solid line) indicate weak independence.

each of these last factors represent minor indicators of application session time according to statistical independence. We supplement these insights with information gain analysis in the next section.

4.3 Information Gain Analysis

To further characterize contextual factor influence on application time, we calculate the *relative information gain* of each factor by measuring the decrease in entropy each brings to the system, or more plainly, the increase in predictability of session times each category of contextual factor gives. The information gain of each contextual factor can be used to guide the design of predictive models.

The entropy of a random variable Y is given as $H(Y) = \sum_i P[Y = y_i] log \frac{1}{P[Y=y_i]}$, where $P[Y = y_i]$ is the probability that $Y = y_i$. The information gain $G(X)$ of a particular factor F with states $f \in F$ is calculated as $G(Y, F) = H(Y) - \sum_{f \in F} \frac{|Y_f|}{|Y|} H(Y_f)$. It is the difference between the total entropy of the original system, and the sum of the entropy of each factor grouping. For comparison purposes, we calculate the *relative information gain*, which normalized the difference in entropy by dividing the result by the total entropy of the system, $H(Y)$.

Figure 6 plots the cumulative distribution of information gain observed by each user in our study for the 5 contextual factors. The figure shows, again, that the temporal components (weekday and hour) along with application name (package name) provide the highest amounts of information gain to the system. Radio type offered moderate information gains, while user activity gave the least by far.

Interestingly, user activity offers the lowest information gain even though our ANOVA analysis ($\S$ 4.2) showed there exists high level of independence between activity subpopulations. This is due to the fact that information gain is not normalized against subpopulation size like ANOVA, and speaks to the need for multiple techniques when designing a prediction model. In the case of user activity, the number of application sessions classified as *stationary* were at least an order of magnitude larger than any of the other activities. Therefore, the entropy of *stationary* sessions (which is weighted by $\frac{|Y_f|}{|Y|}$) is very close to the total entropy of the system.

5. MOBILE APP PREDICTION

We now outline a procedure for modelling and predicting application session times. We first formalize the bounds of prediction error by calculating the maximum error allowable to still offer

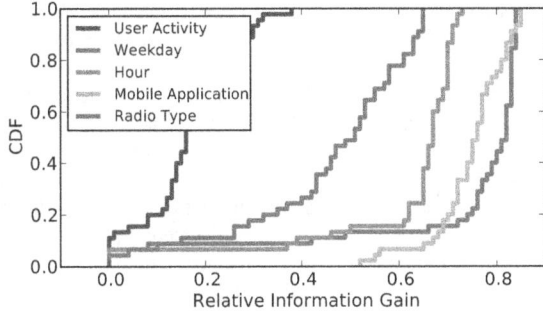

Figure 6: Relative information gain for contextual factors for application session time. Application name, and temporal components have large information gains for study users.

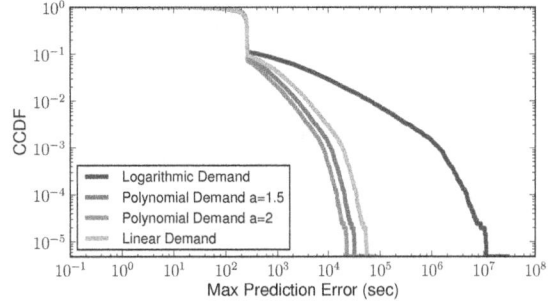

Figure 7: Maximum prediction error ($e_t = |t_p - t|$) tolerable for session prediction to improve against the current model. While each demand model differs on its tail behavior, errors for each demand model are very similar, and heavily dependent on $\bar{t}$, which in our study is 258.9 seconds.

more accurate information than the average session time. Using this model, we compute the potential cost of inaccurate prediction on advertisers and publishers before presenting preliminary work toward session time prediction.

5.1 Prediction Error Bounds

Since ad sales are closed *before* the user has even begun viewing an ad, it is impossible to know the actual session length at bidding time, making it necessary to use an estimate. We formalize the bounds of prediction error by calculating the maximum error allowable to still offer more accurate information than the average session time, $\bar{t}$. With prediction, there always exists some error, e_t, between the predicted session time, t_p, and the actual session time, t.

We define the loss due to prediction error as the difference in price between the predicted session time, and the price of the actual session time, $|P(t_p) - P(t)|$. This cost due to any prediction error can only be determined by knowing the shape of the advertiser demand function, $P(t)$. This is due to our definition of loss being based on the price differential between actual and predicted session times, therefore the shape of the price (demand) curve is integral to the overall loss. We compare this prediction loss to the difference in price between that of mean session time and the price of the actual session time, $|P(\bar{t}) - P(t)|$.

We look at the results from our estimation of advertiser demand curves using linear, polynomial and logarithmic growth functions. We look for conditions where the loss from prediction is less than the loss from the current model.

$$|P(\bar{t}) - P(t)| > |P(t_p) - P(t)| \qquad (2)$$

Using linear demand where $P(t) = Ct + b$, we can reduce Equation 2 to $|\bar{t} - t| > |t_p - t|$, or more simply, when the error from prediction is less than the distance to the session time mean. Using a polynomial demand where $P(t) = Ct^a + b$ and $a > 1$, we can reduce Equation 2 to $|\bar{t}^a - t^a| > |t_p^a - t^a|$, the value of session time here depends on the magnitude of the demand exponent, along with prediction accuracy. Using logarithmic demand where $P(t) = C\log(t) + b$, Equation 2 reduces to $|\log(\frac{\bar{t}}{t})| > |\log(\frac{t_p}{t})|$.

Using the distribution of application session times collected from our user study (§ 3), we simulate the maximum value of prediction error, e_t which can be tolerated for our prediction model using the three possible demand curves described above. Figure 7 shows the maximum prediction error for Equation 2 to hold using all application session times taken from our experiments. The Figure shows the high similarity in allowable prediction error for the

different demand curves, diverging only above the 90th percentile among all curves. This similarity shows that for the vast majority of cases, the advertiser demand function has a minimal effect on the bounds of prediction error.

5.2 A Naïve Prediction Model

Using the data collected from our experiments (§ 3), and our contextual factor analysis (§ 4) we constructed and evaluated a naïve prediction model for mobile application sessions. Due to the complex interactions between contextual factors and app session time, we chose to use a decision tree classifier to predict session times over other classifiers and regression models. Each class is generated taking an equal percentile from the overall training set distribution. Using a classifier over potential regression models reduces overall accuracy since the predicted value is the average value taken for a given classification; however, we found this to be more accurate when compared to regression models such as linear or decision-tree regression.

We analyzed the accuracy of our predictive models through the classification accuracy, the percentage of session times which are correctly placed in the right class. To evaluate our prediction model, we split our dataset into a training and validation set. Since our dataset encompassed a two week period, we use the first week of data for model training and the second week as a validation set for our models. This allows us to compare the success of several different classifier models and class sizes. We found that decision trees provided the most accurate predictor of mobile application session times, when compared with other common classifiers such as support vector classifiers (SVCs) and Naive Bayes classifiers. Unsurprisingly we found that as we increased the number of classes we see classifier accuracy decrease substantially.

Application session times are continuous values, and the classifier accuracy does not capture the absolute error obtained by the prediction. For instance, if a session was classified incorrectly, but still placed in an adjacent class, the prediction might still be beneficial. We therefore also measure the absolute prediction error of our predictive model, defined as the difference between the predicted session time and the actual session time from our testing set. Since our predictions are based on classes, the predicted time is taken to be the average session time in each class from the training set. Figure 8 shows this prediction error for our prediction model, the mean error, and a random distribution sampling. Our classifier outperforms mean error in over 90% of cases.

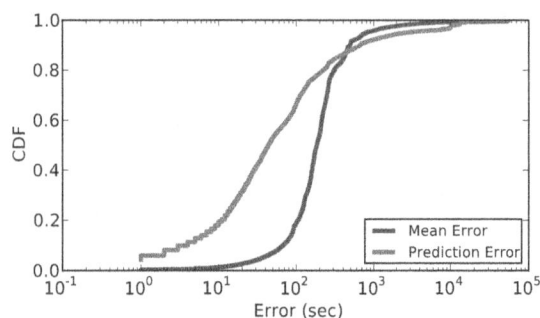

Figure 8: Prediction error for simple decision tree classifier and 10 classes, compared to the mean error. Our prediction model outperforms mean error in over 90% of cases.

6. RELATED WORK

Several recent efforts have looked at the impact of device context on mobile device usage patterns, and understanding user engagement and application usage for individuals. Research on user engagement has focused on determining dominant factors for user viewing or for developing predictive models for engagement in online videos (e.g., [1, 3]) .

Other projects have explored application usage and prediction on mobile devices (e.g., [2, 12, 13, 15, 16]) considering contextual factors such as time of day and location to predict, for instance, the next application to be launched. Understanding the effect of context on device usage has important implications on system performance enhancements, device preloading and prefetching, and application design.

Our work is complementary to these efforts. We approach the problem of usage prediction not from the individual applications, but from the level of the entire device, and bringing in additional contextual information such as user activity (e.g., walking, standing), network state, total phone session and performance. By focusing on device engagement, we are able to understand usage patterns across classes of applications and over short individual application sessions. Ourgoal is to better understand the effect that each of these contextual elements has on device and application usage, and, use this information to reliably predict session times for devices and applications.

Due to their large role in financing mobile applications, mobile advertisements have recently been studied in the contexts of fraud [9], contextual effectiveness [11], and network and power usage on mobile devices [14]. Closest to our work is by Mohan et al. which studied the efficacy of prefetching mobile advertisements [10]. Part of their analysis was to look at the entropy of application session lengths from a large historical sample, finding that prediction is indeed feasible. Our work extends their initial analysis, taking into account a large variety of user contexts, and implementing a first attempt at mobile session prediction from this context.

7. CONCLUSION AND FUTURE WORK

The usage patterns of mobile users, and thus their engagement times, may be in conflict with the effectiveness of current ads. While users engagement with mobile apps can range from a few seconds to several minutes, the current format of ad auctions dictates that ads are priced, sold and configured prior to actual viewing, *regardless* of the actual exposure time. We argue that the wealth of easy-to-gather contextual information on mobile devices is sufficient to allow advertisers to make better choices by *effectively predicting exposure time*. Building on a two-week-long user study in two markets we analyzed mobile device usage patters. We used factor analysis to derive a simple predictive model and show that is able offer improved accuracy compared to mean session time over 90% of the time. We made the case for including predicted ad exposure time in the price of mobile advertisements and posit that such information could significantly impact the effectiveness of mobile advertisement, giving publishers the ability to tune campaigns for engagement length and enabling a more efficient market for ad impressions, select appropriate media for an ad impression and lowering the cost to users including network utilization and device power. In ongoing work, we are exploring better prediction models and evaluating the benefits of estimated session times in other contexts, including media selection and network usage.

8. ACKNOWLEDGEMENTS

We would like to thank our shepherd, Alex Snoeren, and the anonymous reviewers for their valuable feedback and assistance. This work was supported in part by the National Science Foundation through award CNS 1218287.

9. REFERENCES

[1] A. Balachandran, V. Sekar, A. Akella, S. Seshan, I. Stoica, and H. Zhang. Developing a predictive model of quality of experience for Internet video. In *Proc. ACM SIGCOMM*, 2013.

[2] M. Böhmer, B. Hecht, J. Schöning, A. Antonio Krüger, and G. Bauer. Falling asleep with angry birds, facebook and kindle: A large scale study on mobile application usage. In *Proc. of MobileHCI*, 2011.

[3] F. Dobrian, V. Sekar, A. Awan, I. Stoica, D. Joseph, A. Ganjam, J. Zhan, and H. Zhang. Understanding the impact of video quality on user engagement. In *Proc. ACM SIGCOMM*, 2011.

[4] X. Dreze and F.-X. Hussherr. Internet advertising: Is anybody watching? *Journal of interactive marketing*, 17(4):8–23, 2003.

[5] eMarketer. Driven by facebook and google, mobile ad market soars 105% in 2013 - emarketer. http://bit.ly/1lOsFlh.

[6] D. G. Goldstein, R. P. McAfee, and S. Suri. The effects of exposure time on memory of display advertisements. In *Proc. of EC*, 2011.

[7] D. G. Goldstein, R. P. McAfee, and S. Suri. Improving the effectiveness of time-based display advertising. In *Proc. of EC*, 2012.

[8] M. H. Kutner, C. J. Nachtsheim, and J. Neter. *Applied Linear Regression Models*. McGraw-Hill/Irwin, fourth international edition, 2004.

[9] B. Liu, S. Nath, R. Govindan, and J. Liu. Decaf: detecting and characterizing ad fraud in mobile apps. In *Proc. USENIX NSDI*, 2014.

[10] P. Mohan, S. Nath, and O. Riva. Prefetching mobile ads: Can advertising systems afford it? In *Proc. of Eurosys*, 2013.

[11] S. Nath, F. X. Lin, L. Ravindranath, and J. Padhye. Smartads: bringing contextual ads to mobile apps. In *Proc. of MobiSys*, 2013.

[12] A. Parate, M. Böhmer, D. Chu, D. Ganesan, and B. M. Marlin. Practical prediction and prefetch for faster access to applications on mobile phones. In *Proc. of UbiComp*, 2013.

[13] C. Shin, J.-H. Hong, and A. K. Dey. Understanding and prediction of mobile application usage for smart phones. In *Proc. of UbiComp*, 2012.

[14] N. Vallina-Rodriguez, J. Shah, A. Finamore, Y. Grunenberger, K. Papagiannaki, H. Haddadi, and J. Crowcroft. Breaking for commercials: characterizing mobile advertising. In *Proc. IMC*, 2012.

[15] Y. Xu, M. Lin, H. Lu, G. Cardone, N. Lane, Z. Chen, A. Campbell, and T. Choudhury. Preference, context and communities: a multi-faceted approach to predicting smartphone app usage patterns. In *Proc. of ISWC*, 2013.

[16] T. Yan, D. Chu, D. Ganesan, A. Kansal, and J. Liu. Fast app launching for mobile devices using predictive user context. In *Proc. of MobiSys*, 2012.

Policy-Carrying Data: A Privacy Abstraction for Attaching Terms of Service to Mobile Data

Stefan Saroiu, Alec Wolman, Sharad Agarwal
Microsoft Research

Abstract: Despite decades of work on privacy-protecting systems, mobile user privacy remains at the mercy of cloud service providers. This paper proposes a different approach – let users attach Terms of Service (ToS) to their data before uploading it to the cloud. We propose an abstraction, called policy-carrying data (PCD), that lets users specify and attach ToS to their data. PCD guarantees that cloud providers claim they are compliant with the ToS policy before they are able to access the data. To offer this guarantee, PCD relies on attribute-based encryption. We present PCD's semantics, its properties, and describe how PCD can be added to JSON or REST. Our hope is that PCD opens a different research path – designing privacy abstractions that provide legal ammunition for mobile users against misuse of their data.

1. INTRODUCTION

Despite its importance, protecting the privacy of mobile users' data stored in the cloud remains an elusive goal. The current landscape is very one-sided: cloud providers maintain control over how users' data is gathered, stored, managed, and used. On the other side, users are given only two choices. One is to abandon using the cloud and all apps' functionality requiring access to private data (e.g., GPS locations, users' profiles, etc...). The other choice is to lose control of their data and simply trust the cloud providers to treat private data sensibly.

This lopsided situation is further exacerbated by the business model of many cloud providers, where they partner with third-party ad networks to generate revenue. Both cloud providers and their partner ad networks have been shown to aggressively mine private data in ways that erode the privacy of most mobile users [16, 20, 12]. Even worse, there is evidence that cloud providers are forced by their local governments to further violate customers' privacy in the name of national security [14].

In response to this "privacy crisis", systems and tools have been developed to offer strong privacy protection for users' cloud data, such as information flow control [31, 7, 11], secure and trusted operating systems [29, 6, 18, 17], secure hypervisors [28, 23, 26, 32], and novel anonymization and encryption schemes [30, 8, 9, 22, 21, 25]. Despite their high degree of technical sophistication,

these tools have yet to empower users with control over their cloud data.

This paper considers an alternative to building systems with strong cloud privacy protections. We advocate a much simpler approach – let users attach *terms of service* (ToS) to their data before it is uploaded to the cloud. Such a solution is similar to how valuable data is treated in other cases. For example, websites routinely publish their ToS dictating how users must treat the websites' data, programmers attach licenses to their code before publishing it online, applications ask users to click on a EULA before installation, and DVD producers force viewers to watch a short "do not copy this DVD" preview before any content is viewed. While these solutions cannot actually prevent data from misuse, they are *legally binding*: data owners can take legal action when a violation is detected. This provides a much-needed re-leveling of the playing field because it gives users additional leverage against cloud providers.

We believe that attaching terms of service to data is a problem of technical nature that the research community can help solve. We propose an abstraction, called *policy-carrying data (PCD)*, that helps to implement such privacy mechanisms. PCD binds a user's data to a policy that specifies the conditions under which data can be used, and offers the following guarantee: the cloud provider must explicitly opt-in to the user-specified policy before it can even access the data. As a result, if policy violations are discovered, the cloud provider cannot claim a lack of knowledge of user's desired policy associated with the data.

To offer this guarantee, PCD relies on encryption. While encryption is typically used to protect data confidentiality, PCD uses encryption in a different way: to force the decrypting party (i.e., the cloud) to claim it is compliant with the policy attached to the data. This is done using ciphertext-based attribute-based encryption (CP-ABE), a form of encryption that can be loosely thought as "encrypting data with a policy". To decrypt successfully, cloud providers must construct a list of attributes compliant with the policy specification; if the attributes are not compliant, decryption fails. An additional benefit of CP-ABE is that it allows policies to be specified in a human-readable form, such as XML.

While PCD does not guarantee that cloud providers do not abuse private data, it provides one form of a customer-dictated "EULA" listing the conditions under which data can be used. An example policy indicates that a GPS reading can only be used once and then must be deleted, or that it cannot be shared with any third-party; another example indicates that photos can only be stored on servers located inside the US. Cloud providers could choose to violate these policies. However, when policy violations are caught, they are likely to be much costlier to cloud providers because the violations were done knowingly and deliberately. We believe that this mechanism increases the likelihood that cloud providers will treat

3. MODEL AND SEMANTICS

The policy-carrying data (PCD) abstraction allows a mobile user's data to be bound to a user-defined policy. PCD offers two primitives: *encapsulate* and *descapsulate*. Encapsulate is performed by a user and takes as input the privacy-sensitive data and a policy, and outputs ciphertext. The reverse operation, decapsulate, is done by the cloud provider and takes as input the ciphertext. By construction, the decryption keys correspond to the set of policies the cloud provider claims it adheres to. Decapsulate decrypts properly *if and only if* the cloud provider claims it is compliant with the policy specified at encapsulation time, during encryption.

3.1 Model

With our abstractions, each cloud provider has a configuration, which is a set of human-readable attributes from a taxonomy of attributes (a strawman example was presented in Table 2). This configuration is published to a trusted provider, such as a certificate authority (CA). This is a one-time step; the CA generates a set of credentials based on these configurations and passes them to the cloud provider. PCD guarantees that the credentials can decapsulate only data whose policy is met by the configuration of the cloud provider.

The explicit step of publishing the configuration offers assurance because the cloud states to a third-party (i.e., the CA) a set of privacy measures. For example, the cloud can state that it never stores credit card information, it does not perform face recognition, or that it uses highly secure software and hardware to handle users' data.

However, PCD also allows for the cloud provider to act as a CA. This offers a weaker form of assurance because the cloud does not have to reveal its configuration to a third-party. Section 4 will provide a more in-depth discussion of the separation between the cloud provider and the CA.

3.2 PCD-based ToS

PCD lets users specify their own terms of service. The same way how websites require their users to click "Agree" on the ToS, PCD require websites to interpret their user's policy to access and use their data. We believe this requirement is sufficient to render the policy attached to the data as legally binding. When violations occur, customers (whether users or other businesses) can take the website to court.

While customers have the option of constructing their own policies for the PCD abstraction, it also possible for a third-party (similar to ToS;DR) to pre-construct a fixed set of policies and label them, perhaps using a color-coding scheme. A green policy could represent a case when the customer uses a non-restrictive policy (e.g., the website can use the GPS location for showing ads), where as a red policy a very restrictive policy (e.g., the website must discard the GPS location as soon as the Web request is answered).

3.3 Trade-off: Policy Restrictiveness vs. Level of Service

The question raised now is: "Why would a user choose any policy other than the most restrictive one so that the user's privacy is maximized?" While the user is free to select any policy, the service provider may use policies to determine what quality of service to offer their users. Depending on the service, the provider may have a number of quality knobs that can be adjusted:

- auto policy discount
- location service accuracy
- search query accuracy
- freshness of web service data

- personalization features
- speech recognition accuracy
- online storage size

For example, if a user restricts their auto insurance company from retaining GPS traces gathered from their phone, then the insurance company may not give the user certain policy discounts. This enables a trade-off between the user's need for privacy and the insurance company's need for risk mitigation. Similarly, an online file storage service may offer less free storage capacity to a user who restricts their data to be stored only in certain datacenter locations. This allows a trade-off between the user's need for protection (e.g, from certain governments) and the storage provider's need for limiting cost in expensive datacenter locations.

3.4 Bootstrapping PCD

One obstacle to deploying PCD is requiring cloud providers to implement our abstraction. One possibility to help bootstrap our system is via a proxy. This proxy could interpret the policies attached to the users' data and decide which cloud provider is best suited with meeting this policy. Effectively, the proxy's role is to construct a set of attributes and values that correspond to each cloud provider. While such a proxy could help speed the adoption of PCD, its existence also raises privacy risks because it would be exposed to all its users' data.

4. CRYPTOGRAPHIC SUPPORT

PCD relies on Ciphertext Policy Attribute-Based Encryption (CP-ABE), a type of public-key encryption in which data is encrypted using a policy, and the decryption keys is dependent on a set of attributes. Decryption is possible only if the set of attributes satisfies the policy. PCD relies on a certificate authority (CA). The CA generates a master private key and a master public key. Encryption is done using the master public key and a user-specified policy. A cloud provider must present a set of attributes to the CA. The CA uses its master secret key to return the cloud provider's decryption key embedding the corresponding attributes. The decryption key can be used successfully against all ciphertexts whose policies are satisfied by the cloud provider's set of attributes.

These are the steps to use CP-ABE in the content of policy-carrying data:

1. CA generates public and private master keys, ($\text{MasterK}_{\text{pub}}$ and $\text{MasterK}_{\text{priv}}$)

2. Cloud provider presents the set of attributes to the CA ($\text{Attrib}_{\text{provider}}$). CA uses private master key $\text{MasterK}_{\text{priv}}$ to generate a decryption key embedding these attributes ($K(\text{Attrib}_{\text{provider}})$).

3. User encrypts data D with policy P and CA's public master key $\text{MasterK}_{\text{pub}}$, producing ciphertext C. User uploads C to provider.

4. Provider decrypts C using its decryption key $K(\text{Attrib}_{\text{provider}})$. If decryption is successful, provider's attributes match the user-specified policy P.

The separation between the CA and the cloud provider (i.e., the principal attempting to decrypt) is crucial to the security of CP-ABE because the CA must guard the secrecy of the secret master key. However, in our case, CP-ABE is used only to guarantee that the cloud provider interprets the user's privacy policy. This guarantee can be met even when the cloud provider also acts as the CA. To decrypt, the cloud provider must use the master secret key and a set of attributes to generate a decryption key. This step is where

Figure 1: CP-ABE: on the left, the CA is separate from the cloud provider; on the right, the CA and the cloud provider are the same. (icons by Freepik [1]/CC BY 3.0.)

the PCD guarantee is met: the cloud provider must use a set of attributes meeting the policy specification to generate a decryption key capable of decrypting the ciphertext.

Figure 1 illustrates the two cases: on the left the CA is a separate entity than the cloud provider, on the right the cloud provider and the CA is the same entity. The case on the left is important to ensure the security of CP-ABE. On the right, ABE is insecure because the cloud provider is the CA, and thus possesses the master private key.

Both cases provide the PCD guarantee – the cloud provider must generate a decryption key whose attributes match the policy, thus having to interpret the policy. However, there is an additional important distinction. On the left, the cloud provider states its configuration to a third-party, a step that can be independently verified. For example, an external audit could verify the configurations claimed by a cloud provider; such an audit could be useful to settle disputes. On the right, the cloud provider takes no external, independently verifiable step to reveal its privacy configurations to a third-party.

4.1 Why CP-ABE?

A legitimate question is why does PCD need to rely on a relatively uncommon form of encryption (CP-ABE)? Why can't PCD use a more common cryptographic scheme, like RSA? To answer these questions, we start by first describing a possible implementation of PCD using RSA and then list its drawbacks.

Mobile users can take their polices and the data to upload and XOR them together. This XOR-ed blob (i.e., policy $\oplus$ data) could be then encrypted with the cloud provider's public key. The user uploads both the ciphertext and the policy. The cloud provider must use its RSA private key to obtain the XOR-ed blob, and then XOR it with the policy to decrypt the data.

$$\text{Encryption:RSA\_pubkey(policy} \oplus \text{data)} \tag{1}$$

$$\text{Decryption:RSA\_privkey(ciphertext)} \oplus \text{policy} \tag{2}$$

CP-ABE offers two advantages over traditional encryption. First, CP-ABE offers policies with multiple clauses linked by conjunctive and disjunctive operators. Traditional encryption does not extend naturally to support policies with multiple "and" and "or" operators. Second, although the cloud provider needs the user's policy to be able to decrypt, its use of the policy is mundane. The cloud provider uses the policy as one of the inputs to the decryption function without having to interpret it. It's similar to how the cloud provider uses other RSA decryption parameters, such as the type of the padding scheme or the length of the key. In contrast, with ABE, the cloud provider itself must generate the set of policies it adheres to. Only after these policies are generated, the cloud provider can obtain the decryption keys. With ABE, the cloud provider has no choice but to claim it adheres to the right policy.

5. POSSIBLE IMPLEMENTATIONS

While there is no single standard on how web services are implemented today, we believe that most Web frameworks are amenable to adding the PCD abstraction to users' data. This subsection presents preliminary designs to adding PCD to two popular Web standards: JSON [5] and REST [24].

JavaScript Object Notation (JSON). JSON is an open standard that uses human-readable text to transmit data objects in a key-value pair format. For example, a GPS location in JSON could be:

```
{
    ``firstName'': ``Barack'',
    ``lastName'': ``Obama'',
    ``latitude'': ``38.8951N'',
    ``longitude'': ``77.0367W''
}
```

Since PCD is human-readable, incorporating PCD into a JSON protocol is trivial. For example, adding policy 1 from Table 1 to this example would become:

```
{
    ``firstName'': ``Barack'',
    ``lastName'': ``Obama'',
    ``lat'': 0x53c5b77d34713801e61bd5a5b00a4aea,
    ``long'': 0xf38f927640da51fdacdb93243317b0de,
    ``PCD'': ``data_retention_limit = one time
            AND service_name = Bing Maps
            AND anonymization_scheme = k-anonymity''
}
```

Representational State Transfer (REST). In REST, data objects are identified using URIs, such as http://example.com/ GPS. The common way to upload a value using REST is to issue an HTTP PUT request to the URI. For example:

```
PUT /GPS/coordinates?firstName=Barack&\
    lastName=Obama&\
    lat=0x53c5b77d34713801e61bd5a5b00a4aea&\
    long=0xf38f927640da51fdacdb93243317b0de \
    HTTP/1.1
Host: www.example.com
X-PCD: data_retention_limit = one time
        AND service_name = Bing Maps
        AND anonymization_scheme = k-anonymity
```

Other Formats. For Web services that do not follow JSON or REST, the PCD policy can be transmitted through a Web cookie. The server must read the cookie and interpret the policy before decrypting the passed-in data objects.

6. ADDITIONAL USES

In recent years, sophisticated privacy tools have been developed to control the amount of information disclosed to a website or a third-party. However, the parameterization of these tools is often under-specified or entirely under the control of the website. An additional use of PCD, beyond just specifying the desired algorithm, is to offer users a way to initialize the parameters (or the configuration) of a website's privacy tools. This section lists a set of privacy tools, their configuration parameters, and how PCD can let users define their input values.

k-Anonymity. k-Anonymity [30] maps sensitive data to a set of identifiers in such a way that they are indistinguishable among k individuals. The value of k is crucial to the privacy of this scheme – a higher value of k offers stronger privacy. With PCD, different users could choose different value of k for their data.

l-Diversity. l-Diversity [22] is an extension of k-Anonymity that aggregates sensitive data into a set of equivalence classes, such that sensitive data has diverse values within each class. l-Diversity is stronger than k-Anonymity because it reduces the likelihood of reversing the anonymization in case the sensitive data has a homogeneous distribution, or when the attacker has additional background knowledge about the data. As before, users could define the l-diversity metric the website must apply to the data classes.

t-Closeness. t-Closeness [21] partitions the sensitive data into equivalence classes in such a way that the distance between the overall distribution of sensitive values and the distribution in each class must be bounded by t. There are several metrics that measure distance between distributions, and, with PCD, users can decide on the metric.

Differential privacy (DP). DP [8, 9] provides an intuitive formalization of privacy. Given a dataset and a query, DP measures how much information is revealed by answering the query. Information is revealed when an attacker who knows the query answer is more likely to guess the existence of a data item in the dataset. Any query answered on the dataset leaks some information, however certain queries leak more information than others. The amount of privacy loss is controlled by injecting noise in the query answer.

DP frameworks offer two knobs. First, a noise knob controls how much "noise" data to inject in the query answer if set to high, the query answer has low privacy loss, but it is also more inaccurate, and vice-versa. Noise is generated dynamically for each query answer; if the same query is repeated, the answer changes from one run to another based on the random noise. The second parameter is the privacy budget of the entire dataset. The privacy lost by each query answer is deducted from this privacy budget. Once it reaches zero, the system refuses to answer any additional queries on this particular dataset. While we do not expect average Web users to be able to parameterize a DP framework, PCD still allows users to select DP configurations pre-defined by third-parties.

7. BRIEF PERFORMANCE EVALUATION

An area of concern is the performance of CP-ABE. To investigate the suitability of CP-ABE as an abstraction mechanism, we perform the following brief performance evaluation. We encrypt a 1KB data item using different policies with increasing levels of complexity. We vary the number of attributes in the policy from one to ten and measure the performance of encrypt and decrypt of CP-ABE.

Our setup uses an NVIDIA Jetson Tegra K1 platform equipped with 2 GB of RAM and an 4-Plus-1 quad-core ARM Cortex A15

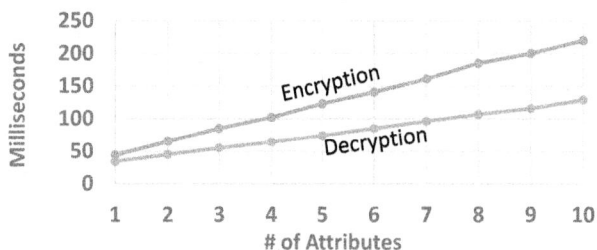

Figure 2: Performance of CP-ABE encryption and decryption.

CPU running at a maximum clock speed of 2.3 GHz. We use a publicly-available implementation of CP-ABE found at http://hms.isi.jhu.edu/acsc/cpabe/, and we repeat each experiment 100 times and report the average. We checked that all our experiments have low variance.

Figure 2 illustrates the performance of encrypt and decrypt as a function of policy complexity. This Figure shows two findings. First, the overhead of CP-ABE is not high; even with complex policies, CP-ABEs' performance is measured in tens of milliseconds. Second, decryption is quite fast (it is less expensive than encryption, a finding consistent with previously reported evaluations of attribute-based encryption). Fast decryption indicates that cloud providers need not worry about the performance overhead due to PCD.

8. RELATED WORK

Our PCD abstraction is inspired by Excalibur [27], which offers policy-sealed data, another abstraction for building trusted cloud services. Like PCD, Excalibur uses CP-ABE to encrypt customer data and bind it to a customer-chosen policy. However, unlike PCD, Excalibur is primarily a security mechanism. Excalibur combines a hypervisor, verified security protocols, and TPM-based attestation to ensure that customer-encrypted data can only be decrypted on cloud servers whose software and hardware configuration is compatible with the customer-specified policy. As a result, Excalibur imposes a high barrier on the cloud-service infrastructure. In contrast, our goal with PCD is just to ensure that the cloud provider explicitly opts-in to the customer policy – no heavy-weight enforcement mechanisms are necessary.

Prior work [15] has proposed middleware for anonymizing user location data along spatial or temporal dimensions. TaintDroid [10] takes an altogether different approach – it traces the flow of private user data through mobile app code to identify when it leaves a mobile device. Similarly, PMP [3] detects when apps use private data. It uses crowdsourcing to determine whether an app should have access to that data, but does not address privacy once the data leaves the app. Other work [20] has studied the economics of mobile app advertising and presents a framework for dynamically obfuscating user data to achieve a revenue target. All this work is complementary – PCD would enable users of these techniques to specify conditions on what levels of anonymity and privacy they desire once data has left the device and reached the cloud.

Privacy legal scholars have previously argued for a *contractual* approach to online privacy [4]. Their argument stems from the lack of consensus among people about *how* important privacy is. Current legal efforts to protect privacy are not sensitive to the individual levels of privacy desired by an individual. A law offers too little privacy for some, and too much for others. Instead, a contractual solution is preferable, where individuals can enter separate contracts that dictate their privacy needs. PCD offers a straightforward mechanism for implementing a contractual approach to privacy.

9. CONCLUSIONS

This paper proposes policy-carrying data (PCD), a privacy abstraction for mobile services. With PCD, users construct a policy expressing how their private data must be treated by the cloud. PCD guarantees that cloud providers claim to be compliant with the specified policy before getting access to the data. This paper describes how attribute-based encryption can be used to offer the PCD abstraction. It also provides a strawman PCD design and taxonomy, and a preliminary performance evaluation. We hope that PCD can offer an alternative approach to offering cloud services with strong privacy guarantees.

10. REFERENCES

[1] Freepik. https://www.freepik.com, 2014.

[2] Terms of Service Didn't Read. https://tosdr.org/, 2014.

[3] Y. Agarwal and M. Hall. ProtectMyPrivacy: Detecting and Mitigating Privacy Leaks on iOS Devices Using Crowdsourcing. In *ACM MobiSys*, 2013.

[4] S. Bibas. A Contractual Approach to Data Privacy. Faculty Scholarship. Paper 1016, 1994.

[5] T. Bray. RFC 7159: The JavaScript Object Notation (JSON) Data Interchange Format. http://www.rfc-editor.org/info/rfc7159, 2014.

[6] X. Chen, T. Garfinkel, E. C. Lewis, P. Subrahmanyam, C. A. Waldspurger, D. Boneh, J. Dwoskin, and D. R. Ports. Overshadow: A virtualization-based approach to retrofitting protection in commodity operating systems. In *ASPLOS*, 2008.

[7] S. Chong, J. Liu, and A. C. Myers. Sif: Enforcing Confidentiality and Integrity in Web Applications. In *USENIX Security Conference*, 2007.

[8] C. Dwork. Differential Privacy. In *ICALP*, 2006.

[9] C. Dwork, F. McSherry, K. Nissim, and A. Smith. Calibrating Noise to Sensitivity in Private Data Analysis. In *IACR Theory of Cryptography Conference*, 2006.

[10] W. Enck, P. Gilbert, B. gon Chun, L. P. Cox, J. Jung, P. McDaniel, and A. N. Sheth. TaintDroid: An Information-Flow Tracking System for Realtime Privacy Monitoring on Smartphones. In *USENIX OSDI*, 2010.

[11] D. B. Giffin, A. Levy, D. Stefan, D. Terei, D. Mazières, J. C. Mitchell, and A. Russo. Hails: Protecting Data Privacy in Untrusted Web Applications. In *USENIX OSDI*, 2012.

[12] P. Gill, V. Erramilli, A. Chaintreau, B. Krishnamurthy, K. Papagiannaki, and P. Rodriguez. Follow the money: Understanding economics of online aggregation and advertising. In *IMC*, 2013.

[13] E. Goldman. How Zappos' User Agreement Failed In Court and Left Zappos Legally Naked. Forbes – http://www.forbes.com/sites/ericgoldman/2012/10/10/how-zappos-user-agreement-failed-in-court-and-left-zappos-legally-naked/, 2012.

[14] G. Greenwald and E. MacAskill. Boundless Informant: the NSA's secret tool to track global surveillance data. The Guardian – http://www.theguardian.com/world/2013/jun/08/nsa-boundless-informant-global-datamining, 2013.

[15] M. Gruteser and D. Grunwald. Anonymous Usage of Location-Based Services Through Spatial and Temporal Cloaking. In *ACM MobiSys*, 2003.

[16] S. Guha, B. Cheng, and P. Francis. Privad: Practical privacy in online advertising. In *USENIX NSDI*, 2011.

[17] C. Hawblitzel, J. Howell, J. Lorch, A. Narayan, B. Parno, D. Zhang, and B. Zill. Ironclad Apps: End-to-End Security via Automated Full-System Verification. In *USENIX OSDI*, 2014.

[18] G. Klein, K. Elphinstone, G. Heiser, J. Andronick, D. Cock, P. Derrin, D. Elkaduwe, K. Engelhardt, M. Norrish, R. Kolanski, T. Sewell, H. Tuch, and S. Winwood. seL4: Formal Verification of an OS Kernel. In *ACM SOSP*, 2009.

[19] M. A. Lemley. Terms of Use. *Minnesota Law Review*, 91, 2006.

[20] I. Leontiadis, C. Efstratiou, M. Picone, and C. Mascolo. Don't kill my ads! balancing privacy in an ad-supported mobile application market. In *HotMobile*, 2012.

[21] N. Li, T. Li, and S. Venkatasubramanian. t-Closeness: Privacy beyond k-anonymity and l-diversity. In *ICDE*, 2007.

[22] A. Machanavajjhala, D. Kifer, J. Gehrke, and M. Venkitasubramaniam. l-Diversity: Privacy Beyond k-Anonymity. In *ICDE*, 2007.

[23] J. M. McCune, Y. Li, N. Qu, Z. Zhou, A. Datta, V. Gligor, and A. Perrig. TrustVisor: Efficient TCB Reduction and Attestation. In *IEEE Symposium on Security and Privacy*, 2010.

[24] C. Pautasso, E. Wilde, and R. Alarcon. *REST: Advanced Research Topics and Practical Applications*. Springer, 2014.

[25] R. A. Popa, C. M. S. Redfield, N. Zeldovich, and H. Balakrishnan. CryptDB: Protecting Confidentiality with Encrypted Query Processing. In *ACM SOSP*, 2011.

[26] H. Raj, D. Robinson, T. Tariq, P. England, S. Saroiu, and A. Wolman. Credo: Trusted Computing for Guest VMs with a Commodity Hypervisor. Technical Report MSR-TR-2011-130, Microsoft Research, 2011.

[27] N. Santos, R. Rodrigues, K. Gummadi, and S. Saroiu. Policy-Sealed Data: A New Abstraction for Building Trusted Cloud Services. In *USENIX Security Conference*, 2012.

[28] A. Seshadri, M. Luk, N. Qu, and A. Perrig. SecVisor: A Tiny Hypervisor to Provide Lifetime Kernel Code Integrity for Commodity OSes. In *ACM SOSP*, 2007.

[29] A. Shieh, D. Williams, E. G. Sirer, and F. B. Schneider. Nexus: a new operating system for trustworthy computing. In *ACM SOSP*, 2005.

[30] L. Sweeney. k-Anonymity: A Model for Protecting Privacy. *International Journal on Uncertainty, Fuzziness and Knowledge-based Systems*, 10(5), 2002.

[31] S. Zdancewic, L. Zheng, N. Nystrom, and A. C. Myers. Untrusted Hosts and Confidentiality: Secure Program Partitioning. In *ACM SOSP*, 2001.

[32] F. Zhang, J. Chen, H. Chen, and B. Zang. CloudVisor: Retrofitting Protection of Virtual Machines in Multi-tenant Cloud with Nested Virtualization. In *ACM SOSP*, 2011.

Sound Shredding: Privacy Preserved Audio Sensing

Sumeet Kumar, Le T. Nguyen, Ming Zeng, Kate Liu, Joy Zhang
Carnegie Mellon University
Moffett Field, California, USA
{sumeet.kumar, le.nguyen, ming.zeng, kate.liu, joy.zhang}@sv.cmu.edu

ABSTRACT

Sound provides valuable information about a mobile user's activity and environment. With the increasing large market penetration of smart phones, recording sound from mobile phones' microphones and processing the sound information either on mobile devices or in the cloud opens a window to a large variety of mobile applications that are context-aware and behavior-aware. On the other hand, sound sensing has the potential risk of compromising users' privacy. Security attacks by malicious software running on smart phones can obtain in-band and out-of-band sound information to infer the content of users' conversation. In this paper, we propose two simple yet highly effective methods called *sound shredding* and *sound subsampling*. Sound shredding mutates the raw sound frames randomly just like paper shredding and sound subsampling randomly drops sound frames without storing them. The resulting mutated sound recording makes it difficult to recover the text content of the original sound recording, yet we show that some acoustic features are preserved which retains the accuracy of context recognition.

Categories and Subject Descriptors

H.4 [**Information Systems Applications**]: Miscellaneous; H.5.5 [**Information interfaces and presentation (e.g., HCI)**]: Sound and Music Computing

Keywords

Sound sensing; sound shredding; sound subsampling; user privacy; context recognition

1. INTRODUCTION

Mobile sound sensing, which uses acoustic attributes collected by mobile devices has been found useful in diverse scenarios of context awareness. Because audio data may contain unique fingerprints, allowing sound sensing software to extract and recognize meaningful events, many applications and systems have already applied sound sensing to im-

prove their approaches. For instance, SurroundSense [2] uses acoustic and other attributes to identify user motions and SensOrchestra [4] leverage sounds and images to recognize the location from where those data were collected. These research results clearly demonstrate that sound sensing could be of significant value in context recognition.

In a typical audio-based application, sounds are collected by mobile devices (either phones or tablets), and stored in storage like SD cards. These mobile devices are usually equipped with high sample rate microphones, which are useful for audio-based applications such as phone conversation, speech recognition, and sound sensing etc. However, the benefit entails the risk of privacy when it comes to collecting audio data. The raw audio data from the microphone are insecure and could easily be replayed. The replayed sound, even at a low sampling rate, may reveal the identity and other sensitive information about the users. Thus the raw sounds may be abused to disrupt the privacy guarantees for users. The problem becomes more obvious in case of continuous sampling applications such as MobiSens [13].

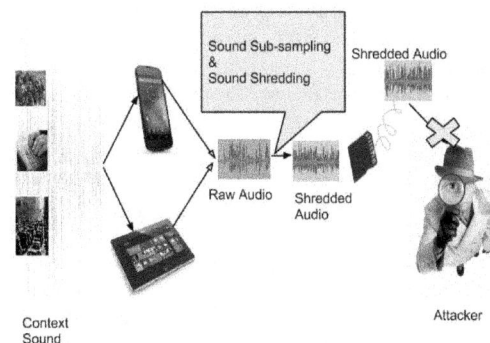

Figure 1: Shredded and sub-sampled audio could not be easily reconstructed, making it difficult for an attacker to sniff any sensitive information.

The main contributions of this paper are:

- **Two methods to preserve audio privacy:** We address the concern of privacy guarantees that may be undermined by malicious software intending to sniff information from raw sounds, by preprocessing raw sounds with sound shredding and subsampling.

- **Experiments and evaluation of proposed methods:** The goal of the two proposed methods is to preserve the user's privacy without significantly decreasing context recognition accuracy. Therefore, we present the results of context recognition accuracy as well as gender and speaker recognition accuracy using shredded and subsampled sound in section 5. In addition, we also propose a sound reconstruction model using frequency content of shredded audio and quantify our findings in this section.

The rest of the paper is organized as follows. We discuss related work in section 2. Then We define a threat model in section 3 that describes the possible attacks against users' privacy. Our sound shredding and sub-sampling methods are described in section 4. In section 5, the experiments and results are elaborated and evaluated. We conclude our work in section 6.

2. RELATED WORK

Sound sensing has been shown to be useful in many context aware applications. Eronen, A.J. [6] demonstrated the usefulness of audio in recognizing environment around a device. Similarly Chu [5] used environmental sounds for the understanding context. SensOrchestra [4] achieved 87.7% recognition accuracy in determining location using audio and image. In addition to context recognition, sound can also be used for other informations. For instance, StressSense [11] used human voice recorded by smartphones to recognize stress. These experiments demonstrate the usefulness of acoustic features.

Although there is a plenty of research on using audio sensing, not much has been done on securing the collected audio data. Klasnja [9] through his work on privacy, shows strong aversion to audio sensing. He mentions "Reactions to the raw audio were nearly unanimously negative. Only two of the 24 participants (8.3 %) would consider a microphone that continuously recorded raw audio". Unfortunately, not many sound sensing applications take the privacy implications into account, therefore introducing potential attacks against user privacy.

One way to improve privacy is by extracting audio features and discarding raw audio, though now it is generally accepted that MFCC are poor features for maintaining privacy because they reveal speech [10]. The PCA of audio spectrogram is proposed to detect non-speech sounds and prevent speech reconstruction intelligently [3, 10] using filters to omit the audio. In addition, there are encryption techniques available to secure audio data, e.g. audio features encrypted by LSH key is devised to hide speech while providing cues for prosody and recognition of conversations [14]. All above methods though suitable on server, cannot be used on mobile phones. The limitations on mobile phones demand a technique, which could easily be implemented and does not consume much power, even if the application runs continuously. Through our experiments, we show that some light-weighted techniques are possible which can be executed on a mobile phone and still be effective in improving the privacy.

3. THREAT MODEL

Sensitive information is often communicated verbally because audio is generally more ephemeral than an email or a SMS text message. However, emails and text messages are often encrypted by the applications that store them, which is rarely the case with audio data collected by sound-sensing applications. Because many sound-sensing applications collect data continuously, the audio data could reveal sensitive information.

In this paper, we are concerned with securing audio data from attackers and malicious software. To provide a clear outline of the threat model, we identify three roles involved: a user, a mobile sensing application and an attacker. A user allows a mobile sensing application to use microphone for collecting contextual information. The application continuously records audio, stores it on the phone and later uses it for context recognition tasks. The application is supposed to provide privacy guarantees to the user, but often makes no attempt to encrypt the audio data. We assume that an attacker can then get an access to the unencrypted audio files containing sensitive information (e.g., by physically stealing the device or by tricking a user to install seemingly-benign app, which will search for unencrypted audio files on the device).

To achieve the goal of privacy preserved sensing, we propose that the operating system preprocesses the audio using sound shredding, sound subsampling or both, before forwarding it to the context sensing application (as shown in Figure 1). Note that we assume that the operating system is trusted, but that the apps with access to audio data are not. For the purposes of this preliminary work, we additionally assume that an attacker has access to a limited corpus of short audio clips and cannot gain additional sensitive information about one clip from another.

4. METHODOLOGY

In this section, we introduce the technique of context recognition using audio data. Then we propose two ways to improve users privacy while collecting audio data, namely "Sound Sub-sampling" and "Sound Shredding".

The architecture of system involves mobile and server. Audio snippets are obtained from mobile OS, which after shredding and sub-sampling are stored on local memory. The stored data is later sent to server for analysis.

4.1 Context Recognition using Audio data

We define context as background environment in which an activity happens. For example, when a person is taking out money from an ATM, taking out money is an activity whereas ATM room is the context. The process of context identification involves data collection, features extraction and context recognition using machine learning as discussed below:

Audio data collection: Audio data could be collected using any device with a microphone. For our experiment, a total of 35 sounds samples were recorded with a sampling rate of 8KHz sampled at 16 bit using a Nexus 4 phone.

Features extraction: First, the audio data is framed using a sliding window with window size of 30 ms, and for each of these audio frames, Mel-frequency cepstral coefficients (MFCC) of 12 vector length are calculated.

Context Recognition: Our experiment uses two machine learning algorithms namely K Nearest Neighbor (KNN) and Support Vector Machine for context classification using MFCC features.

4.2 Sound Subsampling

Identifying speech from an audio source requires a fairly continuous data but that is not the case with context recognition, which can often be extracted from a few segments of sound e.g. if a person is driving his car as well as talking to his fellow rider, the extraction of speech requires a continuous sample whereas the background noise of a moving car on the road can be extracted from even a few audio segments. In fact, the context recognition like driving a car does not require a continuous sample. At the same time if continuous sample is not collected, it makes it difficult to retrieve speech information. Hence, if context recognition is the primary goal, users privacy could improve by storing sub-samples of audio data.

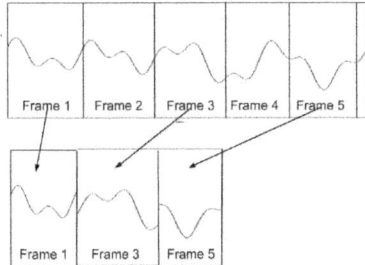

Figure 2: Sound Sub-sampling at the rate of 50%

We define Sub-sampling as the process of collecting only a part of the raw data e.g. a subsampling at 20% means only 20% of audio data is stored, i.e. only two frames out of ten audio frames are stored and rest are discarded. Figure 2 demonstrates the process of sub-sampling at 50% where every second frames is dropped during audio data collection.

4.3 Sound Shredding

Subsampling of audio is good way to reduce speech information in the audio data, but even sub-sampling at a lower rate could still give away information. One possible way to further improve user privacy is by randomizing the sound data. We noticed that sound features like MFCC are extracted from audio frames of 20-40 ms duration. These features do not change even if the sound frames are randomized as long as the frames are not changed internally.

We define Sound Shredding as randomizing the audio frames in a sound snippet. We randomize sound by selecting an audio frame and moving it to a random location in the sound snippet i.e. if a frame is located at i index in the collection of audio frames that makes the sound snippet, we generate a random number between 0 and i, and move the frame at the generated random number. We do the same with all the frames that make the sound snippet.

Figure 3 shows the process of sound shredding. Shredded audio becomes difficult to reconstruct and replay as later demonstrated in the experiments section 5.

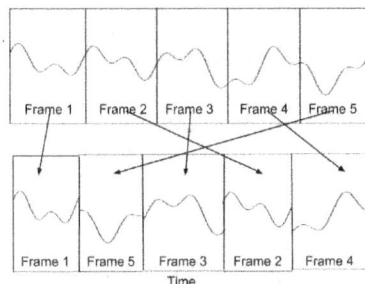

Figure 3: Sound shredding

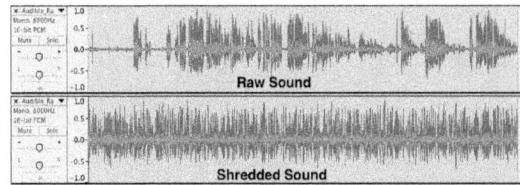

Figure 4: Sound Shredding: Raw data and shredded data

Figure 4 shows the data collected by shredding. As the data is randomized during collection, the shredded data looks very different from sub-sampled data.

4.4 Sound Shredding and Sound Sub-sampling

In some cases of context recognition, sound shredding and sound sub-sampling can be combined for improved privacy.

5. EXPERIMENTS AND RESULTS

In this section, we describe our experiments that are divided in four parts. First we conducted experiments to determine the effect of sound shredding and sound sub-sampling on context accuracy. Then we conducted a user study to find changes in user privacy by replay of privacy preserved audio. Next we used a speech recognition engine to determine gender and speaker identification accuracy. At the end we designed and evaluated a speech reconstruction model based on frequency content of shredded audio.

5.1 Context Recognition

Audio data for the experiments was collected using a Nexus 4 phone by reading its microphone at 8000 HZ using single audio channel. In total we collected thirty-five sound samples in different contexts including: student faculty meeting, friends talking during lunch, walking, brewing coffee in cafeteria, students talking in a meeting, classroom, guest talk, laboratory etc. The experimenter used the context as the label for the audio. For each of the contexts, three sound snippets of approximately 2 minutes duration were recorded. We divided the raw audio snippet in frames of 30 ms, which were used to extract the MFCC(12) features. For testing the algorithms accuracy, we divide the entire set of MFCC features in to training and test data. We used 80% of the data set as training data and the rest as test data. To classify the context, we used proven KNN and SVN algorithms. A collection of vectors made of 12 coefficients of MFCC and the audio label was used as input to the classification algorithms. The training and testing data were used as input to the above two algorithms for the context recognition accuracy. We used Java-ML [1] for running experiments, which provides an easy interface to get the classification results.

The experiments were run with varying degree of sub-sampling (10% to 100%).

Figure 5 shows the trend of changes in the accuracy of SVN and KNN algorithms with changes in sub-sampling percentage. The results show a slow decrease in recognition accuracy with increased sub-sampling (increased frames dropping) till the sub-sampling percentage is around 70%. But after 80% sub-sampling there is a steep decrease in context recognition accuracy.

In addition, the experiments were also run with sub-sampled shredded sound with varying degree of sub-sampling (10% to 100%).

Policy	Specification
1	data_retention_limit = one time *and* service_name = Bing maps *and* anonymization_scheme = k-anonymity
2	data_retention_limit = one day *and* is_BitLocker_present = true *and* share_with_3rd_party = false
3	(data_location = EU *and* share_with_3rd_party = true) *or* (data_location = US and share_with_3rd_party = false)

Table 1: Examples of more sophisticated policies.

Data	Precision	Use	Threat Model	Location	Retention
meta-data	precise	actual service	national govnmt.	US	one-time
contents	k-anonymity	improve service	foreign govnmt.	Canada	one day
password	l-diversity	targeted ads	HDD theft	EU	one year
location	t-closeness	3rd-party	memory attacks	Asia	until accnt. is closed
payment	diff. privacy			Caymans	forever

Table 2: Taxonomy of attributes for PCD.

their mobile users' data according to their wishes. Cloud providers may choose to offer degraded service to those users that specify overly onerous ToS.

2. TOS-BASED POLICIES

2.1 Brief Background on ToS

Terms of Service (ToS) are a set of rules which one must agree to abide by in order to use a service. Websites often define ToS to state their users' rights and responsibilities as well as the website's limitations of liability. ToS can be subject to change; whenever the ToS change, websites must once again seek the consent from their users [13].

ToS are often long and complicated. It is widely believed that Web users often accept the websites' ToS without understanding them or even bothering to read them. ToS;DR [2] is a recent project that aims at reviewing all websites' ToS policies and rating them according to a color-coding scheme. With their tools, whenever a user encounters a new ToS, the user can immediately evaluate the ToS's restrictiveness by its color shade: solid green meaning "best ToS" to solid red meaning "this ToS raises very serious concerns".

Courts have overwhelmingly sided with enforcing online ToS [19]. There are a few exceptions when courts ruled against enforcing the ToS. The courts aimed to protect consumers from certain clauses they considered unreasonable, such as *onerous arbitration* clauses (i.e., in case of a dispute, the user agrees to settle it only through the arbitration mechanism described by the ToS) and *forum selection* clauses (i.e., any litigation resulting from the contract will be initiated in a specific jurisdiction or court). These clauses are not considered unreasonable when the plaintiff is a business because courts presume that businesses are "sophisticated economic entities" and know what they are doing when accessing another company's website.

2.2 Examples of Policies

Many ToS-based policies are possible. Some users would prefer policies that are simple and easy to understand. Example of simple policies that appeal to many users are:

1. When uploading a credit card number, a user may attach a policy that restricts its use to a single transaction. With such a policy, the cloud provider can use the credit card for a one-time charge, but is not allowed to store the number for future transactions.

2. When uploading a personal photo to a social networking site, a user may attach a policy forbidding any attempt to interpret the photo's content beyond simply rendering the photo, such as performing face recognition or object detection on the photo.

3. When uploading personal health data to the cloud (e.g., a mobile app that measures the user's pulse, or any form of health care records), a user may attach a policy that forbids sharing with a third-party, and requires data to always be stored in encrypted form.

4. When using a mobile payment application, a user may attach a policy that forbids any form of customer profiling on the data.

Privacy-savvy users may define more sophisticated policies on their data that go beyond these simple examples, and describe features related to the software and hardware they require from cloud providers. For example, policies can use the following types of features:

1. Features related to data privacy. Examples are data retention limits, the degree of data shareability (e.g., whether it can be shared with 3rd parties), or the type of anonymization scheme required (e.g., hashing, k-anonymity, differential privacy).

2. Software-related features. Examples are: encrypted filesystem (e.g., BitLocker), verified OSes (e.g., seL4 [18], IronClad [17]), or specific versions of software.

3. Physical/Hardware-related features. Examples are: geographic locations of data-centers, or the presence specialized hardware such as a Trusted Platform Module (TPM) or a Hardware Security Module (HSM).

Table 1 shows a few examples of more sophisticated policies. Each policy is a set of constraints linked by conjunction or disjunction operators. Each constraint tests a condition over an attribute which can be a string or a number. The condition can be an equality (e.g., attribute=value) or an inequality in case of numbers that span a *finite set*. Examples of finite sets are the set of past released version numbers for a piece of software, or the set of days of the week. Unfortunately, the cryptography underlying our abstraction cannot support infinite or uncountable sets. The set of natural numbers is countably infinite, and the set of real numbers is uncountable.

2.3 Taxonomy for Constructing Policies

Our vision is that a common set of policies will become de-facto standards that users will pick from when requesting protection for their data. This is similar to how Creative Commons (a non-profit organization) has defined a set of simple licenses for sharing content, or how ToS;DR has defined a color-coded scheme for interpreting EULAs.

Table 2 presents one taxonomy example as a starting point. Broadly, users may apply the same policies to most of their metadata, such as call logs and web access logs, and a separate set of policies to data contents, such as photographs and chat messages. We expect users to treat a few data items differently – location, credit card numbers, and passwords. Each data item may have multiple policies that allow different uses depending on the granularity of the data.

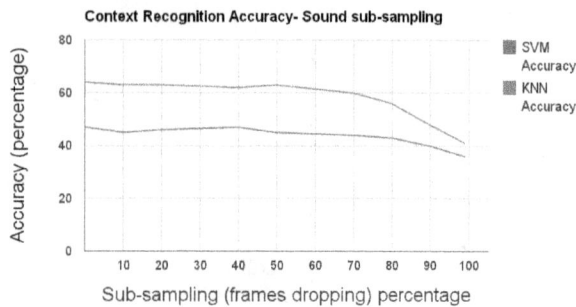

Figure 5: Context Recognition Accuracy vs. Sound sub-sampling percentage

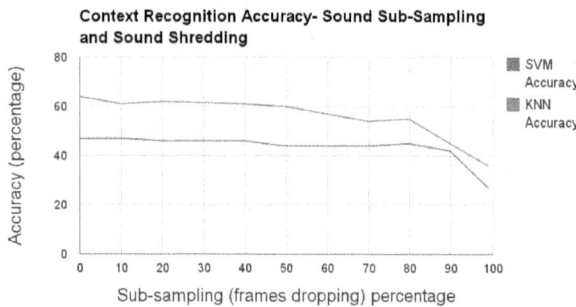

Figure 6: Context Recognition Accuracy vs. Sound sub-sampling percentage for shredded sound

Figure 6 shows the trend of change in accuracy of SVN and KNN algorithms with change in sub-sampling percentage for shredded audio. The results show a slow decrease in recognition accuracy with increased sub-sampling (increased frames dropping) till the sub-sampling percentage of 80%. But after around 80% sub-sampling, there is a steep decrease in the context recognition accuracy.

The above experiments and results indicate that shredding and sub-sampling of audio data can lead to improved data privacy without losing much on recognition accuracy, if sub-sampling and shredding has positive impact on users privacy. The impact of sub-sampling and shredding on privacy is discussed next.

5.2 Privacy-preservation User Study

The user study involved playing different sounds (shredded and sub-sampled) in front of users. As they hear the sound, they rated the sound on speech recognition, recognition of count of people in conversation and gender identification. Parameters and scale used for user study:

1. Speech recognition (1- 5)

2. Count of people in conversation (1-5)

3. Gender identification (1- 5)

The scale used was 1-5, where 1 meant "Not at all" and 5 meant "Yes, I can". Over all, 10 students took the survey and the responses were averaged to use in the graph.

The data obtained was aggregated in a chart format shown in Figure 7. As it can be observed the speech recognition, one of the major concern is user privacy drastically improves by sound shredding in which audio frames are randomized. In addition, the possibility of counting people decreases with shredding as well as sub-sampling. The gender identification

showed least improvement, but still improves by 10-25%. Overall sound shredding with subsampling rate of 20% gives the best result in terms of privacy preservation.

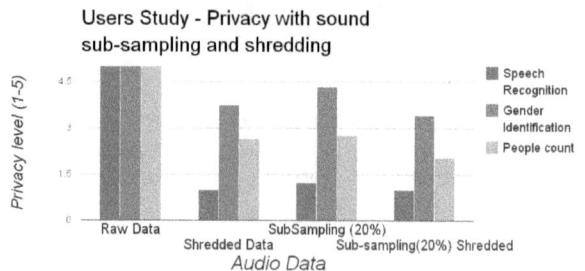

Figure 7: The user study results indicate that sound shredding can effectively protect user privacy. The speech recognition rates decrease significantly by using our approaches. The scale used was 1-5, where 1 meant "Not at all" and 5 meant "Yes, I can"

5.3 Computer-based Recognition

In the previous experiment, we studied how well can people recognize the gender, the identity and the speech given shredded and subsampled audio signal. In the following, we evaluate computer-based recognition techniques using a similar criteria. This simulates the situation of having an attacker, who gets an unauthorized access to the audio files.

We use 330 speech snippets with an average duration of 10 seconds collected from 8 users (4 male, 4 female) [8]. For gender and speaker identification we use the open source LIUM toolkit [12], which has pre-trained gender recognition model. To train the speaker identification model for our evaluation, we use one audio snippet for each user in the dataset.

As illustrated in Figure 8, subsampling and shredding does not have a significant effect on both gender and speaker identification. This confirms the results of the user study.

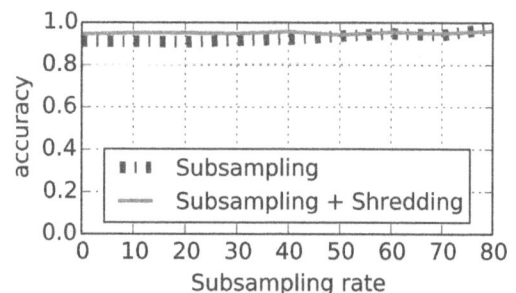

Figure 8: Subsampling and shreadding does not have a significant effect on gender prediction.

To recognize the speech we use the speech recognition system presented in Kim et al. [8]. The performance of speech recognition is measured in Word Error Rate (WER), where the smaller WER, the more content is recovered. The WER for the original signal is 5.70%. As shown in Figure 10, with low subsampling rate, one can recover the speech relatively well. However, if an audio signal is shredded, no speech information can be recovered.

From the presented results we can observe that through shredding and subsampling the sound signals do not loose information about the gender and user identity. However, no speech content can be recovered if the audio is shredded or

138

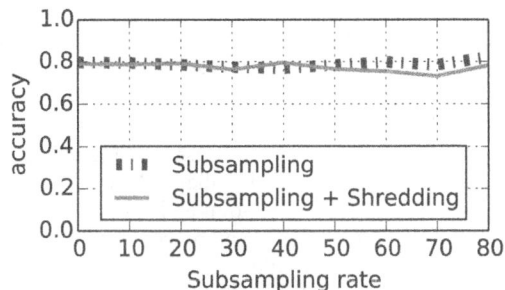

Figure 9: Subsampling and shreadding does not have a significant effect on speaker identification.

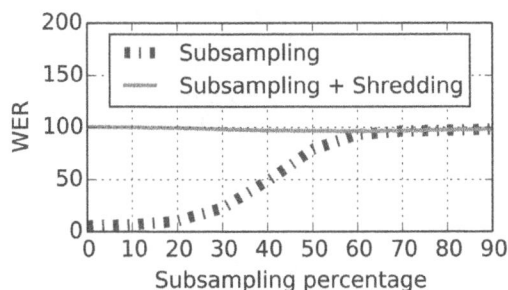

Figure 10: Speech content cannot be recovered if the audio is shredded or subsampled with high rate.

subsampled with a high rate. This property is highly desirable in many applications such as social life-logging. These applications aim to measure how much social interaction did a user have and how many people she met over the day without needing to know the content of user's conversations.

5.4 Speech Reconstruction Attacks

In shredded audio, all components of the original audio are present and so it is theoretically possible to reconstruct the sound, though it may be infeasible to do so because of computational challenges. As in the case of paper shredding challenge by Darpa [7], there are no single known efficient solution to reconstruct shredded sound. Possible solutions would involve a combination of approaches. Here we describe two possibilities.

5.4.1 Brute force attack

If we take a small sound sample of 10 seconds and frame width of 15 ms, there are apprximately 667 frames in the sound sample. There are n! different ways of arranging n distinct objects into a sequence, so these 667 frames can be rearranged in 667! ways. O(n!) calculations are computationally very expensive e.g. 100! is approximately 9.332622e+157, which indicates that our computer could easily run out of processing capability. Also, we need to consider the cost of analyzing the audio of each of the arrangements to get the text back, which can be either done manually or by using a speech processing system, and incurs additional cost.

5.4.2 Reconstruction based on frequency content

Shredded audio contains all frequencies present in the original audio, but they loose their original order because of shredding. The diagram 11 compares spectogram of original audio and shredded audio, where original audio was shredded in 12 pieces, looking at which one gets an impression that it could be possible to rearrange the frames back. We

designed an experiment to do the same and tried a greedy algorithm approach to reconstruct the audio.

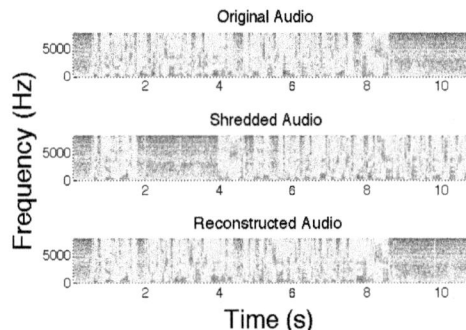

Figure 11: Spectrogram of Original, Shredded and Reconstructed audio. The original audio was split in 12 pieces and shredded. In this case, the greedy algorithm could partially reconstruct the original audio. As the no of divisions (split) increases, it becomes increasingly difficult to reconstruct the original audio as shown in figure 12.

Assume we have original signal O, the shredded signal S and the reconstructed signal R. We compute d(O, S) and d(O, R), where d() is Euclidian distance function comparing two audio encodings. We define audio encodings as the arrangement of audio frames e.g. an audio signal O can be represented as a string abcdef.... where each character represents an audio segment, whereas a shredded audio S will be represented as dbmkc.... comprising entirely of characters present in audio O, but in a random order. We compute d(O,S) as the Euclidian distance between strings abcdef.... and dbmkc...., where each character represents a number e.g. a=1, b=2 etc. In addition, we also calculate similarity between O and R using Longest common subsequence (LCS) algorithm which uses abcdef... and dbmkc... as two strings obtained from the method described above.

To reconstruct signal O from signal S, we take inspiration from paper shredding experiment [7] where right edge of a shredded part matches the left edge of the shredded part on the right. Similarly, for audio spectrogram, the frequencies present on the right most window of a segment will be similar to frequencies present in the left edge of the segment on the right. Based on this idea, we compute spectrogram of segments of shredded audio, which gives amplitude and phase of all frequencies present in smaller segments d,b,m,k.... Then we start with the first frame of shredded signal S, namely d and use greedy approach to search the remaining frames in S, to find the closest match for frequency amplitude present in the rightmost window of segment d. If closest match of d gives k, then we construct signal as "dk" and then start another greedy search for k. This way we can reconstruct complete audio R like "dkmabc....". We then compute d(O,R), the Euclidian distance comparing O and R. The measure of d(O,R) gives us how much successful we are in reconstructing the shredded audio. In addition to the Euclidian distance we also calculated similarity using Longest common subsequence algorithm.

The results shown in figure 12 reveals that the thinner the shredding is, the more difficult it is to reconstruct the audio. The audio signal which was divided in 5 or lesser segments, it was possible to reconstruct the audio, but as the number of divisions increase (shredding thickness decreases),

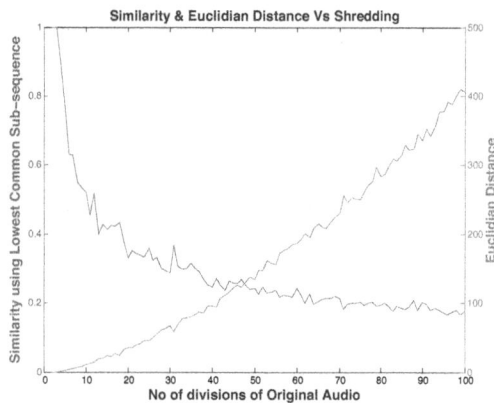

Figure 12: Euclidian distance and Similarity (using longest common sub-sequence) between Original and Reconstructed audio Vs No of divisions of Original Audio. The result indicates that the thinner the shredding, the more difficult it becomes to reconstruct the original audio.

it becomes increasingly difficult to reproduce the original audio based on frequency content.

6. CONCLUSION AND FUTURE WORK

Audio is a valuable source of contextual information, which is crucial for many context-aware mobile applications. However, beside context information the captured audio signals often contain sensitive speech content. In this work, we show that sound shredding and subsampling are effective means for making speech not recognizable, while preserving sufficient information for context, gender and speaker recognition. Through the experiments, we showed that no speech content could be recognized from the processed signal by either human or automated computer techniques.

In future work, further studies are needed to understand the effectiveness and robustness of the proposed approaches. Since both sound shredding and subsampling are meant to be run directly on mobile devices, additional experiments are needed to analyze the battery consumption and the computational complexity of these approaches. Although we provided a theoretical analysis of attacks aiming at reconstructing the original signal, more sophisticated attacks needs to be explored to study the effectiveness of the proposed approaches.

7. ACKNOWLEDGEMENT

This research is supported in part by the National Science Foundation under the award of 1346066: SCH: INT: Collaborative Research: FITTLE+: Theory and Models for Smartphone Ecological Momentary Intervention.

We would like to thank all the reviewers for their insightful comments and suggestions which have greatly helped us to improve our work.

8. REFERENCES

[1] T. Abeel, Y. Van de Peer, and Y. Saeys. Java-ml: A machine learning library. *J. Mach. Learn. Res.*, 10:931–934, June 2009.

[2] M. Azizyan, I. Constandache, and R. Roy Choudhury. Surroundsense: mobile phone localization via ambience fingerprinting. In *Proceedings of the 15th annual international conference on Mobile computing and networking*, MobiCom '09, pages 261–272, New York, NY, USA, 2009. ACM.

[3] F. Chen, J. Adcock, and S. Krishnagiri. Audio privacy: reducing speech intelligibility while preserving environmental sounds. In *Proceedings of the 16th ACM international conference on Multimedia*, pages 733–736. ACM, 2008.

[4] H.-T. Cheng, F.-T. Sun, S. Buthpitiya, and M. Griss. Sensorchestra: Collaborative sensing for symbolic location recognition. In M. Gris and G. Yang, editors, *Mobile Computing, Applications, and Services*, volume 76 of *Lecture Notes of the Institute for Computer Sciences, Social Informatics and Telecommunications Engineering*, pages 195–210. Springer Berlin Heidelberg, 2012.

[5] S. Chu, S. Narayanan, and C.-C. J. Kuo. Environmental sound recognition with time-frequency audio features. *Trans. Audio, Speech and Lang. Proc.*, 17(6):1142–1158, Aug. 2009.

[6] A. Eronen, V. Peltonen, J. Tuomi, A. Klapuri, S. Fagerlund, T. Sorsa, G. Lorho, and J. Huopaniemi. Audio-based context recognition. *Audio, Speech, and Language Processing, IEEE Transactions on*, 14(1):321–329, Jan 2006.

[7] T. Geller. Darpa shredder challenge solved. *Commun. ACM*, 55(8):16–17, Aug. 2012.

[8] J. Kim and I. Lane. Accelerating large vocabulary continuous speech recognition on heterogeneous cpu-gpu platforms. In *Acoustics, Speech and Signal Processing (ICASSP), 2014 IEEE International Conference on*, pages 3291–3295. IEEE, 2014.

[9] P. Klasnja, S. Consolvo, T. Choudhury, R. Beckwith, and J. Hightower. Exploring privacy concerns about personal sensing. In *Proceedings of the 7th International Conference on Pervasive Computing*, Pervasive '09, pages 176–183, Berlin, Heidelberg, 2009. Springer-Verlag.

[10] E. C. Larson, T. Lee, S. Liu, M. Rosenfeld, and S. N. Patel. Accurate and privacy preserving cough sensing using a low-cost microphone. In *Proceedings of the 13th international conference on Ubiquitous computing*, pages 375–384. ACM, 2011.

[11] H. Lu, D. Frauendorfer, M. Rabbi, M. S. Mast, G. T. Chittaranjan, A. T. Campbell, D. Gatica-Perez, and T. Choudhury. Stresssense: detecting stress in unconstrained acoustic environments using smartphones. In *Proceedings of the 2012 ACM Conference on Ubiquitous Computing*, UbiComp '12, pages 351–360, New York, NY, USA, 2012. ACM.

[12] S. Meignier and T. Merlin. Lium spkdiarization: an open source toolkit for diarization. In *CMU SPUD Workshop*, volume 2010, 2010.

[13] P. Wu, J. Zhu, and J. Y. Zhang. Mobisens: A versatile mobile sensing platform for real-world applications. 18, February 2013.

[14] D. Wyatt, T. Choudhury, and J. Bilmes. Conversation detection and speaker segmentation in privacy-sensitive situated speech data. In *INTERSPEECH*, pages 586–589, 2007.

Author Index

Achtzehn, Andreas 63
Adkins, Joshua 27
Agarwal, Sharad 129
Ajay, Jerry Antony 105
Amos, Brandon 51
Baker, Mary 93
Banerjee, Suman 69
Barría Castillo, Irving Antonio 63
Borriello, Gaetano 15
Brockmeyer, Monica 39
Bustamante, Fabián 123
Campbell, Bradford 27
Cha, Hojung 33
Challen, Geoffrey 99, 105
Chen, Zhuo 51
Corner, Mark 1
Dell, Nicola 15
DiRienzo, Nick 105
D'Silva, Krittika 15
Du, Hao 45
Dutta, Prabal 27
Erman, Jeffrey 57
Flinn, Jason 111
Georgiev, Petko 117
Gilbert, Benjamin 51
Gopalakrishnan, Vijay 57
Gummeson, Jeremy 93
Ha, Kiryong 51
Halepovic, Emir 57
Han, Bo 87
Harkes, Jan 51
Hu, Wenlu 51
Ikematsu, Kaori 3
Jackson, Neal 27
Jain, Ankur 45

Jana, Rittwik 57
Jin, Xin 57
Jun, Byungjin 123
Kennedy, Oliver 105
Kim, Dongwon 33
Kim, Kyu-Han 93
Klugman, Noah 27
Kumar, Sumeet 135
Lane, Nicholas D. 117
Lee, Kyungmin 111
Leng, Ning 69
Li, Jiangtao 21
Li, Liqun 21
Liu, Angli 21
Liu, Kate 135
Lu, Feng 45
Mähönen, Petri 63
Maiti, Anudipa 99, 105
Metri, Grace 39
Mohapatra, Prasant 9
Nandugudi, Anandatirtha 105
Nguyen, Le T. 135
Noble, Brian 111
Noh, Hae Young 81
Pan, Shijia 81
Park, Sewook 33
Pathak, Parth H. 9
Patro, Ashish 69
Petrova, Marina 63
Pillai, Padmanabhan 51
Qian, Feng 87
Qian, Yuqiu 81
Ra, Moo-Ryong 87
Rexford, Jennifer 57
Richter, Wolfgang 51

Riihihjärvi, Janne 63
Rula, John P. 123
Saroiu, Stefan 129
Satyanarayanan, Mahadev 51
Shantharam, Sriram 105
Shen, Guobin 21
Shi, Jinghao 105
Shi, Weisong 39
Siio, Itiro 3
Sinha, Rakesh K. 57
Snoeren, Alex C. 45
Srinivasa, Guru Prasad 105
Srivastava, Animesh 93
Sun, Chao 21
Terzis, Andreas 45
Velibeyoglu, Irem 81
Voelker, Geoffrey M. 45
Wang, Ningning 81
Wolman, Alec 129
Xu, Chao 9
Zachariah, Thomas 27
Zeng, Ming 135
Zhang, Joy 135
Zhang, Pei 81
Zhang, Tan 69
Zhang, Zengbin 75
Zhao, Ben Y. 75
Zhao, Feng 21
Zheng, Haitao 75
Zhu, Yanzi 75
Zhu, Yibo 75
Ziarek, Lukasz 105
Zou, Xuan Kelvin 57